Order and Rivalry

The First World War transformed the legal and geopolitical framework for international trade by decentring Europe in global markets. *Order and Rivalry* traces the formation and development of multilateral trade structures in the aftermath of the First World War in response to the marginalization of Europe in the world economy, the use of private commerce as a tool of military power, and the collapse of empires across Central and Eastern Europe. In this accessible study, Madeleine Lynch Dungy highlights the 1920s as a pivotal transition phase between the network of bilateral trade treaties that underpinned the first globalization of the late nineteenth century and the institutionalized regime of international governance after 1945. Focusing on the League of Nations, she shows that this institution's legacy was not to initiate a linear forward march towards today's World Trade Organization, but rather to frame an open-ended and conflictual process of experimentation that is still ongoing.

Madeleine Lynch Dungy is a researcher at the Norwegian University of Science and Technology.

Order and Rivalry

Rewriting the Rules of International Trade after the First World War

Madeleine Lynch Dungy

Norwegian University of Science and Technology

 CAMBRIDGE
UNIVERSITY PRESS

CAMBRIDGE
UNIVERSITY PRESS

Shaftesbury Road, Cambridge CB2 8EA, United Kingdom

One Liberty Plaza, 20th Floor, New York, NY 10006, USA

477 Williamstown Road, Port Melbourne, VIC 3207, Australia

314–321, 3rd Floor, Plot 3, Splendor Forum, Jasola District Centre, New Delhi – 110025, India

103 Penang Road, #05–06/07, Visioncrest Commercial, Singapore 238467

Cambridge University Press is part of Cambridge University Press & Assessment, a department of the University of Cambridge.

We share the University's mission to contribute to society through the pursuit of education, learning and research at the highest international levels of excellence.

www.cambridge.org
Information on this title: www.cambridge.org/9781009308908

DOI: 10.1017/9781009308892

First published 2023

A catalogue record for this publication is available from the British Library.

ISBN 978-1-009-30890-8 Hardback

Cambridge University Press & Assessment has no responsibility for the persistence or accuracy of URLs for external or third-party internet websites referred to in this publication and does not guarantee that any content on such websites is, or will remain, accurate or appropriate.

For my parents

Contents

Acknowledgements

I will always be grateful to the teachers that I had as an undergraduate at the University of Wisconsin–Madison. Laird Boswell, Laurence Dickey, Robert Freeland, and Ullrich Langer provided models of academic inquiry and inspired me to pursue my own graduate research.

I first began working on the League of Nations as an MSt student at the University of Oxford, under the supervision of Patricia Clavin. Patricia opened up the field of international history for me through her foundational research on the workings of the League's Economic and Financial Organization, and she has provided invaluable feedback on successive versions of this project.

I collected the bulk of my archival material as a PhD student at Harvard University, under the supervision of Alison Frank Johnson, with funding from the Weatherhead Centre, the Krupp Foundation, the Georges Lurcy Charitable and Educational Trust, and the John Clive Fellowship Fund. Alison offered constant support and encouragement as I explored a very muddled set of archives. She showed me the richness of Central European history and the region's pivotal place in the League of Nations. I also benefitted greatly from working with the other two members of my dissertation committee. Erez Manela helped me to refine the structure of my argument and to appreciate the peculiarities of US internationalism. Mary Lewis guided me through the complex legal and institutional ramifications of European trade policy in the colonial world. I owe a particular debt of gratitude to the archivists and librarians who assisted my research. I would especially like to thank Jacques Oberson and Lee Robertson at the League of Nations Archives, Manuela Haselmayr at the Archiv der Wirtschaftskammer Wien, and Birgit Gummersbach, Claus-Friedrich Laaser, Guido Warlimont, and Bernhard Klein at the Kiel Institut für Weltwirtschaft (IfW). Fellow historians have also helped me get a handle on some of the more complex archival material that I encountered. Notably, Gunnar Take's generous advice made the IfW archive much more intelligible to me, while conversations with Thomas David clarified the idiosyncratic organization of the International Chamber of Commerce.

Thank you to Youssef Cassis, Valentina Sandu-Dediu, and Madeleine Herren-Oesch for giving me the opportunity to revise my manuscript while working at European University Institute in Florence, the New Europe College in Bucharest, and the Institute for European Global Studies at the University of Basel. Béla Kapossy and Mats Ingulstad made it possible for me to finish the book with generous research support from the College of Humanities at the École Polytechnique Fédérale de Lausanne and the Fate of Nations project at the Norwegian University of Science and Technology, respectively. I am grateful to Sophus Reinert for helping me decide how to pitch the book. The staff at Cambridge University Press have offered crucial assistance throughout the publishing process, and the two readers sharpened the manuscript a great deal through their careful comments.

Finally, I would like to thank my family. My four parents and my sister and brother have always been there to buck me up in moments of doubt, and they have encouraged me by the example of their own creativity and tenacity. Throughout the research and writing process, my husband, Graham Clure, has kept me grounded with his unfailing good sense, analytical clarity, and humour. The research trips that we took together are the best memories that I have from working on this book.

None of the chapters in *Order and Rivalry* has been previously published. Some of the phrasing and some of the archival material have been presented in a different form in the following publications: Madeleine Lynch Dungy, 'The Global Agricultural Crisis and British Diplomacy in the League of Nations in 1931', *Agricultural History Review*, 65 (2017), 297–319; Madeleine Lynch Dungy, 'The Economic and Social Impact of the LoN and the ILO: Economic and Monetary Achievements', in Bernard Lescaze and Olga Hidalgo-Weber (eds.), *100 Years of Multilateralism in Geneva from the LoN to the UN* (Suzanne Hurter Editions, 2020), 283–97; Patricia Clavin and Madeleine Dungy, 'Trade, Law, and the Global Order of 1919', *Diplomatic History*, 44 (2020), 554–79, reproduced by permission of Oxford University Press; Madeleine Lynch Dungy, 'Writing Multilateral Trade Rules in the League of Nations', *Contemporary European History*, 30 (2021), 60–75, reproduced by permission of Cambridge University Press; Madeleine Lynch Dungy, 'International Commerce in the Wake of Empire: Central European Economic Integration between National and Imperial Sovereignty', in Peter Becker and Natasha Wheatley (eds.), *Remaking Central Europe: The League of Nations and the Former Habsburg Lands* (Oxford University Press, 2021), 213–40, reproduced by permission of Oxford University Press.

Organizational Abbreviations

AAA	American Arbitration Association
ABCEI	Association belge de coopération économique internationale (Belgian Association for International Economic Cooperation)
AMTC	Allied Maritime Transport Council
ASTWIK	Abteilung für Statistische Weltwirtschaftskunde und Internationale Konjunkturforschung (Department of Statistical World-Economic Research and International Business-Cycle Research), part of the IfW
CAED	Comité d'action économique et douanière (Committee of Economic and Customs Action)
CCFA	Comité commercial franco-allemand (Franco-German Commercial Committee)
DFWV	Deutsch-Französischer Wirtschaftsverein (German–French Economic Association), counterpart to the CCFA
EFO	Economic and Financial Organization of the League of Nations
EIS	Economic Intelligence Service of the League of Nations
EU	European Union
GATT	General Agreement on Tariffs and Trade
ICC	International Chamber of Commerce
ICIC	International Committee on Intellectual Cooperation
IFLNS	International Federation of League of Nations Societies
IfW	Institut für Seeverkehr und Weltwirtschaft (Institute for Sea Traffic and World Economy), later renamed the Institut für Weltwirtschaft und Seeverkehr
IPU	Inter-Parliamentary Union
MWT	Mitteleuropäische Wirtschaftstagung (Central European Economic Conference)
NSDStB	Nationalsozialistische Deutsche Studentenbund (National Socialist German Student Association)
RTAA	Reciprocal Trade Agreements Act

OECD	Organization for Economic Co-operation and Development
SSRC	Social Science Research Council
UDE	Union Douanière Européenne also known as Europäischer Zoll-Verein (European Customs Union)
WTO	World Trade Organization

Note that archival abbreviations are listed in the bibliography.

Introduction

The interwar period marked the end of a dramatic expansion in international trade. The First World War did not destroy the commercial networks that had underpinned nineteenth-century globalization, but it did reroute and repurpose them to serve military ends. It transformed the legal and geopolitical context of international trade by precipitating the collapse of continental empires across much of Eurasia and decentring Europe in global markets.[1] From 1913 to 1928, Europe's share of total world trade dropped by roughly 16 per cent, due to a relative decline in direct imports and exports as well as transit trade.[2] In an attempt to give structure to a world economy in flux, many Europeans embraced new multilateral methods in the 1920s, using the League of Nations as their institutional canvas. They disavowed the laissez-faire liberalism of the past, concluding that markets would have to be actively propped open using international rules and institutions.[3] Internationalists came to this common project with widely varying geopolitical ambitions, and competition between divergent models of regional, global, and imperial order generated much of the momentum behind multilateral innovation in interwar trade politics. Yet, this underlying conflict also meant that any institutional compromise that could be reached was provisional and fragile.[4]

---

[1] A. Estevadeordal, B. Frantz, and A. M. Taylor, 'The Rise and Fall of World Trade, 1870–1939', *The Quarterly Journal of Economics*, 118/2 (2003), 359–407; P. Clavin, 'Defining Human Security: Roads to War and Peace, 1918–45', in C.-C. W. Szejnmann (ed.), *Rethinking History, Dictatorship, and War: New Approaches and Interpretations* (Continuum, 2009), pp. 69–83; A. Tooze and T. Fertik, 'The World Economy and the Great War', *Geschichte und Gesellschaft*, 40/2 (2014), 214–38.

[2] A. G. Kenwood and A. L. Lougheed, *Growth of the International Economy, 1820–2015*, 4th ed. (Routledge, 1999), 213; M. B. Miller, *Europe and the Maritime World: A Twentieth-Century History* (Cambridge University Press, 2012), 242–3.

[3] On this point, I am in full agreement with Q. Slobodian, *Globalists: The End of Empire and the Birth of Neoliberalism* (Harvard University Press, 2018).

[4] R. Boyce, *The Great Interwar Crisis and the Collapse of Globalization* (Palgrave Macmillan, 2009).

The multilateral trade experiments of the 1920s did not durably revive globalization, but they did alter expectations about what kinds of problems trade policy could be asked to address, on what scale, and through what channels. Those assumptions were encoded in legal norms and institutional practice in the League of Nations and in the associational networks that formed around it. This book traces that process of innovation through public administration, think tanks, policy advocacy, and organized business by focusing on one prominent actor in each area. It centres on the four main European belligerents in the First World War – Austria, Britain, France, and Germany – because much of the book is concerned with the long transition from war to peace. Of course, the United States was also an important belligerent, and it figures prominently in the second and third chapters, covering the war and the peace negotiations. The United States was not very involved in League-led trade cooperation until the arrival of Cordell Hull as Secretary of State in 1933 (as explained in the Conclusion). It is also true that the export-dependent neutral states of Northern Europe and the imperial successor states of Central and Eastern Europe had distinctive interests in international trade politics, and their perspectives are also included when discussing specific initiatives. This analysis extends recent scholarship on the genesis of international economic governance in the League era by revealing the particular lines of cleavage in trade and showing how the commercial treaty system inherited from the nineteenth century was reconfigured around multilateral institutions in the 1920s.[5]

The collection of bilateral trade agreements that had been concluded in the final decades of the nineteenth century remained the foundation for trade regulation in the 1920s. These agreements were linked together through most-favoured-nation (MFN) clauses, which guaranteed that treaty partners would receive all tariff concessions and regulatory advantages that were afforded to third parties, at least according to the most robust interpretation. In the nineteenth century, MFN was celebrated as a framework for open markets, but it was also a baseline against which regional and imperial discrimination could be articulated. Trading powers used various techniques to build substructures within the over-arching regime of MFN treaties: some made the transfer of benefits between partners 'conditional' on securing equivalent counter-concessions, some carved out special advantages for colonial partners,

---

[5] Y. Decorzant, *La Société des Nations et la naissance d'une conception de la régulation économique internationale* (Peter Lang, 2011); P. Clavin, *Securing the World Economy: The Reinvention of the League of Nations, 1920–1946* (Oxford University Press, 2013).

and some 'specialized' tariff concessions so narrowly that they would only apply to one partner's particular exports. Thus, in the nineteenth century, MFN was both a tool to knit markets together and to divide them into preferential blocs, and that dual function was institutionalized through the Paris Peace Settlement and the League of Nations. The League provided a central point of integration for the diffuse network of bilateral treaties by establishing a standard formulation of the MFN principle. At the same time, the League also opened legal space for smaller groupings to develop within the standardized global treaty network by defining an exemption from MFN norms for free trade areas. The League thus framed a novel regime of multi-layered trade governance which generated opportunities for regulatory innovation but also created considerable tension. The interplay between regional and global structures made foreign trade a powerful matrix for projects to reorder the world, first in the League and then in the later General Agreement on Tariffs and Trade (GATT) and World Trade Organization (WTO).

Multilateral trade policy has not figured prominently in the standard narrative of the war and its aftermath, which has focused heavily on the issue of reparations. Financial constraints did weigh heavily on trade in the 1920s, but international policy in these two spheres operated quite differently. In the realm of finance, cooperative lending schemes had a concrete impact on markets, moving considerable sums of money around to facilitate the reconstruction of the gold standard and to sustain the cycle of war debts and reparations. International financial cooperation often encroached on domestic systems of taxation and production, as Jamie Martin has shown.[6] In contrast, multilateral trade initiatives intervened much less directly in markets and instead supported high-level policy coordination and normative standardization. That pattern began to shift during the Great Depression, as more intrusive intergovernmental commodity agreements proliferated, with backing from the League. In the 1920s, the more abstract quality of trade cooperation made it a platform for grand projects to reconfigure relations between states and markets.

Trade and finance were clearly separated in the League's organigram. Under the umbrella of its Economic and Financial Organization (EFO), trade was handled through the Economic Committee. This body did consider trade credit and some aspects of foreign direct investment, but a separate Financial Committee addressed most other matters of

---

[6] J. Martin, *The Meddlers: Sovereignty, Empire, and the Birth of Global Economic Governance* (Harvard University Press, 2022).

banking, monetary policy, and investment. Working alongside the EFO, the League Transit Organization dealt with shipping, often in cooperation with the Economic Committee. The semi-autonomous International Labour Organization was responsible for employment policy. The divisions between the League's technical bodies mirrored standard divisions at the national level between ministries of finance, commerce, transit, and labour. Members of the Economic Committee were technically appointed as independent experts by the League Council, but they came recommended by home governments, and most of them were lead national trade negotiators. The Economic Committee was quite small when compared to today's sprawling World Trade Organization. The committee's composition varied, but it hovered around one dozen members. An overwhelming majority of them came from Europe, and most from Western Europe. A system of geographic representation ensured that the non-European views were voiced by a member from Japan, a member from Latin America, a member from India or the British Dominions, and, starting in 1928, a member from the United States. Non-European participation in the sub-committees that actually fleshed out the details for individual projects remained very limited due to the greater expense and travel time involved in sending qualified experts to Geneva from overseas.[7]

In the 1920s, League trade policy thus focused heavily on Europe and responded to the geopolitical tensions there which stemmed from the First World War, centring on 'the German problem'. Before 1914, Germany had become the nucleus of European trade treaties by leading several successive rounds of negotiations. The Treaty of Versailles cut the centre out of the European treaty system by stripping Germany of MFN rights for five years, constraining its negotiating capacity. Although Germany's wings were clipped temporarily in 1919, it gained tremendous regional clout as the only great power left standing in Central and Eastern Europe. In territorial terms, Germany came out of the Paris Peace Settlement relatively intact, while the surrounding empires utterly disintegrated.[8] This power shift in the east also heightened friction in Western Europe. Without a Russian partner on Germany's eastern flank, France faced a powerful neighbour with a potentially expansive hinterland. After first attempting a policy of confrontation which culminated in the occupation of Germany's industrial heartland in the Ruhr in 1923, the French government embraced a more collaborative approach, aiming to bind

---

[7] P. Clavin and J.-W. Wessels, 'Transnationalism and the League of Nations: Understanding the Work of Its Economic and Financial Organisation', *Contemporary European History*, 14/4 (2005), 465–92.

[8] A. J. P. Taylor, *The Origins of the Second World War* (Fawcett, 1961), 44–52, 66–77.

Germany in a network of European partners through multilateral rules.[9] As French leaders well understood, the architecture of German power in Europe also depended to a large extent on decisions made in Vienna. Austria sought to leverage its position as a weak but decisive intermediary between east and west, balancing its close bonds to Germany with its ties to the Habsburg successor states.[10]

Many Europeans concluded that managing these complex dynamics would require a more sophisticated form of multilateral organization beyond traditional bilateral diplomacy, and League trade policy became a central vehicle for their projects. There was, however, disagreement about whether multilateralism would facilitate or constrain Germany's influence over its neighbours and whether it should anchor Europe within a universal normative framework or bracket its problems within a special regional regime. At issue was not merely Europe's internal relations but also its position in the wider world. Ongoing political conflict in Russia, East Asia, and the Middle East undermined the vast Eurasian continental empires whose stability had enabled Europeans to project power far afield during a long period of colonial expansion.[11] At the same time, nationalist movements and transnational diasporas had begun to mount a forceful challenge to European maritime empire in its outer reaches.[12] Indeed, although Europeans dominated international trade debates in the 1920s, the League also opened new channels for Asians, Africans, and Latin Americans to contest Eurocentrism and to articulate alternative models of economic order.[13]

[9] R. Boyce, *British Capitalism at the Crossroads, 1919–1932: A Study in Politics, Economics, and International Relations* (Cambridge University Press, 1987), 165–77; P. Jackson, *Beyond the Balance of Power: France and the Politics of National Security in the Era of the First World War* (Cambridge University Press, 2013).
[10] A. Suppan, 'Mitteleuropa Konzeptionen zwischen Restauration und Anschluss', in R. G. Plaschka, H. Haselsteiner, A. Suppan, A. M. Drabek, and B. Zaar (eds.), *Mitteleuropa-Konzeptionen in der ersten Hälfte des 20. Jahrhunderts* (Verlag der Österreichischen Akademie der Wissenschaften, 1994), pp. 171–97.
[11] J. Darwin, *After Tamerlane: The Rise and Fall of Global Empires, 1400–2000* (Allen Lane, 2008), 365–424.
[12] E. Manela, *The Wilsonian Moment: Self-Determination and the International Origins of Anticolonial Nationalism* (Oxford University Press, 2009); R. Gerwarth and E. Manela (eds.), *Empires at War, 1911–1923* (Oxford University Press, 2014).
[13] S. Jackson, 'Diaspora Politics and Developmental Empire: The Syro-Lebanese at the League of Nations', *Arab Studies Journal*, 21/1 (2013), 166–90; S. Pedersen, *The Guardians: The League of Nations and the Crisis of Empire* (Oxford University Press, 2015); C. Biltoft, 'The League of Nations and Alternative Economic Perspectives', in J. Ghosh, R. Kattel, E. Reinert (eds.), *New Perspectives on the History of Political Economy* (Edgar Elgar, 2016), pp. 270–80; J. A. S. Román, 'From the Tigris to the Amazon: Peripheral Expertise, Impossible Cooperation and Economic Multilateralism at the League of Nations, 1920–1946', in S. Jackson, A. O'Malley (eds.), *The Institution of*

In the 1920s Europeans confronted far-flung countries that did not want to be led, as well as rising competitors that did not want to lead. The United States notably ended the war with vast economic clout which far outstripped its diplomatic will or capacity, as Adam Tooze has emphasized.[14] Interwar debates about European unity were largely – though by no means exclusively – about how to manage transatlantic relations, with reference to the United States and the larger pan-American project.[15] Britain found itself in a particularly tight position, balancing a commitment to European reconstruction against demands from increasingly assertive Dominions and a fickle Atlantic partner.[16] The analysis presented here refines influential recent scholarship that highlights the importance of US leadership in twentieth-century international relations.[17] While it is certainly true that the dramatic expansion of US influence during the world wars profoundly shaped the development of modern international governance, this book shows that interwar Europe made decisive contributions to that process precisely because it grew weak and unstable. In the 1920s, multilateral experimentation in trade policy was a leaderless competition among rival visions of post-war Europe.

Those European experiments fed into a broader regime of 'global order', defined by Andrew Hurrell as a system of international norms mediating value conflicts and power asymmetries stemming from social, political, and economic change. Hurrell shows that this normative core is constantly being redefined in response to shifting regional structures.[18] Seen in this light, the traditional preoccupation with the 'success' or 'failure' of the League of Nations is misplaced because modern international governance is inherently unstable: global order and disorder are always in dynamic

---

International Order: From the League of Nations to the United Nations (Routledge, 2018), pp. 59–64.

[14] A. Tooze, The Deluge: The Great War and the Remaking of Global Order, 1916–1931 (Allen Lane, 2014).

[15] S. Beckert, 'American Danger: United States Empire, Eurafrica, and the Territorialization of Industrial Capitalism, 1870–1950', The American Historical Review, 122/4 (2017), 1137–70; A.-I. Richard, 'Competition and Complementarity: Civil Society Networks and the Question of Decentralizing the League of Nations', Journal of Global History, 7/2 (2012), 233–56.

[16] A. Orde, The Eclipse of Great Britain: The United States and British Imperial Decline, 1895–1956 (St. Martin's Press, 1996), 41–69; J. Darwin, The Empire Project: The Rise and Fall of the British World-System, 1830–1970 (Cambridge University Press, 2009), 359–417.

[17] P. O. Cohrs, The Unfinished Peace after World War I: America, Britain and the Stabilisation of Europe, 1919–1932 (Cambridge University Press, 2008); Tooze, The Deluge; O. Rosenboim, The Emergence of Globalism: Visions of World Order in Britain and the United States, 1939–1950 (Princeton University Press, 2017); S. Wertheim, Tomorrow, the World: The Birth of U.S. Global Supremacy (The Belknap Press of Harvard University Press, 2020).

[18] A. Hurrell, On Global Order: Power, Values, and the Constitution of International Society (Oxford University Press, 2007).

tension. This insight provides useful guidance for interpreting the recent centennial assessment of the First World War's legacy. Much of the scholarship suggests that the war was both a product and a producer of turbulent international relations.[19] It should be emphasized that conflict was not chaos. The breakdown and reconfiguration of global order during and after the First World War produced distinct geopolitical and institutional patterns, which were reflected in the changing outlook of European trade experts. Prior to the war, they generally conceived of the world economy as an interconnected but diffuse system without a centre. They referred frequently to the 'organization' of economic activity without specifying who directed that process or through what legal channels. In contrast, after 1918, they began to argue that the world economy required a clearly defined institutional nucleus which would provide a firm base to manage the manifold shocks brought by the war. Although bilateral methods continued to dominate European treaty practice through the end of the interwar period, League collaborators defined multilateralism as the new frontier of innovation. This book tells their story.

In the 1920s, international trade politics were dominated by a generational cohort born in the 1870s who reached professional maturity just before the outbreak of the First World War. They were effective institutional entrepreneurs because in 1918 they were sufficiently well established to have extensive organizational resources at their disposal but still young enough to be willing to use those resources in creative ways. In response to tectonic shifts in the international economic and political landscape, they sought to bind the world's governments and markets in a durable system of multilateral coordination. Their macroeconomic objectives were not revolutionary – they generally tried to ease restrictions on foreign trade and restore patterns of economic integration that had been disrupted by the war. There was no systematic effort to use trade policy to manage changing relations between workers and employers or between agriculture and manufacturing. Those issues did periodically appear on the League trade agenda in the 1920s, but it was not until the 1930s that new models of planning and international development directed League economic policy more deliberately towards goals of full employment and balanced economic growth.[20]

---

[19] C. Clark, *The Sleepwalkers: How Europe Went to War in 1914* (Allen Lane, 2012); J. Leonhard, *Der überforderte Frieden: Versailles und die Welt 1918–1923* (C. H. Beck, 2018); R. Gerwarth, *The Vanquished: Why the First World War Failed to End, 1917–1923* (Allen Lane, 2016); E. Conze, *Die große Illusion: Versailles 1919 und die Neuordnung der Welt* (Siedler Verlag, 2018).

[20] Clavin, *Securing the World Economy*, 159–97; C. R. Unger, *International Development: A Postwar History* (Bloomsbury Academic, 2018), 23–78.

The relative absence of social issues from League trade debates in the 1920s must not be interpreted as evidence that interwar liberals were generally hostile towards welfare provision at the national level. Some observers such as Ludwig von Mises did interpret League trade policy in that light.[21] However, restricting social democracy was not the primary intention behind any of the practical trade initiatives discussed in this book. Indeed, most members of the Economic Committee looked favourably on national social insurance, which they saw as an essential complement to a regime of open international trade. For example, Hubert Llewellyn Smith, the British official who was the single most influential figure in early League trade policy, began his career as a union organizer. He joined the civil service as a reform-minded 'New Liberal', with a remit to build-out Britain's collective-bargaining system using the levers of state commercial administration in the Board of Trade. He went on to write the legislation that established Britain's unemployment insurance system in 1911 and served as a mentor to William Beveridge, who later continued that work. Although Llewellyn Smith favoured state-funded welfare programmes, he was sceptical that such programmes could be advanced through standardized international trade norms, given the diversity of local social conditions. It is true that the ILO used a very different regulatory strategy to promote social insurance. The Economic Committee's commercial rules were often quite detailed and prescriptive, but the ILO worked through an arms-length process of standard-setting that left national governments and social partners wide latitude to adapt norms to local circumstances.[22]

In terms of substantive content, League trade norms did not stray far from nineteenth-century trade treaties. The Economic Committee worked to standardize and modestly supplement existing treaties through multiparty agreements. It offered new machinery to write, enforce, and amend collective agreements thus embedding bilateral treaty negotiations in a continuous process of policy coordination. Patricia Clavin has demonstrated that the League of Nations functioned as a porous 'multiverse'. Its operations were repeatedly reconfigured through the integration of new collaborators and ideas, with economic and financial activities gradually assuming greater prominence as political cooperation stalled.[23] This book

---

[21] Slobodian, *Globalists*, 27–54.

[22] This arms-length approach partly reflected the fact that ILO officials wanted to strengthen the self-governance of national insurance funds, which constituted an important base of political support for their work. See S. Kott, 'Constructing a European Social Model: The Fight for Social Insurance in the Interwar Period', in J. Van Daele, M. Rodriguez Garcia, and G. van Goethem (eds.), *ILO Histories* (Peter Lang, 2011), pp. 173–96.

[23] Clavin, *Securing the World Economy*.

reveals how the institutional nexus described by Clavin was grounded in nineteenth-century trade treaties and how the transition from nineteenth-century globalization towards twentieth-century international governance fed through diverse national perspectives and organizational contexts.

The full significance of the leap towards multilateral order in the 1920s becomes clear when it is set against the more decentralized trade politics that predated the First World War. This book situates four influential reformers in the pre-war trade system and then traces their competing efforts to reshape that system in the 1920s using different organizational pathways. It focuses on Hubert Llewellyn Smith, the aforementioned British trade official, who was largely responsible for crafting the basic architecture for multilateral trade treaties in the League; Bernhard Harms, a German academic who built one of Europe's most prominent economic think tanks, the Kiel Institute for World Economy and Sea Traffic (Instiut für Weltwirtschaft und Seeverkehr or IfW); Lucien Coquet, a French lawyer who led a series of policy-advocacy groups dedicated to European unity; and Richard Riedl, an Austrian who became the central point of contact between League trade policy and the International Chamber of Commerce (ICC). Although these men crossed paths, they were not part of a clearly defined coterie. Rather, they were prominent voices in a wider conversation about the changing configuration of international trade, and their organizational trajectories reveal the winding paths along which trade debates developed from the 1880s to the 1920s.

In this book, institutional contextualization will predominate over personal stories. Studying Coquet, Harms, Llewellyn Smith, and Riedl is useful because they expose organizational environments that shaped international trade debates in the 1920s. These men cannot be taken as direct representatives of mainstream trade policy in their home countries, but their multilateral projects were firmly grounded in national and imperial settings and commanded a substantial following. Although this book does not offer a biographical analysis in a conventional sense, it does use some tools of biography to study the processes of institutional transition at work in the interwar period. Tracing individual trajectories exposes the grinding gears of organizational practice. It also highlights the novel opportunities for personal agency that were available in an international system in flux, when internationalists could exert considerable influence by positioning themselves between shifting organizations.[24] This book extends previous

---

[24] I. Löhr, 'Lives beyond Borders, or: How to Trace Global Biographies, 1880–1950', *Comparativ: Lives beyond Borders: A Social History 1880–1950*, 23/6 (2013), 7–21; M. Herren and I. Löhr, 'Being International in Times of War: Arthur Sweetser and the Shifting of the League of Nations to the United Nations', *European Review of History: Revue européenne d'histoire*, 25/3–4 (2018), 535–52; H. A. Ikonomou, 'The Biography As

research emphasizing interactions between nationalism and internationalism to show how such linkages were institutionally articulated through trade policy.[25]

Chapters 1, 2, and 3 run from 1890 to 1920 and follow Coquet, Harms, Llewellyn Smith, and Riedl together as a generational cohort who reached the height of their careers just at the moment when an era of unprecedented global economic integration gave way to a war of unprecedented destruction. Chapters 4, 5, 6, and 7 analyse their different institutional responses to that reversal in four individually focused chapters. Born around 1870, Coquet, Harms, Llewellyn Smith, and Riedl spent their student years in a period of volatility, marked by intense imperial competition, sweeping technological change, and the rise of mass politics coinciding with an extension of voting rights. The 1870s witnessed a deep global economic depression, and the subsequent four decades brought a spectacular but erratic recovery. This belle époque is now often described as an era of globalization, but contemporaries were less fixated on overall levels of economic growth than on its uneven, boom-and-bust character.[26] They witnessed a significant expansion of global commercial interdependence that coincided with the rise of nationalism, jingoistic imperialism, and protectionism. This prompted new efforts to understand and control the mechanics of world trade.

'Organization' became the watchword for trade policy during this period. This term covered a dense collection of rules, information, and institutions, all designed to make trans-border business more intelligible

Institutional Can-Opener: An Investigation of Core Bureaucratic Practices in the Early Years of the League of Nations Secretariat', in K. Gram-Skjoldager, H. A. Ikonomou, and T. Kahlert (eds.), *Organizing the 20th-Century World: International Organizations and the Emergence of International Public Administration, 1920–1960s* (Bloomsbury Academic, 2020), pp. 33–48; B. Reinalda, 'Biographical Analysis: Insights and Perspectives from the IO BIO Dictionary Project', in K. Gram-Skjoldager, H. A. Ikonomou, and T. Kahlert (eds.), *Organizing the 20th-Century World: International Organizations and the Emergence of International Public Administration, 1920–1960s* (Bloomsbury Academic, 2020), pp. 14–32.

[25] See notably, M. Herren, *Hintertüren zur Macht: Internationalismus und modernisierungsorientierte Außenpolitik in Belgien, der Schweiz und den USA 1865–1914* (Oldenbourg, 2000); D. Gorman, *The Emergence of International Society in the 1920s* (Cambridge University Press, 2011); G. Sluga, *Internationalism in the Age of Nationalism* (University of Pennsylvania Press, 2013); Pedersen, *The Guardians*; M. Mazower, *Governing the World: The History of an Idea, 1815 to the Present* (Penguin Press, 2012); G. F. Sinclair, *To Reform the World: International Organizations and the Making of Modern States* (Oxford University Press, 2017); Martin, *The Meddlers*.

[26] The most influential account of nineteenth-century globalization is K. H. O'Rourke and J. G. Williamson, *Globalization and History: The Evolution of a Nineteenth-Century Atlantic Economy* (MIT Press, 1999).

and predictable.[27] This included state-led programmes of 'export-promotion' and changes in private corporate governance, as well as hybrid projects that bridged the two. In the latter decades of the nineteenth century, multinational commercial activity was coordinated by ad-hoc groups of investors, trading houses, and manufacturers who collaborated to exploit new market opportunities created by infrastructural development and colonial expansion. Public trade policy focused on facilitating the exchange of information within these nebulous networks to ensure a modicum of operational and regulatory consistency across markets.[28] This entailed a significant expansion in the laws and institutions buttressing foreign trade, opening new avenues for professional advancement to ambitious educated young men, including Coquet, Harms, Llewellyn Smith, and Riedl. The growth of economic bureaucracy also opened some new professional opportunities for young women, chiefly in information functions, but they had limited access to more mobile and active decision-making roles.

The outbreak of war among Europe's main trading powers in 1914 profoundly disrupted the regulatory fabric of global commerce. War automatically suspended trade treaties between belligerents and halted many private transactions. Both the Allies and the Central Powers quickly introduced measures to transform the world economy into a weapon. The Allied blockade and the German programme of submarine warfare similarly aimed to exploit relations of commercial interdependence to cripple enemy military capacity. Coquet, Harms, Llewellyn Smith, and Riedl all participated in economic warfare. At the same time, they saw that the political instrumentalization of private trade would not be easily reversed, because many areas of economic life would retain new strategic significance in peacetime. Thus, leaders on both sides began to develop multilateral plans to police the world economy after the war while also trying to safeguard their own supply lines. In 1915 and 1916 these multilateral projects coalesced into post-war programmes for customs unions, trade agreements, and punitive restrictions on enemies. Wartime plans for solidarity among military allies set the institutional and geopolitical parameters for later trade debates in the League of Nations. The

---

[27] See for example, J. Hellauer, *Die Organisation des Exporthandels: Eine allgemeine Darstellung und Untersuchung* (Handels-Museum, 1903); G. de Leener, 'L'organisation du commerce d'exportation et la concurrence internationale', in *Ce qui manque au commerce belge d'exportation* (Misch & Thron, 1906), pp. 225–84; 'Trade Organization', *The Encyclopædia Britannica: A Dictionary of Arts, Sciences, Literature, and General Information*, Eleventh ed. (Cambridge University Press, 1910), pp. 135–9.

[28] G. Jones, *Multinationals and Global Capitalism: From the Nineteenth to the Twenty-First Century* (Oxford University Press, 2005), 26, 170, 201–3.

United States contributed decisively to this process through a series of influential policy pronouncements, most famously Woodrow Wilson's Fourteen Points.

At the Paris Peace Conference, proposals for exclusive economic blocs that would prolong wartime alliances vied with projects that aimed to safeguard global market access through universal trade norms. The final peace settlement left the conflict between those approaches unresolved; it combined unilateral restrictions on the defeated states' commercial sovereignty with a universal commitment to 'the equitable treatment of commerce' in the League Covenant. That ambiguous formula reflected deep disagreements among all parties concerning national and imperial economic sovereignty and the relationship between trade and security. In the 1920s, the unfulfilled aspirations for world order that had been awakened during the peacemaking process were projected onto a common institutional canvas in the League of Nations, but they remained rooted in divergent geopolitical programmes. The trajectories followed by Coquet, Harms, Llewellyn Smith, and Riedl reveal how competing national priorities influenced League trade policy through different organizational channels: formal state bureaucracy, economic information, policy advocacy, and business networks.

After the close of the 1919 peace conference, League collaborators moved quickly to improvise economic institutions. Post-war crisis stimulated League action but also limited its scope, since many states clung to trade barriers as a means to manage economic and political instability. In this tumultuous environment, Llewellyn Smith intervened decisively to help create the League's Economic Committee, and he dominated that body until his retirement in 1927. In the 1920s Llewellyn Smith was officially designated as Britain's top economic diplomat, His Majesty's Chief Economic Advisor. He favoured an open, rules-based trade regime, but also insisted that League norms must not threaten the internal cohesion of the British Empire. He facilitated the orderly re-entry of Germany into world markets, while also working to remove Germany from Britain's strategic supply chains, in the name of national security. Llewellyn Smith embraced multilateralism as a framework to manage these competing priorities and established new procedures to write collective trade rules through the League. He was an incremental innovator, with an eye to Britain's delicate international position. He sponsored a series of narrowly focused technical treaties, in coordination with governments, experts, and business leaders.

After Llewellyn Smith initially set the League Economic Committee on a cautious course, Franco-German conflict helped stimulate the development of a more ambitious trade agenda, which found expression in the

League's 1927 World Economic Conference. The Franco-Belgian occupation of the Ruhr in 1923 was a crucial catalyst for change. Bernhard Harms responded by demanding a more broadly institutionalized international economic regime which would include the United States and would cover sensitive issues skirted by Llewellyn Smith, including reparations, raw materials, and colonial markets. Harms had a prominent bully pulpit from which to promote this vision, as the director of the IfW. He used his position to facilitate ongoing policy dialogue among a large community of League collaborators and critics. The 1923 Ruhr crisis prompted Harms to shift the focus of this information network from news to sustained policy research with backing from US philanthropic bodies such as the Rockefeller Foundation. He helped establish a novel think-tank environment that spanned business, academia, and government and became an important base of support for the League. In recognition of his pivotal role in international information networks, Harms was asked to coordinate a massive economic bibliography for the League at the end of the 1920s. His work on that project challenged Llewellyn Smith's attempt to craft a multilateral diplomatic process that preserved states' primacy over outside experts. Furthermore, while Llewellyn Smith held fast to a traditional commitment to free trade based on comparative advantage, Harms was the head of the Friedrich List Society. He argued that an integrated world economy was fully compatible with active industrial policy, backed by limited tariffs on nascent sectors. In Kiel, he gathered experts from across the colonial and non-colonial developing world to discuss these policy options, opening the Eurocentric discussions in Geneva to wider debate and criticism.

Although their methods and goals differed significantly, Harms and Llewellyn Smith were both globalists who shared a strong antipathy to regionalism. In contrast, Lucien Coquet and Richard Riedl were the foremost spokesmen for European unity in League trade debates. They used the 1927 World Economic Conference to launch competing plans for a European sub-unit within the League of Nations. Coquet was an improbable advocate for European reconciliation since he had enthusiastically supported the 1923 Ruhr occupation as an opportunity for French territorial expansion. After the 1924 Dawes Reparations Settlement and 1925 Locarno Accords foreclosed that path, Coquet pivoted towards a pan-European orientation. In effect, he sought to reimpose the temporary constraints that had been placed on German commercial rights through the Treaty of Versailles by applying them to the rest of Europe as well. To advance this goal, he helped rally French politicians and business leaders in a new organization that was simply called the European Customs Union (Union Douanière Européenne, or

UDE). Working in close partnership with the French Ministry of Foreign Affairs, Coquet built out national branches of the UDE across Europe. Coquet and Riedl joined forces in 1929 to promote a proposal for European federation from the French minister of foreign affairs, Aristide Briand, and a parallel plan for a League-sponsored tariff truce. This marked a brief moment of unity when diverse League collaborators tried to work together to respond to the onset of the Great Depression through concerted European tariff reduction. This cooperation quickly lost momentum as the Depression advanced, however. The Briand Plan fragmented into a series of smaller sub-regional projects, including a controversial plan for an Austro-German customs union which was widely condemned as a prelude to full political union or *Anschluss*.

The possibility that general plans for European unity would become a vehicle for German power via *Anschluss* always lurked beneath the surface of League multilateralism in the 1920s. Indeed, this was why Coquet and his associates anchored their work so firmly in the League. The peace treaties had made the League the central bulwark against *Anschluss*, and that makes the story of Richard Riedl – and his collaboration with Coquet – particularly remarkable. In the 1920s, Riedl was a well-known advocate of *Anschluss*, having spent his long career in the in the Vienna Chamber of Commerce and the Austrian Ministry of Commerce advocating ethnic Germans' regional leadership. In 1927, when Coquet launched his movement for a European customs union, Riedl initiated an elaborate programme to use the League to bring about *Anschluss* gradually by embedding Austro-German bilateral economic integration in a multilateral system. He sought to bypass the formal treaty constraints that prevented the Austrian and German governments from pursuing this course by facilitating low-level administrative rapprochement through business organizations, using the Vienna Chamber of Commerce and the ICC.

Initially, the ICC's engagement in League trade policy had focused on specific areas of business regulation, such as commercial arbitration and trade credit. Riedl pushed the ICC into a more political role by intervening in debates about the fundamental architecture of trade treaties. Riedl notably used the ICC to weigh in on the League's standardization of the MFN norm and its efforts to regulate the legal status of foreign commercial agents and firms. Llewellyn Smith had initiated the League's work in both areas, from his perch at the heart of the bureaucratic establishment, and Riedl then intervened to push for deeper engagement with business interests and a more explicit regional cast. In the process, Riedl provoked new debate about the League's authority to mediate relations between national governments and international business. By the end of the 1920s, Riedl grew frustrated with the institutional constraints in the ICC, as a technical body with a diverse membership base that included many opponents of European unity. Throughout the 1920s, the conflict between a logic of trade blocs and a logic of global market integration framed much of the League's economic work. After 1920, Europe's economic and political dominance could no longer be taken for granted and its relationship to the wider world had to be more precisely defined and institutionalized.[29] From Austria and France, Richard Riedl and Lucien Coquet worked in tandem to place regionalism at the heart of the League's trade agenda. Both saw European unity as a solution to 'the German problem', but Riedl sought to enhance German economic influence and Coquet sought to curtail it. For his part, Bernhard Harms was not particularly concerned about strengthening Germany's position in Europe; instead, he focused on restoring his country's overseas commercial relationships. Both Harms and Llewellyn Smith aimed to build a comprehensive system of information and trade rules which would facilitate commercial integration worldwide, but they disagreed fundamentally about the status of European empires. Harms advocated an 'open-door' regime ensuring free access to colonial markets and resources, while Llewellyn Smith insisted that international trade rules must not impinge on British imperial sovereignty. Harms and Llewellyn Smith affirmed the League's authority as an over-arching framework for world economic order but left the conflict over regional and imperial substructures unresolved. The inconclusive confrontation between regionalists, globalists, and imperialists of different stripes produced an unstable multi-level system of trade regulation that turned out to be a remarkably durable institutional legacy of the League, still evident in today's regime of general WTO rules floating above a dense thicket of 'free trade areas'.

The multilateral experiments of the 1920s permanently changed the legal and institutional architecture of foreign trade. The League consolidated the use of MFN to regulate relations between global, regional, and imperial economic programmes within a common international framework. League trade debates privileged the priorities of commercially developed countries in Western Europe but also created a platform to contest their influence.[30] While standardizing formal treaty practice, the

---

[29] Richard, 'Competition and Complementarity', 234–5.
[30] Dissenting voices notably came from League members whose sovereignty was attenuated by structures of imperial dependence or international tutelage, including the British Dominions and the young imperial successor states of Central and Eastern Europe.

League also promoted the interpenetration of public international law (governing relations between states) and private international law (governing relations between firms and individuals). This public–private legal hybridity became a defining feature of twentieth-century global order.[31] Finally, interwar multilateralism shifted trade politics away from one-off treaty negotiations towards ongoing debate and coordination. This process was supported by the international bureaucracy in Geneva and by broader systems of policy research that linked business, academia, and government.[32]

After 1929, the procedural compromises of the 1920s broke down under the pressure of the Great Depression and the increasingly combative power politics that accompanied it. Multilateral models remained influential in Geneva, but the political will to submit national, regional, and imperial ambitions to League mediation rapidly waned across Europe. Nevertheless, trade policy remained a central forum in which the rules-based League order was defied and defended through the end of the 1930s. French and British governments cleaved away from the League by developing preferential imperial trade systems. Nazi leaders pursued eastward expansion through bilateral barter agreements that flouted MFN norms.[33] At the same time, the United States began to engage more actively, though discreetly, in League multilateralism. Cordell Hull, Franklin Roosevelt's Secretary of State, turned to Geneva to advance his hallmark trade agreements programme, which was anchored by the League's standard MFN clause. Hull thus helped open US trade policy to international engagement, laying the groundwork for the United States to assume a leadership role in trade policy after 1945 in the GATT.

The League set many precedents that later underpinned the GATT and the WTO, but this was not a linear process of legal accretion. Multilateral trade policy emerged in the 1920s as field of experimentation that linked together wide-ranging global transformations: the marginalization of Europe in world markets, the growing reliance on foreign trade

Trade policy thus intersected with the conflicting sovereignty claims that Susan Pedersen highlights (S. Pedersen, 'Back to the League of Nations', *The American Historical Review*, 112/4 (2007), 1091–117; Pedersen, *The Guardians*). I analyse this issue in more depth in M. L. Dungy, 'Writing Multilateral Trade Rules in the League of Nations', *Contemporary European History*, 30/1 (2021), 60–75.

[31] Hurrell, *On Global Order*, 95–120.

[32] K. Gram-Skjoldager and H. A. Ikonomou, 'Making Sense of the League of Nations Secretariat: Historiographical and Conceptual Reflections on Early International Public Administration', *European History Quarterly*, 49/3 (2019), 420–44.

[33] A. Hirschman, *National Power and the Structure of Foreign Trade* (University of California Press, 1945).

as a weapon of war, and the shift in European power dynamics tied to the collapse of continental empires. Coquet, Harms, Llewellyn Smith, and Riedl each grappled with these common problems using a distinct set of organizational tools and speaking from a particular national standpoint. Together, they helped initiate debate over the nature, scope, and purpose of multilateral trade politics that is still open today.

1 Organizing Globalization

The decades before the First World War were marked by a complex and rapid set of economic changes which are now frequently described as the first globalization.[1] Spectacular advances in transportation and communications knit together distant markets to an unprecedented degree. From 1860 to 1910, the world's railway networks were extended from 66,000 to 465,000 miles.[2] A series of technical improvements made steam shipping much cheaper and faster, and canal construction greatly shortened the distances to be covered. The telegraph and the gold standard allowed money and information to flow rapidly along these new infrastructural networks.[3] A massive expansion in formal and informal empire institutionally underpinned this commercial integration.[4] Connecting markets more tightly over longer distances drove down prices in Europe and helped transmit shocks more rapidly. A deep global depression starting in 1873 made a significant dent in European foreign trade through the early 1890s, with export growth declining from over 5 per cent to roughly 2 per cent.[5] Mass unemployment brought the 'the social question' to prominence, fostering new currents of transnational intellectual exchange among reformers.[6] In Europe, the depression coincided with a large-scale 'invasion' of commodities from the United States, backed by innovations in agronomy and transportation.[7] From 1870 to 1913, wheat prices fell substantially across Western Europe, provoking demands for agricultural protection in countries with large farming populations and reinforcing

---

[1] O'Rourke and Williamson, *Globalization and History*; J. A. Frieden, *Global Capitalism: Its Fall and Rise in the Twentieth Century* (W. W. Norton, 2006).

[2] Darwin, *The Empire Project*, 114–15.

[3] O'Rourke and Williamson, *Globalization and History*, 33–4; Darwin, *The Empire Project*, 114–15.

[4] Darwin, *After Tamerlane*, 257–8.

[5] P. Bairoch, 'European Trade Policy, 1815–1914', in P. Mathias and S. Pollard (eds.), *The Cambridge Economic History of Europe from the Decline of the Roman Empire* (Cambridge University Press, 1989), pp. 1–160, 45.

[6] D. T. Rodgers, *Atlantic Crossings: Social Politics in a Progressive Age* (Belknap Press, 1998).

[7] Bairoch, 'European Trade Policy', 45–51.

free trade as a strategy to deliver cheap food to city dwellers in Britain and other economies that were firmly oriented towards industrial exports.[8] Yet there was also growing debate in Britain about whether free trade was still a recipe for prosperity as new protectionist industrial titans emerged to challenge British primacy in global markets. The US share of world exports rose from roughly 8 per cent in 1870 to 13 per cent in 1913 and Germany achieved a similar increase, while Britain's export share declined from roughly 20 per cent to 14 per cent over the same period.[9]

Many Europeans attributed the impressive growth rates achieved in the United States to the country's command over supply chains and markets on a continental scale (the final decades of the nineteenth century also saw a strong drive for westward settlement). Admiration for US continental power motivated Europeans to try to construct similarly large and cohesive territorial units. They used new transportation and communications technology to lay claim to inland population, resources, and markets through more comprehensive and intensive territorial administration.[10] Projects to band together in regional customs unions intersected with ambitions for imperial cooperation in a vast vision of 'Eurafrica'.[11] Cooperation was not the dominant principle of European politics during this period, however. Although there was no general European war in this period, neither was there peace. There were many small conflicts and threats of conflict, and violence was extreme in many cases.[12] The international environment was crowded, volatile, and tense, and Europeans responded using new tools of public and private 'organization'. Crucially, 'organization' could be competitive or collaborative and its geographic scope was often ambiguous.

Born within the span of a decade from the mid-1860s to mid-1870s, Lucien Coquet, Bernhard Harms, Hubert Llewellyn Smith, and Richard Riedl came of age in the 1880s when organizational responses to the 1873 depression were being tested. They began life with some social advantages but also faced early obstacles. Their fathers worked in trade and public administration, and a father's profession defined family

---

[8] K. H. O'Rourke, 'The European Grain Invasion, 1870–1913', *The Journal of Economic History*, 57/4 (1997), 775–801.

[9] A. Lewis, 'The Rate of Growth of World Trade, 1830–1973', in S. Grassman and E. Lundberg (eds.), *The World Economic Order: Past and Prospects* (Macmillan, 1981), pp. 11–74, 38–59.

[10] C. S. Maier, 'Consigning the Twentieth Century to History: Alternative Narratives for the Modern Era', *The American Historical Review*, 105/3 (2000), 807; C. S. Maier, *Once within Borders: Territories of Power, Wealth, and Belonging since 1500* (The Belknap Press of Harvard University Press, 2016), 185–232.

[11] Beckert, 'American Danger'.

[12] I. V. Hull, *Absolute Destruction: Military Culture and the Practices of War in Imperial Germany* (Cornell University Press, 2013).

social rank in this period. Coquet's father was a municipal architect in an unfashionable Paris suburb, Llewellyn Smith's was a tea wholesaler, Riedl's was an official in the Austrian tobacco monopoly, and Harms's was a businessman and tax collector. Llewellyn Smith and Riedl both lost their fathers when they were young and had to rely on scholarships to complete their studies. Harms and Coquet travelled widely during their student years. Harms toured France, Spain, and the Netherlands, while Coquet went to Britain and Germany. In Cologne, Coquet married Betty Wolff, whose brother Otto went on to become a major steel magnate and an important figure in the Ruhr occupation of 1923. Coquet, Harms, Llewellyn Smith, and Riedl all pursued university studies in subjects that offered mobility to ambitious members of the middle class. Riedl and Coquet studied law, Llewellyn Smith studied mathematics, and Harms studied political science. During their student years, they were caught in diverse currents of social and political change. Harms and Llewellyn Smith both engaged in debates about 'the social question', Coquet participated in the movement to promote international arbitration, and Riedl was immersed in pan-German nationalism as a fraternity leader.[13]

All four men followed circuitous routes to professional success. Harms did not initially go to university due to ill health; he first completed an apprenticeship in bookbinding with a maternal relative.[14] Although Llewellyn Smith was at the top of his class at Oxford, he decided not to enter the British civil service directly. He took the entrance examination but declined the position that he was offered in the War Office due to his family's Quaker background. Instead, he opted to spend several years in the London social reform scene before joining the Board of Trade (the department that was responsible for domestic and foreign commercial policy in the British government).[15] Riedl also entered the civil service unusually late: he came into the Austrian Ministry of Commerce only

---

[13] L. Coquet, Mémoire de défense, 10 October 1945, AN: F12/9460; Bericht vom 25 November betreffend die vom Advokaten Coquet in Paris betriebene Gründung einer deutsch-französischen Handelsvereinigung, 31 January 1908, PA AA: Paris Gesandtschaft/1432; G.C. von Unruh, Ein bedeutender Nationalökonom aus Ostfriesland, 1964, IfW: Hs, Harms 1; Friedrich Hoffmann, 'Die Geschichte des Instituts für Weltwirtschaft', 3 vols., unpublished manuscript, IfW (1943–5), vol. III, p. 7, IfW; R. Davidson, 'Sir Hubert Llewellyn Smith and Labour Policy, 1886–1916', DPhil thesis, University of Cambridge (1971), pp. 1–8; G. H. Brettner-Messler, 'Richard Riedl – ein liberaler Imperialist: Biographische Studie zu Handelspolitik und "Mitteleuropa"-Gedanken in Monarchie und Erster Republik', PhD thesis, University of Vienna (1998), pp. 10–11.

[14] G.C. von Unruh, Ein bedeutender Nationalökonom aus Ostfriesland, 1964, IfW: Hs, Harms 1.

[15] Davidson, 'Sir Hubert Llewellyn Smith and Labour Policy', p. 15.

after working for twenty years in the Vienna Chamber of Commerce. Moreover, he did not have a doctorate, which made him an outlier in the Austrian ministerial hierarchy.[16] As a lawyer, Coquet specialized in trademark law but was able to forge ties with influential parliamentarians and jurists well beyond his limited professional circle through his participation in the arbitration movement.

At the end of his career Llewellyn Smith recalled the formative environment of social and economic turmoil in which he and his contemporaries spent their student years: 'The era of unquestioned predominance and of unbroken and rapid expansion of British trade had given place to a difficult period of transition, marked by long and often painful readjustments to meet the new conditions of commercial rivalry and economic nationalism with which British traders were everywhere faced in their former overseas markets.' This destabilization led to 'widespread disillusion and depression, the searching for new solutions, and the questioning of conclusions hitherto regarded as fundamental'.[17] A sense of disillusionment may have been particularly acute in Britain because it was falling from a high peak of economic dominance, but globalization provoked a similar exploratory impulse across Europe in the late nineteenth century.

Although there were many parallels in their early experiences, Coquet, Harms, Llewellyn Smith, and Riedl followed divergent career paths that were shaped by their very different personalities. By nature, Harms had a 'tendency towards the large scale' and a curiosity about the world, 'far and wide', according to his assistant. When Harms accepted his professorship in Kiel, he had already booked berths for his family on a steamer to Shanghai to take up a position there. Yet Harms combined a broad perspective with a drive to act as the master of his own defined fiefdom. For example, in his first post as a temporary lecturer in Tübingen, he set up a tennis court on the lawn of his rental house because he thought that the public courts were too crowded.[18] As soon as Harms arrived in Kiel, he worked to cultivate a dedicated network of supporters in business and political circles to carve out his own distinct sphere of activity at the university. Harms and Llewellyn Smith were both system builders, but they had very different methods and goals. Harms had an effusive personality that could fill a room, and he managed to generate a strong gravitational pull around Kiel as a centre for policy debate, drawing in both European and international collaborators. In contrast, Llewellyn Smith focused on refining deep institutional processes, and he stood at the helm

[16] Brettner-Messler, 'Richard Riedl', pp. 13, 22, 44.
[17] H. Llewellyn Smith, 'Introduction', *The New Survey of London Life and Labour*, 9 vols. (P. S. King, 1930), vol. I, pp. 1–57, 1–2.
[18] Hoffmann, 'Die Geschichte des Instituts für Weltwirtschaft', vol. III, pp. 15–16.

of several of the world's most complex economic bureaucracies over the course of his career. He ran Britain's Board of Trade before the war and was largely responsible for constructing its Commercial Intelligence Branch and for leading its work on social protection. During the war, he helped create Britain's Ministry of Munitions before turning his attention to the League's Economic Committee in the 1920s. When he finally retired from the Board of Trade and the League in 1927, the German Foreign Office reported that he would 'not be regretted by the active members of the Economic Committee. He has proven himself to be very bureaucratic, tedious, and fussy'.[19] It was Llewellyn Smith's insistence on formal bureaucratic procedure that made him an effective early innovator, capable of devising a new rule-making routine for the League. Llewellyn Smith's meticulous methods also fitted his understanding of Britain's changing role in the world. He feared that undisciplined international cooperation would sow chaos in the rapidly evolving British Empire.

On the eve of the First World War, Riedl occupied a very similar position to Llewellyn Smith's at the peak of Austria's foreign trade administration, but Riedl was less preoccupied with the construction of concrete institutions and more prone to embark on extravagant policy projects. The Austro-Hungarian foreign minister, Alois von Aerenthal, denounced one of Riedl's plans to negotiate a customs union with Romania in the wake of the Balkan Wars as 'unreal' and 'fantastic', a demonstration of 'how utopian the man's thinking is'. Aerenthal complained that it was irresponsible for Riedl 'to set such goals without specifying the ways and means to get there'.[20] This utopian streak kept Riedl on the periphery of ministerial power in Austria, but his willingness to leap into the unknown later enabled him to push the boundaries of institutional innovation in the League of Nations. Riedl shared with Coquet a propensity towards whimsy, and the two men fed off one another in the 1920s to devise elaborate schemes for European unity that extended outwards from the institutional core that Llewellyn Smith established in the Economic Committee. Coquet and Riedl combined an experimental mindset with deep competence in trade regulation, as trained lawyers, and both privileged technical solutions that skirted open geopolitical conflict. This made them more welcome in national ministries and in the League Secretariat than Richard Coudenhove-Kalergi, the more boisterous and unpredictable standard-bearer for European unity in the interwar years.

[19] Wendler to Referat Völkerbund, Auswärtiges Amt, 8 June 1927, PA AA: Sonderreferat Wirtschaft, R 118453.
[20] Quoted in D. Löding, 'Deutschlands und Österreich-Ungarns Balkanpolitik von 1912–1914 unter besonderer Berücksichtigung ihrer Wirtschaftsinteressen', PhD thesis, University of Hamburg (1969), p. 94.

Riedl and Coquet used many of the same methods, but they operated quite differently. Riedl enjoyed making speeches and cultivated a public persona, while Coquet was shy and self-effacing. At an early meeting in 1907, the German Consul in Paris remarked disdainfully that Coquet was 'without importance or influence'. He was 'a slender, unhandsome person in his thirties with a constant nervous tick affecting one eye. Financially, he does not seem to be doing well at all. His shirtfront greatly needed to be cleaned'. Coquet was, however, determined. He told the consul that he 'would not rest in his efforts to bring about a rapprochement between German and French commercial circles despite all the difficulties'. Over time, Coquet's personal standing in official circles did rise a bit, but he continued to work behind the scenes as an advocate for collective organizational causes and, on occasion, as intermediary for individual patrons such as his brother-in-law Otto Wolff. At any given time, Coquet's Paris office functioned as the headquarters for several different associations and periodicals and as a library of publications from partner groups. Coquet and Riedl were important in the League system not because they built durable institutional structures but rather because they facilitated cooperation across different organizations. Their outreach overlapped, but Riedl focused more on business circles, while Coquet concentrated on semi-diplomatic policy networks. Both men straddled international and European contexts and together they helped configure the institutional interface between regional and global order in the League. They were able to perform this intermediary function effectively because they had already spent several decades moving through the complex associational networks that underpinned international trade politics.

Economic Organization in the Belle Époque

Coquet, Harms, Llewellyn Smith, and Riedl all participated in the movement to monitor and organize foreign trade, which can be traced back to the 1873 depression. The depression prompted European producers to work together to allocate market share and stabilize production through cartels. The cartel movement was concentrated in Europe, underpinned by dense networks of engineers and other technical experts. This regional focus was also explained by the fact that Continental Europeans had limited domestic and imperial markets to cushion a decline in capital-intensive exports.[21] Alongside this private cooperation, there were also

---

[21] W. Kaiser and J. W. Schot, *Writing the Rules for Europe: Experts, Cartels, and International Organizations* (Palgrave Macmillan, 2014), 186–90.

growing demands for state intervention to buffer firms, farmers, and workers from the vagaries of international commerce.[22] This brought a wave of tariff hikes in the late 1880s and 1890s, but the first response from many governments came in the area of commercial information. In the mid-nineteenth century, the most common form of market information that governments had provided to the business community were thick annual consular reports. In the 1880s, ministries of commerce began to transmit smaller items of time-sensitive news in weekly trade bulletins such as Britain's *Board of Trade Journal* or France's *Moniteur Officiel du Commerce Extérieur*. These publications borrowed material from one another and from the sector-specific technical periodicals that were multiplying rapidly during these years, forming a multilateral web of information exchange.

Producing trade bulletins brought significant changes in relations between business and the state. Traditional consular reports mainly surveyed regulations and government-issued statistics. Now, consuls were urged to send practical information about specific products, changing consumer preferences, market opportunities, and commercial practice.[23] Consuls had previously gathered most of their material from government officials in their district. Providing market news on a rolling basis required them to expand ties to the local business elite. They did so by deputizing local traders as 'agents' or 'honorary consuls' and helping to establish expatriate chambers of commerce. By most counts, there were only five such bodies prior to 1880. By 1900 there were more than 50, and by 1914, there were over 150. These chambers served as liaisons between the local business 'colony' and state officials and were often heavily involved in the negotiation of trade treaties.[24] They also performed private regulatory functions, for example by helping to police quality standards. Expatriate chambers of commerce were part of the broader self-organization of the mobile trading elite that culminated in the International Congress of Chambers of Commerce, which met regularly from 1905 to 1914.[25]

---

[22] Bairoch, 'European Trade Policy', 46–51.

[23] This transition is well documented in the successive circulars that the French Ministry of Foreign Affairs sent to consuls over the course of the 1880s explaining their evolving duties in the area of commercial information. These can be found in AMAE: Affaires diverses commerciales/285. Documentation on the procedure for integrating consular information into the *Moniteur Officiel du Commerce Extérieur* can be found in AMAE: Affaires diverses commerciales/286.

[24] C.-G. Drossinis, *Les chambres de commerce à l'étranger* (Payot, 1921), 326–65; Bairoch, 'European Trade Policy', 97–101.

[25] M. Aldous and C. Coyle, 'Examining the Role of a Private-Order Institution in Global Trade: The Liverpool Cotton Brokers' Association and the Crowning of King Cotton, 1811–1900', *Business History Review*, 95/4 (2021), 671–702, 687.

This congress was the forerunner to the International Chamber of Commerce, which was founded in 1920 and became a key partner in League trade policy.[26] 'Trade museums' were another tool that governments began to use in the 1880s to facilitate engagement with the commercial community. These museums exhibited samples of foreign products that were selling well on international markets so that local firms could replicate them. Many of these museums were started from sample collections gathered for World's Fairs. The first was founded in Vienna using samples gathered from the 1873 World's Fair.[27] The largest and most widely admired commercial museum was established in Brussels using samples collected for Belgium's 1880 National Exhibition of the Golden Jubilee. It offered visitors an overview of world markets for any product. The collections were arranged by category, physically juxtaposing samples from all parts of the globe. An information sheet accompanied each sample indicating where the item was produced and sold, any regulatory conditions of sale, as well as packaging requirements. The exhibits covered two-and-a-half floors of a former music hall, and this space also served as the entry point for a larger information system. Visitors were invited to request technical details or physical samples that were not currently on display, and a detailed classification system allowed staff to communicate these queries quickly and precisely to consular staff abroad.[28] The museum visually represented the ethos that guided European trade policy after 1873, which identified the competitive capture of export markets as the main driver for economic growth.

While the commercial museums of the 1880s had focused on goods, the next generation of trade-promoting institutions centred more squarely on people and information, reflecting a growing fixation with news as a tool of political and economic power.[29] The exemplars for this

---

[26] G. Ridgeway, *Merchants of Peace: Twenty Years of Business Diplomacy through the International Chamber of Commerce, 1919–1938*, 2nd ed. (Columbia University Press, 1959), 13–18.

[27] *Das Handelsmuseum in Wien. Darstellung seiner Gründung und Entwicklung, 1874–1919* (Handelsmuseum in Wien, 1920); Bairoch, 'European Trade Policy', 101–3; S. A. Marin, 'Introducing Small Firms to International Markets: The Debates over the Commercial Museums in France and Germany 1880–1910', in H. Berghoff, P. Scranton, and U. Spiekermann (eds.), *The Rise of Marketing and Market Research* (Palgrave Macmillan, 2012), pp. 127–52; D. Muddiman, 'A Brain Centre of Empire: Commercial and Industrial Intelligence at the Imperial Institute, 1886–1903', in T. Weller (ed.), *Information History in the Modern World: Histories of the Information Age* (Palgrave Macmillan, 2011), pp. 108–29.

[28] 'Classe 83: Musées commeriaux', Rapports des Membres du Jury International des Récompenses, vol. V (Commisariat Général du Gouvernement Belge, 1886), 150–64.

[29] H. Tworek, *News from Germany: The Competition to Control World Communications, 1900–1945* (Harvard University Press, 2019), 17–44.

model were the French National Office of Foreign Trade (Office national du commerce extérieur) and the Commercial Intelligence Branch of the British Board of Trade, founded in 1898 and 1899, respectively. Both were located directly in business districts, signalling a commitment to public outreach. The French Office was housed in rooms owned by the Paris Chamber of Commerce, adjacent to its main headquarters. One of the Chamber's leaders emphasized the importance of this close proximity, scoffing at a previous attempt by the government to open an economic information office in the stuffy Parisian ministerial quarter along Rue Varenne: 'You know the respect that ministries inspire: will the members of the public, the general public, ever dare to make the journey to the Rue Varenne to enquire about the price of wallpaper in Yokohama or to verify the creditworthiness of a customer in Constantinople? Surely not!'[30] In order to handle these kinds of queries, the National Office of Foreign Trade, like Britain's Commercial Intelligence Branch, offered a walk-in information service for members of the trading community, drawing on a large archive of carefully indexed press clippings. They maintained vast networks of private correspondents around the world to gather this material and to respond to complex enquiries; Coquet served as one such 'Foreign Trade Advisor'. In Britain, Llewellyn Smith was responsible for supervising the Board of Trade's Commercial Intelligence Branch with guidance from an advisory committee of business leaders, bankers, and public officials.[31] The transition from trade museums to information offices in the 1890s confirmed a shift in the conceptualization of international markets, from a collection of concrete wares on offer to abstract spaces in which advantage depended on information and institutional reach, on 'organization'.[32]

The trade museums in Vienna and Brussels were transformed into information offices in line with these trends. Tellingly, in 1898 the Vienna Museum began to sell its collection of commercial samples to make space for a new Export Academy (today it has become

---

[30] M. Camus et Couvreur, Exposition internationale d'Anvers – Exposition spéciale des Musées commerciaux, 17 October 1894, Archives de Paris: Chambre de commerce et d'industrie de Paris, 2ETP/6/2/12 10.

[31] Commercial Intelligence Committee, *Report of the Departmental Committee Appointed by the Board of Trade to Inquire into and Report upon the Dissemination of Commercial Information and Exhibition of Patterns and Samples* (H. M. G. Stationery Office, 1898). The minutes of the Advisory Committee on Commercial Intelligence are in TNA: BT 11/3.

[32] D. Muddiman, 'From Display to Data: The Commercial Museum and the Beginnings of Business Information, 1870–1914', in W. B. Rayward (ed.), *Information Beyond Borders: International Cultural and Intellectual Exchange in the Belle Époque* (Ashgate, 2014), pp. 263–82.

Austria's largest business school, the Wirtschaftsuniversität Wien).[33] Across Europe, the development of business education supported the expansion of commercial organization by training young men and women to work with new forms of economic information and to navigate new institutions. Female education focused on clerical work and languages, and women were often preferred for documentation roles, filling the backrooms of institutions such as the French National Office of Foreign Trade. This opened a channel for some women to assume a more active role in the production of information as economic journalists.[34] In contrast, male business education cultivated skills required for business negotiation, such as contract law and international politics. Attempts to foster a patriotic commercial elite through business education and information reflected the informal, clannish configuration of European foreign trade before 1914. Diverse and unpredictable conditions in newly opened markets made rigid corporate bureaucracy impractical. Trade was thus managed through minimalist firm structures underpinned by strong social norms.[35]

The futility of state efforts to move beyond the indirect provision of information to try to give companies a concrete national cast was illustrated by the dogged but unsuccessful attempts to do this in the Austrian Ministry of Commerce. In the decade before the First World War, the Ministry disbursed stipends to Austrian trading houses to open new subsidiaries abroad. Stipend recipients had to submit detailed reports accounting for the citizenship of every employee as well as the origins of all the goods sold.[36] Leaders in these subsidiaries were also designated as correspondents of the Vienna Trade Museum, which meant that they were responsible for providing information about local market conditions. Yet the Ministry of Commerce was often forced to appoint correspondents who were junior partners in German or British collaborative

[33] *Das Handelsmuseum in Wien. Darstellung seiner Gründung und Entwicklung, 1874–1919*, 17, 22–3; C. Meyer, *Exportförderungspolitik in Österreich: Von der Privilegienwirtschaft zum objektiven Förderungssystem* (Böhlau, 1991), 115–19.
[34] Office du Commerce, Note pour Monsieur le Ministre, 15 March 1897, AN: F12/9138; Conditions d'admissibilité du personnel de l'Office, undated, AN: F12/9138.
[35] Jones, *Multinationals and Global Capitalism*, 169; M. Aldous, 'Trading Companies', in T. da S. Lopes, C. Lubinski, and H. J. S. Tworek (eds.), *The Routledge Companion to the Makers of Global Business* (Routledge, 2021), 204.
[36] Entwurf eines Uebereinkommens betr. Exposituren des k.k. österr. Handelsmuseums in Rio de Janeiro, Buenos-Aires, Montreal, Calcutta, 10 November 1908, ÖStA: AVA, k.k. Handelsministerium/Allgemeine Registratur/1218; Wiedererrichtung der ho. Expositur in Bombay und Erneuerung des bestehenden Expositurabkommens mit der Firma A. Janowitzer, Wien, 29 September 1911, ÖStA: AVA, k.k. Handelsministerium/ Allgemeine Registratur/1185.

ventures and thus could not be relied upon to give preference to Austrian exports.[37] After he joined the Ministry of Commerce in 1909, Riedl assumed responsibility for the Vienna Trade Museum and for broader programmes to enforce patriotic solidarity in the Austrian commercial community. This experience brought frequent reminders of the country's weakness in international markets.[38] His preoccupation with cultivating ties to Germany can thus be understood, in part, as a response to Austria's failure to break into overseas markets on its own.

Conversely, Germany's private commercial success in this period meant that there was less interest there in Central European solidarity and less demand for state-backed 'export-promotion'. Following the opening of the French National Office of Foreign Trade and the British Commercial Intelligence Branch, German business leaders discussed creating an analogous Reich Trade Office as well as a network of expatriate chambers of commerce.[39] These plans drew support from the small- and medium-sized firms that gathered in the Industrialists' League (Bund der Industriellen) but were opposed by the large-scale heavy industrial firms, which were represented in the Central Association of German Industry (Centralverband deutscher Industrieller). The Industrialists' League argued that the German government should help small exporters both by gathering data on foreign markets and by disseminating information to counter the anti-German biases in British and French news agencies. The large firms in the Central Association of German Industry saw less need for these services, since they had their own methods to prospect for markets and cultivate customers. The German Chancellor Bernhard von Bülow agreed with this view and refused to approve a Reich Trade Office or expatriate chambers of commerce. The Industrialists' League never-theless continued to call for more state support through the outbreak of the First World War.[40] Both Coquet and Harms made their early

---

[37] Abschrift eines Berichtes des k.u.k. Generalkonsulates in Shanghai, 5 April 1911; k. und k. oesterr. – ungar. Konsulat to Handelsministerium, 10 February 1908, ÖStA: AVA, k. k. Handelsministerium/Allgemeine Registratur/1218.

[38] 'Maßnahmen auf dem Gebiet der Exportförderung', *Die Industrie*, 8 January 1910, 2; Meyer, *Exportförderungspolitik in Österreich*, 76.

[39] Muddiman, 'From Display to Data'.

[40] H.-P. Ullmann, 'Staatliche Exportförderung und private Exportinitiative. Probleme des Staatsinterventionismus im Deutschen Kaiserreich am Beispiel der staatlichen Außenhandelsförderung (1880–1919)', *Vierteljahrschrift für Sozial- und Wirtschaftsgeschichte*, 65/2 (1978), 157–216; A. Pohlmann, *Außenwirtschaftlicher Nachrichten-und Auskunftsdienst: Ein etwas verzwickte Geschichte* (Koehler & Hennemann, 1982), 3–12; C. S. Maier, *Recasting Bourgeois Europe: Stabilization in France, Germany, and Italy in the Decade after World War I*, revised ed. (Princeton University Press, 2016), 66–7; Tworek, *News from Germany*, 28.

careers by helping to fill the organizational gap left by their unfulfilled demands. Despite official opposition, in 1908 Coquet managed to create a pair of French and German expatriate chambers of commerce in Berlin and Paris, in all but name. In a technique that he continued to use throughout his career, Coquet exerted influence by building bridges between influential patrons. On the French side, he worked with the Colonial Party and the National Committee of French Foreign Trade Advisors, which was attached to the National Office of Foreign Trade. On the German side, he worked with the Industrialists' League, the German Association of Chambers of Commerce (Handelstag), and the Trade Treaty Association (Handelsvertragsverein).[41] With backing from these organizations, in 1908 Coquet founded a Franco-German Commercial Committee (Comité commercial franco-allemand, hereafter CCFA) in Paris and a corresponding German–French Economic Association (Deutsch-Französischer Wirtschaftsverein, hereafter DFWV) in Berlin.[42] Coquet was thus able to position himself as an intermediary, at a time when he was still an obscure figure. Although Coquet was able to rally business leaders to his cause, French and German diplomatic leaders kept Coquet and the CCFA/DFWV at arm's length. The French Ministry of Foreign Affairs repeatedly refused to give Coquet an official endorsement, beyond a form letter of introduction. It was primarily Jules Cambon, the long-serving French Ambassador in Berlin, who counselled caution.[43] Cambon conceded that 'if it acts with discretion' the CCFA/DFWV might be able to 'provide useful support for the efforts of our administration to improve economic relations of France and Germany'. He emphasized that those who favoured détente with France in the German diplomatic establishment considered this to be 'a matter for chancelleries rather than for public activism', alluding to official German opposition to trade promotion that mixed public and private channels.[44]

---

[41] H. Flinsch, Gründung eines deutsch-französischen Verein zur Förderung der gegenseitigen Wirtschaftsbeziehungen, January 1908, PA AA: Paris Gesandtschaft, 1431; Christian Jecklin, Bericht vom 25. November betreffend die vom Advokaten Coquet in Paris betrieben einer deutsch-französischen Handelsvereinigung, 31 January 1908, PAAA: Paris Gesandtschaft/1431.

[42] C. Jecklin, 29 February 1908; Bericht über die Gründungversammlung, 29 March 1908, PA AA: Paris Gesandtschaft/1431; R. Poidevin, *Les relations économiques et financières entre la France et l'Allemagne de 1898 à 1914* (Armand Colin, 1969), 451–4.

[43] Poidevin, *Les relations économiques et financières entre la France et l'Allemagne de 1898 à 1914*, 450, 455–7.

[44] L'Ambassadeur de la République à Berlin à son Excellence Monsieur le Ministre des Affaires Étrangères, 27 November 1909, AMAE: Correspondance politique et commerciale/Nouvelle Série/Allemagne/81.

Public–private partnerships did carry considerable risks in the muddled European diplomatic environment that Christopher Clark describes in *The Sleepwalkers*.[45] Cambon may well have advised his Paris-based colleagues against cooperation with the CCFA/DVWV precisely because he feared that they would turn this organization against him. The ministerial leadership did, indeed, use their press network to try to derail Cambon's negotiations with Germany in 1911. In the 1920s, the League of Nations made engagement with private auxiliaries a more systematic feature of European diplomacy. The League's sprawling operations were surrounded by a perpetual buzz of press-coverage, and private associations had ample space to intervene in foreign policy debates directly.[46] Interwar governments developed new methods to coordinate with private groups in this complex multilateral setting. For example, the French Ministry of Foreign Affairs created a dedicated League of Nations Service, which worked more harmoniously with Coquet's interwar association to promote a European customs union.

Like Coquet, Harms built up a private information network before 1914, which he then used to engage with national and international economic policy in a more structured way in the 1920s. Harms took a keen interest in the activities of private 'double-state' business associations such as Coquet's CCFA/DVWV, as a substitute for German expatriate chambers of commerce.[47] In 1915, Harms counted nine such organizations, formed with Russian, French, Italian, Greek, Bulgarian, Chinese, Nordic, Latin American, and North American partners.[48] Gustav Stresemann, who went on to guide League collaboration in the 1920s as Germany's foreign minister, founded the German–American association on the eve of the war. Stresemann was also behind a push in the Industrialists' League to unify Germany's private 'double state' associations under a central institution.[49] Harms cultivated close relations with Stresemann and the Industrialists' League during his early career

---

[45] Clark, *The Sleepwalkers*, 168–239.

[46] Clavin and Wessels, 'Transnationalism and the League of Nations'.

[47] See 'Ein deutsche Handelskammer in Genf', *Weltwirtschaftliches Archiv*, 2 (1913), 207–8; 'Die Entwicklung der belgisch-russischen Studiengesellschaft in Brüssel', *Weltwirtschaftliches Archiv*, 2 (1913), 317–18; 'Deutsch-Chinesischer Verband', *Weltwirtschaftliches Archiv*, 3 (1913), 389–90; W. Borgius and J. P. Sevening, 'Die Gründung des internationalen Handelskammer- und Vereinskongresses', *Weltwirtschaftliches Archiv*, 4 (1914), 149–51; 'Gründung eines Deutsch-Amerikanischen Wirtschaftsverbandes', *Weltwirtschaftliches Archiv*, 4 (1914), 151–2.

[48] B. Harms, Zur Wiederanknüpfung und Pflege der weltwirtschaftlichen Beziehungen Deutschlands, 1915, IfW: Hs Harms/8c.

[49] Ullmann, 'Staatliche Exportförderung und private Exportinitiative', 208–9; M. Berg, *Gustav Stresemann: Eine politische Karriere zwischen Reich und Republik* (Muster-Schmidt Verlag, 1992), 34–7.

and shared their ambition to concentrate and institutionalize German commercial information.[50] He declared that 'more and more, a central agency from which the entire world market and world commerce can be observed and researched ... is desperately wanted'.[51] With the German government set against the Industrialists' League's demand for a Reich Trade Office, Harms used his base at the University of Kiel to offer an alternative. He formally opened an Institute for Sea Traffic and World Economy (Institut für Seeverkehr und Weltwirtschaft, hereafter IfW) in February 1914, with Stresemann in attendance at the inaugural ceremony as a founding member.[52] There were many other business leaders present, for Harms's ambition was to collapse the distinction between theory and practice by creating a research organization that would be 'in constant contact with the large export houses, shipping companies, and other world firms'.[53] Heinrich Diedrichsen, a Kiel-based wholesaler and shipowner, helped him gain access to North German commercial elites.[54]

Harms used information to cultivate a wide network of supporters, whom he could rely upon to provide further information, in a virtuous cycle. Beginning in 1913, he started to publish articles from businessmen, politicians, and fellow academics in a semi-annual periodical, the *Weltwirtschaftliches Archiv* (Archive of the World Economy). Each issue contained roughly 1,000 pages of research articles, literature reviews, and news 'chronicles'. The *Weltwirtschaftliches Archiv* served as a medium of exchange that helped Harms amass a large library of journals, government documents, statistical surveys, and business reports, which he collected in a central archive. Archive staff continuously surveyed the international press for noteworthy items, which were then classified in a general database of press clippings. Important items were passed on to the *Weltwirtschaftliches Archiv*, and the full trove of information could be queried by correspondents and students. This kind of database and inquiry service was performed by official trade bureaus in other countries, such as the French National Office of Foreign Trade. In 1911 Riedl created an 'Archive of Political Economy' in the Vienna Trade Museum as part of its transformation into an information office.[55]

---

[50] B. Harms, *Entstehung und Bedeutung der Weltwirtschaftlichen Aufgaben Deutschlands: Vortrag gehalten auf der Generalversammlung des Bundes der Industriellen* (Hauptverband Deutscher Flotten-Vereine im Auslande, 1911).

[51] Quoted in Hoffmann, 'Die Geschichte des Instituts für Weltwirtschaft', 3 vols., unpublished manuscript, IfW (1943–5), vol. I, p. 14.

[52] Hoffmann, 'Die Geschichte des Instituts für Weltwirtschaft', vol. I, pp. 67–69.

[53] Quoted in Hoffmann, 'Die Geschichte des Instituts für Weltwirtschaft', vol. I, p. 10.

[54] Hoffmann, 'Die Geschichte des Instituts für Weltwirtschaft', vol. I, pp. 59–61.

[55] *Das Handelsmuseum in Wien. Darstellung seiner Gründung und Entwicklung, 1874–1919*, 46–7.

Information played an important part in Harms's theoretical conception of the 'world economy' (*Weltwirtschaft*) as a highly documented and regulated system. He defined the world economy as an analogue to the national economy (*Volkswirtschaft*) but acknowledged that the analogy was imperfect. He did not think that there could ever be a 'world state' that exerted the same degree of control over the world economy as European governments held over national economies. Nevertheless, he believed that the proliferation of treaties and international organizations regulating transborder commercial activity constituted a new layer of institutional authority whose cumulative impact could only be properly understood by analysing the world economy as a unit.[56] Niels Petersson suggests that Harms's enthusiasm for international economic law reflected broader aspirations in the German political elite for an organized trade regime and explains that the First World War caused Harms and other German leaders to pivot towards more formal, state-backed institutions.[57] For Harms, the pre-war world economy was a comprehensive network of rules and information that transcended economic administration on a national, regional, and imperial scale even as it buttressed those smaller sub-systems. He thus captured the dynamic tension between a logic of territorially defined trade blocs and a logic of global market integration that later ran through League trade debates.

In Harms's eyes, it was not the growing volume of international trade in the second half of the nineteenth century which justified creating the new concept of world economy, but rather the expansion of international law to govern that trade. He explained that both national economy and world economy 'benefit from positive supportive and regulatory measures that are derived from separate sources of law: from autonomous state legislation on the one hand and from states' collective treaties on the other hand'.[58] He emphasized that treaties were being used to regulate more economic and social activity at a higher level of detail, citing agreements in shipping, resource exploitation, contract procedures, intellectual property, weights and measures, hygiene, and foreign nationals' legal standing.[59] Taken together, these treaties had created a more regimented mode of international politics. Harms memorably declared, 'where previously, to a greater or lesser extent, arbitrariness and indeed often

---

[56] B. Harms, *Volkswirtschaft und Weltwirtschaft: Versuch der Begründung einer Weltwirtschaftslehre* (Gustav Fischer, 1912); D. Plehwe and Q. Slobodian, 'Landscapes of Unrest: Herbert Giersch and the Origins of Neoliberal Economic Geography', *Modern Intellectual History*, 16/1 (2019), 185–215, 193–4.

[57] N. P. Petersson, *Anarchie und Weltrecht: Das Deutsche Reich und die Institutionen der Weltwirtschaft 1890–1930* (Vandenhoeck & Ruprecht, 2009), 151–66.

[58] Harms, *Volkswirtschaft und Weltwirtschaft*, 107.

[59] Harms, *Volkswirtschaft und Weltwirtschaft*, 283.

anarchy reigned, there is now order and norm'.[60] Yet this was a diffuse order without a clear institutional centre.[61]

Trade Treaties As a Source of Provisional Stability

The basic framework for international trade during this period was a network of bilateral treaties that spread across most of Europe, beginning with the Franco-British treaty negotiated by Michel Chevalier and Richard Cobden in 1860. Crucially, these agreements were linked together through most-favoured-nation (MFN) clauses. MFN was a safeguard against discrimination designed to ensure that no single trade partner was favoured above the rest. The 'unconditional' MFN clauses that were used in most European trade treaties guaranteed that concessions granted to one partner would be transferred automatically to all others. In principle, this encouraged trade negotiations by signalling that a treaty would not be undercut by a future agreement granting better concessions to other partners. Armed with this assurance, governments across Europe significantly reduced tariffs through a long series of interlocking bilateral negotiations in the 1860s.[62] There has nevertheless been considerable disagreement among both historians and contemporaries about whether MFN treaties constituted a step towards freer trade and peace or towards protection and international rivalry.

In the nineteenth century, many free traders condemned negotiated tariff reductions through treaties. They drew on the writings of David Ricardo to argue that unilateral tariff reduction carried substantial benefits for the country enacting lower duties by forcing its exporters to concentrate on those areas of production in which they enjoyed a comparative advantage.[63] Recent econometric research suggests that the proliferation of European MFN treaties in the 1860s resulted in lower overall trade growth than unilateral action in preceding decades.[64] This is part of a more general debate about how important tariffs and treaties

---

[60] 'Wo früher mehr oder weniger Willkür, ja oftmals Anarchie herrschte, da ist heute Ordnung und Norm.' From Harms, *Volkswirtschaft und Weltwirtschaft*, 315. This quote was the inspiration for the title of Petersson, *Anarchie und Weltrecht*.
[61] Mazower, *Governing the World*, 44.
[62] R. Pahre, *Politics and Trade Cooperation in the Nineteenth Century: The 'Agreeable Customs' of 1815–1914* (Cambridge University Press, 2008), 283–95.
[63] H. Llewellyn Smith, *The Board of Trade* (G. P. Putnam's Sons, 1928), 62–3; A. Howe, *Free Trade and Liberal England, 1846–1946* (Oxford University Press, 1997), 58–9, 92–4.
[64] O. Accominotti and M. Flandreau, 'Bilateral Treaties and The Most-Favored-Nation Clause: The Myth of Trade Liberalization in the Nineteenth Century', *World Politics*, 60/2 (2008), 147–88.

really were in determining trade patterns in this period. In their influential study of nineteenth-century globalization, Kevin O'Rourke and Jeffrey Williamson argued that the tariff treaties of the 1860s created a 'free trade zone', which was meaningfully undermined by new tariffs after the 1870s.[65] Subsequent studies emphasized that despite tariffs, foreign trade continued to expand until the First World War due to declining transport costs and integrated international capital markets, undergirded by the international gold standard.[66] Starting in the 1870s, most of the major trading powers agreed to maintain their currencies at fixed gold parities. This system supported the development of international trade credit and commercial services, particularly in Britain. Trading houses from around the world held balances in London which they used to finance commodity transactions through bills of exchange. Britain also served as a central nexus for a range of other commercial services including insurance, contract arbitration, and the brokerage of cargo space on ships.[67]

Although commercial treaties were not the only determinant of market integration in the belle époque, they did carry considerable political and organizational weight.[68] Treaties offered more predictability than uncoordinated unilateral action at a time when large-scale industrial production and more complex and sprawling chains of supply and distribution began to necessitate more stable business conditions.[69] Thomas Barclay – a prominent British follower of Richard Cobden who was also Lucien Coquet's early mentor – made this case in an encomium on the centenary of Cobden's birth:

the evil of the day is uncertainty, uncertainty of tariffs, uncertainty of the preservation of peace, financial uncertainty, general uncertainty at home … Fortunately, we are in an era of treaties, postal and telegraphic treaties, telephone treaties, transport treaties, treaties of commerce, treaties of navigation, industrial

---

[65] O'Rourke and Williamson, *Globalization and History*, 95–105.
[66] Notably, Estevadeordal, Frantz, and Taylor, 'The Rise and Fall of World Trade, 1870–1939'.
[67] B. Eichengreen, *Golden Fetters: The Gold Standard and the Great Depression, 1919–1939* (Oxford University Press, 1992), 42–54; Y. Cassis, *Capitals of Capital: The Rise and Fall of International Financial Centres, 1780–2009* (Cambridge University Press, 2006), 84–100; Darwin, *The Empire Project*, 115–16; N. P. Petersson, 'Legal Institutions and the World Economy', in C. Dejung and N. P. Petersson (eds.), *The Foundations of Worldwide Economic Integration: Power, Institutions, and Global Markets, 1850–1930* (Cambridge University Press, 2013), pp. 21–39, 31–3; C. Lemercier and J. Sgard, *Arbitrage privé international et globalisation(s). Rapport de recherche* (Archive ouverte en Sciences de l'Homme et de la Société, 2015), 14.
[68] F. Trentmann, *Free Trade Nation: Commerce, Consumption, and Civil Society in Modern Britain* (Oxford University Press, 2008), 10.
[69] Jones, *Multinationals and Global Capitalism*, 20, 76–90.

treaties, treaties of private international law, treaties of arbitration, treaties of peace without war. It is by treaties that certainty is made to take the place of uncertainty, stability the place of instability.[70]

In a messy commercial environment that was cross-cut by mounting colonial rivalries, Barclay and other Cobdenites concluded that the link between trade and peace could not be taken for granted but rather must be deliberately constructed through formal legal mechanisms.[71] Barclay was an influential advocate of treaty-based cooperation, as a long-standing leader of the British Chamber of Commerce in Paris and a prominent voice in the burgeoning international law community.[72]

The development of the discipline of international law in the second half of the nineteenth century coincided with the practical juridification of international relations. The final decades of the nineteenth century saw a growing volume of increasingly detailed treaties and the addition of legal advisors to the diplomatic corps in most states.[73] Nineteenth-century treaties focused heavily on economic issues – on tariffs, intellectual property, transport, monetary policy, and communication. Many international lawyers, including Thomas Barclay, also wanted to apply formal arbitration mechanisms to politics. The arbitration movement gathered momentum in the Institute of International Law and the Inter-Parliamentary Union and culminated in the Hague Conferences of 1899 and 1907. These conferences produced a Permanent Court of Arbitration and defined the rules of war and, crucially, the rules of neutrality.[74] From the Spanish–American War, to the Boer War and the Russo-Japanese War, a string of limited conflicts demonstrated the wide ramifications of modern industrialized warfare for seafaring and trading nations, whose maritime and commercial resources could easily be drawn into a conflict despite formal neutrality. Concern about this problem was not limited to

---

[70] T. Barclay, *Thirty Years: Anglo-French Reminiscences (1876–1906)* (Houghton Mifflin, 1914), 71–2. On the politics surrounding the Cobden centenary, see Trentmann, *Free Trade Nation*, 134–5.
[71] Howe, *Free Trade and Liberal England, 1846–1946*, 91–2, 301–2.
[72] For a summary of his time in Paris, see Barclay, *Thirty Years*.
[73] E. Keene, 'The Treaty-Making Revolution of the Nineteenth Century', *The International History Review*, 34/3 (2012), 475–500; M. M. Payk, *Frieden durch Recht? der Aufstieg des modernen Völkerrechts und der Friedensschluss nach dem ersten Weltkrieg* (De Gruyter, 2018), 27–62.
[74] M. Koskenniemi, *The Gentle Civilizer of Nations: The Rise and Fall of International Law, 1870–1960* (Cambridge University Press, 2002), 5, 62, 87; C. Kissling, *Die Interparlamentarische Union im Wandel: Rechtspolitische Ansätze einer repräsentativ-parlamentarischen Gestaltung der Weltpolitik* (Peter Lang, 2006), 31–82; M. Abbenhuis, *The Hague Conferences and International Politics, 1898–1915* (Bloomsbury Academic, 2019), 11, 15–16, 153, 164–6.

the 'perpetually neutral' states such as Belgium or Switzerland. For, the world's great military powers were also great trading powers, and they wanted to be able to declare neutrality in the next limited conflict and protect their economic interests. Thus, in the midst of a mounting arms race, European governments came together to write a detailed code of neutrality at the Second Hague Conference in 1907. Those rules framed the sharper division between belligerents and neutrals that emerged during the First World War.[75]

Coquet worked as Barclay's clerk for the Second Hague Conference. Both men saw the Hague conferences as an opportunity to reconceive international law as an ongoing process rather than a fixed edifice, an approach that later continued in the League of Nations. Coquet praised his mentor's pragmatic incrementalism in his French translation of draft treaty clauses that Barclay prepared for the conference. Coquet explained that Barclay was not trying to construct 'a general system' all at once but merely sought to 'introduce a certain fixity, susceptible to further improvement, where incertitude has reigned until now'.[76] In order to support gradual progress, Barclay suggested that the Hague conferences should become 'periodical' as the basis for a permanent 'World Council'. This was one of the key contributions made by the Second Hague Conference in 1907; it opened prospects for a serial sequence of meetings that would facilitate a sustained dialogue among lawyers and governments.[77]

Barclay anticipated the later movement for 'open diplomacy' in the League of Nations by emphasizing the role played by public opinion in foreign relations.[78] A growing newspaper industry provided extensive press coverage of the Hague conferences, disseminating debates about the regulation of war and peace to a wide audience.[79] In the French context, Coquet also praised arbitration treaties as a means to make foreign policy more accessible to public scrutiny, complaining that French diplomacy was a 'haughty and majestic grand dame' which 'only speaks when compelled by a powerful parliamentary group that was constituted solely in order to

---

[75] M. M. Abbenhuis, *An Age of Neutrals: Great Power Politics, 1815–1914* (Cambridge University Press, 2014), 178–218; G. A. Frei, *Great Britain, International Law, and the Evolution of Maritime Strategic Thought* (Oxford University Press, 2020), 110–38.

[76] L. Coquet 'Avant-Propos du Traducteur', in T. Barclay, *La Seconde Conférence de la Haye: modèles des clauses et des conventions* (Pédone, 1907), 7. Coquet's commitment to pragmatism was widely shared in the arbitration movement. See Mazower, *Governing the World*, 90.

[77] Abbenhuis, *The Hague Conferences and International Politics*, 165.

[78] T. Barclay, *Problems of International Practice and Diplomacy* (Sweet and Maxwell, 1907), xii.

[79] Abbenhuis, *The Hague Conferences and International Politics*, 12–13, 157–60, 167.

bring her out of her lethargy' (he was referring to the French parliamentary group for voluntary arbitration, where he had close ties).[80] This was the beginning of Coquet's long career in policy advocacy, which he spent prodding parliamentarians and business leaders to prod governments towards reform. In practice, these efforts did not facilitate wide public engagement, however, since Coquet's collaborative networks never extended beyond a narrow economic and political elite.

During the belle époque, Coquet, Barclay, and other advocates of arbitration hoped that it could be used to defuse colonial tensions. Barclay collaborated with the French Colonial Party to build support for an arbitration agreement between France and Britain, which laid the groundwork for the two countries' imperial quid-pro-quo in Morocco and Egypt as part of the *Entente Cordiale* of 1904. In 1907 Eugène Étienne, the leader of the Colonial Party, tried to replicate this process to bring about a similar colonial settlement with Germany, this time working with Barclay's clerk, Coquet. Étienne opened the pages of the Colonial Party newspaper to Coquet to promote Franco-German arbitration as a path to colonial and commercial rapprochement and also endorsed his plans for French and German expatriate chambers of commerce, in recognition of the way that Barclay had used the British Chamber of Commerce in Paris to advocate arbitration and colonial detente.[81] In the end, Coquet's CCFA was the only practical result of Étienne's machinations and Colonial Party members figured prominently on its board. They continued to emphasize linkages between continental and colonial cooperation, without endorsing a comprehensive vision of Eurafrica.[82] Alongside colonial détente, Coquet also used his new committee to call for a Franco-German commercial treaty, and Barclay pursued a similar British-German agreement. Both men admired the strong emphasis on treaties in German trade policy and cited the country's legalistic approach as a model for others to follow.

---

[80] L. Coquet, 'Fragments d'une etude sur les "Secrets d'États"', *La Justice Internationale*, 25 May 1903, 151.

[81] The Colonial Party over-estimated the role that they and Barclay had played in the *Entente Cordiale* and misunderstood the nature of the new Franco-German tensions that emerged in the wake of the Franco-British settlement. See Poidevin, *Les relations économiques et financières entre la France et l'Allemagne de 1898 à 1914*, 411–57; P. Grupp, 'Eugène Etienne et la tentative de rapprochement franco-allemand en 1907', *Cahiers d'études africaines*, 15/58 (1975), 303–11. On the nebulous influence of the Colonial Party, see C.-R. Ageron, *France coloniale ou parti colonial?* (Presses universitaires de France, 1978).

[82] For discussion of Eugène Étienne's territorial ambitions in Africa in the context of broader debates about continental and imperial consolidation see Beckert, 'American Danger', 1152–3.

Trade Treaties As a System of International Rivalry

Germany became the central pivot of the European treaty system in the 1890s. France had previously occupied that position after it signed a raft of MFN treaties in the 1860s that pooled tariff concessions among a wide network of partners. Germany had enjoyed passive access to this network by securing MFN rights, notably through the 1871 Treaty of Frankfurt, which bound France and Germany to grant one another MFN status after the Franco-Prussian War. In 1892, France's new Méline tariff threatened to upset this arrangement and critically undermine German access to West European markets, at a time when German industrial exports to Russia and the United States were also being squeezed by tariffs. Crucially, the Méline tariff was coupled with a French decision not to renew the numerous European trade treaties that were due to expire in 1892. The new tariff was divided into two fixed tiers, and this left the government relatively little room to negotiate new agreements. As a general principle, treaty partners with MFN status would receive the lower French rate on their exports while the rest would receive the higher rate. As France withdrew from leadership in the European treaty system, the German chancellor, Leo von Caprivi, stepped into the breach by concluding a batch of European treaties. He mainly sought to ensure a continuation of German manufactured exports in Europe, in exchange for limited reductions on German agricultural tariffs.[83] Caprivi emphasized that stability was as important as market access for German industry, declaring 'the first requirement of every industry is being able to count on longer periods of time, knowing what it must adapt itself to'.[84] The Caprivi treaties provided stability for a period of ten years but their planned expiration in 1903 threw European trade policy into disarray by prompting a frenzy of pre-emptive 'fighting tariffs'. Once again, Germany was the pacesetter.

Caprivi's trade policy provoked opposition within Germany from advocates of protection who then built support for tariff hikes under Caprivi's successor, Bernhard von Bülow.[85] Bülow sponsored a new tariff in 1902, which he presented as an opening bid for treaty negotiations. He set a four-year time lag between the tariff's introduction and final implementation in 1906 to leave a window to renegotiate the Caprivi treaties before the new rates took effect.[86] Bülow thus positioned Germany as the central

---

[83] Bairoch, 'European Trade Policy', 54, 61–6; C. Torp, *The Challenges of Globalization: Economy and Politics in Germany, 1860–1914* (Berghahn Books, 2014), 113–17.

[84] Quoted in Torp, *The Challenges of Globalization*, 114.

[85] Torp, *The Challenges of Globalization*, 124–9, 139–202.

[86] Torp, *The Challenges of Globalization*, 203–4; Bairoch, 'European Trade Policy', 74.

hub in the last major round of European trade negotiations before the First World War. Bülow concluded treaties with Russia, Switzerland, Italy, Romania, Belgium, Austria–Hungary, and Serbia. The concessions in these agreements were automatically extended to all third countries with MFN rights in Germany, including France and Britain. Although France and Britain enjoyed basic MFN status in Germany, Coquet and Barclay both argued that the countries should conclude full commercial treaties with Germany that would address their exporters' specific tariff and regulatory concerns. Barclay singled out the 1905 agreement between Germany and Austria–Hungary as an exemplary 'highly-developed' treaty that covered 'almost every conceivable item of the commercial relations of these two countries'.[87] He reported approvingly that in negotiating seven such treaties, Germany had exchanged roughly 3,700 notes and memoranda over two-and-a-half years. He suggested that this information-intensive diplomatic process was, in and of itself, an important contribution to the organization of the European commercial environment.[88]

It is true that structures sprang up across Europe to facilitate consultation with the commercial community about the effects of Bülow's trade policy. In Britain's Commercial Intelligence Branch, Llewellyn Smith devoted considerable resources to tracing the Bülow treaties' ramifications for British exports and querying business leaders about a possible commercial treaty with Germany.[89] Riedl performed a similar function in the Vienna Chamber of Commerce, as a representative of the semi-official Central Authority for the Preparation of Trade Treaties.[90] Within Germany, the Trade Treaty Association, which partnered with Coquet, was originally founded by export-oriented business leaders to protest against Bülow's tariff hike, and then went on to promote commercial treaties in order to mitigate the tariff's effects. Coquet advanced these efforts through his CCFA by collating the French commercial community's demands for an eventual treaty with Germany.[91]

The Bülow treaties were thus minutely analysed across a range of institutional settings, and many observers concluded that the net result

[87] T. Barclay, *Bearing and Importance of Commercial Treaties in the Twentieth Century* (Manchester University Press, 1906), 8.
[88] Barclay, *Bearing and Importance of Commercial Treaties in the Twentieth Century*, 13–14.
[89] The results can be found in: The Board of Trade, *The New German Tariff As Modified by Treaties* (H. M. G. Stationery Office, 1905).
[90] Brettner-Messler, 'Richard Riedl', p. 26.
[91] L. Coquet, 'Commerçants et Agrariens Français et Allemands', *La Dépêche Coloniale*, 17 November 1907; C. Biggeleben, *Das 'Bollwerk des Bürgertums': Die Berliner Kaufmannschaft 1870–1920* (C. H. Beck, 2006); Torp, *The Challenges of Globalization*, 162–3; Maier, *Recasting Bourgeois Europe*, 35.

was an overall increase in tariff rates in Europe, in contrast to today's assumptions about the importance of MFN as an antidote to protectionism. This is because several other states significantly increased national tariffs in preparation for the Bülow round of treaty negotiations, and these fighting tariffs were not fully cancelled out by concessions which formed part of the treaties signed with Germany.[92] Moreover, the Bülow tariff also opened the door to discrimination by sub-dividing many classifications. This 'specialization' limited the spread of treaty concessions through the operation of MFN because Germany could define its tariff reductions so specifically that they would apply only to goods that were produced in one or two countries. Although Germany granted highly selective tariff reductions, it continued to demand full MFN rights in foreign countries with less specialized tariffs. This contributed to a perception in both France and Britain that Germany gained far more than it gave up under the MFN regime. A belief that Bülow's trade policy had been unfair and had encouraged protectionism in Europe later helped persuade US and Allied leaders to impose one-sided constraints on German commercial sovereignty after the First World War.[93]

The Bülow tariff provoked considerable opposition within Germany, stimulating debate about the country's role in the world economy. This was the context in which Bernhard Harms defined his intellectual and organizational agenda. He did not advocate 'universal free trade' in the British mould, which he criticized as the 'universal subservience of the less advanced nations under the supremacy of the leading industrial commercial and maritime powers'.[94] He positioned himself as a follower of Friedrich List (he later became the head of the Friedrich List Society), whom he credited with ensuring that, within Germany, 'world economy and free trade have ceased to be identical concepts'.[95] For Harms, limited protection of nascent industries was desirable and

---

[92] Bairoch, 'European Trade Policy', 72–83.

[93] Econometric studies generally show that Bülow's policies did not significantly increase effective tariff protection in Europe, calculated as the ratio of customs duties to imports. By that measure, the most significant shift towards protection came from the 1870s to the 1890s, with the introduction of agricultural tariffs across much of Europe to guard against the 'invasion' of grain from the New World. See O'Rourke and Williamson, *Globalization and History*, 93–117; K. H. O'Rourke, 'Tariffs and Growth in the Late 19th Century', *The Economic Journal*, 110/463 (2000), 456–83, 261; Torp, *The Challenges of Globalization*, 262–5, 274. At the time, however, most government officials and traders did not use a metric of effective tariff protection. They paid attention to the published nominal tariff rates and thus believed that Bülow's policies triggered the increase and specialization of tariffs, in Germany and across the continent. See, for example, The Board of Trade, *The New German Tariff As Modified by Treaties*.

[94] Harms, *Volkswirtschaft und Weltwirtschaft*, 9–10.

[95] Harms, *Volkswirtschaft und Weltwirtschaft*, 11.

compatible with a strong world economy, but he argued that the Bülow tariff was too high and erred in protecting agriculture.[96] Harms outlined this view in a widely noted speech to the General Assembly of the Industrialists' League in 1911. He argued that Germany needed to foster population growth in the interest of security, and this meant more manufacturing exports and lower tariffs on food and raw materials. He suggested that these principles had guided Caprivi's more moderate tariff policy of the 1890s, paraphrasing a famous speech by Caprivi to the Reichstag: 'we must either export goods or men. As we want to keep men, there is nothing to do but send goods'. According to Harms, this meant, bluntly, 'industrial products out and foodstuffs in'.[97] Harms thus pitted himself against turn-of-the-century advocates of a balanced economy who insisted that Germany should preserve its character as an agrarian state to ensure long-term social and economic stability.[98] Instead, he argued that Germany must turn outwards and seek new markets for its manufactured goods and new sources of raw materials.

Many of the markets and inputs that German industry needed lay in foreign colonies or zones of influence, while Germany's own overseas empire offered relatively limited commercial prospects. Germany's global influence, under the banner of *Weltpolitik*, focused more on commercial penetration and less on colonial expansion, driven by concerns about the country's demographic and industrial development.[99] Harms invoked the US concept of the 'open door' to demand that all trading powers grant one another equal rights in the territories that they controlled. In the second half of the nineteenth century, Europeans had used a combination of trade law and military coercion to vastly extend their commercial and territorial reach, joined in the final stages by Japan and the United States.[100] While Harms looked to the United States to integrate this uneven imperial economic landscape, other Europeans drew

---

[96] Harms, *Volkswirtschaft und Weltwirtschaft*, 10.
[97] Harms, *Entstehung und Bedeutung der Weltwirtschaftlichen Aufgaben Deutschlands*, 13. On press coverage of Harms's speech, see IfW: Hs Harms/10k. On Caprivi's original Reichstag speech in 1891, see H. James, *The End of Globalization: Lessons from the Great Depression* (Harvard University Press, 2001), 15; Torp, *The Challenges of Globalization*, 116.
[98] Torp, *The Challenges of Globalization*, 114–202; D. Blackbourn, 'Das Kaiserreich transnational. Eine Skizze', in S. Conrad and J. Osterhammel (eds.), *Das Kaiserreich transnational: Deutschland in der Welt 1871–1914* (Vandenhoeck & Ruprecht, 2004), pp. 302–24, 307; Petersson, *Anarchie und Weltrecht*, 63; E. Grimmer-Solem, *Learning Empire: Globalization and the German Quest for World Status, 1875–1919* (Cambridge University Press, 2019), 271–4.
[99] Blackbourn, 'Das Kaiserreich transnational. Eine Skizze', 320–1; Grimmer-Solem, *Learning Empire*, 169–72.
[100] Mazower, *Governing the World*, 42.

very different lessons from the US example. For many, the contrast between the thin and unwieldy European colonial empires and the increasingly integrated continental United States confirmed the importance of consolidating access to raw materials and markets on a firm territorial basis.[101] Woodrow Wilson and his team later struggled to combine a general commitment to the open-door doctrine with the United States' narrower regional and imperial economic commitments. US leaders continued to vacillate between these positions as they assumed a more prominent leadership role in international trade policy in the 1930s and 1940s. Both faces of US trade policy featured in League trade debates, with universalists such as Harms emphasizing the country's open-door commitments and regionalists such as Coquet and Riedl highlighting US continental coherence and its policies of imperial and regional preference.

Although the United States drew admiration from diverse European onlookers, there were significant legal and political constraints on the country's commercial leadership before and after the First World War. The United States had comparatively high tariff rates, and the president had limited authority to negotiate their reduction through treaties. Moreover, the United States had long applied an idiosyncratic 'conditional' interpretation of MFN. Most European governments adhered to 'unconditional' MFN, which guaranteed that any trade concessions would automatically be extended to all treaty partners. In contrast, the United States generally transferred treaty concessions from one trading partner to the next only if it secured equivalent advantages from both. This meant that United States could only claim a portion of the concessions shared in common among Europeans and offered each government advantages commensurate to its specific sacrifices.[102] The United States used this policy of reciprocal trade relations to consolidate regional and colonial ties in the Americas and the Pacific. This notably included an abortive preferential agreement with Canada in 1911.[103] Although ultimately unsuccessful, the highly publicized US–Canadian negotiations established a clear analogy between imperial and regional preference

---

[101] Beckert, 'American Danger', 1137–61.

[102] United States Tariff Commission, *Reciprocity and Commercial Treaties* (Government Printing Office, 1919), 18. Bairoch, 'European Trade Policy', 39–40; D. A. Irwin, *Clashing over Commerce: A History of US Trade Policy* (The University of Chicago Press, 2017), 47.

[103] United States Tariff Commission, *Reciprocity with Canada: A Study of the Arrangement of 1911* (Government Printing Office, 1920); R. E. Hannigan, 'Reciprocity 1911: Continentalism and American Weltpolitik', *Diplomatic History*, 4/1 (1980), 1–18; M. Hart, *A Trading Nation: Canadian Trade Policy from Colonialism to Globalization* (University of British Columbia Press, 2002), 80–1.

and helped make Canada a key focal point in debates about the status of trade blocs within in the broader regime of MFN treaties.[104] Indeed, Canada had already ignited conflict over MFN in 1898 when it used its commercial autonomy as a self-governing British colony to introduce one-sided tariff preferences in favour of the United Kingdom. Germany invoked its MFN treaty with the British Empire to claim the benefit of these preferences and thereby triggered a ten-year trade war with Canada. The British government tried to conciliate both sides by denouncing the trade treaty with Germany while continuing to grant it MFN status unilaterally. In return, the German government passed its own unilateral legislation that granted MFN status to Britain and its colonies, apart from Canada, on a renewable basis.[105] This solution prevented a dramatic disruption in commercial traffic between Britain and Germany but still left one of the world's most important bilateral trade relationships on a highly precarious legal footing for roughly fifteen years.

Paradoxically, the right to enact unilateral imperial preferences became an important marker of autonomy as many self-governing colonies shifted to Dominion status in the decade before the First World War.[106] Dominion governments placed firmer territorial boundaries on trade, transit, and resource extraction while the British commercial elite and the officials in the Board of Trade continued to pursue universalist ideals of global free trade underpinned by standardized legal principles.[107] This reflected a commitment to liberal ideals, but it was also based on a clear-eyed understanding of Britain's multilateral trade system. Britain was only able to balance its large deficit in merchandise trade with European and American markets by trading through imperial markets. India was pivotal in the British balance of payments; by selling lots of cheap raw materials on European and American markets and buying a large share of British textile exports, India funnelled foreign exchange back to the United Kingdom.[108] After India gained tariff autonomy in 1919 and began to embrace moderate protection in the 1920s, British exporters

---

[104] W. H. Taft, 'Reciprocity with Canada', *Journal of Political Economy*, 19/7 (1911), 513–26, 515. On the importance of US–Canadian relations in the early formulation of GATT policy on regional 'free trade areas', see K. Chase, 'Multilateralism Compromised: The Mysterious Origins of GATT Article XXIV', *World Trade Review*, 5/1 (2006), 1–30; D. A. Irwin, P. C. Mavroidis, and A. O. Sykes, *The Genesis of the GATT* (Cambridge University Press, 2009), 167–8.
[105] Germany and Canada, March 1904, TNA: FO 64/1643.
[106] F. McKenzie, *Redefining the Bonds of Commonwealth, 1939–1948: The Politics of Preference* (Palgrave Macmillan, 2002), 19–20.
[107] Bairoch, 'European Trade Policy', 112–13; Darwin, *The Empire Project*, 112–79; Beckert, 'American Danger', 1149–50.
[108] Darwin, *The Empire Project*, 182–3.

became more open to imperial preference as a means to preserve their position in the Indian market.[109] Canada's early moves towards imperial preference had already stimulated a campaign for 'tariff reform' within the United Kingdom around the turn of the century. Reformers proposed to reciprocate Canadian preferences by introducing new protective UK tariffs, which would then be moderated by special reductions on colonial imports. The main spokesman for tariff reform, Joseph Chamberlain, presented it as a strategy to gain leverage in bilateral treaty negotiations, following Bülow's model.[110] Britain's policy of unilateral free trade meant that it had no protective duties, only low revenue duties that applied uniformly to imperial and non-imperial imports, and this left the British government with few bargaining chips when faced with a European fighting tariff. In the Board of Trade, Llewellyn Smith was deeply critical of Bülow's tactics and did not think Britain should follow his model. He lamented that Bülow's negotiations 'have not been on the basis of the existing tariff rates but of a new tariff constructed as an engine of warfare ... This is in marked contrast to the results of the Caprivi treaties of 1892, when the concessions represented real reductions in the direction of freer trade'.[111] Llewellyn Smith nevertheless tried hard, though without success, to conclude an Anglo-German commercial treaty after the rupture of 1897. He complained that Germany's revocable MFN grant to Britain left traders 'hampered by the present uncertainty in making future contracts'.[112]

The fact that bilateral trade between Britain and its most important trading partner had been imperilled in 1897 by the independent initiative of a self-governing colony encouraged Llewellyn Smith to help build legal space for imperial preference in Britain's trade treaties, even though he fundamentally disagreed with this policy.[113] Thus, starting in 1905 the UK government began to defend imperial preference in trade treaties by asserting the self-governing colonies' claim to MFN status as long as they granted equal treatment to 'foreign Countries'.[114] This allowed the Board

---

[109] A. Mukherjee, 'British Industrial Policy and the Question of Fiscal Autonomy, 1916–1930', *Proceedings of the Indian History Congress*, 62 (2001), 726–55; Tooze and Fertik, 'The World Economy and the Great War', 235.

[110] Trentmann, *Free Trade Nation*, 28–31, 57–68.

[111] H. Llewellyn Smith, the New German Tariff, 30 May 1905, TNA: FO 64/1643.

[112] H. Llewellyn Smith, German Treaty Negotiations, 25 May 1905, TNA: FO 64/1643.

[113] H. Llewellyn Smith to Foreign Office, 5 March 1906, TNA: FO 368/22; H. Llewellyn Smith, The New German Tariff, 30 May 1905, TNA: FO 64/1643; H. Llewellyn Smith, German Treaty Negotiations, 25 May 1905, TNA: FO 64/1643; Howe, *Free Trade and Liberal England, 1846–1946*, 223.

[114] 'Treaty of Commerce and Navigation between Great Britain and Roumania, October 31, 1905', *Hertslet's commercial treaties* (H. M. G. Stationery Office, 1907),

of Trade to continue to defend a robust, unconditional interpretation of MFN in relations with non-imperial partners while insisting that MFN doctrine did not apply to intra-imperial trade because it was not 'foreign trade'. This remained Britain's basic legal stance towards imperial preference throughout the interwar period and became an important reference point in broader debates about the relationship between trade blocs and universal market regulation.

Britain certainly was not the only country that practised imperial preference during this period. Indeed, other colonial powers such as France or Portugal used tariff discrimination much more systematically.[115] Britain stood out due to the vehemence with which it continued to defend free trade in the wider world, even as it created legal space for imperial solidarity. The United States adopted a somewhat analogous stance, by stridently demanding an 'open-door' in external markets while protecting its own colonial relationships with steep tariff preferences.[116] When Britain and the United States later took the lead in framing the trade terms of the 1919 Peace Settlement, their distinct but similarly contradictory positions on free trade and empire stood as the main impediment to a comprehensive trade policy. Imperial preference then remained a central point of contention throughout the interwar period.

Foreign Trade and the Social Question

There was an important internal social dimension to British debates about tariff reform and imperial preference, as well. Both advocates and opponents of protection claimed that their approach would raise living standards for the working class. Llewellyn Smith's central role in these debates highlights the close links that the depression of the 1870s established between the politics of free trade and social progress. This was especially true in Britain, where the depression fuelled a sharp rise in unemployment from 1.1 per cent in 1873 to 10.7 per cent in 1879.[117]

Llewellyn Smith spent the 1880s as a student in Oxford, during a period of intense political ferment. He arrived in 1883 just at the moment when the publication of the pamphlet *The Bitter Cry of Outcast London* thrust 'the social question' into the centre of public debate by

vol. XXIV, 948–54; G. J. Stanley, Commercial Treaties of the United Kingdom: Report to the President of the Board of Trade on the Treaty of Arrangements of the United Kingdom, September 1917, TNA: BT 274/24.

[115] For a survey of tariff preferences in different colonial systems at the end of the nineteenth century, see, Bairoch, 'European Trade Policy', 107–28.

[116] Bairoch, 'European Trade Policy', 122–3.

[117] G. R. Boyer and T. J. Hatton, 'New Estimates of British Unemployment, 1870–1913', *The Journal of Economic History*, 62/3 (2002), 643–75, 662.

presenting vivid descriptions of urban poverty.[118] Llewellyn Smith helped organize a Social Science Club in Oxford to provide an alternative to the 'propagandism' of *The Bitter Cry*, based on 'knowledge of facts and actual industrial conditions and difficulties'. He also helped found an Adam Smith Society that linked the improvement of living standards to free trade.[119] He allied himself with the 'new Liberals', a loose label adopted by the progressive wing of Britain's Liberal Party. New Liberals did not coalesce around a clearly defined reform programme, but they generally distinguished themselves from the old guard by demanding more active policy intervention to improve working-class living conditions. They remained ideologically aligned with the Liberal Party in their commitment to free trade and their preference for voluntary self-improvement over legal coercion.[120]

After he left Oxford, Llewellyn Smith spent several years immersed in London-based reform movements as a union organizer and a teacher in the Oxford extension programme. He was also the youngest collaborator in a massive Survey of the Life and Labour of the People of London led by the shipping magnate, Charles Booth.[121] Llewellyn Smith was attracted to Booth's belief in social reform based on scientific investigation and public administration rather than pathos and philanthropy. Booth privileged systematic analysis over 'sensational stories' by amassing an enormous volume of data. He gathered abundant statistics about family size, income, and employment along with 450 notebooks of qualitative data from in-person household visits.[122] Through his participation in this project, Llewellyn Smith refined his views on state power and social progress in dialogue with other rising stars in the London reform scene, including Beatrice Potter. She recalled sitting on a London dock at six in the morning with Llewellyn Smith, awaiting a boat of immigrants, as 'good friends and working Comrades', but their friendship quickly cooled.[123] Potter soon married Sydney Webb, and together they advocated a model of socialism that Llewellyn Smith condemned for

[118] A. Mearns, *The Bitter Cry of Outcast London: An Inquiry into the Condition of the Abject Poor* (James Clarke, 1883). On the impact of *The Bitter Cry* in Oxford see, S. Collini, *Liberalism and Sociology: L. T. Hobhouse and Political Argument in England, 1880–1914* (Cambridge University Press, 1979), 54–5.

[119] Davidson, 'Sir Hubert Llewellyn Smith and Labour Policy', pp. 7–8.

[120] P. Clarke, *Liberals and Social Democrats* (Cambridge University Press, 1978), 23–4; Davidson, 'Sir Hubert Llewellyn Smith and Labour Policy', pp. 12–17.

[121] Collini, *Liberalism and Sociology*, 55–6; Davidson, 'Sir Hubert Llewellyn Smith and Labour Policy', pp. 18–19.

[122] For a description of the methods used see, C. Booth (ed.), *Life and Labour of the People in London* (Macmillan and Co., 1892), vol. I, 3–27.

[123] 16 December 1888, *Beatrice Webb's Typescript Diary, 15 February 1886–December 1888*, LSE Digital Library, https://digital.library.lse.ac.uk/objects/lse:yom975poh.

excessively constraining individual autonomy.[124] Llewellyn Smith's divergence from the Webbs became more pronounced as he climbed the ranks of the British civil service. In 1893, Llewellyn Smith was recruited by Liberal Party leaders to run a new Labour Department in Britain's Board of Trade. His first task was to implement a new system of employment arbitration, and he urged the government to 'be most cautious how it interferes and be careful not to try to substitute the physical compulsion of law for the voluntary agreement of the parties'.[125]

Llewellyn Smith combined a light regulatory touch with voluminous data, pushing the Board of Trade to collect more systematic statistics on labour. This gave him a clear vision of rising unemployment around the turn of the century. From 1899 to 1904, the Board of Trade recorded an increase in unemployment from 2 per cent in to 6 per cent.[126] These trends helped fuel criticism of Britain's free trade policy and its growing reliance on income from foreign investment. Chamberlain's programme of tariff reform promised to solve these problems by using the bludgeon of fighting tariffs to lower barriers to British exports and also by cultivating imperial markets through a system of tariff preferences. Chamberlain gathered a large following, but he also provoked a popular campaign in favour of free trade that spread well beyond the Liberal base. In the end, the public debate over free trade and tariff reform hinged largely on the question of which policy would lead to lower urban food prices.[127] From the Board of Trade, Llewellyn Smith supported the Liberal view that free trade offered a path to affordable food that would also safeguard Britain's role as a commercial intermediary to the world.[128]

True to his faith in information, Llewellyn Smith contributed to the fight against tariff reform by coordinating a massive two-volume statistical assessment of Britain's economic performance relative to other large industrial states, the Fiscal Blue Books.[129] The Blue Books sought to counter Chamberlain's claim that the average Briton would have been better off under a protectionist regime such as that of Germany. The Blue Books showed that wholesale and retail prices had declined more rapidly

---

[124] Davidson, 'Sir Hubert Llewellyn Smith and Labour Policy', p. 46.
[125] Quoted in Davidson, 'Sir Hubert Llewellyn Smith and Labour Policy', p. 143.
[126] Boyer and Hatton, 'New Estimates of British Unemployment, 1870–1913', 662.
[127] Trentmann, *Free Trade Nation*, 28–31, 89–91.
[128] Howe, *Free Trade and Liberal England, 1846–1946*, 251–73.
[129] Board of Trade, *British and Foreign Trade and Industry. Memoranda, Statistical Tables, and Charts prepared in the Board of Trade in reference to Various Matters Bearing on British and Foreign Trade and Industrial Conditions* (H. M. G. Stationery Office, 1903); Board of Trade, *British and Foreign Trade and Industry. Second Series of Memoranda, Statistical Tables, and Charts prepared in the Board of Trade in reference to Various Matters Bearing on British and Foreign Trade and Industrial Conditions* (H. M. G. Stationery Office, 1904).

in the United Kingdom than in other industrial states, while workers' wages remained comparatively high. By emphasizing the advantages of low-cost imports for British workers, the Blue Books reiterated a traditional Liberal defence of free trade that dated back to the Anti-Corn Law League. Remarkably, the Blue Books were translated into popular propaganda, as Liberal handbills advertised 'Facts from the Government Blue Book' comparing wages, working hours, and food prices in Britain and Germany. These numbers were illustrated in pictorial form; two unequal loaves of bread were used to illustrate that 'half an hours skilled labour in England purchases 3 times as much Bread as half an hours skilled labour in Germany'.[130] The Blue Books' dense factual content drew popular interest partly because they fit into a more sensational and widely influential campaign focused on dramatizing the misery of 'the hungry forties' before Britain had repealed the corn laws. The free trade message carried the day, achieving a strong electoral victory for the Liberal Party in 1906. Upon victory, the Liberals appointed Lewellyn Smith as Permanent Secretary of the Board of Trade (the department's most senior bureaucrat), a position that he kept through the end of the First World War.[131]

Victory in the 1906 election forced Liberal leaders to offer their own response to the social ills that Chamberlain had highlighted. They did so by sponsoring landmark legislation on social insurance as part of 'the people's budget' of 1910. Instead of regulating foreign trade and investments, they opted to protect workers from the vagaries of free markets through domestic social insurance. Llewellyn Smith took the lead in writing new plans for individual unemployment insurance. He noted that 'the growing social concern for the maintenance of stability is the counterpart of the growing conviction that, with the world-wide development of industry, the causes of fluctuations and irregularity are becoming continually more incalculable and their effects more unavoidable by unaided individual effort'.[132] In other words, social insurance was an essential complement to globalization. Llewellyn Smith strove to implement this ideal by writing a bill for national unemployment insurance, which was packaged together with a plan for employer-subsidized health coverage as the 1911 National Insurance Act.[133] Through this legislation,

---

[130] Quoted in Trentmann, *Free Trade Nation*, 91, Colour Plate VIII.
[131] Davidson, 'Sir Hubert Llewellyn Smith and Labour Policy', p. 177; Howe, *Free Trade and Liberal England, 1846–1946*, 251–73; Trentmann, *Free Trade Nation*, 31–9.
[132] H. Llewellyn Smith, 'Economic Security and Unemployment Insurance', *The Economic Journal*, 20/80 (1910), 513–29, 517.
[133] Davidson, 'Sir Hubert Llewellyn Smith and Labour Policy', pp. 212–16; *National Insurance Bill (Part II: Unemployment): Explanatory Memorandum* (H. M. G. Stationery Office, 1911).

Llewellyn Smith helped lay the cornerstone of the modern British welfare state and brought into government a new cohort of reformers who ensured its future development, notably William Beveridge.

In Germany, Harms shared Llewellyn Smith's interest in state policy on foreign trade and social protection. He began his career by publishing a long study of the mid-century German socialist, Ferdinand Lassalle, whom he praised for recognizing the 'rule of growing state activity' at an early date. Harms predicted that future governments would be expected to regulate economic and social life around the world as minutely as medieval city-states had done at the local level. He wrote:

Today it appears to us self-evident that the state protects agriculture, promotes trade and industry, impedes competition from other industrial countries, seeks to prevent the decline of craft production, regulates working hours, closes firms that are hazardous to health, etc., etc., ...

This change in the goals of state activity will continue in the future, for it follows as a natural necessity from the increase and differentiation of our social body conditioned by the industrial transformation of our economic life. The more densely populated the marginal zones of subsistence become, the more difficult it will be for individuals to claim a place, and the more necessary the help of the state will be in the search for new and broader employment opportunities. The tenterhooks of production will be extended, the national economy will be interlinked with the world economy, trade will span the globe – and everywhere one needs the wise state, which one expects to establish the legal and also to a large extent economic preconditions for such expansion.[134]

Harms's vision of a competitive scramble for land and raw materials driven by demography echoed new debates about 'geopolitics' which were emerging in Germany around this time.[135] He advocated more forceful state intervention than Llewellyn Smith did in part because he was preoccupied with the ratio between Germany's population and its limited natural resource base, which was a less urgent concern in the vast British Empire.

Harms spent his early years in Kiel conceptualizing a regulated 'world economy' that would guarantee global commercial access to a country like Germany that had a large population and a small overseas empire. He was particularly concerned about commercial competition in territories that were not formal colonies but faced heavy outside political interference. Each issue of his *Weltwirtschaftliches Archiv* included a 'Chronicle of Open-Door Regions'. Interestingly, it was always an Austrian, Siegmund

---

[134] B. Harms, *Ferdinand Lassalle und seine Bedeutung für die deutsche Sozialdemokratie* (G. Fischer, 1909), 93–4.
[135] A. Bashford, *Global Population: History, Geopolitics, and Life on Earth* (Columbia University Press, 2016), 55–60.

Schilder, who wrote that segment. Schilder moved in the same professional circles as Richard Riedl in Vienna, serving for a time as the secretary of the Vienna Trade Museum, under Riedl's supervision. Whereas Schilder and Harms emphasized diffuse competitive dynamics on global markets, Riedl saw a world divided into internally cohesive imperial power blocs. This difference in outlook reflected Riedl's much deeper commitment to ethnic German nationalism.

Trade and Nationalism in the Tinderbox of Europe

Riedl was exposed to German nationalism at a young age. His paternal family who took charge of his upbringing after his parents' early death were based in Egerland, an area in northern Bohemia with a large German population. Egerland was a hub for German nationalism in the Habsburg Empire. After the territory was later ceded to Czechoslovakia in 1918, it became a central base for the interwar pan-German movement. When Riedl went to the University of Vienna, he maintained his regional roots by becoming a leader in the Albia fraternity, which had been founded by Bohemian Germans. 'Albia' was the medieval name for the Elbe River which connected Bohemia to the North Sea through Hamburg; this name communicated the fraternity's pan-German orientation and fit Riedl's worldview well. Throughout his career, Riedl was fixated on Austria's commercial dependence on North German ports. His early professional activities focused on 'export-promotion', which entailed the cultivation of trade networks and infrastructural links to the north, through Germany, and to the south, through the Mediterranean. He did this work in the Vienna Chamber of Commerce from 1890 to 1909, eventually rising to the highest-ranking administrative position. In 1909 he joined the Austrian Ministry of Commerce as the Director of the Commercial Policy Department.[136]

Riedl's German nationalism made him an outlier in the Habsburg bureaucracy, which was built around non-national loyalty to the emperor.[137] Most forms of nationalism fit uneasily in most areas of Habsburg bureaucracy, but there was a particularly sharp tension between Riedl's German nationalism and his efforts to develop Austrian foreign trade institutions. For, German nationalism in Austria was closely associated with anti-Semitism during this period. At the same time, Jews played a prominent role in the country's foreign trade and continued to

---

[136] Brettner-Messler, 'Richard Riedl', pp. 12–20, 44–5.
[137] A. Suppan, '"Germans" in the Habsburg Empire: Language, Imperial Ideology, National Identity, and Assimilation', in C. W. Ingrao and F. A. J. Szabo (eds.), *The Germans and the East* (Purdue University Press, 2008), pp. 147–269, 162–3.

identify strongly with German culture, especially in Vienna.[138] Riedl responded to these complexities by adopting different attitudes towards Jews in different settings. As a student, he participated in new racially charged strains of German nationalism, which barred Jews from German culture based on their family background. Jewish exclusion became a defining feature of the Austrian fraternity movement just at the moment when Riedl was moving into its ranks. Significantly, the future Zionist leader Theodor Herzl was one of the very last Jewish members who tried to claim a German identity as a member of the Albia fraternity. Three years before Riedl joined, Herzl resigned in protest against Albia's increasingly racialized anti-Semitism.[139] Riedl confirmed this trend when he wrote the first general agreement for Austria's German-nationalist fraternities, the *Linzer-Delegierten-Convent* in 1890, in which all member associations excluded Jews on racial criteria.[140] Riedl remained active in fraternity alumni networks after he graduated from the University of Vienna. In 1908 he helped found a German Club in Vienna as a non-party social venue for other alumni of nationalist fraternities and remained one of its most prominent leaders for the remainder of his career.[141] Many club members were highly critical of Jewish involvement in Austrian trade.[142] Riedl does not seem to have openly endorsed such views himself, but he did foster a German nationalist environment in which they flourished.[143]

In his professional activity in the Vienna Chamber of Commerce and the Ministry of Commerce, Riedl conformed to the more pragmatic

---

[138] S. Beller, 'Germans and Jews as Central European and "Mitteleuropäisch" Elites', in P. M. R. Stirk (ed.), *Mitteleuropa: History and Prospects* (Edinburgh University Press, 1994), pp. 61–85, 75–6, 78; M. Richarz, 'Berufliche und soziale Struktur', in S. M. Lowenstein, P. Mendes-Flohr, P. G. J. Pulzer, and M. Richarz (eds.), *Deutsch-jüdische Geschichte in der Neuzeit: Umstrittene Integration 1871–1918* (C. H. Beck, 1997), pp. 39–62, 55.

[139] K. Beck, *Wiener akademische Burschenschaft Albia, 1870–1930* (Selbstverlag der Wiener akademische Burschenschaft 'Albia', 1930), 38; J. Kornberg, *Theodor Herzl: From Assimilation to Zionism* (Indiana University Press, 1993), 49–51.

[140] Beck, *Albia*, 61–71; Brettner-Messler, 'Richard Riedl', pp. 17–18.

[141] Beck, *Albia*, 140–1.

[142] *Satzungen des Vereins 'Deutscher Klub'* (Vernay, 1908); 'Die wirtschaftliche Macht des Judentums in Deutschösterreich', *Mitteilungen des Deutschen Klubs*, 11 (1924); L. Erker, A. Huber, and K. Taschwer, *Deutscher Klub: Austro-Nazis in der Hofburg* (Czernin, 2018).

[143] The anti-Semitism in the 1908 German Club stands in contrast to the more inclusive culture that prevailed in a parliamentary German Club that had been founded in the 1880s. The leadership of this earlier organization included German nationalists with a Jewish background, such as Heinrich Friedjung (P. Pulzer, 'Rechtliche Gleichstellung und öffentliches Leben', in S. M. Lowenstein, P. Mendes-Flohr, P. Pulzer, and M. Richarz (eds.), *Deutsch-jüdische Geschichte in der Neuzeit: Umstrittene Integration 1871–1918* (C. H. Beck, 1997), pp. 151–92, 184.

cultural anti-Semitism that prevailed there. Assimilated Jews who had valuable expertise or personal connections could gain limited access to these institutions.[144] Riedl collaborated with many colleagues and indeed many German nationalists with a Jewish background. He notably developed close ties to the historian Heinrich Friedjung, who came from a Jewish family in Moravia. Like Riedl, Friedjung advocated a pan-German continental bloc as a counterweight to European maritime empires.[145] Indeed, Riedl may have owed his appointment to the Ministry of Commerce in 1909 to his participation in Friedjung's 'Oriental Committee' to promote pan-German control of the Balkans, since the Ministry's director was also a member.[146] Riedl shared Friedjung's fixation on the Balkans and argued that Austria should seek to position itself there as an 'intermediary between kindred Germany and the Orient'. He argued that the German drive to extend its influence in the Middle East – for example, through the Berlin–Baghdad Railway – left Austria 'only a short time' to act.[147] Although he advocated a closer partnership with Germany, Riedl remained committed to the preservation of the Habsburg Empire as an independent regional actor and did not seek formal union before 1918. This aligned him with mainstream German foreign policy, which was premised on close collaboration with an independent Austria, from Bismarck to Bülow.[148]

Austria's regional commercial role was constrained by the complex internal politics of the Dual Monarchy. The Austrian Ministry of Commerce had to contend with competing trade institutions in the cities under its remit, such as Trieste and Prague.[149] The most fundamental conflict was with Budapest. According to the terms of the 1865 agreement that established the Dual Monarchy, Austria and Hungary each had separate Ministries of Commerce but shared a diplomatic service. Thus, although Austria and Hungary competed for the same export markets in the Balkans, they had to rely on common consuls and embassies to do so. Moreover, the two halves of the Monarchy had very different commercial priorities. Austria had sizeable manufacturing and service sectors, while Hungary was more focused on agriculture and food processing.[150]

[144] Pulzer, 'Rechtliche Gleichstellung und öffentliches Leben', 186.
[145] H. Friedjung, *Das Zeitalter des Imperialismus, 1884–1914* (Neufeld und Henius, 1919), vol. 3.
[146] Brettner-Messler, 'Richard Riedl', pp. 59–60.
[147] 'Industrieller Klub. 28. Monatsversammlung. Handelskammersekretär Richard Riedl', *Die Industrie*, 15 February 1908, 4.
[148] Suppan, '"Germans" in the Habsburg Empire', 172–3.
[149] Meyer, *Exportförderungspolitik in Österreich*, 76–8.
[150] 'Industrieller Klub. 28. Monatsversammlung. Handelskammersekretär Richard Riedl', *Die Industrie*, 15 February 1908, 4.

Riedl participated in Franz Ferdinand's projects to reduce Hungarian influence in the Dual Monarchy by forming a new Slavic unit as a base from which to cultivate closer partnerships with the independent Balkan states. The Habsburg heir was, in part, looking for options to counter Russian pan-Slavic agitation. Russia's defeat by Japan in 1905 had made this threat more urgent by inflaming Russian nationalism and shifting its focus to the Eastern Mediterranean. Austria–Hungary's annexation of Bosnia in 1908 further stimulated the pan-Slav movement.[151] Riedl argued that Austria must try to pre-empt Russian influence and make itself the patron of emerging Balkan nations. He declared that ethnic Germans possessed an exceptional 'political creative force' (*politischer Gestaltungskraft*) that endowed them with a vocation for leadership over other nationalities in the region.[152] Riedl's regional aspirations were rooted in a belief that the world was being divided into large imperial units, but he was careful to differentiate his plans for continental solidarity in Europe from outright colonial empire. For example, he defended a scheme for a customs union with Romania as,

a decisive step towards the goals of uniting Central European states in a great whole dominating access to the east, of establishing a solid foundation for the peace of the continent, and of countering the expansionary policies of colonial states with the power of a Central European organization reposing on free treaty commitments among nations.[153]

Thus, although Riedl's regional vision was deeply rooted in his belief in German superiority, he proposed to implement it through treaties among sovereign states rather than formal colonial subordination.[154] This strategy foreshadowed his later efforts to encode regional hierarchy in international trade law in the League of Nations.

Riedl praised the treaty network that Caprivi had built in the 1890s as the beginnings of a regional 'tariff system' that stretched 'from the Mediterranean to the Baltic'. Nevertheless, this system was a 'half measure' because it did not 'take the last step', which was 'to exempt the

---

[151] Löding, 'Deutschlands und Österreich-Ungarns Balkanpolitik', p. 10, 92 n. 42; D. Lieven, *Towards the Flame: Empire, War and the End of Tsarist Russia* (Allen Lane, 2015), 207–17.

[152] Quoted in Brettner-Messler, 'Richard Riedl', p. 217.

[153] Quoted in Brettner-Messler, 'Richard Riedl', p. 148.

[154] While Riedl presented Austria's regional ambitions as a reaction against European colonial expansion, a growing body of scholarship has revealed the myriad ways in which Austria participated indirectly in European maritime empire in the late nineteenth century. See W. Sauer (ed.), *K.u.k. kolonial – Habsburgermonarchie und europäische Herrschaft in Afrika* (Böhlau, 2002); Florian Krobb (ed.), 'Colonial Austria: Austria and the Overseas' special issue of *Austrian Studies* (2012); A. Frank, 'The Children of the Desert and the Laws of the Sea: Austria, Great Britain, the Ottoman Empire, and the Mediterranean Slave Trade in the Nineteenth Century', *The American Historical Review*, 117/2 (2012), 410–44.

concessions that the members of the treaty system granted one another from the most-favoured-nation claims of outside states'. Riedl suggested that the formation of such a bloc would have enabled Europeans to raise duties selectively against New World farmers, while leaving the European agricultural market relatively open. He later concluded that this solution would have reduced political tensions in the run-up to the First World War, lamenting that Austria–Hungary had been forced to abandon tariff preferences favouring Serbian pig exports in the name of MFN during negotiations for the Bülow treaties. He concluded that 'seldom has the link between economic policy and peace been so clearly demonstrated'.[155]

Trade As a Factor in European Security

During the belle époque, there was a widespread belief that trade and peace were closely connected, but there was also considerable disagreement about the precise nature of that link. In the run-up to the First World War, perhaps the best-known proponent of the view that trade led to peace was the British journalist Norman Angell, who was later a founding member of Coquet's interwar association for a European customs union. In his 1909 bestseller, *The Great Illusion*, Angell argued that modern trading powers could no longer secure advantages against one another through outright military conquest and any attempt to do so would disrupt their reciprocal economic relations and leave all parties worse off. He highlighted the dense international capital links that had developed in the late nineteenth century, underpinned by expanding networks of transit, communication, and law.[156] In 1913, Bernhard Harms's journal published a lengthy critique of *The Great Illusion*, by Hermann Levy, a German scholar of the British Empire, followed by a rejoinder from Angell. Levy argued that territorial annexation could confer long-term benefits for economic development that outweighed the short-term economic disruptions highlighted by Angell. Gaining more resources, more people, and a more expansive commercial infrastructure would increase a state's overall 'productive capacity' and enable its firms to capture economies of scale.[157] Angell responded that Britain had been

---

[155] R. Riedl, 'Äußere Handelspolitik', in V. Mataja (ed.), *Lehrbuch der Volkswirtschaftspolitik* (Österreichische Staatsdruckerei, 1931), pp. 441–521, 472–3.

[156] N. Angell, *The Great Illusion: A Study of the Relation of Military Power to National Advantage* (William Heinemann, 1909).

[157] H. Levy, 'Weltwirtschaft und territoriale Machtpolitik. Einige Bemerkungen kritischer Art über Norman Angell's Friedensargument', *Weltwirtschaftliches Archiv*, 1 (1913), 349–60.

able to secure many organizational advantages without direct territorial control; the domination of Britain's laws, language, and commercial practice in the world economy resulted more from country's preponderant position on capital markets than from its formal colonial claims.[158]

In a speech to the German Navy League in 1910, Harms offered a somewhat different critique of the Angellian view that international economic integration made military power less relevant. He conceded that outright war with England would be 'folly' for Germany: 'We should be so extraordinarily satisfied with the trend of our economic development on the world market, and above all with our success relative to England, that we have absolutely no reason to risk all this in a war.'[159] He nevertheless argued that a strong navy played an essential role in peacetime commercial expansion:

If some power was in the position in South America, Morocco, Turkish Asia, or China, to exert pressure on state authorities, such that our imports were disadvantaged relative to those of other states or our economic activity in new countries was otherwise constricted, this would be a grievous impediment to our economic development. A free path for peaceful competition is for us a condition of life![160]

Harms contributed to the ongoing effort to build up German sea power by giving courses at the Naval Academy in Kiel. The titular head of the German Navy, Prince Heinrich of Prussia, was the IfW's official patron, and Harms personally taught his son.[161] Although Harms saw a strong navy as a crucial asset for commercial competition, he also understood that Germany was in no position to engage in real naval conflict since Britain had a considerable lead in warship construction.[162] Harms concluded that Britain's global maritime dominance appeared 'entirely secure for the foreseeable future' and advised against confrontation.[163]

In Britain, Llewellyn Smith similarly urged caution when discussing a hypothetical conflict with Germany. In 1911 and 1912, he represented the Board of Trade in an inter-ministerial inquiry into 'Trading with the Enemy'. This body was charged with assessing possibilities to exert pressure on Germany in an eventual war by restricting commercial traffic.

---

[158] N. Angell, 'Weltwirtschaft und territoriale Machtpolitik. Eine Erwiderung', *Weltwirtschaftliches Archiv*, 3 (1914), 367–82.
[159] B. Harms, 'England und Deutschland', *Deutsche Revue*, 35 (1910), 17.
[160] Harms, 'England und Deutschland', 18.
[161] G. Take, '"Die Objektivität ist durch sein Wesen verbürgt": Bernhard Harms' Gründung des Kieler Instituts für Weltwirtschaft und sein Aufstieg im Ersten Weltkrieg', *Demokratische Geschichte*, 26 (2015), 13–74, 24.
[162] Clark, *The Sleepwalkers*, 150. [163] Harms, 'England und Deutschland', 7–8.

It anticipated the modified blockade that Britain did eventually impose on Germany, but this strategy had only very limited support in the British government before the outbreak of war.[164] Indeed, as Gabriela Frei emphasizes, British leaders were heavily preoccupied with defining the country's rights and duties as a neutral, since that was the position that Britain had usually occupied in the limited wars of the nineteenth century. Moreover, its extensive commercial networks left it highly exposed to conflict around the world.[165] If Britain had much to lose as a passive neutral, Llewellyn Smith argued that it also had little to gain by waging active economic warfare against its rivals. He warned that 'it was quite possible ... that we might inflict greater suffering on ourselves than on Germany' by trying to cut bilateral trade.[166]

Llewellyn Smith was concerned about two issues which would continue to preoccupy him during the war. Firstly, he worried that the measures required to halt trade with Germany would antagonize neutral states and undermine Britain's commercial influence. A large share of German foreign trade went through the ports of Antwerp and Rotterdam, which meant that Britain's key trade partners, Belgium and the Netherlands, would be caught in the crossfire. Secondly, Llewellyn Smith was also concerned about the direct impact on British industry. He noted that two-thirds of British export revenue came from the German market, and Germany could easily replace most of its British suppliers.[167] Llewellyn Smith's involvement in munitions production during the early years of the war did persuade him that Britain should permanently reduce trade with Germany in a few strategic sectors, but he opposed schemes for general post-war restrictions on raw materials.

Llewellyn Smith's discomfort with a confrontational economic policy reflected a misalignment between the disruptive demands of total war and the trade institutions of the belle époque, which were designed to promote stability above all else. In a 1911 speech, Llewellyn Smith had declared, 'one of the most significant and important economic tendencies of the present day is the growing recognition of the importance of security and regularity in all operations of industry and commerce'.[168] The outbreak of war in 1914 injected a large measure of unpredictability into economic life, as commercial resources were gradually reoriented towards military ends in

---

[164] H. Strachan, *The First World War: To Arms* (Oxford University Press, 2001), 401.

[165] Frei, *Great Britain, International Law, and the Evolution of Maritime Strategic Thought*.

[166] Minutes of Fifth Meeting, 9 February 1912, Report and Proceedings of the Standing Committee of the Committee of Imperial Defence on Trading with the Enemy, 1912, TNA: CAB/16/18A.

[167] N. A. Lambert, *Planning Armageddon: British Economic Warfare and the First World War* (Harvard University Press, 2012), 155–66.

[168] Llewellyn Smith, 'Economic Security and Unemployment Insurance', 516.

fits and starts. The tools of trade politics that were handed down from the belle époque shaped how this new war economy was interpreted. The associations, laws, and information networks that had been created to manage world markets before 1914 gave a veneer of coherence to rather impromptu systems of economic mobilization. The blurry boundaries between public administration and private commerce meant that independent commercial opportunism was presumed to have a political motive. Before 1914, the sources of uncertainty in global markets were many and diffuse. From 1914 to 1918, both sides grew convinced that enemy governments were systematically trying to bend the entire world economy towards war (the Allies came much closer to achieving that feat, in practice). The new prospect of world economic warfare – both actual and imagined – persuaded Coquet, Harms, Llewellyn Smith, and Riedl that private trade relations could be harnessed to political ends on a grand scale, a possibility which supported both international rivalry and cooperation during the 1920s.

2   The World Economy at War

In August 1914, the outbreak of war fully suspended some commercial relationships and reconfigured many others. Wartime economic restrictions varied considerably from state to state, but everywhere policies of sequestration and expropriation began to disentangle the web of multinational capital that had underpinned international trade. The war did not roll back global market integration across the board, however. Indeed, many firms moved into new markets and forged distant business partnerships to fill gaps in their supply chains and meet the resource demands of large-scale industrialized war.[1] Llewellyn Smith and Riedl both participated directly in the administration of the war economy at a high level, while Bernhard Harms and Lucien Coquet focused their energies on information exchange and policy planning as they prepared for a more sharply politicized post-war trade environment. Coquet was the only one of the four men who served in the military; he was enlisted in 1915 as a secretary and translator attached to the French General Staff in Paris.[2] This posting enabled him to keep up his associational activity as a member of France's Committee of National Foreign Trade Advisors.

In 1914–15, leaders on both sides scrambled to compensate for input shortages and to ramp up munitions output. The war exposed dependence on imports of strategic materials, prompting efforts to exploit enemies' commercial vulnerabilities through the tools of blockade and submarine warfare. As European belligerents struggled to secure their

---

[1] A. C. Bell, *A History of the Blockade of Germany and of the Countries Associated with Her in the Great War, Austria-Hungary, Bulgaria, and Turkey, 1914–1918* (H. M. G. Stationery Office, 1937), 176–9; Miller, *Europe and the Maritime World*, 240–42; E. Storli, 'The Global Race for Bauxite, 1900–1940', in R. S. Gendron, M. Ingulstad, and E. Storli (eds.), *Aluminium Ore: The Political Economy of the Global Bauxite Industry* (UBC, 2013), pp. 24–52; Tooze and Fertik, 'The World Economy and the Great War'; N. Mulder, *The Economic Weapon: The Rise of Sanctions as a Tool of Modern War* (Yale University Press, 2022), 53–60.

[2] Bureau de recrutement militaire de Versailles, Registre matricule, Lucien Coquet, Archives départementales des Yvelines, Montigny-le-Bretonneux: 1R/RM 234.

supply lines, they also began to devise legal and institutional safeguards to ensure permanent access to strategic materials. This brought a rupture with the pre-war assumption that markets should be left to allocate productive capacity, but the depth and institutional character of that shift varied from country to country. Keenly aware of their severe resource shortages and limited commercial reach abroad, leaders in France and Austria devised elaborate plans to transform military alliances into permanent economic partnerships that would continue after the war. Some German and British leaders expressed sympathy for this logic of trade blocs, but most sought to preserve open markets with the hope of restoring their wide-ranging commercial networks after the war. Starting in 1916, US President Woodrow Wilson also began to call for an open world economy, in order to sustain the dramatic increase in US commercial influence during the war and to counteract the politicization of European trade relations.

The Wartime Transformation of Economic Administration

By spring 1915, European belligerents began to dramatically retool national economic administration, as they faced a war that was more resource-intensive than they had anticipated. Before 1914, state trade policy was generally limited to providing information, legal protection, and physical infrastructure. During the war, bureaucrats began to intervene more directly in processes of production, exchange, and consumption. Most governments shed these functions after 1918 (to a much greater extent than they later did after 1945). Nevertheless, the wartime experiments in economic administration did produce new patterns of organizational practice that persisted at both the national and the international level.

The British case illustrates the wartime transformation of economic administration particularly vividly. Before the war, the British state had deliberately avoided meddling in production to allow for the free play of comparative advantage, but it pivoted towards deep intervention in supply chains by 1915.[3] As Britain's top commercial bureaucrat, Llewellyn Smith was at the very heart of the country's war economy. His protégé William Beveridge later wrote that during the war Llewellyn Smith was 'at the top of his powers and his amazing industry. There seemed to be no

---

[3] S. Broadberry and P. Howlett, 'The United Kingdom during World War I: Business As Usual?', in S. Broadberry and M. Harrison (eds.), *The Economics of World War I* (Cambridge University Press, 2009), pp. 206–34, 213–14.

limit to the things he could find time to think of'.[4] Llewellyn Smith notably played a leading role in creating a new Ministry of Munitions in 1915 after a shell shortage contributed to a highly publicized British defeat at Aubers Ridge.[5]

Llewellyn Smith was responsible for defining the bureaucratic organization of the Ministry of Munitions, and he proposed a traditional departmental configuration with himself at its nucleus, as general secretary. Within this formal framework, the businessmen and private experts who staffed the ministry had wide latitude to innovate.[6] The Ministry of Munitions quickly ballooned into a massive organization; the headquarters staff rose from an initial count of 200 to 25,000 at the Armistice. By 1917 there were 40,000 employees across the United Kingdom with an additional 8,000 in the United States.[7] The diversity of the Ministry of Munitions' staff was celebrated as a unique asset. Christopher Addison, who became minister of munitions in December 1916, declared that 'the Ministry presents perhaps the most remarkable aggregation of men and women of diverse qualifications and attainments that has ever been got together in this country or in the world'. He marvelled that people 'from every branch of commerce and industry are serving with us (often as volunteers); scientists, lawyers, literary men, commercial men, travellers, soldiers, sailors, and I know not what besides, are working in our ranks'.[8] There were many similarities in the organization of the Ministry of Munitions and the early League of Nations. Both relied on a diverse array of experts as employees and unpaid consultants, and both had relatively fluid institutional structures. Llewellyn Smith worked tenaciously to impose a minimum degree of bureaucratic discipline in these dynamic environments.

During his time as general secretary of the Ministry of Munitions, Llewellyn Smith was forced to watch the administrative separation of labour and trade policy, two spheres which he had worked hard to connect. During the early years of the war, he was responsible for managing wartime shortages of skilled labour. He relaxed restrictions on

[4] W. Beveridge, 'Sir Hubert Llewellyn Smith', *The Economic Journal*, 56/221 (1946), 143–50, 145.

[5] Davidson, 'Sir Hubert Llewellyn Smith and Labour Policy', p. 314; D. French, 'The Military Background to the "Shell Crisis" of May 1915', *Journal of Strategic Studies*, 2/2 (1979), 192–205, 311–12.

[6] *History of the Ministry of Munitions*, 12 vols (H. M. G. Stationery Office, 1922), vol. II, part 1, pp. 151–3.

[7] C. Wrigley, 'The Ministry of Munitions: An Innovatory Department', in K. Burk (ed.), *War and the State: The Transformation of the British Government, 1914–1919* (Routledge, 1982), pp. 32–56, 42–4; J. A. Fairlie, *British War Administration* (Oxford University Press, 1919), 107.

[8] *History of the Ministry of Munitions*, vol. II, part 1, p. 166.

output per worker and recruited more women into the labour force, arousing the ire of union leaders.[9] They responded by forcing the Ministry of Munitions and the Board of Trade to cede their authority over labour supply to a new Ministry of Labour in 1916. The Labour Party and the unions had been demanding a dedicated ministry for many years before the war, but Llewellyn Smith had consistently opposed them, declaring:

It would be most undesirable to have a Minister of Labour supposed to stand for the 'Labour' side of each economic question, and a Minister of Commerce taking the other side. But, beyond this, experience shews that the best guarantee for wise dealing with matters, relating either to labour or commerce, is to deal with each in the light of the other; i.e. to keep questions of the 'condition of the people' in mind in dealing with a commercial question, and to remember the effects on commerce and foreign competition, when dealing with such matters as the regulation of labour.[10]

This 'New Liberal' ideal of integrated economic administration reached its apogee in 1911 when Llewellyn Smith and Beveridge founded Britain's national unemployment insurance administration within the Board of Trade, but this apparatus was transferred only five years later to the Ministry of Labour.[11] Across Europe, the First World War confirmed labour as a separate policy sphere, by centralizing the administration of national employment and by politically empowering unions.[12] This administrative distinction was later mirrored at the international level through the separation of the League's Economic and Financial Organization and the International Labour Organization (ILO).

During the war, Llewellyn Smith continued to argue that employment and trade must be closely coordinated to manage Britain's mounting balance of payments problems. He was a leading proponent of the view that Britain should keep up its exports to try to cover rising imports from the United States, and he tried hard to ensure that military recruitment left sufficient skilled workers for private industry.[13] Any imports that were not matched by exports would have to be funded by taking on new US debt and selling off investments. This would force Britain to intervene in novel ways in private financial markets while also limiting its political

---

[9] *History of the Ministry of Munitions*, vol. I, part 4, p. 12; Davidson, 'Sir Hubert Llewellyn Smith and Labour Policy', pp. 339–79.
[10] Quoted in Davidson, 'Sir Hubert Llewellyn Smith and Labour Policy', p. 381.
[11] Davidson, 'Sir Hubert Llewellyn Smith and Labour Policy', pp. 380–95.
[12] Maier, *Recasting Bourgeois Europe*, 43–77.
[13] War Policy. Report and Supplementary Memoranda of a Cabinet Committee, 12 October 1915, TNA: CAB 24/1/32; *History of the Ministry of Munitions*, vol. IV, part 3, pp. 31–6; Lambert, *Planning Armageddon*, 327–30, 418.

room for manoeuvre over the long term.[14] Anxious to avoid these dangers, the Board of Trade probably over-estimated British exporters' capacity to compete directly on US markets at a time when the circuitous multilateral trade networks that Britain had used to earn dollars before the war were being squeezed by shipping constraints. In the end, the British trade deficit with the United States increased more than six-fold over the course of the war, but this paled in comparison to the French transatlantic trade deficit, which increased sixteen-fold.[15]

Weaponizing Foreign Markets: Blockade and Submarine Warfare

As the belligerents all struggled to maintain their own trade networks to support wartime production, they also moved to cut enemy supply lines. The Allies relied on tools of blockade while the Central Powers used submarine warfare. Both approaches were fundamentally premised on the pre-war understanding of the world economy as a deeply integrated system but posed fundamentally new legal and operational challenges. In wartime, expansive commercial networks became a potential source of weakness because they entailed dependence on strategically vulnerable supply lines. The confrontation between Germany and Britain had the most significant implications for trade politics because they were the belligerents with the most extensive commercial links with one another and with the rest of the world. The tit-for-tat escalation of submarine warfare and blockade had profound effects on coalition partners with weaker underlying economic capacity and on neutral states that were caught in the middle.

Llewellyn Smith and other leaders in the Board of Trade tried to resist the Admiralty's drive to weaponize foreign trade. Britain never declared a formal blockade against Germany because it could not be fully enforced and would thus violate international law. In lieu of an official blockade, Britain cobbled together an elaborate regime of 'economic warfare' to impede trade into and out of Germany, directly and through neutral ports. The Admiralty, the Foreign Office, and the Board of Trade all shared responsibility for the administration of this system, but the Board of Trade was often a reluctant partner.[16] In the initial

---

[14] H. Strachan, *Financing the First World War* (Oxford University Press, 2004), 161–223; Tooze, *The Deluge*, 36–8.
[15] M. Horn, *Britain, France, and the Financing of the First World War* (McGill-Queen's University Press, 2002), 86–7.
[16] Lambert, *Planning Armageddon*, 348–52. H. Llewellyn Smith to W. Runciman, 24 July 1915, Bodleian Library: Asquith Papers/MS 29.

rules on 'trading with the enemy' that were adopted in autumn 1914, the Board demanded relatively light restrictions on British exports of 'war-like stores' to avoid ceding markets to neutral suppliers. At the same time, the Board tried hard to maintain harmonious trade relations with neutral partners. It resisted the new interpretation of international law that the Foreign Office devised to empower the Royal Navy to ration goods passing through neutral countries, permitting the passage of just enough food and essential raw materials to meet local needs. The Navy initially seized food shipments only when it could prove that they were destined for enemy armies. It began to broaden its seizures in spring 1915 in response to expanding state control over the German food supply, which made it more difficult to differentiate provisions destined for civilian and military use.[17]

Trade through neutral states was rationed unevenly, based on their own varying interpretations of neutrality, their geopolitical leverage, and the counter-pressures exerted by the Central Powers. The Swiss, whose neutral status was formally enshrined in international treaties dating back to the close of the Napoleonic Wars, were relatively unconcerned about demonstrating neutrality. The Swiss freely played their neighbours off one another, as Allied restrictions on Swiss trade were enforced conjointly by France, Britain, and Italy. The Swiss manufactured munitions for the Allies, in violation of neutrality under international law, even as they extracted allowances from the Allies to continue to trade actively with the Central Powers so as to preserve lucrative links to the German engineering sector. The Allies restricted trade through the Netherlands more tightly, even as the Dutch government took greater pains to demonstrate formal compliance with international norms of neutrality. The Dutch were keenly aware of their dependence on British goodwill in the Netherlands East Indies, which they were powerless to defend militarily (in contrast, the Swiss had no vulnerable overseas outposts to worry about). Thus, the Dutch adhered to the Allied blockade assiduously while loudly protesting the violations of international law that it entailed. The government managed to distance itself from the actual implementation of the blockade by outsourcing it to a private Netherlands Overseas Trust. The Allies attempted to replicate this business-led model with the Scandinavian neutral states but encountered considerable resistance. Sweden had substantial leverage because it controlled important

[17] Bell, *A History of the Blockade of Germany and of the Countries Associated with Her in the Great War, Austria-Hungary, Bulgaria, and Turkey, 1914–1918*, 173–9, 540–41; Lambert, *Planning Armageddon*, 210–11, 223, 259, 277; I. V. Hull, *A Scrap of Paper: Breaking and Making International Law during the Great War* (Cornell University Press, 2014), 158–9, 171–6.

transport routes to Russia and the Baltic Sea, but Norway's heavy dependence on imports of food and other raw materials from Britain left it more vulnerable. In one of the most aggressive wartime moves against a neutral state, Britain withheld coal shipments to Norway in an unusually cold winter to pressure the government to halt exports of pyrites to Germany, an important input for ammunition. In the resource-rich northern neutrals, Allied economic controls focused as much on restricting production for use by the Central Powers as on limiting the trans-shipment of foreign supplies.[18]

As neutral states were drawn into the Allied apparatus of economic warfare, they were also hit hard by German submarine warfare. Submarine warfare reflected a logic of total war that implicated civilians as victims and participants.[19] The German public perceived the block-ade as a campaign of indiscriminate starvation and demanded equiva-lent reprisals against British civilians. The U-boat figured prominently in popular fantasies because it was a new and relatively untested tech-nology and so held seemingly infinite promise.[20] The novelty of the submarine also meant that its status under international law was unclear. In February 1915, the German government declared the waters around Great Britain to be a 'war zone' in which enemy and neutral ships could be sunk without warning. This contravened international prize law for conventional cruisers, which only allowed the sinking of commercial vessels after the passengers and crew had disembarked. The German government initially argued that normal 'cruiser rules' did not apply to submarines, but some officials, including the Chancellor Theobald von Bethmann Hollweg, worried that that this stance would damage political relations with neutral states. After the United States forcefully protested the sinking of British passenger ships carrying US citizens – most famously, the *Lusitania* – the German government agreed in autumn 1915 to apply cruiser rules to U-boat engagement with neutral and enemy passenger ships. It extended this policy to cover enemy commercial vessels in spring 1916. Although it was brief, the

[18] P. Salmon, *Scandinavia and the Great Powers, 1890–1940* (Cambridge University Press, 1997), 129–46; P. Moeyes, 'Neutral Tones: The Netherlands and Switzerland and Their Interpretations of Neutrality 1914–1918', in H. Amersfoort and W. Klinkert (eds.), *Small Powers in the Age of Total War, 1900–1940* (Brill, 2011), pp. 57–84; Miller, *Europe and the Maritime World*, 227–8.

[19] H. Jones, 'The Great War: How 1914–18 Changed the Relationship between War and Civilians', *The RUSI Journal*, 159/4 (2014), 84–91.

[20] Strachan, *The First World War: To Arms*, 418–19; A. Watson, *Ring of Steel: Germany and Austria-Hungary at War, 1914–1918* (Allen Lane, 2014), 236–41; Grimmer-Solem, *Learning Empire*, 523–5.

interval of unrestricted submarine warfare in 1915 provoked a substantial reinforcement of the Allied blockade.[21]

In the Austrian Ministry of Commerce, Riedl saw first-hand the tightening of the Allies' commercial vice around Central and Eastern Europe in 1914 and 1915. While the Allies constrained Austrian shipping in the Mediterranean, the blockade on Germany also had a profound impact on the Austrian economy because it depended heavily on trade through North German ports. The declaration of war automatically triggered laws in Austria–Hungary and Germany that prohibited foreign trade in strategic commodities, and those laws had not been coordinated to exempt trade between the two belligerents. Consequently, in September 1914, Austria–Hungary faced critical shortages of many inputs that it normally imported through Germany. For example, before the war, Austrian spinners had bought 65 per cent of their raw cotton from the United States, through Bremen. When that supply chain was disrupted in 1914 – partly by the war and partly by a bad US harvest – they struggled to compensate with alternative imports through Trieste. Austria's Mediterranean port had never developed sufficient warehouse capacity to support a large wholesale trade, nor could it offer financial and organizational resources equivalent to the Bremen Cotton Exchange.[22] In September 1914, Riedl made an urgent trip to Germany to negotiate the trans-shipment of paid-up Austro-Hungarian orders that were sitting in Hamburg and Bremen, and he also ensured that Austrians would be able to buy a share of any further stocks that Germany could obtain of cotton, wool, metal, saltpetre, and synthetic chemicals.[23] Thus, in the first weeks of the war, Riedl took the full measure of Austria's dependence on German commercial infrastructure. This experience reinforced his commitment to Austro-German economic solidarity, over the long term.

Riedl also believed that the internal organization of the Austrian war economy required administrative harmonization with Germany. As a corollary to the September Agreement on raw materials, Riedl also helped create internal mechanisms for Austrian resource distribution that mirrored those in Germany. In both Austria and Germany, the impetus to organize commodity markets for war production initially came from private industrialists. Walther Rathenau, the head of the German engineering behemoth, Allgemeine Elektricitäts-Gesellschaft, led a new War Raw

---

[21] Hull, *A Scrap of Paper*, 240–57.

[22] R. Riedl, *Die Industrie Österreichs während des Krieges* (Carnegie Endowment for International Peace, 1932), 335–7.

[23] Riedl, *Die Industrie Österreichs während des Krieges*, 24–6, 334–7; Brettner-Messler, 'Richard Riedl', pp. 261–4.

Materials Department (*Kriegsrohstoffabteilung*) in the Prussian War Ministry. This body oversaw the formation of a series of industry-led Raw Materials Corporations (*Kriegsrohstoff-Gesellschaften*) that managed the allocation of commodities. In Austria, Riedl oversaw the creation of an analogous set of Centrals (*Zentralen*) to interface with German institutions and handle internal distribution. The first Centrals were formed with private funds as profit-making enterprises, but Riedl incorporated them into the September Agreement. His willingness to use state power to support the self-organization of industry reflected the deep ties that he had developed with the business community during his long stint at the Vienna Chamber of Commerce. The Austrian Centrals and German Raw Materials Corporations were created by business leaders to compensate for bureaucratic deficiencies at the state level, and they expanded into a fully fledged administrative apparatus in response to the extension of the Allied blockade starting in spring 1915. By the end of the war, there were roughly ninety Centrals and two hundred Raw Materials Corporations.[24]

Economic Information and the Self-Mobilization of Business

Austrian and German leaders focused public attention on the blockade as the primary reason for food and raw material shortages to draw attention away from their own bureaucratic mismanagement, and, in the process, they spread a narrative of the war that emphasized trade. Germans grew convinced that Britain was using the blockade to undercut their position in foreign markets.[25] The Allied governments reinforced this view by using their pre-war information networks to encourage expatriate commercial communities to take over German clients. These campaigns to 'capture enemy trade' gave superficial coherence to opportunistic private attempts to exploit market distortions resulting from the war. This reinforced Germans' and Austrians' fears that the Allies were planning to continue commercial warfare in peacetime and encouraged the Central Powers to develop their own plans to promote patriotic solidarity on foreign markets after the war.

Through the IfW's wartime publications, Bernhard Harms painted Allied economic warfare with a broad brush, and he reached a growing audience of German business leaders. The network of financial sponsors and news correspondents that he had built up before the war gave the IfW

---

[24] Riedl, *Die Industrie Österreichs während des Krieges*, 27–9; Brettner-Messler, 'Richard Riedl', pp. 264–5; Watson, *Ring of Steel*, 208.
[25] Watson, *Ring of Steel*, 229.

a crucial advantage as German information channels were constricted. Heidi Tworek explains that the Allies engaged in a deliberate campaign to limit German access to information by destroying communications infrastructure during the war, and this encouraged the German elite to regard news as a tool of power politics.[26] Beginning in autumn 1915, the IfW implemented a multi-pronged publication strategy to disseminate different kinds of information on the global war economy to different groups of readers. It continued to produce its biannual research periodical, the *Weltwirtschaftliches Archiv*, but shifted its focus to the war. From 1915 to 1918 the IfW also published a monograph series entitled 'The Economic War', *Der Wirtschaftskrieg*, with each volume covering efforts by a different enemy state to 'combat German trade and promote their own economic activity'. In 1915, the IfW began to issue a running bulletin of 'War-Economy News', the *Kriegswirtschaftliche Nachrichten*, at a rate of three issues per week. This was a compilation of short reports from the international press and private correspondents.[27] It served as a medium of communication among IfW members; they supplied much of its material, and they all automatically purchased a subscription as a component of their membership fees. The IfW underwent its most dramatic expansion during the years when it was publishing the *Kriegswirtschaftliche Nachrichten*. It grew from 175 members in June 1914 to 5,304 in 1918.[28] The *Kriegswirtschaftliche Nachrichten* presented an expansive vision of the war by tracing its ramifications in global markets. It portrayed spontaneous private initiatives that were directed against Germany or the other Central Powers as part of a sweeping 'private side-war' that would continue after the end of the conflict. The newspaper covered 'all efforts that have the goal of using the present obstruction of German world economic activity to usurp German business relationships'.[29] This encompassed state policy, private business, and the vast web of associations that fell in-between.

Edith Oske, who ran the news archive at the IfW that fed into the *Kriegswirtschaftliche Nachrichten*, singled out expatriate chambers of commerce as sites for particularly frenzied organizational innovation during the war. As discussed in the previous chapter, these associations had become an important interface between mobile business communities and governments

[26] H. Tworek, 'Magic Connections: German News Agencies and Global News Networks, 1905–1945', *Enterprise and Society*, 15/4 (2014), 672–86.
[27] Zur Entwicklung des Nachrichtendienstes des Instituts für Seeverkehr und Weltwirtschaft in Kiel, undated, IfW: Hs N.A./1.
[28] Liste der Mitglieder der Gesellschaft zur Förderung des Instituts für Seeverkehr und Weltwirtschaft an der Universität Kiel, 10 June 1914, Stadtarchiv Kiel/32893; Hoffmann, 'Die Geschichte des Instituts für Weltwirtschaft', vol. I, pp. 21–3.
[29] 'Vorbemerkung', *Kriegswirtschaftliche Nachrichten*, 1 November 1916, 1.

before 1914, and also offered a channel of professional mobility for ambitious young men such as Coquet. The IfW had been monitoring expatriate chambers of commerce prior to the war and closely followed their wartime activities, publishing over one hundred articles on the topic in the *Kriegswirtschaftliche Nachrichten*. The war caused a proliferation of expatriate chambers of commerce; over fifty were established from 1914 to 1918.[30] Oske linked this spike to broader changes in commercial activity, explaining,

the development of chambers of commerce abroad reflects the tendencies that currently dominate international economic life: the growing conviction in the necessity of economic organization, the strengthening of the national principle, the transfer of the war to the economic domain.[31]

Oske noted that international chambers of commerce, which had grouped together European expatriates of different nationalities in major trading cities before the war, were dissolving into competing national organizations. For example, the pre-war International Chamber of Commerce in Shanghai was replaced with distinct British and French chambers, which were both explicitly anti-German in orientation.[32] The war did not politicize expatriate chambers of commerce; they were already political. The war did encourage these kinds of organizations to demonstrate their national and imperial allegiances in a more assertive way. Philip Dehne explains that expatriate business leaders often ran ahead of their home governments in their ambition to exploit the wartime distortion of overseas markets, mixing motives of profit and patriotism.[33]

British and French policies helped create an impression that more or less spontaneous initiatives in overseas commercial communities were part of a coordinated commercial offensive from the Allies. The French and British governments both launched official campaigns in autumn 1914 to 'capture enemy trade'.[34] In Britain, this campaign was orchestrated by the Board of Trade's Commercial Intelligence Branch, under

[30] Drossinis, *Les chambres de commerce à l'étranger*, 326–65.

[31] E. Oske, 'Neuerrichtung von Auslandshandelskammern', *Weltwirtschaftliches Archiv*, 9 (1917), 104–6; See also E. Oske, 'Neugründungen von internationalen Vereinen und Gesellschaften', *Weltwirtschaftliches Archiv*, 8 (1916), 447–50; E. Oske, 'Neugründungen von internationalen Vereinen und Gesellschaften', *Weltwirtschaftliches Archiv*, 10 (1917), 439–41; E. Oske, 'Neuerrichtung von Auslandshandelskammern', *Weltwirtschaftliches Archiv*, 12 (1918), 414–24.

[32] Oske, 'Neuerrichtung von Auslandshandelskammern', 104. See also 'China. Französische Handelskammer', *Kriegswirtschaftliche Nachrichten*, 6 March 1916, 125; 'China. Tätigkeit der englischen Handelskammer in Shanghai', *Kriegswirtschaftliche Nachrichten*, 14 July 1916, 404.

[33] P. A. Dehne, *On the Far Western Front: Britain's First World War in South America* (Manchester University Press, 2009).

[34] Miller, *Europe and the Maritime World*, 224.

Llewellyn Smith's supervision. The Board published a series of brochures on new overseas sales opportunities in 'branches of trade in which enemy competition abroad has been especially acute'.[35] By December 1914, it had issued roughly four-dozen such brochures.[36] It also organized 'Exchange Meetings' which allowed British manufacturers to inspect samples of products that had previously been sourced from Germany and Austria–Hungary and to meet the commercial intermediaries who traded those goods. There had been eleven Exchange Meetings by the end of 1915.[37] The first, in September 1914, focused on toys and was attended by more than six hundred manufacturers and traders.[38] In May 1915, the Commercial Intelligence Branch followed up the Exchange Meetings with a 'British Industries Fair' which exhibited British-made alternatives to German and Austro-Hungarian exports.[39]

Similar initiatives were sponsored in France by the National Office of Foreign Trade. In August 1914, the Office issued a circular to all of France's expatriate chambers of commerce and consular posts asking them to report open contracts with German and Austrian exporters that might be taken over by French firms. This information was then distributed as pamphlets to a list of 1,000 private correspondents of the Office, to all mainland chambers of commerce, and to the major French producer syndicates. The Office continued to develop this '*Dossiers Commerciaux*' service throughout the war. It used this channel to disseminate general information about Austro-Hungarian and German organizational practices (for example related to trade credit, insurance, and transport) and to provide lists of firms that had represented Austro-Hungarian and German exporters on foreign markets.[40] Interestingly, although Coquet disbanded his Franco-German Commercial Committee, its sister organization in Berlin continued to function as a zombie information service which turned against the French. It used its accumulated knowledge of the French commercial bureaucracy to track the wartime sequestration of German

---

[35] *Report to the Board of Trade by the Advisory Committee on Commercial Intelligence, with Reference to Their Proceedings October 1913 to October 1917* (H. M. G. Stationery Office, 1917), 11.

[36] 'German and Austrian Foreign Markets: Further Issue of Special Memoranda', *Board of Trade Journal*, 10 December 1914, 684–5.

[37] *Report to the Board of Trade by the Advisory Committee on Commercial Intelligence, with Reference to Their Proceedings October 1913 to October 1917*, 12.

[38] 'Samples of German, Austrian, and Hungarian Goods: "Exchange Meetings" of Manufacturers and Buyers', *Board of Trade Journal*, 1 October 1914, 21.

[39] *Report to the Board of Trade by the Advisory Committee on Commercial Intelligence, with Reference to Their Proceedings October 1913 to October 1917*, 12–13.

[40] Letter from le Directeur de l'Office national du commerce extérieur to Monsieur le Ministre du Commerce de l'Industrie, des Postes et des Télégraphes, 19 December 1914, AN: F12/9289; Dossiers Commerciaux, November 1914–April 1917, AN: F12/9289.

property as well as Allied initiatives to take over German export markets. It published this material in a new periodical on the 'German-French Trade War', the *Deutsch-Französische Handelskrieg*.[41] For his part, Coquet drew on his pre-war experience to intervene as an expert on German commercial chicanery in the same organizational forums that he had used before the war, including the Committee of Foreign Trade Advisors, attached to the National Office of Foreign Trade.

In practice, French and British attempts to exploit the wartime stoppage of European trade to promote their own national exports yielded limited results. Producers outside Europe, especially in the United States, were in a much better position to scoop up Austro-Hungarian and German customers. British and French shipping and commercial infrastructure was tied up in the war effort and could not be wasted in the laborious process of cultivating new markets. There was also much duplication and competition between British and French initiatives; the Commercial Intelligence Branch and the National Office of Foreign Trade shared materials with one another, but only after a considerable delay.[42] Their programmes were nevertheless lumped together in German publications such as the *Kriegswirtchaftliche Nachrichten* or the *Deutsch-Französische Handelskrieg*. These publications noted the great fanfare surrounding the fairs, exchange meetings, and other Allied efforts to 'capture enemy trade' but had limited means to assess the results on the ground. They amplified the perception that Allied economic warfare threatened to undermine the Central Powers' future position in the world economy. Leaders on all sides drew the conclusion that private trade networks would remain a tool of power politics after the war and would thus have to be subject to greater institutional oversight.

Economic Security in Mitteleuropa

The formation of a seemingly coherent system of Allied economic warfare which stretched deep into private commerce reinforced Riedl's belief that the world was being divided into rival power blocs. During the war, he participated in German nationalist debates about the future of Central Europe and emerged as a leading advocate for a regional customs union. In 1915, Riedl circulated a draft treaty that would unite Austria–Hungary and Germany behind a common external tariff but maintain lower 'intervening tariffs' between the states, to be gradually reduced at fixed

---

[41] *Deutsch-Französische Handelskrieg*, 1914–1919.
[42] Letter from le Directeur de l'Office national du commerce extérieur to Monsieur le Ministre du Commerce de l'Industrie, des Postes et des Télégraphes, 30 November 1914, AN: F12/9289.

intervals. They would also harmonize their commercial laws and administration.[43] This arrangement would be open to other states from the Baltic to the Balkans, forming a vast continental grouping with Germany and Austria–Hungary at its core. Riedl explained that 'uniting the two Central Powers is for each of them a prerequisite for the association of other smaller powers, desired by one side or the other as the basis for a true world policy [*Weltpolitik*] of central European nations, ensuring the independence of these nations with respect to the great world powers'.[44] Thus, he did not pursue a united Mitteleuropa as a closed autarkic system but rather as a springboard for access to global markets. He planned to regulate relations between his proposed regional bloc and the wider world through traditional MFN treaties. This was partly in deference to German leaders, who were deeply committed to MFN, although Riedl also saw MFN treaties as means for Austria to continue its own pre-war drive to expand overseas export markets.[45]

In 1915, Riedl incorporated his plan for a customs union into an influential proposal for Central European solidarity, the *Denkschrift aus Deutsch-Österreich* (Memorandum from German-Austria). The *Denkshrift* was written by a group of officials and intellectuals who gathered around the Austrian historian Heinrich Friedjung. They were also in contact with the German politician Friedrich Naumann, whose more popular tract, *Mitteleuropa*, was published around the same time. The two texts had very different emphases and audiences, however.[46] Naumann disdained technical detail, arguing that it was a waste of time to 'tinker too much with tariff laws' because 'first we must ensure that we have the great masses behind us'.[47] In contrast, the *Denkschrift* offered precise administrative prescriptions and was only published for private circulation among officials. It justified Central European union based on the wartime transformation of international law:

The security and the expansion of internationality [*Internationalität*] was the prerequisite for the independence of a large number of states, which, if dependent solely on their own resources, could not have developed. The war brought an end

---

[43] R. Riedl, Entwurf eines Zollvereinsvertrages, March 1915, ÖStA, HHStA: NL Baernreither/30; R. Kapp, 'The Failure of the Diplomatic Negotiations between Germany and Austria-Hungary for a Customs Union, 1915–1916', PhD thesis, University of Toronto (1977), pp. 132–43; J. Vermeiren, *The First World War and German National Identity: The Dual Alliance at War* (Cambridge University Press, 2016), 173–4.

[44] Besprechung bei Kaz. Dr. Marchet, 4 May 1915, ÖStA, HHStA: NL Baernreither/30.

[45] Besprechung bei Kaz. Dr. Marchet, 4 May 1915, ÖStA, HHStA: NL Baernreither/30; Sitzung bei Exz. Marchet, 5 May 1915, ÖStA, HHStA: NL Baernreither/30.

[46] Kapp, 'The Failure of the Diplomatic Negotiations between Germany and Austria-Hungary', pp. 149–55; Brettner-Messler, 'Richard Riedl', pp. 222–8; Watson, *Ring of Steel*, 263.

[47] II. Sitzung, 26 March 1915, ÖStA, HHStA: NL Baernreither/30.

to this system of medium or small economic bodies that want to be called independent and yet are not self-reliant. We have witnessed a mockery of the most widely recognized international law, the trampling of the principles of the protection of private property, of trade and transit, and of neutrality. In such a manner, life-giving internationality was taken from small governmental and economic bodies. Even after the conclusion of peace, a reversal is highly unlikely ... power as such will play an even greater role in relations among countries than before. Therein lies an undeniable incentive for the two empires at the centre of Europe to establish and develop their military and economic union.[48]

Thus, the *Denkschrift* argued that the war had produced a new field of intensified power politics, which forced small states to join larger regional groupings. In the 1920s, this logic continued to motivate Riedl to pursue union with Germany.

In 1915–16, the *Denkschrift* circulated widely in Austrian and German official circles and notably made a strong impression on Bethmann Hollweg and on the Austro-Hungarian military chief of staff, Franz Conrad von Hötzendorf. They had both begun to contemplate a permanent Central European union to defuse tensions concerning territory occupied by the Central Powers, especially Russian Poland.[49] Although leaders in Austria–Hungary might have accepted a customs union with Germany in response to these geopolitical exigencies, they were unwilling to support it as a ploy to extend the influence of ethnic Germans within the Dual Monarchy. Both Karl von Stürgkh and István Tisza, the top Austrian and Hungarian political leaders, took this view. In contrast, Bethmann Hollweg responded positively to German nationalist propaganda from Vienna, especially the *Denkschrift*, and he explicitly linked partnership with Austria–Hungary to ideals of pan-German cultural solidarity. This raised Tisza's hackles and doomed the project.[50] The Austrian minister of commerce fumed that 'there were certain undercurrents in the top levels of the Austrian bureaucracy that combined the economic reorganization of Central Europe with national-imperialist plans and thereby compromised this programme, which otherwise was fully justified in economic and geopolitical

---

[48] *Denkschrift Aus Deutsch-Österreich* (Hirzel, 1915), 71. Glenda Sluga shows that before 1914 'internationality' was understood as the infrastructural, legal, and cultural framework for nation states. See Sluga, *Internationalism in the Age of Nationalism*, 12–17.

[49] Georges-Henri Soutou indicates that the war stimulated German interest in a Central European customs union for political rather than economic reasons. It was a means to ensure regional dominance without large territorial annexations that would disrupt the internal political balance within Germany by adding minorities. See G.-H. Soutou, *L'or et le sang: Les buts de guerre économiques de la Première Guerre mondiale* (Fayard, 1989), 22–3, 39–43, 82–91.

[50] Soutou, *L'or et le sang*, 90–95.

terms'.[51] After the negotiations for a customs union fell through, Austrian leaders excluded Riedl from high-level diplomatic negotiations with Germany through the end of the war in order to limit the influence of German nationalism.[52]

Although Riedl's wartime plans for a Germanic Mitteleuropa initially proved counterproductive, they formed the basis for much of his future multilateral work in the League of Nations. In the 1920s, he continued to promote the formation of a vast regional union around an Austro-German core, in which intervening tariffs would be reduced at regular intervals by a fixed percentage. He also insisted that a regional bloc along these lines was compatible with an open international trade regime based on MFN. Riedl's geographic focus shifted westwards in the 1920s: he later included France in his plans but excluded Hungary. The institutional sinews also changed: he began to advocate multilateral agreements coordinated by the League of Nations rather than bilateral treaties negotiated independently by governments. He remained convinced that universal international institutions could not offer a substitute for regional integration, and he supported the League only insofar as he believed it would be possible to create robust European and Austro-German substructures within it. In sum, Riedl maintained a fundamental distrust of 'internationality' through the 1920s.

Economic Security among the Allies

As Riedl was developing his plans for an economic Mitteleuropa during the early years of the war, Coquet and Llewellyn Smith were pursuing inter-Allied solidarity. By 1916, a clear logic of economic blocs had emerged on the Allied side as well as among the Central Powers. As Georges-Henri Soutou has demonstrated, this symmetry was not produced by a tit-for-tat escalation of war aims but rather a common impulse, borne of total war, to safeguard future national security by consolidating access to raw materials and markets.[53] The Allies held an economic conference focused on these goals in Paris in June 1916, during

---

[51] Quoted in Kapp, 'The Failure of the Diplomatic Negotiations between Germany and Austria-Hungary', p. 282.
[52] '6.12.1916', H. Wildner and R. Agstner (eds.), *1915/1916, Das etwas andere Lesebuch zum 1. Weltkrieg. Heinrich Wildner: Tagebuch* (Lit Verlag, 2014), 196; Kapp, 'The Failure of the Diplomatic Negotiations between Germany and Austria-Hungary', 195–283. Jan Vermeiren argues that most Germans who supported the ideal of Mitteleuropa during the First World War were motivated by general geopolitical calculations rather than a sense of cultural or political solidarity with German-speakers outside the German Reich. See Vermeiren, *The First World War and German National Identity*, 120–45.
[53] Soutou, *L'or et le sang*, 265.

their second major offensive on the Somme, which saw an unprecedented level of heavy bombardment. This massive deployment of industrial resources underlined the intention of Allied policies for the Paris Economic Conference: limit German and Austria–Hungarian production during the war and enhance the Allies' long-term self-reliance in strategically important resources.

The 1916 Paris Economic Conference was the brainchild of Étienne Clémentel, who had become the French minister of commerce the previous year. Clémentel originally hoped to use the conference to lay the groundwork for a thorough economic transformation at both the national and international level. The war brought a profound dislocation of French industry, as Germany rapidly invaded the north-eastern territories which produced most of the country's coal, steel, and textiles.[54] As minister of munitions, Albert Thomas sought to rationalize France's remaining manufacturers by placing them in groups to regulate prices, wages, and production. Clémentel devised a similar strategy to regulate post-war foreign trade.[55] He was particularly anxious to secure stable supplies of materials such as metals, textiles, and chemicals to feed the development of export industries.[56] To this end, he proposed to create an inter-Allied office that would keep a common ledger of resources and needs and allocate supplies first to the Allies, then to the neutrals, and finally to the defeated states (as a reward for good behaviour). Thus, raw materials would become a central tool to enforce the political terms of the peace.[57] As Nicholas Mulder shows, Clémentel's plans later fed into the regime of targeted economic sanctions in the League of Nations. Initially, however, he envisaged a more comprehensive trade policy tied to a programme of national economic modernization.[58]

Clémentel blended a traditional conception of power politics with a new desire to construct a rules-based multilateral economic order.[59] At a meeting of the International Parliamentary Commercial Conference which Coquet helped organize in spring 1916 to drum up

---

[54] P.-C. Hautcoeur, 'The Economics of World War I in France', in S. Broadberry and M. Harrison (eds.), *The Economics of World War I* (Cambridge University Press, 2009), pp. 169–205, 172–3.

[55] M. Trachtenberg, '"A New Economic Order": Étienne Clémentel and French Economic Diplomacy during the First World War', *French Historical Studies*, 10/2 (1977), 315–41, 318; R. F. Kuisel, *Capitalism and the State in Modern France: Renovation and Economic Management in the Twentieth Century* (Cambridge University Press, 1981), 43; Maier, *Recasting Bourgeois Europe*, 74–5.

[56] Conférence des Alliés dans l'ordre économique: Mesures transitoires, Proposition II, undated, AN: F12/7988.

[57] Programme de la conférence économique de Paris, Section B Article 2, June 1916, AN: F12/7988; Trachtenberg, 'A New Economic Order', 318–20.

[58] Mulder, *The Economic Weapon*, 73.   [59] Jackson, *Beyond the Balance of Power*, 174–7.

support for the Paris Economic Conference, Clémentel called upon the Allies to form 'an economic bloc against which the *Weltpolitik* of pan-Germanism will shatter'.[60] This would require economic coordination on a global scale. Indeed, there was a fundamental geopolitical tension at the heart of Clémentel's vision: it was, in essence, a project for security in Western Europe, but it depended on the participation of overseas partners, both colonial and non-colonial, that held most raw materials.[61] Their participation could not be taken for granted at a moment when colonial governments were claiming greater commercial and political autonomy from metropolitan overlords. Facing complex economic demands from the Dominion governments, the British refused categorically to discuss imperial economic relations at the Paris Economic Conference.[62]

In the end, the Paris resolutions on raw materials were kept quite vague.[63] The Allies simply committed to 'render themselves independent of the enemy countries in so far as regards the raw materials and manufactured articles essential to the normal development of their economic activities'.[64] This wording left latitude to negotiate intra- and inter-imperial relations and gave Clémentel space to pursue his own plans for regional customs unions within Europe. Prior to the Paris Economic Conference, he had been exploring prospects for a bilateral customs union with Belgium. Some Belgian leaders endorsed this idea, eager to moderate Germany's strong pre-war influence in industry, shipping, and banking; but others feared that a bilateral arrangement with France would compromise the links to Britain that underpinned Belgian global exports. Belgium's complex trilateral relations with France, Britain, and Germany remained a pivotal factor in European trade debates throughout the 1920s. Although it was a small country, Belgium was a major commercial player. It was one of the most dynamic industrial economies in Western Europe – it led the world in per capita manufactured exports in 1913, and it had an edge in growth sectors such as electrical engineering. Moreover, the First World War highlighted

---

[60] *Conférence Parlementaire Internationale du Commerce, Deuxième Assemblée* (Félix Alcan, 220). This event was held under the umbrella of the Inter-Parliamentary Union and gathered the Allied politicians who were responsible for trade policy to discuss post-war cooperation.
[61] H. Hauser, L'Approvisionnement de l'Allemagne en matières premières après la guerre, undated, AN: F12/7988.
[62] A. Orde, *British Policy and European Reconstruction after the First World War* (Cambridge University Press, 1990), 8–9.
[63] W. Runciman to E. Clémentel, 12 February 1916, AMAE: Guerre 1914–1918/1216; Orde, *British Policy and European Reconstruction*, 8.
[64] *Recommendations of the Economic Conference of the Allies* (H. M. G. Stationery Office, 1916), 8.

Belgium's pivotal geopolitical position and the strategic value of its heavy industry and shipping. After 1918, Belgium became a bridge between the European belligerents and neutral states, since it abandoned neutrality (until 1936), but its leaders nevertheless continued to share the neutrals' deep commitment to international law and open markets.[65]

Belgium's low tariffs made a full customs union with France difficult, especially as protectionist pressure mounted in French parliamentary and industrial circles. For his part, Clémentel hoped to return to France's 1914 tariff and even to push further and offer preferential reductions to Allied and imperial partners, up to a full customs union. This system of preference would require a wholesale break with MFN, but it was an expansionary programme, not an inward-oriented regime of protection, at least in Clémentel's original formulation. He hoped to boost French productivity significantly through domestic economic reforms and sought new post-war export markets to support this growth.[66] Thus, Clémentel linked his plans for the multilateral organization of world markets to the internal modernization of the French economy, and Coquet participated in both parts of this programme. Coquet contributed a series of studies on the fashion sector to a survey of French domestic production conducted by Clémentel's deputy, Henri Hauser, to prepare the post-war French economy.[67] In the final years of the war, Clémentel and Hauser invested considerable institutional resources in economic planning, but their idiosyncratic liberal vision encountered strong resistance from protectionist forces at home and from foreign Allies who were reluctant to compromise traditional free trade principles in order to participate in a regime of multilateral preference.

At the 1916 Paris Economic Conference, British and French leaders were able to reach a firmer agreement on negative measures against Germany than on positive measures for post-war trade cooperation among Allies. Hubert Llewellyn Smith worked with the president of the Board of Trade, Walter Runciman, on British preparations for the conference. As the scion of a prominent shipping family and a leading Liberal

---

[65] Soutou, *L'or et le sang*, 189–91; É. Bussière, *La France, la Belgique et l'organisation économique de l'Europe, 1918–1935* (Comité pour l'histoire économique et financière de la France, 1992), 14–39; D. Laqua, *The Age of Internationalism and Belgium, 1880–1930: Peace, Progress and Prestige* (Manchester University Press, 2013), 145–70.

[66] Trachtenberg, 'A New Economic Order', 315, 318–20; Kuisel, *Capitalism and the State in Modern France*, 37–48; Soutou, *L'or et le sang*, 296–302; L. Badel, *Diplomatie et grands contrats: l'État français et les marchés extérieurs au XXe siècle* (Publications de la Sorbonne, 2010), 40.

[67] Coquet wrote studies on couture, lingerie, fur, umbrellas, corsets, perfume, and lace for *L'Enquête sur la production française et la concurrence étrangère* (Association Nationale d'Expansion Économique, 1917).

MP, Runciman shared Llewellyn Smith's commitment to open markets. They countered Clémentel's proposal for a general system of trade preferences with a more targeted proposal for the Allies to withhold MFN status from the Central Powers during post-war reconstruction while upholding MFN rights in other treaties.[68] Although this was a much less sweeping change than Clémentel demanded, it was still a significant break with precedent. It differed markedly from the trade provisions of the 1871 Treaty of Frankfurt which marked the end of the Franco-Prussian War, in which France and Germany had guaranteed one another MFN status.[69] In contrast, the Allies signalled their intention to force the Central Powers to adhere to norms of free trade in any future peace settlement without accepting reciprocal obligations themselves. Both the French and the British justified this deviation from the precedent of 1871 on the grounds that the reciprocal MFN provisions in the Treaty of Frankfurt had disproportionately benefitted Germany as the stronger exporter. In addition to this historical rationale, the British plan to strip Germany and Austria–Hungary of MFN rights was also motivated by the view that 'the Allied Countries had allowed themselves to drift into a state of dangerous dependence upon potential enemies' before 1914. Withholding MFN status from the Central Powers after the war would give Allied governments more space to shelter 'essential industries' from German competitors. During the early years of the war, British military production was hampered by critical shortages of materials that had previously been supplied by Germany, including synthetic medicines, optical glass, smelted zinc, engine alternators, and chemical dyes. Llewellyn Smith grappled first-hand with these shortages in the Ministry of Munitions.[70]

Llewellyn Smith identified chemical dyes as 'far the most characteristic case' of an 'essential industry' warranting future protection. He estimated that before the war Britain imported 90 per cent the chemical dye it used and that 90 per cent of those imports came from Germany.[71] After 1914, this heavy dependence undermined Britain's military production and its balance of payments. To support its pre-war dye industry, Germany had set up extensive facilities to harvest toluene, a by-product of tar distillation that could be used to make dyes and, crucially, to make TNT. When

---

[68] Trachtenberg, 'A New Economic Order', 322; Soutou, *L'or et le sang*, 249.
[69] B. Dedinger, 'The Franco-German Trade Puzzle: An Analysis of the Economic Consequences of the Franco-Prussian War', *The Economic History Review*, 65/3 (2012), 1029–54, 1043–4.
[70] Soutou, *L'or et le sang*, 84, 167, 189. Memorandum on the Paris Economic Conference, 30 June 1916, Bodleian Library: Asquith Papers/ MS 30.
[71] Minutes of Evidence taken before the Committee on Commercial and Industrial Policy, Evidence of Hubert Llewellyn Smith, 14 September 1916, TNA: BT 55/10.

the war broke out, Germany rapidly converted its tar distillation facilities to manufacture explosives. Meanwhile, Britain's TNT production was hamstrung by shortages of toluene, and its textile exports – an important source of foreign currency – lacked dye. The British government responded by creating extensive new tar distillation works during the war as part of a domestic synthetic dye industry, using expropriated German industrial assets.[72] In order to preserve this strategic capacity in peacetime, Britain passed the Dyestuffs Import Regulation Act in 1920 as a prelude to the more general Safeguarding of Industries Act the following year.[73] This legislation sheltered Britain's dye market with a prohibition on imports and 'safeguarded' domestic production of several thousand other items that were deemed to have strategic value with a 33.3 per cent tariff.[74]

Britain's tariffs to shelter strategic industries affected only a small share of the national economy, but these limited moves towards protection nevertheless loomed large in international trade debates because they entailed novel forms of discrimination. Many measures were specifically directed against Germany, and empire trade benefitted from a special reduction on UK tariffs starting 1919, thus introducing a limited measure of imperial preference.[75] These advantages and disadvantages were more form than substance, but they nevertheless undermined British claims to embody universal ideals of international free trade.[76] In all belligerent states, the war forged new links between trade and production as factors

[72] War Cabinet, Scheme for the Development of the British Dye Industry, 8 January 1918, TNA: CAB 24/4/38; Position of the Dye-Making Industry, Memorandum by the President of the Board of Trade, 29 November 1920, TNA: CAB 24/115/92; *History of the Ministry of Munitions*, vol. VII, part 1, pp. 5, 58, part 4, pp. 11–12, 33–4; Jones, *Multinationals and Global Capitalism*, 204; P. Högselius, A. Kaijser, and E. van der Vleuten, *Europe's Infrastructure Transition: Economy, War, Nature* (Palgrave Macmillan, 2015), 147.

[73] Position of the Dye-Making Industry, Memorandum by the President of the Board of Trade, 29 November 1920, TNA: CAB 24/115/92; Safeguarding of Industries Bill, Memorandum by the President of the Board of Trade, 29 December 1920, TNA: CAB 24/117/74.

[74] Safeguarding of Industries Bill, Memorandum by the President of the Board of Trade, 29 December 1920, TNA: CAB 24/117/74; F. W. Hirst, *Safeguarding and Protection in Great Britain and the United States* (Macmillan, 1927), 16–17; Llewellyn Smith, *The Board of Trade*, 185–8; B. D. Varian, 'The Growth of Manufacturing Protection in 1920s Britain', *Scottish Journal of Political Economy*, 66/5 (2019), 703–11.

[75] I. M. Drummond, *British Economic Policy and the Empire, 1919–1939* (Allen and Unwin, 1972), 51–70; C. Kindleberger, 'Commercial Policy between the Wars', in S. Pollard and P. Mathias (eds.), *The Industrial Economies: The Development of Economic and Social Policies* (Cambridge, 1989), 161–2.

[76] J. Lacour-Gayet, *La réforme douanière* (Comité d'action économique et douanière, 1926), 14–15; D. Serruys, *Commercial Treaties: Tariff Systems and Contractual Methods* C.E.I. 31 (League of Nations: 1927); B. Harms, 'Strukturwandlungen der Weltwirtschaft', *Weltwirtschaftliches Archiv*, 25 (1927), 1–58, 32.

of national security, which made it nearly impossible to attain universal international economic norms in the 1920s. Multilateral trade negotiations in Geneva became a contest to determine which state could impose the combination of general rules and specific exemptions that best suited its security needs. Llewellyn Smith created space in Geneva for a dynamic tension between universal and particular policy goals by clinging tenaciously to ideals of global free trade even he worked to enhance his own country's strategic autonomy. During the war, Llewellyn Smith and Runciman defended general legal commitments to neutrals in debates about the blockade and about future treaty policy. Notably, they sought to preserve Britain's wide web of MFN treaties in Latin America, East Asia, and Europe, which they saw as a crucial safeguard for open markets. Llewellyn Smith was particularly concerned about the danger of US expansion in Latin America, where Britain had held a preponderant commercial position until 1914.

The Challenge from the United States

As the European belligerents sank ever more of their economic resources into the war effort, the United States emerged as a large supplier of war material and finance while also increasing its trade with the rest of the world, especially with Latin America. Significantly, the Panama Canal began operations in 1914, opening a new commercial pathway between North and South America just as European trade was hit by wartime restrictions. Wilson's secretary of the treasury, William McAdoo, later recalled that 'the entire structure of commerce' in South America 'went to pieces' during the war: 'the South Americans were like the customers of a store that has burned down; they were looking for a place to spend their money'.[77] Even before the war began, Wilson had already started to lay the groundwork for a concerted programme of southward economic expansion.[78]

Shortly after assuming the presidency in 1913, Wilson passed the Federal Reserve Act, which allowed US banks to establish foreign branches that could accept bills of exchange. This enabled US banks – especially the National City Bank of New York – to cut into London's

---

[77] Quoted in B. Albert and P. Henderson, *South America and the First World War: The Impact of the War on Brazil, Argentina, Peru, and Chile* (Cambridge University Press, 1988), 61.
[78] Christopher Capozzola has demonstrated that the wartime expansion of US financial and commercial influence was accompanied by a reinforcement of hard power in the formal US Empire and beyond. See C. Capozzola, 'The United States Empire', in R. Gerwarth and E. Manela (eds.), *Empires at War, 1911–1923* (Oxford University Press, 2014), pp. 235–53.

dominant position in trade credit during the war. City Bank alone opened fifty-seven new foreign branches from 1914 to 1920.[79] McAdoo convened a Pan-American Financial Conference in 1915 to help direct these private initiatives into a system of hemispheric economic integration.[80] A strong navy was another central component of Wilson's programme to project US economic influence. In summer 1916, he announced a massive naval construction programme that put the United States on track to equal British tonnage in a few years. This was partly a response to the opening of the Panama Canal and partly a bid to prevent Europeans from trampling on neutral rights in the future.[81] Freedom of the seas was initially at the heart of Wilson's post-war vision. He identified it as the '*sine qua non* of peace, equality, and cooperation' in his first sketch for a peace plan announced in January 1917.[82]

Although Wilson's expansionist programme did originally include trade treaties, he made little practical progress on that front. In 1913, he sponsored a tariff cut that also included authorization to negotiate a new round of preferential trade agreements based on the traditional US doctrine of 'conditional' MFN. In contrast to his Republican predecessors, who had pre-emptively raised tariffs to pressure US trade partners to make concessions, Wilson pre-emptively lowered rates as a conciliatory opening gambit to induce partners to grant the United States favourable treatment. This strategy did not bear fruit in Europe, where 'fighting' tariffs had become the norm. Most European leaders did not reciprocate Wilson's 1913 tariff cuts with significant concessions. For example, France granted the United States less than one hundred of the roughly six hundred tariff reductions that it accorded to European partners with unconditional MFN rights.[83] Thus, even before the war, many of Wilson's advisers had begun to question the wisdom of the traditional US policy of trade preferences based on conditional MFN.

Wilson and his advisors concluded that trade preferences were politically dangerous in the context of 1916 Paris Economic Pact as well as rumoured plans for Mitteleuropa in Germany and Austria–Hungary. They feared that without forceful US intervention to keep global markets open, European belligerents would durably divide the post-war

[79] A. E. Eckes and T. W. Zeiler, *Globalization and the American Century* (Cambridge University Press, 2003), 47; Cassis, *Capitals of Capital*, 151.

[80] Albert and Henderson, *South America and the First World War*, 61.

[81] Tooze, *The Deluge*, 35–6.

[82] W. Wilson, 'A League for Peace', 22 January 1917, 64th United States Congress, 23rd Session, Senate Document No. 685.

[83] C. M. Barnes, Denunciation of Commercial Conventions by France, 1 June 1918, USNA: RG 256, Economic Records, box 107/folder 231.

world economy into exclusive zones of influence.[84] In January 1916, the National Foreign Trade Council, an association of export-oriented US business leaders, called upon Wilson to create a permanent body to define US trade policy on a 'scientific basis'.[85] In April 1917, just five days before the United States joined the war, he responded by appointing a new Tariff Commission with instructions to 'investigate the Paris Economy Pact and similar organizations and arrangements in Europe'.[86] From 1916 to 1918, the Tariff Commission undertook a sweeping investigation of the implications of the war for international trade law.[87]

Many German leaders looked to the United States to advocate open international trade policy after the war, even as they feared growing US economic clout. Bernhard Harms had already identified the United States as a potential champion for 'open-door' trade policies before the war and shared Wilson's deep hostility to the Paris Economic Conference. In autumn 1916, Harms presented a detailed account of the conference to a meeting of IfW members. He specifically denounced the proposal, written by Llewellyn Smith, to withhold MFN status from Germany and Austria–Hungary after the war. Harms argued that the Central Powers should not impose this type of unilateral tariff discrimination against the Allies, even if they achieved an overwhelming victory. Like most of Germany's leaders, he calculated that the country had more to gain from universal open markets than from exclusive privileges. Consequently, Harms recommended that the Central Powers use the peace settlement to impose strong, uniform trade rules that would bind allies and enemies alike, including universal MFN rights. He affirmed that Germany had 'a great interest' in the formation of a 'system of commercial policy' based on universal MFN, at least during the period of reconstruction.[88] Official German post-war planning also focused on promoting the wide application of the MFN principle. Georges-Henri Soutou interprets this as an 'offensive' policy, because German officials

---

[84] E. S. Rosenberg, *Spreading the American Dream: American Economic and Cultural Expansion, 1890–1945* (Hill and Wang, 1982), 67; D. M. Kennedy, *Over Here: The First World War and American Society* (Oxford University Press, 2004), 309–10; Soutou, *L'or et le sang*, 320–21.

[85] Soutou, *L'or et le sang*, 317.

[86] U.S. Code, Title 19, Chapter 4, Subtitle II, Part II, §1332, Cornell Law School Open Access, www.law.cornell.edu/uscode/text/19/1332.

[87] United States Tariff Commission, *Reciprocity and Commercial Treaties*.

[88] B. Harms, 'Die Zukunft der Weltwirtschaft', *Vom Wirtschaftskrieg zur Weltwirtschaftskonferenz: Weltwirtschaftliche Gestaltungstendenzen im Spiegel gesammelter Vorträge* (Gustav Fischer, 1927), pp. 1–68, 59.

calculated that expansive MFN rights would enable them to make considerable inroads into French and Italian markets.[89]

For Harms, the arena for post-war commercial competition was not Europe but the world. He predicted that the most significant outcome of the war would be a rebalancing of economic relations between Europe, as a whole, and the United States. He argued that the United States would benefit from the wartime development of manufacturing capacity outside Europe because this meant that, in the future, foreign trade would rarely involve a simple exchange of raw materials for finished goods. It would depend increasingly on complex relationships of technical cooperation and market sharing between more and less established manufacturers, supported by foreign direct investment and mediated by sophisticated regulatory institutions on both sides.[90] This new model of investment-backed trade would favour the United States, which, under McAdoo, took over a large share of Europe's pre-war investments and capital reserves and began to use these resources to make inroads in Asian and Latin American markets.

Harms foresaw that US global economic preponderance would increase as the war dragged on and European belligerents were sapped of their 'financial strength'. He predicted, presciently:

The main consequence of the war will be a significant shift in power. This would certainly occur in any case, even if the war should end with a clear victory for one side or the other. Only the victor would participate in this shift in a positive sense, while otherwise the entire transformation will solely benefit neutrals, and above all America. We must be clear about this: the longer the war lasts, the more the centre of gravity for world-economic activity will shift from Europe to America ... I do not rule out the possibility that one day future historians will judge that European states in the second decade of the twentieth century tore each other apart in a great war in blind disregard for their collective interests for the benefit of Americans.[91]

Ironically, Harms's fear that the United States was accumulating overwhelming global influence led him to embrace a policy that guaranteed this outcome:a the resumption of unrestricted submarine warfare. Harms recognized that this policy would likely damage German relations with the United States in the short term. He believed, however, that Germany's only hope was a rapid victory, and this depended on cutting off the Allies, especially Britain, from overseas commercial networks.

---

[89] Soutou, *L'or et le sang*, 594.   [90] Harms, 'Die Zukunft', 62.
[91] Harms, 'Die Zukunft', 24. See also B. Harms, 'Der Außenhandel der Vereinigten Staaten von Amerika', *Weltwirtschaftliches Archiv*, 6 (1915), 341–8; B. Harms, 'Bestrebungen der Amerikaner, ihr Wirtschaftsleben durch den Krieg zu befruchten', *Weltwirtschaftliches Archiv*, 5 (1915), 385–8.

As the war dragged on, the instrumentalization of trade relations for military ends stimulated plans for institutional innovation in peacetime. Schemes for a limited decoupling of strategic industries from enemy suppliers vied with more ambitious proposals for large preferential blocs. Both approaches entailed more concerted multilateral management of trade policy than had been practised before 1914. The war shattered the pre-war system of bilateral trade treaties and opened debate about how it should be reconstructed. At the two extremes, Étienne Clémentel called for a full break with MFN, while most German economic leaders, including Harms, demanded a firm and universal MFN pact. Britain assumed an intermediate position, proposing targeted MFN restrictions against Germany alongside a general regime of open global markets that would include the United States but would also allow space for imperial preference. This ungainly British compromise became the basis for the actual trade terms of the 1919 Peace Settlement, but that solution contained many gaps and contradictions which left openings for alternative peace projects to be revived in the League of Nations.

3 Planning the Peace

Winter 1916–17 brought a brief lull in a rapidly escalating conflict as both sides regrouped and began to plan for peace. The long British-led offensive on the Somme ended in November with only minimal territorial gains for the Allies, despite a massive outlay of men and material that stretched Allied finances. The Battle of the Somme persuaded the German High Command to pursue its own ambitious programme of armament production and to resume unrestricted submarine warfare to try to secure a decisive edge.[1] German attacks on neutral merchant ships helped push Wilson into the war in April 1918 with a mission to moralize international relations. At the same time, submarine warfare also stimulated Allied efforts to make supply lines more secure and more efficient by coordinating their economic administration in innovative ways, providing a template for new forms of economic discrimination that sat uneasily with Wilson's vision of the peace. The final years of the war saw competing projects to consolidate territorial resource blocs as a foundation for peacetime economic recovery. After these plans faltered, Wilsonian ideals were fused to a pared-down model of Allied economic control at the Paris Peace Conference. The minimalist legal framework for international trade in the final League Covenant excluded the defeated states and left open many important policy questions, notably issues related to imperial preference, French security along the Rhine, and the Austro-German relationship. In the 1920s, Coquet, Harms, Llewellyn Smith and Riedl picked up this unfinished business in their multilateral projects, drawing on the new organizational structures that developed around foreign trade policy during and after the war.

A New Architecture of Confrontation and Cooperation

In 1917, Germany's decision to resume unrestricted submarine warfare reaffirmed the Allies' determination to exclude the Central Powers from post-war international trade institutions. By that time, Harms had already

---

[1] Strachan, *The First World War: To Arms*, 932–3, 1085–8; Tooze, *The Deluge*, 53–8.

concluded that only outright victory would secure German commercial rights, and he joined many other experts to help the German Admiralty make a case for submarine warfare. One of the most influential experts was Hermann Levy, a frequent contributor to Harms's *Weltwirtschaftliches Archiv*. It was Levy who had penned the critique of Norman Angell for the journal's inaugural issue in 1913. At that time, he had contested Angell's claim that modern warfare could not bring economic advantage. During the war, Levy and Harms went a step further and argued that submarine attacks could transform Britain's market dominance into a source of weakness by targeting its central axes of commercial integration, especially its wheat supply. In autumn 1916, Harms declared that Germany must 'swipe the world-economic trump cards so ruthlessly from [Britain's] hands, that its adequate supply in food, raw materials, and manufactures is impossible'.[2] Harms and Levy both argued that this strategy required Germany to sink merchant vessels on a large scale and thus to abandon the international 'cruiser rules' that had restrained such attacks in 1915 and 1916. In January 1917, the German government adopted this policy, hoping to accelerate victory and avoid plunging weary soldiers into another protracted battle. This proved a gross miscalculation; the German U-boat campaign did not sink sufficient tonnage to critically damage the Allied war economy but did help pull the resource-rich United States into the war on the Allied side.[3] The tightening of the blockade squeezed German food supplies. From 1916 to the end of the war, average monthly grain imports to Germany declined by 63 per cent and meat imports fell by 95 per cent.[4]

The uptick in German U-boat attacks did not undermine Allied supply lines to the same extent, in part because the Allies reorganized trade and shipping on a cooperative basis, with important institutional consequences. By November 1917, they had created a series of committees to manage different commodity flows, with central coordination ensured by an Allied Maritime Transport Council (AMTC). Most of this cooperation proceeded through relatively informal advisory channels, with key operational roles assigned to private experts who had experience in shipping and commodity trading. The AMTC was able to centrally allocate raw

---

[2] Harms, 'Die Zukunft', 21.
[3] A. Offer, *The First World War: An Agrarian Interpretation* (Clarendon Press of Oxford University Press, 1989), 354–67; Take, '"Die Objektivität ist durch sein Wesen verbürgt": Bernhard Harms' Gründung des Kieler Instituts für Weltwirtschaft und sein Aufstieg im Ersten Weltkrieg', 59–62; Watson, *Ring of Steel*, 417–23; Tooze, *The Deluge*, 56–8; Hull, *A Scrap of Paper*, 263–6; Grimmer-Solem, *Learning Empire*, 530, 579.
[4] A. Ritschl, 'The Pity of Peace: Germany's Economy at War, 1914–1918 and Beyond', in S. Broadberry and M. Harrison (eds.), *The Economics of World War I* (Cambridge University Press, 2009), pp. 41–76, 58.

materials among the Allies by controlling information and transport. It kept a common balance sheet of imports for the Allies and then distributed available tonnage to meet these requirements. Clémentel hoped that a similar arrangement could be used to facilitate trade in raw materials among the Allies after the war ended.[5] In spring 1918, he told the French Senate, 'existing bodies have shown that it is easy for the Allies and neutral powers, however numerous, to apply an allocation mechanism. The proof is there. Thus, when the time comes, it will be easy to launch a comprehensive organization'.[6] In fact, Clémentel's British and US counterparts were reluctant to extend the principles of Allied resource cooperation far into peacetime and instead proposed to restore free trade in a more institutionalized form. MFN was a key point of divergence between French and Anglo-American visions of post-war economic order.

Clémentel demanded a radical break with MFN to create space for a permanent organization of commodity markets along preferential lines. There was backing across the French political and economic elite for a turn away from MFN, and Clémentel was trying to ensure that this policy would not simply bring a pivot towards protectionism. He hoped to ratchet down tariffs through negotiation and called upon the Allies to denounce all their existing MFN treaties so that they would be free to conclude preferential trade agreements among themselves. He envisaged a nesting arrangement that would differentiate between imperial, Allied, and neutral partners. This was partly a strategy to cover France's resource needs and partly a bid to contain German commercial influence.[7] Clémentel's trade proposals found favour in Britain with Edward Carson, who chaired the Economic Offensive Committee. Carson criticized the British Government's failure to follow through on the resolutions on raw materials adopted at the 1916 Paris Economic Conference and advocated a full weaponization of trade policy in peacetime. In striking language, he affirmed that 'there should be as little disagreement' about preserving the capacity to wage a 'post-bellum trade war' against Germany 'as there would be in regard to the desirability of maintaining an army and navy'. Carson endorsed Clémentel's proposal to convene a special conference to stage a mass denunciation of MFN treaties among all the Allies, to allow latitude for a system of

---

[5] J. A. Salter, *Allied Shipping Control: An Experiment in International Administration* (The Clarendon Press, 1921), 91–3; Soutou, *L'or et le sang*, 513–15; Mazower, *Governing the World*, 143; Miller, *Europe and the Maritime World*, 213–24; Martin, *The Meddlers*, 33–4.

[6] 'Sénat, séance du 7 février 1918', *Journal officiel de la République française*, 72.

[7] Soutou, *L'or et le sang*, 296–302.

anti-German trade preferences. The Foreign Office and the Board of Trade strongly objected to this course of action.[8]

Llewellyn Smith took the lead in defending MFN against Carson's coterie. In a presentation to Parliament, he enumerated the many practical difficulties that Clémentel's planned preferences would pose for Britain. He also helped to prepare a lengthy cabinet memorandum that analysed Britain's pre-war treaty policy and emphasized the importance of trade with neutral partners. He suggested that if Britain denounced its MFN treaties with neutral states, it would open Latin America and Scandinavia to US and German schemes for restrictive regional solidarity. More generally, an upsurge in regionalism around the world could threaten the integrity of the British Empire by exerting a centrifugal pull in far-flung colonies. According to this logic, a global economy fragmented into small and open markets was a political precondition for a cohesive British Empire.[9] Llewellyn Smith saw MFN as the main legal mechanism to preserve that state of diffuse openness. He therefore fought vigorously to uphold the system of MFN treaties inherited from the nineteenth century but temporarily reduced German and Austro-Hungarian room for manoeuvre within it. The successive presidents of the Board of Trade during the war, Walter Runciman and Albert Stanley, shared Llewellyn Smith's commitment to preserve free trade, while allowing a limited departure to guard against Germany, and they gave him full rein to pursue that strategy.[10]

Llewellyn Smith and his fellow free traders in London wanted to encourage Wilson's moves to open US trade policy, hoping to push him away from regional schemes that threatened British interests (memories of the 1911 plan for a preferential trade agreement between the United States and Canada were still fresh). British leaders were also keen to allay Wilson's fears that Allied plans to restrain German commercial sovereignty would dent peace prospects. Shortly before the United States joined the war, Wilson announced that one of the four fundamental 'bases of peace' should be a 'mutual agreement not to take part in any joint economic action by two or more nations which would in effect constitute an effort to throttle the industrial life of any nation or shut it off from fair and equal opportunities of trade with the nations thus in

---

[8] E. Carson, Memorandum on Economic Offensive, September 1917, G 156, TNA: CAB 24/4/6.

[9] Darwin, *After Tamerlane*, 337–8.

[10] Post-bellum Tariff Policy and British Commercial Treaties (undated) Bodleian Library: Asquith Papers/MS 29; Minutes of Evidence taken before the committee on Commercial and Industrial Policy, 14 September 1916, TNA: BT 55/10; Commercial Treaties of the United Kingdom (1917), TNA: BT 274/24; Soutou, *L'or et le sang*, 523.

concert or with the rest of the world'.[11] This was a criticism of the Paris Economic Pact, but it was not intended to limit US regional or colonial influence. Indeed, Wilson was not above using the war to give his own exporters an advantage over German competitors. Even before the United States declared war, the government had begun to confiscate German ships, patents, and other industrial assets and to pursue German export markets in Latin America.[12] Nevertheless, Wilson saw US power as a force for international peace, in contrast to divisive European imperialism.[13]

Indeed, many of Wilson's advisors insisted that the United States must adopt a more assertive trade policy, with the economist Frank Taussig emerging as a particularly strong advocate for greater international engagement. Wilson appointed Taussig as chair of the US Tariff Commission in 1917 with a mission to define a new trade policy adapted to the United States' changing role in the world. The Tariff Commission conducted a thorough survey of US treaty practice since the country's founding and delivered this report to the president on the eve of the Paris Peace Conference.[14] It argued that the United States should participate fully in the international treaty system after the war and must therefore abandon its traditional commitment to preferential trade relations, based on conditional MFN. For, conditional MFN was not a tool of global leadership but rather a means to carve out niche advantages through 'frequent and repeated special negotiations, constant bargaining'.[15] The Tariff Commission linked this piecemeal approach to a broader policy of international disengagement and counselled against both:

An opportunist attitude was natural so long as the United States kept aloof from foreign complications and was intent upon avoiding them. Now, however, the situation is completely altered. The United States has become committed to far-reaching participation in world politics. The American Government can no longer shape its commercial negotiations solely with reference to the results of each particular arrangement. It must consider the world at large and must shape

---

[11] W. Wilson to R. Lansing, 9 February 1917, *The Papers of Woodrow Wilson Digital Edition* (University of Virginia Press, 2017), http://rotunda.upress.virginia.edu/founders/WILS-01-41-02-0179.

[12] Kennedy, *Over Here*, 311–16; R. W. Tucker, *Woodrow Wilson and the Great War: Reconsidering America's Neutrality, 1914–1917* (University of Virginia Press, 2007); K. Steen, *The American Synthetic Organic Chemicals Industry: War and Politics, 1910–1930* (The University of North Carolina Press, 2014), 78–171.

[13] Tooze, *The Deluge*, 53–4.

[14] United States Tariff Commission, *Reciprocity and Commercial Treaties*. Douglas Irwin argues that this report 'proved to be one of the most influential government documents on trade since Alexander Hamilton's *Report on Manufactures*'. See Irwin, *Clashing over Commerce*, 362.

[15] United States Tariff Commission, *Reciprocity and Commercial Treaties*, 42.

its commercial policy in conformity with the political and humanitarian principles which govern its general attitude in the international sphere.[16]

Although the Tariff Commission was highly critical of conditional MFN, it did not recommend that Wilson formally abandon that policy as part of the peace settlement. Taussig predicted that doing so would provoke the ire of protectionists in the US Congress and told Wilson that 'substantially the same result could be achieved by adopting and pressing a general policy of commercial treaties based in fact on the most-favoured-nation basis'.[17] Thus, Taussig and his commission concluded that US trade policy should be guided by a vaguer norm of 'equality of treatment'.[18] That language came from the third of Wilson's famed Fourteen Points, which called for 'the removal as far as possible, of all economic barriers and the establishment of an equality of trade conditions among all nations consenting to the peace'.[19] Announced in January 1918, Wilson's Fourteen Points sketched a vision of post-war order based on ideals of open diplomacy, free trade, and disarmament, which would all be institutionalized through a 'general association of nations', looking forward to the future League of Nations.[20]

Failed Attempts to Establish Post-war Resource Blocs to the East and West

The Fourteen Points were a response to peace negotiations between Soviet Russia and the Central Powers at Brest-Litovsk in winter 1917–18. Over the course of 1917, the Russian Revolution intersected with Wilson's drive to transform the war into a principled crusade, reframing the peace process around a new set of normative commitments. In spring 1917, the revolutionary Russian government announced a new agenda, the 'Petrograd Formula', which included a right to national self-determination for subject peoples, as a means to undermine the remaining empires of Central and Eastern Europe. This strategy ultimately succeeded, but only through a messy series of unintended

[16] United States Tariff Commission, *Reciprocity and Commercial Treaties*, 10.
[17] Frank Taussig, F.W.T. on Memorandum by A.A.Y. entitled 'Possible International Action with Respect to Tariffs', undated, USNA: RG 256, Economic Records, box 111/folder 316.
[18] United States Tariff Commission, *Reciprocity and Commercial Treaties*, 10.
[19] *President Woodrow Wilson's Fourteen Points* (Avalon Project at Yale Law School Lillian Goldman Library), https://avalon.law.yale.edu/20th_century/wilson14.asp. Wilson drafted Point III himself, with support from his advisor Edward M. House. See 'From the Diary of Colonel House', 9 January 1918, *The Papers of Woodrow Wilson Digital Edition*, http://rotunda.upress.virginia.edu/founders/WILS-01-45-02-0528.
[20] *President Woodrow Wilson's Fourteen Points*.

consequences. Russia's revolutionary government tried to push the Allies to adopt the Petrograd Formula through a disastrous last-ditch summer offensive. The Russians failed in their immediate military objectives but did manage to foster leftist support in Allied countries for a moralized peace programme. It was, however, not the Allies but the Central Powers who first responded to the call for self-determination in their peace talks with the newly triumphant Bolsheviks at Brest-Litovsk. Yet it quickly became evident that self-determination would provide political cover for a protectorate regime that would give Germany and Austria–Hungary broad economic and diplomatic control over Ukraine and the Baltic states without forcing them to absorb new minority populations.[21]

The path to German supremacy in Central and Eastern Europe was clearly outlined in the trade terms of the Treaty of Brest-Litovsk signed in March 1918 and the Treaty of Bucharest with Romania that followed shortly thereafter. Both agreements included reciprocal MFN rights, but those commitments did not cover most of Central and Eastern Europe. Russia and Romania agreed not to claim any advantages that Germany and Austria–Hungary might grant one another or their neighbours through customs unions.[22] This signalled the German intention to use MFN keep markets open in Western Europe and the wider world while forming a secure hinterland to the east through customs unions. French leaders perceived both components of this programme to be aggressive. The Ministry of Commerce emphasized that a regime of global free trade enforced through MFN would disproportionately benefit Germany: 'after having destroyed the economic equipment of invaded countries through systematic destruction, [Germany] demands the free play of unequal competition from its disarmed rivals'. This point was under-scored with a quote from Harms about Germany's determination to 'reconquer the position that it occupied in world commerce'. While the French feared Germany's global ambitions, they also saw the regional preferential arrangements in the eastern peace treaties as a dangerous plot to consolidate a powerful 'Mitteleuropa' with commercial 'tentacles' that would extend from Scandinavia to the Middle East. Both Britain and

---

[21] W. Baumgart, *Deutsche Ostpolitik, 1918: Von Brest-Litowsk bis zum Ende des Ersten Weltkrieges* (Oldenbourg, 1966), 1–28; Tooze, *The Deluge*, 109–20; Watson, *Ring of Steel*, 492–8; Payk, *Frieden durch Recht?*, 99–101; L. Wolff, *Woodrow Wilson and the Reimagining of Eastern Europe* (Stanford University Press, 2020), 80–82.

[22] *Peace Treaty of Brest-Litovsk* (Avalon Project at Yale Law School Lillian Goldman Library), https://avalon.law.yale.edu/20th_century/bl34.asp; *The Treaty of Peace between Roumania and the Central Powers, Signed at Bucharest 7 May 1918* (US Government Printing Office, 1918).

France later cited the treaties of Brest-Litovsk and Bucharest to justify their own demands to withhold MFN from the defeated states in 1919.[23] The Central Powers' bid to form a regional resource base through the eastern peace treaties did not yield the hoped-for supplies but did strengthen Clémentel's resolve to organize commodity markets on the Allied side. Clémentel concluded that the Allies must counterbalance the Central Powers' gains on the 'territorial map' with their own advantages on the 'economic map'. At the same time, he presented the control of raw materials as a 'powerful tool of negotiation' that could be used to enforce Wilsonian ideals. He argued that US entry into the war on the side of the Allies, followed by a string of other resource-rich countries in South America, made it possible to envisage comprehensive control of many raw materials.[24] Yet the United States did not formally join the Allied economic agencies until October 1918, and many members of Wilson's entourage were reluctant to submit US resources to foreign control, especially Herbert Hoover, the US 'food czar'. For his part, Wilson was more open to helping the Allies access the raw materials that they needed for reconstruction and to countenance temporary economic pressure on the defeated states after the war to ensure their compliance with the peace terms. Thus, against Hoover's advice, Wilson agreed to continue the blockade during the armistice period and to keep Allied economic agencies in place to handle immediate post-war relief under the aegis of a new Supreme Economic Council (SEC). Maintaining the blockade was important for the Allies because it offered a potential framework to regulate German access to commodity markets on a more durable basis.[25] Yet in peacetime, Wilson was only willing to allow raw materials to be used as a political bludgeon in the League's formal sanctions regime and not as part of standard trade policy, as Clémentel hoped.[26]

The conflict between US and Allied positions on raw materials came to a head at a fateful meeting of the SEC in April 1919.[27] The Allies were concerned about both surpluses and shortages coming out of the war. They formed a united front on the problem of

---

[23] Ministère du Commerce et de l'Industrie, *Tableau des conditions économiques de la Paix Allemande*, September 1918, AN: F12/7985; Jackson, *Beyond the Balance of Power*, 171–3; Soutou, *L'or et le sang*, 637–58, 677–84, 746–7.

[24] 'Sénat, séance du 7 février 1918', 71–2; Soutou, *L'or et le sang*, 487.

[25] M. Trachtenberg, *Reparation in World Politics: France and European Economic Diplomacy, 1916–1923* (Columbia University Press, 1980), 327–8; Soutou, *L'or et le sang*, 515–19, 828, 834; Offer, *The First World War: An Agrarian Interpretation*, 376–85; P. A. Dehne, *After the Great War: Economic Warfare and the Promise of Peace in Paris 1919* (Bloomsbury Academic, 2019), 77–107.

[26] Mulder, *The Economic Weapon*, 84–127.   [27] Soutou, *L'or et le sang*, 835.

surplus. Producers in Britain, France, and Italy all ended the war with stockpiles of material that had been purchased from the United States at high prices during the war. During reconstruction, they wanted to force Germany to purchase from these Allied stockpiles at the same prices paid by their own producers. Robert Cecil, the British chair of the SEC, avowed to being a staunch 'free-trader' but nevertheless argued that 'it was necessary to let down gradually from the high prices of the war'. As Britain's former minister of blockade, he suggested that some of the wartime trade restrictions could be left in place temporarily to support the equalization of input prices between the defeated and the victorious states. The US representative on the SEC, Bernard Baruch, refused to play along, declaring sanctimoniously, 'I don't mind seeing this beast being cut up, but I won't take any part in the cutting'. Concretely this meant that US producers would be free to sell Germany raw materials at the 'lowest market price'. Cecil pointed out that this was far from a disinterested policy. Under normal market conditions, Germans would not buy from the Allies' expensive stockpiles – they would purchase inputs directly from the United States at lower prices. This would boost the already buoyant US economy and also place German producers in a position to undersell their Allied competitors on post-war export markets. Baruch refused to budge, however.[28]

Cecil demanded temporary Allied coordination to manage problems of post-war surplus, but he shared Baruch's scepticism of French plans to handle problems of shortage by preserving the Allies' wartime mechanisms to allocate raw materials and shipping space. British and US leaders agreed to targeted measures to help France make up for critical shortages during reconstruction, for example in cotton and coal, but they were unwilling to apply a 'principle of priority to Allied needs' across the board. Cecil's caution stemmed in part from the Dominions' resistance to outside control over their natural resources in an imperial or an Allied framework.[29] Cecil also argued that there would be relatively few instances of post-war resource scarcity, and these could be handled on a case-by-case basis. Clémentel pointed out that even where no verifiable shortage existed, prices might be bid up if producers anticipated that demand would rise.[30]

---

[28] Supreme Economic Council, Raw Material Section, Stenographic Record of Meeting of 4 April 1919, 180.05301/5, USNA: RG 256, Microfilm 184/134. On Cecil's role in the SEC and the 1919 peace negotiations, see Dehne, *After the Great War*.

[29] Soutou, *L'or et le sang*, 816; Dehne, *After the Great War*, 43–50.

[30] Supreme Economic Council, Raw Material Section, Stenographic Record of Meeting of 4 April 1919, 180.05301/5, USNA: RG 256, Microfilm 184/134.

Quite apart from the macroeconomic mechanics of post-war transition, for Clémentel there were more fundamental issues at stake concerning the new role that foreign trade was required to play in international relations after the war. In strikingly clear language, Clémentel argued that commercial warfare against Germany must continue for political reasons. In the SEC, he announced that 'America was committing the gravest error in history in considering that the war was over at the date of the Armistice, and in being so intent on restoring liberty of trade'. He took the contrary view that 'the economic war was just beginning, to last for twenty-five years'. The trade war 'would not cease until the restoration of economic equilibrium'. After the April meeting of the SEC dashed Clémentel's hopes for Allied cooperation in raw materials, he shifted his attention away from the peace negotiations towards a parallel set of private talks among business leaders to create a new International Chamber of Commerce (ICC). In 1920, Clémentel became the first president of the ICC. He briefly tried to use this organization to promote private cooperation in raw materials but ran up against British and US opposition in that forum as well.[31] In the 1920s, Clémentel's protégés in the French Ministry of Commerce remained committed to multilateral trade policy as a tool of French security, working through the League of Nations and private European trade associations such as Lucien Coquet's UDE.

In sum, the experience of economic warfare produced two distinct models of multilateral economic pressure. Targeted and time-limited economic sanctions could be used to punish or threaten wayward states, and Nicholas Mulder has traced how that approach developed through the League's regime of political arbitration.[32] Alongside international sanctions, the tools of mainstream trade policy could also concentrate strategic supply lines in friendly territory and withhold resources from potential enemies on a broader and more durable basis, through prohibitions and preferences. Clémentel provided the fullest articulation of that approach during the war and the peace talks. In 1919, British and US leaders aligned against Clémentel to defend 'equitable treatment' as the normative foundation for international trade policy, barring a generalized system of preferences. At the same time, they did make exceptions for

---

[31] Boyce, *British Capitalism at the Crossroads*, 27–8; C. Druelle, 'Un laboratoire réformateur, le département du commerce en France et aux États-Unis de la Grande Guerre aux Années Vingt', PhD thesis, Institut d'Études Politiques (2004), 282; C. Druelle-Korn, 'Étienne Clémentel président-fondateur de la Chambre de commerce internationale', in M. C. Kessler and G. Rousseau (eds.), *Étienne Clémentel (1864–1936) Politique et action publique sous la Troisième République* (Peter Lang, 2018), pp. 419–34.

[32] Mulder, *The Economic Weapon*.

their own regional and imperial preferences. In the 1920s, increasingly strident demands for regional and imperial solidarity and for national security widened the legal space for trade preferences. At the end of the 1920s, the League outlined a special allowance for preferential relations within multilateral trade blocs without abandoning its baseline commitment to 'equitable treatment'. It thus framed out a powerful but inherently unstable regime of multi-layered trade regulation in which preferential free trade areas could be used to exert pressure directly by excluding specific states and indirectly by influencing universal trade norms. This process was distinct from the development of formal sanctions and operated through different institutional channels, in the League's Economic Committee rather than its regime of political arbitration.

Trade and Reparations

The failure of Clémentel's plans for inter-Allied preferences had important consequences not only for trade policy, but also for reparations. At the Paris Peace Conference, the French negotiators hardened their demands for reparations from Germany after Clémentel's proposals for Allied resource cooperation failed, as Marc Trachtenberg has demonstrated. From the outset, the French delegates insisted that they could only ease reparation demands on Germany if the Allies were willing to cooperate among themselves to facilitate economic reconstruction and security. Since Britain and the United States offered neither credit nor trade commitments, direct reparations were the only available tool left to safeguard the French economy vis-à-vis Germany. Demanding a high sum could force Britain and the United States to contribute directly to French reconstruction through cooperation on raw materials.[33] French leaders were also under pressure to push for high reparations due to dissatisfaction in the government with the treaty provisions concerning hard security, since France's military leaders did not trust British and US promises to guarantee French territory against renewed German aggression.[34]

The trade and financial terms of the Paris Peace Settlement remained closely linked in practice, although formally separated in the treaties. In the 1920s, an interconnected network of war debts and reparations left the European belligerents desperate to earn dollars through exports, but

---

[33] Trachtenberg, *Reparation in World Politics*, 31–40; Orde, *British Policy and European Reconstruction*, 34.
[34] A. Sharp, *The Versailles Settlement: Peacemaking in Paris, 1919* (Palgrave Macmillan, 1991), 100, 113.

the US market remained heavily protected as a series of Republican presidents reversed Wilson's drive to lower tariffs.[35] In the 1920s, the reintroduction of the gold standard exacerbated transatlantic financial imbalances resulting from the war. Many European governments were only able to stabilize their currencies on a fixed gold peg with the support of large loans from Wall Street, and these loans would have to be repaid from trade revenue.[36] Although new US loans to Europe delayed financial reckoning until the end of the 1920s, Germany would ultimately only be able to fund the cycle of war debts and reparations by vastly increasing its exports, undercutting the Allies' foreign trade. In 1919, John Maynard Keynes had advocated a sweeping programme of debt forgiveness and financial cooperation in part to avoid this outcome. He proposed elaborate international financial engineering but was much more modest in his trade objectives (he called for a simple 'Free Trade Union').[37] In contrast to Clémentel, who hoped to revise the economic 'equilibrium' between France and Germany, Keynes was quite content to leave German commercial might intact. Indeed, he believed that the Continent would not function without a strong German centre, and many British officials agreed.[38]

In internal British debates, Llewellyn Smith sided with Keynes to demand low reparations and to urge moderation in the trade terms of the peace settlement.[39] A 1916 memorandum from the Board of Trade – which included a study of reparations from Keynes – argued that any restrictions on German commercial sovereignty should be purely in the interest of 'economic defence'. For, 'the permanent crushing of the commercial and industrial power of Germany, even were it practicable, would not be to the eventual advantage of this country, while the attempt to effect it (though doomed to failure) would alienate the good opinion and outrage the moral sense of the civilized world'. The Board of Trade did nevertheless push for some constraints on the German economy, insisting that the peace treaties should grant 'none of the usual provisions of a commercial treaty', and should notably withhold MFN rights. Llewellyn Smith maintained this

---

[35] US Democrats were critical of the Republican's protectionism on these grounds, as were the US businessmen involved in the negotiation of reparations and war debts, such as Owen Young. See Cohrs, *The Unfinished Peace*, 83.

[36] P. Clavin, *The Great Depression in Europe* (St. Martin's Press, 2000), 7–39.

[37] J. M. Keynes, *The Economic Consequences of the Peace* (Macmillan and Co., 1919), 248–50.

[38] Keynes, *The Economic Consequences of the Peace*, 13–14, 275–6; R. Skidelsky, *John Maynard Keynes: Hopes Betrayed, 1883–1920* (Macmillan, 1983), 391; A. M. Carabelli and M. A. Cedrini, 'Keynes and the Complexity of International Economic Relations in the Aftermath of World War I', *Journal of Economic Issues*, 44/4 (2010), 1009–28, 1013–14.

[39] Skidelsky, *Hopes Betrayed*, 356.

ambivalent attitude towards Germany in the peace negotiations and the early 1920s. He worked to reintegrate Germany into the world economy but supported the decision to impose MFN obligations unilaterally on the defeated states (a policy that Keynes criticized).[40] The unilateral trade provisions in the Peace treaties rankled in Germany because they were set against the universalist backdrop of the League of Nations.

Article 23(e) of the League Covenant included a commitment 'to secure and maintain equitable treatment for the commerce of all Members'.[41] At the same time, the individual peace treaties imposed a unilateral obligation to grant the victors MFN rights for a period of five years.[42] This was an inversion of the 1916 Paris Economic Pact. In 1916, the Allies had agreed to withhold MFN treatment *from* the Central Powers. In contrast, the 1919 peace treaties imposed an obligation *on* them to accord the Allies MFN status. The Allies could voluntarily choose to reciprocate this obligation (as the United States eventually did in 1923), and this made it possible to construe the peace treaties as consistent with Wilson's Fourteen Points. In his path-breaking study of interwar trade politics published thirty years later, Albert Hirschman described the Paris Economic Pact and the Fourteen Points as 'twin conflicting fountainheads' of international economic order. He observed that 'the silence concerning the commercial policy of the Allies' in 1919 eliminated the 'open contradiction' between them.[43]

The MFN norm was formulated more precisely in the peace treaties than it had been in the Paris Economic Pact. The pact had contained one sentence which bound the Allies not to grant the Central Powers MFN status; the 1919 peace treaties included four lengthy articles that obligated the defeated states not to engage in specific forms of discrimination. The peace treaties stipulated that the regulatory and tariff burdens on trade from the Allied and Associated States could not be more onerous than the burden imposed on trade from any other country. Furthermore, any legal advantage granted to one Allied or Associated State would have to be extended automatically to all the others. These clauses were standard across all the peace treaties and formed the legal foundation for a range of other trade provisions covering shipping, indications of origin, and the legal treatment of foreign firms. They also provided the starting point for the League's own standardization of the MFN norm at the end of the 1920s.

---

[40] Economic Desiderata in the Terms of Peace, February 1917, TNA: CAB 29/1.

[41] *The Covenant of the League of Nations* (Avalon Project at Yale Law School Lillian Goldman Library), http://avalon.law.yale.edu/20th_century/leagcov.asp.

[42] Articles 264–7, *The Treaty of Peace between the Allied and Associated Powers and Germany* (H. M. G. Stationery Office, 1920).

[43] Hirschman, *National Power and the Structure of Foreign Trade*, 65–6.

Qualified Commercial Sovereignty in the League of Nations

Although the defeated states faced the most stringent constraints on their commercial sovereignty, the peacemakers applied a range of other restrictions across the League system. The most ambitious proposal tabled was to extend the commercial obligations that were imposed on the defeated powers to the victors, through a supplementary Convention on Equality of Trade Conditions.[44] Llewellyn Smith helped write the British version of this agreement, which included a general commitment to unconditional MFN as well as rules concerning transit rights, intellectual property, and other regulations.[45] This would not have established full reciprocity in the trade terms of the peace, because the defeated states still would have been excluded from the benefits of this MFN pact. The asymmetry between victors and vanquished would have been lessened, however, because Allied economic sovereignty also would have been subjected to detailed international prescriptions. Moreover, binding the Allies together in a multilateral trade system would have made it easier to restore the defeated states' MFN rights through a single legal act instead of through a series of tortuous bilateral negotiations over several years, as actually occurred once the defeated states regained their commercial sovereignty in 1925. The primary motivation behind Britain's Draft Convention on Equality of Trade Conditions was not to achieve a more even-handed peace, but rather to pre-empt Wilson.[46] Dominion leaders voiced concern that Wilson would try to establish an international trade regime that interfered with British imperial preference.[47] The US draft agreement on 'equality of trade conditions' did indeed subject British imperial preference to international oversight, without prohibiting it entirely.[48] This proposal was fundamentally incompatible with the

---

[44] In January 1919, Wilson instructed British and US legal advisers David Hunter Miller and Robert Cecil to write a draft of the League Covenant to form the basis for negotiations. Wilson himself led the negotiations and ensured that the US–British draft underwent minimal modifications. See M. MacMillan, *Paris 1919: Six Months That Changed the World* (Random House, 2002), 90–94.

[45] 'Equality of Trade Conditions: American Draft, British Draft and Notes', in D. H. Miller, *The Drafting of the Covenant*, 2 vols (G. P. Putnam's Sons, 1928), vol. II, 18–21.

[46] Draft Convention for 'Equality of Trade Conditions', Explanatory Note, 20 January 1919, TNA: FO 608/72.

[47] H. Llewellyn Smith to B. Baruch, 6 February 1919, 181.17/13, USNA: RG 256, Microfilm 820/154; Economic Commission, Section on Permanent Commercial Relations, Sub-Commission on Customs Regulations, Duties, and Restrictions, 12 March 1919, 181.171101/1, USNA: RG 256, ACNP Microfilm 820/155.

[48] 'Equality of Trade Conditions: American Draft, British Draft and Notes', in Miller, *The Drafting of the Covenant*, 17.

Board of Trade's legal stance, according to which imperial preference was a matter of internal and not 'foreign' trade and so fell outside the purview of international treaties.

The First World War rekindled debate about imperial preference in Britain by demonstrating the strategic importance of the Empire's economic and political cohesion. This led to the creation of an Imperial War Cabinet in 1917 that included leaders from India and the Dominions.[49] But the policy of imperial preference remained divisive because it could not be implemented effectively in Britain without first introducing protective duties on food imports, which made up most imperial trade. As prime minister, David Lloyd George categorically refused to introduce such 'food taxes', although he endorsed the general principle of imperial preference in 1917. He was responding to public outcry in Britain over rising wartime consumer prices.[50] By 1917, British food prices were more than 200 per cent higher than pre-war levels, leading to bread riots.[51] Lloyd George saw the Russian Revolution as evidence of the political dangers posed by expensive food.[52] Dominion leaders accepted that the war was not a propitious moment for Britain to raise preferential tariffs on agricultural staples to benefit empire trade, but they wanted to ensure that the peace settlement would not foreclose this policy option. Within the Imperial War Cabinet, Dominion leaders singled out Wilson's commitment to 'equality of trade conditions' as the main obstacle to future imperial preference.[53] In 1919, the British government took only hesitant steps in the direction of imperial preference by introducing special reductions for empire trade in existing tariffs without adding new protection for the staple goods that mattered the most to the Dominions. Britain created space in international trade law for a more comprehensive regime of imperial reference but did not use that space until the Ottawa Imperial Conference of 1932.[54]

Although the British moves towards imperial preference during and after the war were largely limited to legal signals, they aroused concern in the United States. The issue of imperial preference divided Wilson's

---

[49] Tooze, *The Deluge*, 180–81.

[50] Minutes of a Meeting of the Imperial War Cabinet, 24 April 1917, TNA: CAB 23/40/11.

[51] Trentmann, *Free Trade Nation*, 194–6.

[52] Minutes of a Meeting of the Imperial War Cabinet, 24 April 1917, TNA: CAB 23/40/11.

[53] Committee of the Prime Ministers of the Dominions: Imperial War Cabinet Meeting, 21 June 1918, TNA: CAB 23/44A/14.

[54] Drummond, *British Economic Policy and the Empire*, 51–70; McKenzie, *Redefining the Bonds of Commonwealth*, 20; Trentmann, *Free Trade Nation*, 331–2.

advisors. They focused their analysis of trade policy on 'economic penetration' by 'great powers' in less developed regions of Asia, Africa, and the Americas, both colonial and non-colonial. British imperial preference was seen as a geopolitical threat because it gave legal sanction to wider 'zones of influence' which would be based on privileged relations with one 'great power'.[55] The economist Allyn Young initially wanted the United States to sponsor a universal MFN pact that would prohibit preferences in the British Dominions altogether and impose an 'open door' in all colonies without tariff autonomy.[56] Others considered this formula untenable, including Frank Taussig.[57] Taussig argued that the US government could not abandon its own preferential colonial arrangement with the Philippines nor could it 'overtly' embrace the European conception of MFN.[58] Anglo-American conflict over imperial preference was the main reason why the two powers did not adopt a more comprehensive multilateral approach to trade at the Paris Peace Conference, according to David Hunter Miller, the US legal adviser who was responsible for co-writing the original draft of the League Covenant, together with Robert Cecil.[59] They agreed to include a general placeholder clause on 'equitable treatment of commerce' in Article 23(e) in lieu of a detailed trade pact, establishing a legal basis to revisit the work that was left undone at the peace conference.

After the negotiations for a general agreement on equality of trade conditions stalled, Llewellyn Smith pushed to impose its provisions selectively on the 'new states' of Central and Eastern Europe. He originally tried to demand that the new states grant full MFN rights to the Allies, using the same language as the Treaty of Versailles, but this was

---

[55] G. Lawrence, *The Inquiry; American Preparations for Peace, 1917–1919* (Yale University Press, 1963), 294–5; As Adam Tooze observes, US opposition to European 'economic penetration' was not a principled rejection of imperial hierarchy but rather a bid to curb geopolitical rivalries that were deemed inimical to US global power. See Tooze, *The Deluge*, 15–16.

[56] A. A. Young, Possible International Action with Respect to Tariffs, 6 January 2018, USNA: RG 256, Economic Division, box 112/ folder 321.

[57] Letter to R. Lansing (unsigned), 3 March 1919, 181.17/22, USNA: RG 256, Microfilm 184/154.

[58] F. Taussig, Comment by F.W.T. on Memorandum by A.A.Y., undated, USNA: RG 256, box 111/ folder 316; A. Young, Memorandum on the Program of the Economic Drafting Committee, 6 February 1919, 181.17/6, USNA: RG 256, Microfilm 820/154.

[59] D. H. Miller to E. M. House, 1 December 1918, FRUS, *The Paris Peace Conference, 1919*, vol. I, ed. J. V. Fuller (1942), doc. 387; S. Mezes to D. H. Miller, Dr Young's Memorandum 'Possible International Action with Respect to Tariffs', 19 January 1918, USNA: RG 256, Economic Division, box 112/ folder 321; 'Equality of Trade Conditions: American Draft, British Draft and Notes', in Miller, *The Drafting of the Covenant*, 16–22.

watered down. Ultimately, the new states merely agreed not do anything that would stand in the way of a future free trade pact.[60] These provisions were included in supplementary treaties that the new states were obliged to sign in Paris in order to authorize League oversight of their policies concerning ethnic minorities. The trade terms in these 'minorities treaties' were relatively uncontroversial compared to the hotly contested provisions related to population sovereignty.[61] The peace settlement nevertheless introduced an important legal distinction in League trade law between the new states and the older great powers, since the latter were not singled out for special economic rules of any kind. Significantly, the peace settlement also required the new states to join a long list of nineteenth-century technical treaties, for example on intellectual property and telegraph standards. Thus, submission to international economic law became a condition of statehood, with the League of Nations standing as the institutional gatekeeper.[62]

It was quite fitting that trade and population politics were joined together in the minorities treaties because concerns about discrimination against foreign commercial agents in Central and Eastern Europe became a core preoccupation of League trade policy in the 1920s. Both Llewellyn Smith and Riedl later sponsored League trade norms governing the 'the treatment of foreigners'. Their efforts met with strong resistance in many of the imperial successor states, where the League's moves to protect traders were seen as a further infringement on population sovereignty. As Susan Pedersen has demonstrated, the League of Nations provided an innovative institutional framework to define gradations of economic and political sovereignty, making the path to

---

[60] Economic Commission. Draft Convention Regulating the Commercial Relations of the New States, 3 March 1919, 181.1702/4, USNA: RG 256, Microfilm 184/155; Economic Commission. Section dealing with permanent commercial relations, 10 March 1919, 181.17101/1, USNA: RG 256, Microfilm 184/155.

[61] On debates about the League's minorities' treaties and Central European population politics, see M. Mazower, 'Minorities and the League of Nations in Interwar Europe', *Daedalus*, 126/2 (1997), 47–63; C. Fink, *Defending the Rights of Others: The Great Powers, the Jews, and International Minority Protection, 1878–1938* (Cambridge University Press, 2004), 133–294; C. Biltoft, 'The Meek Shall Not Inherit the Earth: Nationalist Economies, Ethnic Minorities, and the League of Nations', in C. Kreutzmüller, M. Wildt, and M. Zimmerman (eds.), *National Economies: Volks-Wirtschaft, Racism and Economy in Europe Between the Wars* (Cambridge Scholars Publishing, 2015), pp. 138–54; T. Zahra, *The Great Departure: Mass Migration from Eastern Europe and the Making of the Free World* (W. W. Norton & Company, 2016), 110–12; Wolff, *Woodrow Wilson and the Reimagining of Eastern Europe*, 168–227.

[62] The Committee on New States. 16th Meeting, 3 June 1919, 181.23201/16, USNA: RG 256, Microfilm 184/155; *Minorities Treaty Between the Principal Allied and Associated Powers (the British Empire, France, Italy, Japan and the United States) and Poland, Signed at Versailles 28 June 1919* (Ungarisches Institut München), www.forost.ungarisches-institut.de/pdf/19190628-3.pdf.

modern statehood a drawn-out and internationally supervised process. This dynamic can be seen in the League's oversight of minority politics in the imperial successor states of Central and Eastern Europe, and in its regime of tutelage in 'mandated' colonies.[63] Jamie Martin shows that the League's lending programmes to support currency stabilization and economic development also posed a novel challenge to sovereignty by bringing international officials deep into domestic economic activity. However, as Martin explains, trade policy did not intervene directly in local systems of production and consumption until the commodity agreements of the 1930s.[64] Thus, coming out of the First World War, international conflicts over commercial sovereignty were less about unwanted outside interference in domestic affairs and more about the formal differences in countries' tariff and treaty rights.

In 1919 the continental Empires of Central and Eastern Europe were divided into new nation states according to a (rough) principle of 'self-determination', but Germany's overseas colonies were assigned to new imperial overlords as League 'mandates', as were former Ottoman dependencies. The uneven application of self-determination in 1919 helped to fuel nationalist fervour in mandated territories, which fed into demands for local autonomy in trade policy.[65] Ex-Ottoman mandates such as Syria–Lebanon had a sizeable local business elite and a large commercial diaspora, who mobilized around the League's Permanent Mandates Commission to challenge the economic prerogatives claimed by new imperial rulers.[66] Many European peacemakers argued that the mandates should function as internationally supervised free trade zones, with equal access to resource concessions and markets for all outside powers. In the end, a formal open-door regime was applied to most of the Middle Eastern and African mandates. Mandatory powers pledged to ensure 'complete economic, commercial, and industrial equality' among nationals from League member countries and to award resource concessions 'without distinction on grounds of nationality'. In practice, the League did little to enforce the open-door rule, however. In League trade treaties, mandates were generally covered by a blanket 'colonial clause' that left imperial powers full latitude to determine whether and how to extend international norms

---

[63] Pedersen, 'Back to the League of Nations'; Pedersen, *The Guardians*, 9–10.
[64] Martin, *The Meddlers*.   [65] Manela, *The Wilsonian Moment*.
[66] Jackson, 'Diaspora Politics and Developmental Empire: The Syro-Lebanese at the League of Nations'.

to all dependent territories. Germans forcefully contested these imperial carve-outs as they worked to reclaim commercial access to former colonies.[67]

Germany and 'Equality of Trade Conditions'

During the peacemaking process, conflicting attitudes about empire were bound up with differing conceptions of Germany's role in the international trade system in Wilson's entourage. Opinions notably diverged over Bernhard von Bülow's pre-war strategy to raise 'fighting tariffs' as an opening bid for treaty negotiations. Frank Taussig saw such competitive tactics as a natural feature of international trade negotiations and argued that the US government should also arm itself with 'bargaining tariffs', declaring, 'we wish a fair field, an honorable rivalry'.[68] He saw colonies as important bargaining chips in international trade negotiations and insisted that Germany 'is fairly entitled to demand colonies of her own' in order to avoid being 'handicapped' by trade restrictions in foreign colonial territories, especially the British Dominions.[69] In contrast, Allyn Young disapproved of 'bargaining tariffs', on principle. He believed that Bülow had used MFN irresponsibly and undermined international stability, and he thus agreed with the Allies that Germany's negotiating capacity should be hamstrung after 1918. Young affirmed that 'Germany is perhaps primarily responsible for the origin and development of the present European system of discriminatory tariffs'. This justified corrective action, for 'if Germany is bound for the present to the observance of the principle of equality and uniformity, it is likely in the long run to have a wholesome effect upon other European tariff systems and make it easier to secure a general observance of the principle of non-discriminatory tariffs'. Young concluded that the unilateral MFN obligations imposed on Germany in the Treaty of

---

[67] A. Anghie, *Imperialism, Sovereignty, and the Making of International Law* (Cambridge University Press, 2005), 141–4; Pedersen, *The Guardians*, 195–237; M. Ingulstad, 'Regulating the Regulators: The League of Nations and the Problem of Raw Materials', in A. R. D. Sanders, P. T. Sandvik, and E. Storli (eds.), *The Political Economy of Resource Regulation: An International and Comparative History, 1850–2015* (UBC Press, 2019), pp. 229–57, 235–6.

[68] F. Taussig, How to Promote Foreign Trade, May 1918, USNA: RG 256, Economic Division, box 112/folder 321; F. Taussig, Memorandum on Bargaining Tariffs and Commercial Treaties in European Countries, 26 January 1918, USNA: RG 256, Economic Division, box 107/folder 231.

[69] F. Taussig, Colonial Tariffs and the Open Door, 18 October 1918, USNA: RG 256, Economic Division, box 107/folder 230.

Versailles were therefore 'in accordance with the President's principle of "equality of trade conditions"'.[70] In Kiel, Harms enthusiastically embraced Wilsonian 'equality of trade conditions', and identified Germany as a defender of this ideal rather than its opponent. In a speech to the German Society of International Law (Deutsche Gesellschaft für Internationales Recht), he outlined a post-war regime of 'world trade law' that would 'ensure equality of rights' among all former belligerents. Using the idiom of US trade policy, he demanded the universal 'recognition of the "open door" in commercial exchange'. For Harms, this meant a blanket prohibition against discriminatory policies in independent nations, formal colonies, or informal spheres of influence, implemented through a comprehensive MFN pact. In effect, he combined the most ambitious elements of British and US post-war trade policy in a single, sweeping multilateral programme. He proposed an explicit affirmation of unconditional MFN (as the British demanded) and the extension of that norm to cover all colonial territories (as US free traders such as Allyn Young demanded).[71]

Harms looked to the future League of Nations to institutionalize his new regime of 'world trade law'. He worked with other members of the German Society for International Law to write the economic clauses of a draft of the League Covenant in autumn 1918. In February 1919, this draft text made its way via Swedish diplomatic channels to Wilson's team in Paris, where it reportedly sparked 'particular interest'.[72] In practice, US leaders dismissed a very similar official proposal that the German government submitted to the peace conference. Although the German draft plans for the League had little concrete impact on the peace negotiations, they set a high benchmark against which German internationalists measured the work of the League in the 1920s.[73] By trying to use the League to implement a universal MFN pact that would cover both the imperial and non-imperial world, Harms sought to prevent the formation

---

[70] A. Young, Memorandum for Mr. Lamont, 5 April 1919, USNA: RG 256, Economic Division, box 108/folder 256.
[71] 'Völkerrechtliche Sicherungen der wirtschaftlichen Verkehrsfreiheit in Friedenzeiten', in B. Harms (ed.), *Vom Wirtschaftskrieg zur Weltwirtschaftskonferenz*, pp. 69–168, 141–54.
[72] J. Grew to I. N. Morris, 27 February 1919, 185.111/101, USNA: RG 256, Microfilm 184/321.
[73] T. Niemeyer (ed.), *Der Völkerbundsentwurf der Deutschen Gesellschaft für Völkerrecht. Vorschläge für die Organisation der Welt* (Verlag Hans Robert Engelmann, 1920), 9–10; H. Wehberg (ed.), *Der Völkerbund-Vorschlag der deutschen Regierung: Flugschrift der Deutschen Liga für Völkerbund* (Verlag Hans Robert Engelmann, 1920), 16–17. On the history of the German drafts of the League Covenant, see Koskenniemi, *The Gentle Civilizer of Nations*, 219–21; H. Gründer, *Walter Simons als Staatsmann, Jurist und Kirchenpolitiker* (Schmidt, 1975), 68–73; J. Wintzer, *Deutschland und der Völkerbund, 1918–1926* (Schöningh, 2006), 139–53.

of exclusive power blocs. He argued that 'political customs alliances' would lead to 'terrible chaos' and would perpetuate 'measures of economic warfare' in peacetime.[74] He condemned both regional and imperial tariff preferences as sources for rivalry and instability in the world economy. In contrast, Llewellyn Smith worked to prevent the formation of regional economic unions in Europe, East Asia, and the Americas in order to preserve the internal cohesion of the British Empire. Meanwhile, in Austria, Riedl advocated the formation of a continental Mitteleuropa as a counterweight to maritime empires.

Anschluss and Central European Commercial Order

In the final months of the war, as Bernhard Harms was preparing for the reintegration of Germany into the world economy, Richard Riedl backed a last-ditch attempt to secure a customs union between Germany and Austria–Hungary. Most German economic officials shared Harms's strong commitment to MFN and prioritized global over regional commercial relationships, but many of Germany's political leaders supported a customs union with Austria–Hungary for strategic reasons. The Chancellor Georg von Hertling believed that a customs union would be the easiest and most legally defensible means to ensure Austria's long-term cooperation as a gateway to South-Eastern Europe. Prevailing treaty practice exempted full customs unions from MFN, so this course of action would not disrupt Germany's commercial relations with third parties. Hertling hoped to finalize an agreement for a Central European customs union before the end to the war and present it as a *fait accompli* at the peace negotiations. He tabled an initial plan for a customs union in a meeting at Spa in May 1918 and then sought to hasten the final negotiations as the military tide turned against the Central Powers during the summer.[75] German and Austro-Hungarian delegations met in Salzburg from July to October 1918 to hammer out the terms for a customs union. They agreed to a preliminary arrangement in August and then began to define a common tariff scheme before the Austrian emperor finally called off the proceedings in the run-up to the Armistice. The main Austrian negotiator was Richard Schüller, a trade official who was both a collaborator and rival to Riedl. In 1918, Schüller, along with most other Austrian and Hungarian political leaders, opposed a customs

---

[74] Harms, 'Völkerrechtliche Sicherungen', 155.
[75] Soutou, *L'or et le sang*, 710–15; A. Müller, *Zwischen Annäherung und Abgrenzung: Österreich-Ungarn und die Diskussion um Mitteleuropa im Ersten Weltkrieg* (Tectum, 2001), 289–306.

union with Germany as a degrading form of vassalage that would inflame tensions among the Dual Monarchy's constituent nationalities, just as they were starting to claim independence.[76] Riedl swam against the current of official opinion and argued that a customs union with Germany was, in fact, the only way to hold the Dual Monarchy together because Austria–Hungary was too weak to counter separatist movements on its own.[77] In Vienna, he held a series of meetings with economic leaders to try to propagate this message, in parallel with Schüller's official negotiations in Salzburg. Riedl warned that without German backing, Austria–Hungary would become like 'Portugal', a country 'equipped with all the symbols of state sovereignty', but which 'in its own house possesses no authority'. It 'must always bend to the will of a foreign state' and 'is forced into trade treaties in which economic power must be given away bit by bit'.[78] In other words, Riedl believed that Austria–Hungary would have more domestic and international authority if it shared power with Germany than in isolation. Moreover, Riedl's experience in organizing the Austrian war economy had made him acutely conscious that Germany had strong material leverage over Austria; it possessed a 'range of instruments of power to let us feel our economic dependence: deliveries of coal, potash, machines, etc'.[79] Germany's urgent desire to conclude a customs union before the Armistice gave Austria–Hungary a limited window to extract concessions. If that opportunity was squandered, Riedl predicted that Austria–Hungary would eventually be forced into Germany's orbit on less generous terms. He recommended that Austria–Hungary keep demands for transitional tariffs to a minimum to secure concessions on other issues, for example on the political status of Poland. In Salzburg, Schüller took the opposite tack, negotiating a complicated set of tariff preferences with German counterparts that fell far short of a passable customs union.[80]

The Salzburg Agreement was never put to the test, but it would have been difficult to reconcile with the post-war strategy advocated by Harms and by most economic officials in Berlin. They planned to reclaim access

---

[76] Watson, *Ring of Steel*, 537; Müller, *Zwischen Annäherung und Abgrenzung*, 293–9; Soutou, *L'or et le sang*, 716.

[77] Protokoll über die Am Dienstag, den 30 Juli 1918 im Handelsministerium abgehaltene Besprechung über die Richtlinien für die wirtschaftspolitischen Verhandlungen zwischen Oesterreich-Ungarn und Deutschland, 30 July 1918, ÖStA, AVA: NL Riedl/61.

[78] Protokoll über die am 3. August 1918 in H.M. fortgesetzte Besprechung über die Richtlinien für die wirtschaftlichen Verhandlungen zwischen Oesterreich-Ungarn und Deutschland, 3 August 1918, ÖStA, AVA: NL Riedl/61, AVA, ÖStA; also quoted in Müller, *Zwischen Annäherung und Abgrenzung*, 315.

[79] Quoted in Müller, *Zwischen Annäherung und Abgrenzung*, 307.

[80] Protokoll, 30 July 1918, ÖStA: AVA, NL Riedl/61.

to global markets through uniform, treaty-based trade law. MFN was the cornerstone of this strategy, but standard treaty practice exempted only full customs unions from MFN, and not partial preferences such as those agreed at Salzburg. In the 1920s, when Austria had become Riedl's fabled 'Portugal', he devoted himself to resolving the legal tension between open global markets based on MFN and regional solidarity between Austria and Germany, using the multilateral levers of the League of Nations and the ICC. In the process, he helped define the institutional architecture for preferential free trade agreements.

The collapse of the Austro-Hungarian Empire turned Riedl's vision for a united Mitteleuropa on its head but also brought Riedl back into the corridors of power in Vienna. In autumn 1918, the Austro-Hungarian Empire splintered into eight new or newly reconfigured 'successor states', divided by seven thousand kilometres of customs borders. Riedl and other Austrians frequently claimed that the end of empire impoverished Central and Eastern Europe by shredding its economic fabric, and this view gained wide currency in the interwar period and in subsequent historiography. Econometric research now suggests that the borders of the successor states roughly corresponded to ethnic and linguistic divisions that had already started to constrain trade relations in late-imperial Austria–Hungary.[81] Moreover, the protectionism that deepened those economic fault lines in the 1920s stemmed as much from a global decline in commodity prices that hit the successor states hard as it did from 'nationalist' policies of export promotion or import substitution. As Jens-Wilhelm Wessels demonstrated, the most fundamental problem for Austrian exporters in the 1920s was farmers' declining purchasing power in the region. That problem was not primarily caused by the break-up of the Habsburg Empire but by low levels of agricultural productivity and glutted markets, especially in grains.[82] Stimulated by the war, world wheat output grew more quickly than consumption in the 1920s, exerting downward pressure on prices. East European farmers struggled to compete on export markets and consequently had less money to spend on traditional imports from Austria.[83]

Although the end of the Habsburg Empire affected Austrian exports less directly than many contemporaries believed, it did have very

---

[81] N. Wolf, M.-S. Schulze, and H.-C. Heinemeyer, 'On the Economic Consequences of the Peace: Trade and Borders After Versailles', *The Journal of Economic History*, 71/4 (2011), 915–49.

[82] J.-W. Wessels, *Economic Policy and Microeconomic Performance in Inter-war Europe: The Case of Austria, 1918–1938* (Steiner, 2007), 143–55.

[83] C. H. Feinstein, P. Temin, and G. Toniolo, *The European Economy between the Wars* (Oxford University Press, 1997), 72; Clavin, *The Great Depression in Europe, 1929–1939*, 78–81.

significant institutional consequences for the region's economy, which Riedl experienced directly in his position in the Austrian Ministry of Commerce. He took for granted that 'German-Austria', as the country was initially called, would simply join the rump German Reich. He believed that union between Austria and Germany (*Anschluss*) was desirable partly because it would allow for a geographic division of labour in the two countries' commercial institutions. Austria's loss of territory in 1918 had left it more heavily dependent on exports while undercutting its organizational access to foreign markets. The Vienna Trade Museum reported that it preserved only 46 of its roughly 500 pre-war collaborators around the world.[84] A memorandum on Austria's post-war fiscal position explained that 'Austria has almost completely lost its consular apparatus and as a small state does not have access to resources to build a network of consular representatives abroad that meets the needs of its foreign commerce'. Facing dire post-war shortages of hard currency, Austria 'must limit itself to maintaining representatives in neighbouring states, in the successor states and the Balkans and in the most important European countries'. For commercial representation further afield, Austria would have to 'seek a solution in dependence on similar institutions in foreign states. Here is meant, in particular, the German Reich'.[85] This strategy was aligned with Riedl's long-held view that Austria should position itself as an intermediary between Germany and Eastern Europe.

Austria's post-war Social-Democratic government shared Riedl's desire to pursue *Anschluss*.[86] In spring 1919, the foreign minister included Riedl in his efforts to conclude a union with Germany in a bid to pre-empt the post-war territorial settlement. Riedl was responsible for negotiating the trade provisions and favoured a full customs union, but he also insisted on Austria's right to negotiate separate treaties with the other imperial successor states. Riedl thus tried to devise a model of Austro-German union that would allow Vienna to preserve an independent sphere of influence in the former Habsburg Empire.[87] The Austrian and German peace treaties cut short efforts in this direction by explicitly barring *Anschluss*. More precisely, *Anschluss* was made contingent on

---

[84] Meyer, *Exportförderungspolitik in Österreich*, 132.
[85] Information für den Herrn Staatssekretär für Handel und Gewerbe, Industrie und Bauten, betreffend die finanzielle Lage des Handelsmuseums, 4 August 1920, ÖstA, AVA: NL Riedl/74.
[86] J. Thorpe, 'Pan-Germanism after Empire: Austrian "Germandom" at Home and Abroad', in G. Bischof, F. Plasser, and P. Berger (eds.), *From Empire to Republic: Post-World War I Austria* (UNO Press 2010) 257–62; Erin R Hochman, *Imagining a Greater Germany: Republican Nationalism and the Idea of Anschluss* (Cornell University Press 2016), pp. 38–41.
[87] Brettner-Messler, 'Richard Riedl', p. 298.

unanimous approval from the League Council, giving the permanent French member an effective veto.[88] Riedl argued that this prohibition – which ran against pro-*Anschluss* public sentiment in Austria – revealed that Wilson's principle of national 'self-determination' was merely a fig leaf for power politics. He claimed that Wilson used 'this idealistic phrase' to mask 'the eminently materialistic aspiration to place more than a third of the inhabited world in a condition of permanent economic atomization, perhaps in such advanced fragmentation, confusion, and conflict, that it will be possible for the more organized political and economic bodies of the world to dominate here without using the force of arms'.[89] Riedl also strongly objected to the requirement that Austria and Germany individually grant the Allies MFN status for five years (although this requirement was made reciprocal in the Austrian case after three years).[90] Significantly, Riedl did not propose to overturn the MFN provisions in the peace treaties, but to extend them. Like Harms, he wanted to make the MFN obligations that had been imposed on the defeated states binding for all League members, but unlike Harms, he included an exemption for tariff preferences within empires and between neighbouring states.[91] Riedl saw the League as a universal regulatory framework that could encompass both regional and imperial sub-units. He continued to try to implement this vision for the remainder of the 1920s, first in his role in the Ministry of Commerce and then as Austria's top diplomat in Germany from 1921 to 1925. When he ran up against official opposition to his plans for Austro-German rapprochement, he moved into private commercial channels, working through the Vienna Chamber of Commerce and the ICC.

Over the course of the 1920s, Riedl and Coquet embraced convergent visions of multilateral order. Both men tried to define a European commercial sub-structure within the League to facilitate regulatory standardization and concerted tariff reductions. However, Coquet and Riedl arrived at this common regional programme from different starting points and used it to pursue divergent geopolitical ends. Indeed, there was a striking symmetry between Riedl's and Coquet's ambitions the end of the war. Riedl tried to expand German territorial power to the east, while

---

[88] Article 88, 'The Treaty of Peace between the Allied and Associated Powers and Austria'; Article 80 'The Treaty of Peace between the Allied and Associated Powers and Germany'.

[89] R. Riedl, 'Die Wirtschaftspolitik der Entente und Wilsons vor dem Frieden', *Deutsche Review*, 45/1 (1920), 97–117, 117.

[90] R. Riedl, Denkschrift über die Möglichkeiten einer Erweiterung dem Österreichischen Wirtschaftsgebietes, April 1926, ÖStA. AVA: NL Riedl/80.

[91] R. Riedl, *Bemerkungen zu den deutschösterreichischen Friedensbedingungen. Handelspolitischer Teil* (Deutschösterreichische Staatsdruckerei, 1919), 18–19.

Coquet sought to reduce it in the west by hiving off Alsace-Lorraine and the neighbouring German Rhineland. Riedl invoked the ideal of self-determination, and Coquet sought to limit its application.

French Security on the Rhine

In the final years of the war, Coquet became quite active in French debates about the restoration of Alsace-Lorraine. There was broad support across the French political spectrum for that goal, but Coquet was especially invested in it. His father had fought in the Franco-Prussian War and then continued to work to recover the 'lost provinces' as a member of the irredentist association, the Patriot League (Ligue des patriotes).[92] Coquet's pre-war Franco-German Commercial Committee strove to facilitate French trade with Alsace-Lorraine to prepare for an eventual territorial transfer. During the war, Coquet became the general secretary of a Republican Committee of Alsace-Lorraine(Comité républicain d'Alsace-Lorraine). It primarily worked to oppose plans to hold a plebiscite in Alsace-Lorraine in the name of self-determination.[93] Many of Wilson's advisors initially favoured a plebiscite, as did several prominent French socialists.[94] Based on his pre-war engagement with business leaders in Alsace-Lorraine, Coquet knew that enthusiasm for reunification with France was uneven there. Local producers in sectors such as textiles and wine did not want to lose access to German markets and feared French competition. Coquet thus opposed a post-war plebiscite and undertook a long campaign to shape public opinion in favour of reunification with France.[95] He founded a newspaper dedicated to this cause in 1918, *La Revue d'Alsace et de Lorraine*, which also became a central bullhorn for Rhineland separatism.[96]

Coquet had widened his gaze from Alsace-Lorraine to the neighbouring German Rhineland during the war, following the current of mainstream official opinion. In the latter years of the war, many French leaders began to demand control over German territory along the

---

[92] L. Coquet, Mémoire de défense, 10 October 1945, Affaire Éditions Elcé, AN: F12/9640; L. Badel, *Un milieu libéral et européen: le grand commerce français, 1925–1948* (Comité pour l'histoire économique et financière de la France, 1999), 31.

[93] 'Les Echos', *Le Matin*, 29 June 1917; L. Coquet, G. Geville, and L. Guillet, 'Pour l'Alsace-Lorraine', *La Presse*, 20 August 1917, 2.

[94] V. Prott, *The Politics of Self-Determination: Remaking Territories and National Identities in Europe, 1917–1923* (Oxford University Press, 2016), 70–75.

[95] L. Coquet, 'L'Avenir économique de l'Alsace-Lorraine', *Revue Politique et Parlementaire*, 10 November 1917, 219–20.

[96] W. A. McDougall, *France's Rhineland Diplomacy, 1914–1924: The Last Bid for a Balance of Power in Europe* (Princeton University Press, 1978), 59.

Rhine for strategic reasons, but they disagreed about practical details. Some officials hoped to divide the Rhineland into one or more independent buffer states, under international supervision. Others wanted the Rhineland to remain part of a radically decentralized Germany. Most demanded, at a minimum, that the Allies occupy German territory on the left bank of the river as well as the bridgeheads on the right bank. US and British leaders ultimately agreed to a time-limited occupation along these lines, as leverage to ensure the delivery of reparations. They refused, however, to alter the political status of the German Rhineland permanently. During the peace negotiations, the French prime minister, Georges Clemenceau, agreed to abandon French plans for an autonomous Rhineland in exchange for promises of military and financial assistance from the Allies. When that support failed to materialize in the early 1920s, the Rhineland began to loom larger in the French security calculus.[97]

The principle of regional autonomy could be used to draw the Rhineland away from Germany and to anchor Alsace-Lorraine more firmly in France. During the war, Clémentel and Hauser hatched grand plans to reorganize the French economy along federal lines.[98] They initially hoped to form regional economic parliaments representing farmers, workers, and business. In 1918 they scaled back this vision to form regional associations of chambers of commerce, linked to new local branches of the National Office of Foreign Trade.[99] Clémentel initiated these reforms as minister of commerce and continued to pursue them after he left this post and assumed leadership of France's National Committee of Foreign Trade Advisors (at the same time as he took the helm of the ICC).[100] Clémentel and Hauser began their programme by creating the 'Eastern' economic region in 1918, in a bid to reintegrate Alsace-Lorraine by strengthening its financial and infrastructural connections with the surrounding area.[101]

Coquet offered his services as a publicist to the regionalist cause, presenting his *Revue d'Alsace et de Lorraine* as a clearinghouse for 'all

[97] McDougall, *France's Rhineland Diplomacy*, 15–96; Sharp, *The Versailles Settlement*, 106–12; Jackson, *Beyond the Balance of Power*, 276–315.

[98] Kuisel, *Capitalism and the State in Modern France*, 43–6; Soutou, *L'or et le sang*, 143–8; Badel, *Un milieu libéral et européen*, 30–31; H. Hauser, *Les Régions économiques* (Librairie Bernard Grasset, 1918), 64.

[99] Projet de division de la France en régions économiques, August 1917, AN: F 12/8037; Hauser, *Les Régions économiques*, 56–8.

[100] A. Megglé, *Atlas, Guide Économique et Touristique des Régions de France et d'Algérie* (Comité National des Conseillers du Commerce Extérieur de la France, 1922–8); Badel, *Diplomatie et grands contrats*, 64–5.

[101] Hauser, *Les Régions économiques*, 47, 66–7.

economic information of interest to the Eastern Region'.[102] Clémentel and Coquet's shared commitment to regional autonomy predated the First World War, when both had tried to use indications of origin to promote decentralized economic administration. Clémentel had praised Coquet's efforts in this direction in the Chamber of Deputies. Before 1914, Coquet had seen regionalism as a means to prepare for the transfer of Alsace-Lorraine to France by opening channels of communication. After 1918, he sought to complete that transition by promoting the construction of railways and tunnels in order to secure a pivotal position for Alsace-Lorraine both in France and in Europe.[103] On the front page of the first issue of *La Revue d'Alsace et de Lorraine*, he boldly declared that 'the Port of Strasbourg must become largest centre for the distribution of merchandise in Central Europe'.[104] Hauser shared this ambition and saw transport infrastructure as a critical factor for regional development strategies, more generally.[105] Hauser argued that regions were a source of economic dynamism because their geometry was more variable than larger national units. He reflected that 'a region is a rather unstable equilibrium between changing elements; it is a harmony that can always be modified'.[106] This controlled flux was a feature of small regions within states and larger regions that grouped multiple states together. It was no coincidence that Hauser, Clémentel, and Coquet all advocated regional autonomy within France and European unity beyond its borders. In the 1920s, they looked to the League of Nations to implement this complex system of multi-level governance.

Alongside his work for *La Revue d'Alsace et de Lorraine*, Coquet used a range of other information channels to support Clémentel and Hauser's programme to regionalize the French economy. In 1924, Coquet published a detailed survey of the different administrative reforms introduced by Clémentel, whom he hailed as the 'principal creator of economic

---

[102] *La Revue d'Alsace et de Lorraine*, 18 December 1918, 1.

[103] L. Coquet, La Percée des Vosges: Rapport général présenté aux Ministres, aux Membres des Parlements, des Chambres Consultatives, et des Conseils Généraux et Municipaux de France et d'Allemagne (Comité commercial franco-allemand, 1909); L. Coquet, 'L'Avenir économique de l'Alsace-Lorraine'; L. Coquet, 'La Percée des Vosges', *La Revue d'Alsace et de Lorraine*, 18 December 1918, 3; L. Coquet, Mémoire de défense, 10 October 1945, AN F12/9640; Kuisel, *Capitalism and the State in Modern France*, 38.

[104] L. Coquet, editorial preface to 'Le Port de Strasbourg', *La Revue d'Alsace et de Lorraine*, 18 December 1918, 1; Henri Hauser highlighted this article in his personal copy of the journal, found in AN: F12/7988. This file also contains Hauser's own reflections on the Port of Strasbourg. See Henri Hauser, Note sur le rapport de M. Peirotes, Adjoint au Maire, relatif au Port de Strasbourg, 19 January 1919.

[105] Troisième rapport sur la mission de M. Henri Hauser auprès des Chambres de Commerce d'Alsace et de Lorraine, 27 January 1919, AN: F12, 8044.

[106] Hauser, *Les Régions économiques*, 39.

regionalism'.[107] At the time, Coquet was the general delegate for a Federation of Provincial Associations(Fédération des sociétés provinciales), which functioned as a clearinghouse for information on French regionalist movements. Coquet corresponded with local associations across the country and collected their publications in a 'regionalist documentary library' in his Paris office. This same space served as the headquarters for the *La Revue d'Alsace et de Lorraine*, as well as an Economic Office of the Rhine, which backed Otto Wolff's bid to advance Rhineland autonomy through the Cologne steel trade.[108] In sum, Coquet was a busy organizational beaver in the early 1920s, building information networks to advocate regional devolution, with an aim to anchor Alsace-Lorraine more securely in France while also facilitating Rhineland separatism.

Shifting the Relationship between Commercial Information and Foreign Policy

Coquet's journalism aligned with a growing tendency across Europe to recast commercial information as a tool of security and geopolitics. At the close of the war, all belligerent governments conducted a thorough overhaul of trade-promoting institutions and endeavoured to unify the sprawling systems of economic information that had been inherited from the belle époque. These changes were introduced through a process of competitive emulation, fuelled by a sense of vulnerability vis-à-vis overseas powers and by an expectation that European exporters would have to compete aggressively to reclaim their lost markets after the war.[109]

During this period, most European governments made attempts to integrate commercial and consular services, which had been separated between Ministries of Commerce and Ministries of Foreign Affairs in most countries. In 1917, Llewellyn Smith's Commercial Intelligence Branch was absorbed by a new Department of Overseas Trade, which the Board of Trade supervised jointly with the British Foreign Office. This new department was responsible for managing Britain's commercial attachés and for collating all economic reports received from consular and diplomatic posts.[110] Inter-ministerial collaboration was not harmonious, however. Llewellyn Smith worked hard to circumscribe the department's authority in order to keep most information functions within the Board of

---

[107] L. Coquet (ed.), *La France régionale: Annuaire régionaliste, touristique, économique et répertoire illustré des grandes marques françaises* (Dubois et Bauer, 1924), 18.
[108] Coquet, *La France régionale*, 15.   [109] Badel, *Diplomatie et grands contrats*, 39–62.
[110] F. M. G. Willson and D. N. Chester, *The Organization of British Central Government, 1914–1956* (Allen and Unwin, 1957), 69; *Memorandum with Respect to the Reorganisation of the Board of Trade* (H. M. G. Stationery Office, 1918).

Trade.[111] In France, Clémentel was more successful in his efforts to secure a wholesale transfer of the commercial attaché service from the Ministry of Foreign Affairs to the Ministry of Commerce, but this move left considerable resentment in the diplomatic corps.[112]

The German government made the biggest structural change by agreeing to create a centralized trade institution in Berlin after resisting that course since the 1880s, but momentum for this reform project quickly flagged. Bernhard Harms played a central role in this process. This was fitting, since he had conceived of the IfW, in part, as a means to compensate for the absence of official German trade promotion. In recognition of that earlier history, Gustav Stresemann asked Harms to present a proposal for a new state trade office at a meeting in 1915 of the War Committee of German Industry (Kriegsausschuss der deutschen Industrie).[113] This committee was a cooperative venture between the Industrialists' League and the Central Association of German Industry. The simple fact that those two bodies had joined forces was significant because they had evinced very different attitudes about trade policy before the war. In 1915, Stresemann gave Harms the documents that the Industrialists' League had collected as part of its fifteen-year campaign for a Reich Trade Office.[114] The Central Association of German Industry had largely been responsible for blocking that campaign.[115]

Harms used Stresemann's material to prepare a lengthy memorandum for the War Committee of German Industry that surveyed Germany's recent institutional history and proposed future reforms. He observed that although the German government had not sponsored formal trade-promoting institutions, informal organizations had proliferated. For example, in lieu of officially sanctioned expatriate chambers of commerce, German business leaders had created private 'double-state' institutions, which effectively served the same purpose (including Coquet's German–French Economic Association). Alongside these de facto expatriate chambers of commerce, Harms also noted the proliferation of independent economic information services in Germany, such as the IfW.[116] These private bodies supplemented the limited information that

---

[111] [illegible signature] to A. Steel-Maitland, E Crowe, V. Wellesley, 8 September 1917, TNA: BT 13/34; Boyce, British Capitalism at the Crossroads, 29–30.

[112] Badel, Diplomatie et grands contrats, 55–9.

[113] Bericht über die gemeinschaftliche Sitzung der Ausschüsse des Bundes der Industriellen und des Centralverbandes Deutscher Industrieller, 21 September 1915, PA AA: NL Stresemann/152.

[114] These documents can be found in IfW: Hs Harms/12.

[115] Ullmann, 'Staatliche Exportförderung und private Exportinitiative'.

[116] B. Harms, Zur Wiederanknüpfung und Pflege der weltwirtschaftlichen Beziehungen Deutschlands (University of Kiel, 1915), 15–16.

the German Ministry of the Interior provided through its monthly summary of foreign trade laws and statistics, the *Deutsches Handels-Archiv*, and its circular of commercial news, the *Berichten über Handel und Industrie*.[117]

The outbreak of war renewed calls to unify Germany's various public and private trade-promoting bodies under a central institution in Berlin. Harms declared that 'there has never been a time in which the urgency of such an effort was so great'. He argued, however, that the state could not simply 'absorb' the multiplicity of private organizations that had already sprouted across Germany. Rather, it should aim to facilitate cooperation among them to produce a composite picture of the world economy.[118] Harms recommended that the new office promote inter-organizational dialogue through specific, targeted initiatives. It could work to improve German access to specific markets (he suggested Brazil and China) and specific commodities (he suggested raw cotton). It could also push for the multilateral standardization of key regulations (he suggested loading rules at ports). Harms saw an important role for the IfW in this process, as a bridge between 'science' and 'practice'.[119] In the 1920s, Harms built the IfW into a forum for inter-organizational dialogue between business, academia, and policy, but its ties to the German state were more tenuous than he initially envisioned.

In response to calls from Harms and other German leaders for more central coordination, plans were laid in 1917 for a new Foreign Trade Bureau (Außenhandelsstelle). Harms agreed to allow it to publish the weekly paper that the IfW had introduced during the war, and which had since been transformed from the 'War Economy News' into the peacetime 'World Economy News' or *Weltwirtschaftliche Nachrichten*. Harms duly moved eight of the IfW's staff members and a large store of its news archive to Berlin in autumn 1918. In the ministerial shake-up that accompanied the formation of the Weimar Republic, plans for the Foreign Trade Bureau shifted from the Reich Economic Office to the Foreign Office. The Foreign Office demanded that the IfW relinquish all editorial authority over the *Weltwirtschaftliche Nachrichten* and permanently cede its staff and news archive. Harms flatly rejected this proposal; he wanted a partnership and not outright institutional annexation. Ultimately, the IfW did end up ceding its news operations wholly to a new semi-official German

---

[117] Pohlmann, *Außenwirtschaftlicher Nachrichten-und Auskunftsdienst*, 8–9.
[118] B. Harms, *Zur Wiederanknüpfung und Pflege der weltwirtschaftlichen Beziehungen Deutschlands*, 16–18.
[119] Bericht über die gemeinschaftliche Sitzung der Ausschüsse des Bundes der Industriellen und des Centralverbandes Deutscher Industrieller, 21 September 1915, PA AA: NL Stresemann/152.

Economic Service (Deutscher Wirtschaftsdienst) under financial pressure from post-war inflation.[120] Although the IfW lost its role in German commercial news, this change enabled a clearer focus on bibliographic research and policy outreach. In the 1920s Harms latched onto the new information-rich mode of trade policy that was developing around the League of Nations while also reaching across the Atlantic to private US philanthropic bodies that were working to sustain Wilson's internationalism.

In 1919, the United States was a problematic torchbearer for international trade cooperation. Through the war, it had gained overwhelming financial leverage over Europeans, and this also increased its heft in foreign trade. Yet the United States was not institutionally equipped to assume global leadership in the international trade system. Wilson demanded open markets but would not give that commitment legal teeth by formally endorsing unconditional MFN. Nor did he have sufficient executive authority to negotiate trade treaties. That change did not come until Cordell Hull and Franklin Roosevelt sponsored the Reciprocal Trade Agreements Act in 1934. Wilson did nevertheless start to construct the multilateral framework into which Hull later inserted himself by investing the League of Nations with a general remit to promote the 'equitable treatment' of foreign trade. It was Europeans who gave flesh to that commitment in the 1920s. Their sustained rivalries – in the absence of a clear hegemon – made them potent multilateral innovators.

The main trade provisions of the 1919 peace settlement were intended, and functioned, as temporary legal placeholders. Although 'equitable treatment' was an import from the United States, in the 1920s Europeans made this concept their own. It became the vessel for their unrealized ambitions for multilateral economic order that had taken shape during the war. As Glenda Sluga has explained, Geneva did not become a cosmopolitan melting pot in the 1920s. Indeed, the juxtaposition of national and imperial programmes often served to reinforce a sense of difference. Every autumn, delegations lined up at the League Assembly to affirm their distinctive national positions in an elaborate international pageant.[121] Behind the scenes, the League's technical economic work remained grounded in wartime conflicts over territorial control, market access, and resource security. Those conflicts hung in suspense through

---

[120] An die Mitglieder der Gesellschaft zur Förderung des Instituts für Weltwirtschaft und Seeverkehr. Den 'Weltwirtschaftlichen Nachrichten' zum Abschied, September 1922, IfW: Hs K.N.W.N. u. Wi.D; Pohlmann, *Außenwirtschaftlicher Nachrichten-und Auskunftsdienst*, 17, 23–4; Tworek, *News from Germany*, 101, 107.

[121] Sluga, *Internationalism in the Age of Nationalism*, 49–61.

the 1920s, providing much of the motivation for experimentation in international trade policy. The League was able to encompass widely varying trade programmes in the 1920s in part because its initial economic mission was so vaguely defined. Coquet, Harms, Llewellyn Smith, and Riedl were all dissatisfied with the 1919 Peace Settlement for different reasons and sought redress through a range of organizational channels. Their divergent but overlapping trajectories reveal how the League multiverse was rooted in the experience of the war and in the nebulous system of economic organization that preceded it.

4   From Bilateral to Multilateral Trade Treaties

Although it had been badly bruised by the war, the network of bilateral trade treaties inherited from the nineteenth century remained the basic framework for trade policy, supplemented by new general multilateral rules. This cooperation advanced relatively modest practical objectives, but it reconfigured the architecture of international trade politics in important ways. More than any other single figure, Hubert Llewellyn Smith embodied the complex transition from nineteenth-century bilateral trade treaties to twentieth-century international economic governance. He had been Britain's lead trade negotiator before the First World War and proudly claimed the legacy of Richard Cobden, who had initiated the country's programme of MFN treaties in 1860. After the war, he pivoted towards multilateral negotiation and became the dominant member of the Economic Committee of the League of Nations. He built up this body into a platform for regulatory standardization, crafting a new multilateral rule-making process. Fittingly, Llewellyn Smith's last act in 1927 before he retired from the Economic Committee and from Britain's Board of Trade was to initiate the League's standardization of the MFN norm. That process confirmed the League as the guardian and arbiter of bilateral treaty law inherited from the nineteenth century and inaugurated a twentieth-century model of international organization in which bilateral agreements were subjected to multilateral scrutiny and coordination from Geneva. That basic organizational principle is still at the heart of today's WTO.

In the Economic Committee, Llewellyn Smith tried to construct a model of multilateral policy in which national trade officials would keep a firm hold on the levers of power but would also be able to engage with a range of outside experts. As Britain's representative, he steadfastly defended national interests, as he understood them, and expected his counterparts to do this same. Indeed, he believed that the main purpose of multilateral institutions was to bring together authoritative officials to discuss conflicting national viewpoints and to seek limited areas for compromise. Under Llewellyn Smith's leadership, early League trade

117

policy was directed towards two general objectives. Firstly, he worked to contain new administrative trade restrictions that had been introduced during and after the war, such as customs formalities and quotas. This activity had a narrow scope, but it brought far-reaching changes in institutional practice. Additionally, Llewellyn Smith also helped to standardize norms of commercial practice related to contract arbitration, bills of exchange, intellectual property, and trade representation.

At a general level, Llewellyn Smith avoided radical change and strove to use the League to shore up Britain's imperial system and its position in the wider world. He had to balance complex objectives: decoupling militarily important sectors of the British economy from German suppliers while reintegrating Germany in the world economy; promoting reconstruction in Central and Eastern Europe while preventing the formation of regional economic blocs that would threaten the internal cohesion of the British commercial system; building an integrated global regulatory regime while allowing India and the Dominions to pursue their own programmes of protection and imperial preference in an increasingly autonomous way. Ultimately, Llewellyn Smith's aspirations for stability in an unstable world exceeded the organizational capacity of both the League and the British diplomatic establishment. He nevertheless left behind a considerable legacy in treaty law and practice by developing institutional processes that other innovators then used to push the League in new directions after his departure. At the League's World Economic Conference in 1927, a new cohort of reformers, including Coquet, Harms, and Riedl, stepped in to demand more direct intervention in relations of production and consumption and more space for regional integration. This conference symbolically marked the end of post-war reconstruction and the beginning of a more experimental phase in League trade cooperation. It was also the endpoint for Llewellyn Smith's League career.

Restoring the Infrastructural Foundations of International Trade

When the League of Nations opened its doors in 1920, the first order of business was to complete the practical transition from war to peace. That transition was long and rocky in much of Europe. Foreign trade recovered slowly, hindered by initial shortages of transport capacity and credit.[1] At the beginning of 1920, the League reported that quarterly exports were down by roughly half in France, Italy, and Britain, when compared against 1913 averages. The situation was even worse for some of the commercially

---

[1] Miller, *Europe and the Maritime World*, 245.

dependent neutrals, notably in Denmark, Sweden, and the Netherlands.[2] To the east, young states with limited infrastructural and fiscal resources faced food shortages, an influenza epidemic, galloping inflation, and ongoing political and military conflict.[3] Immediate emergency relief came from independent aid organizations and from remnants of the Allied military administration operating under the aegis of the SEC.[4] Llewellyn Smith represented Britain on the SEC, where he worked with General Henry Osborne Mance to facilitate the reconstruction of Europe's war-torn transport system. Mance had been the Director of Railways and Roads at the British War Office and served alongside Llewellyn Smith on Britain's delegation to the Paris Peace Conference. Together, they prepared a set of transit conventions for the conference. These agreements did not make it into the final peace settlement but did give the League a clear blueprint for an international transit regime.[5] In order to prepare the League's work, Llewellyn Smith set up a temporary Communications Section within the Board of Trade in 1919 with Mance as director. Mance used this base to maintain British military transport missions across Central and Eastern Europe to assist aid distribution, while also managing preparations for a General Conference on Communications and Transit, hosted by the League in Barcelona in 1921.[6]

Llewellyn Smith led the British delegation to Barcelona, and he frequently looked back on that event as an example of successful international negotiations. The Barcelona Conference produced a set of treaties to frame a new Organization for Communications and Transit within the League, transferring to Geneva the infrastructural work that Mance had been coordinating out of London on behalf of the SEC.[7] Llewellyn Smith

---

[2] 'Table XXVI. – Statement Showing the Fluctuations in the Weight of Imports into and Exports from the Under-mentioned Countries during the Period Specified', *Supreme Economic Council: Monthly Bulletin of Statistics*, 1/12 (1920), 26.

[3] R. Gerwarth and J. Horne (eds.), *War in Peace: Paramilitary Violence in Europe after the Great War* (Oxford University Press, 2012); B. Cabanes, *The Great War and the Origins of Humanitarianism: 1918–1924* (Cambridge University Press, 2014); P. Clavin, 'The Austrian Hunger Crisis and the Genesis of International Organization after the First World War', *International Affairs*, 90/2 (2014), 265–78; Gerwarth, *The Vanquished*; Leonhard, *Der überforderte Frieden*.

[4] Decorzant, *La Société des Nations et la naissance d'une conception de la régulation économique internationale*, 152–61; Dehne, *After the Great War*, 77–106.

[5] International Rivers Draft Convention, 10 February 1919, TNA: FO 608/72; Draft Convention Providing for Freedom of Transit, 20 January 1919, TNA: FO 608/72.

[6] Correspondence concerning the operation of the SEC communications section within the Board of Trade can be found in TNA: BT 65/2.

[7] In the League, 'technical' bodies were differentiated from those with an explicit political function such as those responsible for disarmament or Mandate administration. Politics nevertheless intervened in 'technical' bodies charged with health, trade, finance, and transit.

deliberately intervened to direct the Barcelona Conference towards the creation of permanent international administration through the conclusion of multilateral treaties. During the opening debates, he solemnly announced that he had plenipotentiary powers to sign binding conventions at the conference and urged the other delegates to obtain similar authorization.[8] Llewellyn Smith helped assert the League's legal authority over transit, but he also circumscribed that authority in order to accommodate the shifting position of the British Empire in the world.

Llewellyn Smith ensured that the proceedings at the Barcelona Conference and the subsequent work of the League's Transit Organization focused on inland transport and excluded maritime shipping.[9] This policy was aligned with Britain's efforts to preserve its capacity for maritime warfare and to fend off US demands for full freedom of the seas. In 1921, the British Admiralty resolutely defended the tools of blockade and contraband control at the Washington Naval Conference, leaving US advocates of neutral rights profoundly dissatisfied with the disarmament settlement agreed there.[10] Unresolved conflict over freedom of the seas resurfaced after the United States co-sponsored a pact to outlaw war in 1928. European internationalists hoped to link this agreement to the League's sanctions regime, and Nordic states tried to use the opportunity to strengthen neutral commercial rights. The British Admiralty was unyielding, however.[11] Llewellyn Smith had defended neutral commercial rights in internal Cabinet debates during the war, but he supported Britain's blockade regime on the international stage in the 1920s. Here as in other areas, he built multilateral legal space for policies that he privately opposed, in deference to his home government. He was both a determined internationalist and a dedicated civil servant, with deep institutional loyalties both to the League and to the British government. The interplay between these loyalties can also be seen in his careful defence of imperial preference.

At Barcelona, foreign governments expressed considerable confusion about the status of the British Empire in the League. This confusion stemmed from the fact that India and the Dominions had tariff autonomy and were separate members of the League. Thus they each individually had the right to participate or abstain from League economic treaties. In

---

[8] Report by the British Delegate on the Proceedings and Results of the League of Nations Conference on Transit and Communications, held at Barcelona, 10 March to 20 April 1921, TNA: FO 371/6146.

[9] H. Llewellyn Smith, Merchant Shipping Section of the Trade Questionnaire, 10 January 1921, LON: Economic Committee, Papers, 1920–22, B 18.

[10] D. J. Lisio, *British Naval Supremacy and Anglo-American Antagonisms, 1914–1930* (Cambridge University Press, 2014), 109.

[11] Mulder, *The Economic Weapon*, 220–45.

Barcelona, Llewellyn Smith performed elaborate legal acrobatics to devise a treaty formula that would both affirm the British Empire as a cohesive political unit and simultaneously allow India and the Dominions to opt in or out of League transit cooperation. He did this by securing an explicit proviso stipulating that the Barcelona conventions would not apply to internal trade within the British Empire.[12] This aligned with the doctrine of *inter se* according to which India and the Dominions were subject to international law in their relations with outside powers but not in their interactions with other parts of the Empire. This principle was intended to ensure that the League would reinforce rather than undermine British imperial rule by guarding against external interference in intra-imperial relations and preventing India and the Dominions from using the League to air their grievances against London. Yet, *inter se* covered widely varying attitudes towards imperial unity and independent statehood.[13]

In terms of international trade, arguably the most significant change was India's formal adoption of tariff autonomy in 1919. India had long been the linchpin of the British trade system, as Britain's export surplus there helped to counterbalance its large commercial deficits elsewhere. Admittedly, India's tariff autonomy was far from complete during the interwar period, as London officials kept close watch on moves towards tariff-backed industrial development (indeed, Llewellyn Smith led a commission that helped define the terms for Indian fiscal administration as part of a more general civil service reform in 1919).[14] India's limited moves towards economic self-government did nevertheless level off imports from Britain during the interwar period, as British imbalances with the United States and the rest of the New World ballooned.[15] Moreover, although Britain exerted considerable influence over India's representation in the League, Indian delegates frequently used Geneva as a platform to defend protection for nascent industry.[16] In 1932, one of India's delegates to the League, Jehangir Coverjee Coyajee, looked back

---

[12] League of Nations, *General Conference on Freedom of Communications and Transit*, C.15. M.10.1921.VIII (League of Nations, 1921).

[13] McKenzie, *Redefining the Bonds of Commonwealth*, 20–21; L. Lloyd, 'Loosening the Apron Strings', *The Round Table*, 92/369 (2003), 279–303, 283–5; Gorman, *The Emergence of International Society in the 1920s*, 23; Darwin, *The Empire Project*, 393–410.

[14] *Llewellyn Smith Report: Report of the Government of India Secretariat Procedure Committee, 1920* (National Institute of Public Administration, reprint 1963), 10–13; B. Chatterji, *Trade, Tariffs, and Empire: Lancashire and British Policy in India, 1919–1939* (Oxford University Press, 1992).

[15] Tooze and Fertik, 'The World Economy and the Great War', 235.

[16] A. V. Shenoy, 'The Centenary of the League of Nations: Colonial India and the Making of International Law', *Asian Yearbook of International Law*, 24 (2018), 3–23.

on the country's record of international engagement and reflected that 'our country has consistently emphasized the rational, moderate and scientific character of that system of Discriminating Protection which is at present in operation in India'.[17] Interestingly, Coyajee compared India's international defence of moderate protection to views voiced in Geneva by the Hungarian economist, Elemér Hantos. Yet in the Economic Committee, Llewellyn Smith struggled to devise an institutional formula that would encompass the British Empire and post-imperial Central Europe, despite the growing awareness of structural similarities on the ground.

In 1921, Llewellyn Smith foresaw that the constitutional complexity of the British Empire might become a stumbling block for wider multilateral cooperation. He noted that his interlocutors at Barcelona obligingly strove 'to overcome and not to accentuate any difficulties arising out of the special position of the British Empire in the League'. He warned colleagues in London that it was 'extremely difficult for foreigners to understand the somewhat anomalous constitution and internal structure of the British Empire, and had any of the States represented at Barcelona been desirous of making trouble their representatives could have made it very difficult to arrive at any generally satisfactory result'.[18] Thus, Llewellyn Smith worked hard to preserve the status of the British Empire as an autonomous but segmented sub-unit within the League but he also understood that doing so would constrain Britain's leadership capacity. Consequently, he aired on the side of caution, seeking consensus, working incrementally, and avoiding bold provocation. His limited ambitions allowed him to focus on crafting a new multilateral process, with important consequences for the subsequent history of international trade policy in the interwar period and beyond.

As the first major multilateral economic settlement concluded under League auspices, the Barcelona Conference provided a template for future cooperation. The Barcelona conventions established a new international rule-making process in which a small expert committee prepared a set of draft agreements with assistance from League bureaucrats. These drafts were then circulated among political and business leaders for consultation before final diplomatic negotiations at a large conference, open to all interested governments. Llewellyn Smith repeated this exercise several times in the first half of the 1920s, helping to create standard procedures that other League collaborators could then adapt to their own objectives. The League Secretariat also supported the development of

[17] J. C. Coyajee, *India and the League of Nations* (Thompson and Co., 1932), 100.
[18] H. Llewellyn Smith to D. Lloyd George, 26 May 1921, TNA: FO 371/6146.

a multilateral routine by ensuring a baseline of legal and institutional continuity between successive initiatives. Indeed, Llewellyn Smith was able to exert decisive influence over the League's early trade policy in part because he worked well with his British compatriots who were serving in the Secretariat's Economic and Financial Section, including the section's head statistician, Alexander Loveday, and its director, Arthur Salter. Yet by his own admission, Salter was mainly interested in finance in the 1920s and left his deputy, Pietro Stoppani, to manage most trade matters. Elisabetta Tollardo explains that Stoppani was an Italian liberal who had lived in the United States for many years before returning to Italy to fight in the war. He thus spoke English fluently, and his focus on back-room technical work enabled him to develop a strong bond with Salter and the other members of the Secretariat while also maintaining distant but harmonious relations with the Fascist government. By the time Stoppani joined the League's Economic and Financial Organization in 1923, its basic institutional architecture had already been defined.[19]

The Genesis of the League's Economic and Financial Organization

Shortly after the League began operations in 1920, the Secretariat established an Economic and Financial Section to prepare for a financial conference in Brussels.[20] Unlike the Barcelona Conference, this event did not yield any firm legal commitments, but it did pass a resolution that led to the formation of the League's Economic and Financial Organization (EFO). The fully formed EFO encompassed the Economic and Financial Section of the Secretariat as well as two consultative bodies, the Financial Committee and the Economic Committee, with the latter focused on trade. Both committees answered to the Council and to the Second Committee of the Assembly, which was responsible for supervising the 'technical' work of the League (as distinct from 'political' work such as disarmament).[21] Llewellyn Smith held strong views regarding the internal composition of Economic Committee. Along with many other British leaders, he strove to use the League to facilitate high-level policy coordination but prevent rogue initiatives from independent experts in Geneva.[22] He advocated a small

---

[19] A. Salter, Appointments Committee, 19 January 1928, LON: Personnel Files, Pietro Stoppani, S 888/3392; E. Tollardo, *Fascist Italy and the League of Nations, 1922–1935* (Palgrave Macmillan, 2016), 219–25.
[20] Clavin, *Securing the World Economy*, 17.
[21] Clavin and Wessels, 'Transnationalism and the League of Nations', 469–80.
[22] Memorandum by Sir P. Lloyd Greame, 9 September 1920, TNA: BT 198/6.

Economic Committee that would include only 'appropriate ministers of the principal States or of their authorized representatives'. In his view, 'one of the principal advantages to be hoped for from the establishment of the League' was to enable national officials to 'conduct the business of their own Countries with full understanding of what is being done and aimed at by their colleagues throughout the world'.[23] That vision was partly a continuation of the Allies' wartime economic administration and partly a new departure.

Arthur Salter, who had steered the Allies' economic apparatus and also supervised the formation of the EFO in the 1920s, agreed that international cooperation in the League would depend upon 'ensuring direct contact between those who exercise responsible authority in the several countries', noting that this principle had been important to the success of the Allies' technical agencies.[24] Along with Salter, many alumni from inter-Allied bodies held prominent positions in the early League Secretariat, including Jean Monnet, who served as a deputy secretary-general.[25] Yet Salter also highlighted discontinuities between the Allied economic system and the League. Wartime bodies had participated directly in economic operations in order to advance precise practical objectives. In contrast, the League was responsible for coordinating 'policy-formation' in a more abstract and open-ended way.[26] To perform this new task, the League's Economic Committee formed in 1920 as a compact, consultative, ten-member body. Seats were allocated on a national basis. Members were technically appointed as independent experts by the Council, but they came on the recommendation of their home governments. Thus, although membership on the Economic Committee was not formally reserved for ministerial officials, as Llewellyn Smith wished, in practice national trade negotiators did fill most seats.[27]

Alexander Loveday emphasized the value of the Economic Committee as a deliberative body when he took stock of the EFO's record in 1938. He argued that the Economic Committee's main contribution had been to

---

[23] H. Llewellyn Smith, The Economic Organisation of the League of Nations: Note for Mr Balfour, 15 October 1920, TNA: FO, 371/5481.

[24] Salter, *Allied Shipping Control*, 274.

[25] Decorzant, *La Société des Nations et la naissance d'une conception de la régulation économique internationale*, 110–348; Y. Decorzant, 'La Société des Nations et l'apparition d'un nouveau réseau d'expertise économique et financière (1914–1923)', *Critique internationale*, 52/3 (2011), 35–50.

[26] Salter, *Allied Shipping Control*, 274; Martin, *The Meddlers*, 58–9.

[27] Clavin and Wessels, 'Transnationalism and the League of Nations', 471; Decorzant, *La Société des Nations et la naissance d'une conception de la régulation économique internationale*, 389–92.

gather top trade officials two to three times per year for lengthy private discussions. He remarked, 'the value of the meeting lies in the act of meeting, and that is particularly the case when the persons in question would normally only meet otherwise to negotiate'.[28] He explained, 'there is, I believe, a very real advantage in their coming together in this way to sit round a table instead of sitting on opposite sides of it, and in discussing their difficulties and preoccupations in common, not in competition. It paves the way for later bilateral negotiations'.[29] While it is true that the Economic Committee did embed bilateral negotiations in a process of ongoing multilateral consultation, multilateralism did not always attenuate competition in trade policy. Indeed, it often raised the stakes. In the Economic Committee, rivalry was not simply about gaining a relative advantage in one bilateral relationship but rather about setting the terms of engagement for a whole group of partners. Multilateral projects also carried additional weight because they defined the structural relationship between trade and other dimensions of the world economy.

Money, Finance, and Trade in the Wake of the First World War

The EFO's founding conference at Brussels emphasized the interdependence between trade liberalization and currency stabilization, but those objectives did not fit together neatly. The Brussels Conference responded to fears that post-war financial disorder would snowball into a sustained global recession and that Bolshevik forces would take the opportunity to expand westward. Immediately after the war, commodity prices shot up worldwide. The Board of Trade reported that British wholesale prices increased by roughly 40 per cent from summer 1919 to summer 1920.[30] This inflation was partly a continuation of wartime trends and partly fuelled by an increased demand for raw materials as firms restocked and governments began to rebuild. The Brussels Conference gathered a large group of financial experts to assess these conditions and to devise an international agenda to guide post-war reconstruction.[31] Delegates at Brussels argued that post-war inflation must be controlled through the elimination of budget deficits. They advised fiscal restraint as well as

---

[28] A. Loveday, 'The Economic and Financial Activities of the League', *International Affairs*, 17/6 (1938), 788–808, 790.

[29] Loveday, 'The Economic and Financial Activities of the League', 791.

[30] 'Table X – United Kingdom – Board of Trade Index Number' *Supreme Economic Council: Monthly Bulletin of Statistics*, 1/12 (1920), 11.

[31] Decorzant, *La Société des Nations et la naissance d'une conception de la régulation économique internationale*, 233–90; Clavin, *Securing the World Economy*, 17–22.

concerted efforts to promote economic growth through freer flowing trade and credit.[32] Many delegates insisted that stabilizing the international monetary system by restoring the gold standard was an essential prerequisite for more open trade. Governments were using 'antidumping' tariffs to compensate for price competition tied to the depreciation of foreign currencies. At the same time, states with weak currencies introduced new quantitative restrictions to conserve hard foreign currency for essential imports.[33]

The withdrawal of the United States from the League project further complicated the linkages between trade, money, and finance. By the early 1920s, the United States had become the world's main creditor and had accumulated a large share of the global gold supply. Yet officials there did not yet appreciate the level of institutional coordination required to restore a basic level of function to the international financial system under these conditions.[34] The pivotal role played by US monetary policy in the world economy was demonstrated vividly in 1920, when the country's Federal Reserve Board raised interest rates to arrest domestic post-war inflation. This drew gold towards the United States and forced Britain and other governments to raise interest rates and cut spending to maintain currency reserves and stay on track for a return to the gold standard. The general movement towards monetary and fiscal stringency in 1920 produced a global deflationary crisis.[35] From 1920 to 1922 US wholesale prices declined by 37 per cent and British wholesale prices declined by 48 per cent.[36] The US government responded with the steep Fordney-McCumber tariff of 1922, which made it harder for Europeans to earn the money they owed US banks through exports.[37] US tariffs also made it more difficult to secure participation in League-led tariff cooperation among Europeans because they were unwilling to open their markets without assurance that the United States would do the same. Shortly after raising its tariff in 1922, the United States formally adopted the standard 'unconditional' interpretation MFN. This gave US leaders new leverage to demand any tariff concessions that Europeans made to one another. They used their financial clout to force European governments to grant the United States highly asymmetrical tariff reductions on the basis of MFN, offering little in exchange.[38] The combination

[32] Eichengreen, *Golden Fetters*, 155–6.   [33] James, *The End of Globalization*, 116–17.
[34] Eichengreen, *Golden Fetters*, 153–63.
[35] Boyce, *British Capitalism at the Crossroads*, 35–41; Eichengreen, *Golden Fetters*, 153–9; Tooze, *The Deluge*, 354–65.
[36] A. Lewis, *Economic Survey, 1919–1939* (Blakiston Co., 1950), 33.
[37] Boyce, *The Great Interwar Crisis*, 83–5; Irwin, *Clashing over Commerce*, 352–65.
[38] P. Guillen, 'La politique douanière de la France dans les années vingt', *Relations Internationales*, 16 (1978), 315–31, 323–4.

of high US tariffs and forceful unilateral demands for trade concessions helped motivate Coquet, Riedl, and others to try to build a system of regional European integration that would exempt European trade cooperation from transatlantic MFN claims.

Alongside the general problems posed by transatlantic imbalances, Britain faced unique challenges stemming from its decision to rejoin the gold standard at the pound's pre-war parity of $4.86 to preserve the credibility of the City as a hub for international finance.[39] Devaluation could imperil the quite successful efforts to restore London's strong position in trade credit in the 1920s, as competition from New York banks mounted.[40] Yet a strong pound also hurt Britain's foreign trade by undercutting its exporters' competitiveness. In the 1920s, many other European governments opted to return to the gold standard at parities that were far below pre-war levels, most notably France. British economic officials initially predicted that a temporary bout of domestic unemployment would restore Britain's competitive position relative to economies with weaker currencies. They assumed that unemployment would produce wage and price reductions that would eventually give British exports an edge in international markets, but this never happened. As Keynes famously observed, wages had become 'sticky' by the 1920s, as more institutionalized labour markets and production processes impeded broad pay cuts. This led to a sustained pattern of high unemployment, high wages, high prices, and low growth. From 1921 to 1928, British unemployment never fell below 10 per cent and then it climbed steeply. In response, both workers and industrialists began to call for trade protection. In this context, Llewellyn Smith struggled to secure domestic backing for international trade liberalization.[41]

A Cautious Agenda for the 'Equitable Treatment of Commerce'

In Geneva, Llewellyn Smith steered the League trade agenda away from bold reform. Although formal leadership in the Economic Committee rotated on an annual basis, Llewellyn Smith kept a firm hand on its operations as the permanent chairman of a standing Sub-Committee on the Equitable Treatment of Commerce. He formed this Sub-Committee in 1921 to 'report on the meaning and scope' of Article 23(e) of the League Covenant, which defined the trade mission of the League as

[39] Boyce, *British Capitalism at the Crossroads*, 52–3.   [40] Cassis, *Capitals of Capital*, 163.
[41] Boyce, *British Capitalism at the Crossroads*, 35–78; Eichengreen, *Golden Fetters*, 153–67; Clavin, *The Great Depression in Europe*, 75; Trentmann, *Free Trade Nation*, 320–30.

promoting the 'equitable treatment for the commerce of all Members'.[42]
Nearly every major initiative handled by the Economic Committee filtered through Llewellyn Smith's sub-committee during his tenure from
1921 to 1927. In line with his cautious pragmatism, this body tackled a set
of specific, manageable tasks. The members decided against, 'the barren
academic labour of attempting to frame a definition of "equitable treatment"' and instead proceeded by 'enumerating the various classes of
practices which, in their judgment, clearly violated the principle of the
equitable treatment of commerce'.[43] This meant that the Economic
Committee sponsored a long series of small treaties in succession,
which enabled it to gradually establish a multilateral rule-making routine.
Although this piecemeal approach carried institutional advantages for the
young League of Nations, it marked a significant retreat when compared
to the proposals for a comprehensive commercial code that had been
considered at Paris Peace Conference in 1919.

German leaders were sensitive to the rupture between the lofty rhetoric
of the peace negotiations and the Economic Committee's practical activity because they were powerless to bridge that gap before Germany joined
the League in 1926. Some of the most perceptive criticism of the early
Economic Committee came from remote observers in Germany. As
Llewellyn Smith was outlining his modest vision for the League's trade
work, Bernhard Harms published an article in the *Weltwirtschaftliches
Archiv* which set out a more ambitious alternative agenda. The author
was Hans Wehberg, an international lawyer who worked for Harms
during the war and then became a key leader in the German League of
Nations Union. In 1920, Wehberg offered an expansive programme for
League trade policy based on the German draft of the League Covenant
that he and Harms had helped write in 1918. Measured against that
baseline, Wehberg considered Article 23(e) to be a very thin foundation
for international economic cooperation. He nevertheless declared that the
creation of a formal system of multilateral governance in Geneva was 'a
great advance' and predicted that, 'from this point, the number of economic questions tackled by the League will grow due to the force of
facts'.[44] He counselled against focusing on specific forms of discrimination, as Llewellyn Smith opted to do in the Sub-Committee on Equitable
Treatment. Rather, Wehberg endorsed Harms's plan to forge
a comprehensive international commercial community based on

---

[42] Article 23, *The Covenant of the League of Nations*.
[43] 'Reports by the Economic Committee. Report on Equitable Treatment of Commerce,
September 1922', *League of Nations Official Journal*, April 1923, 468–472.
[44] H. Wehberg, 'Verkehrsfreiheit und Völkerbund', *Weltwirtschaftliches Archiv*, 15 (1919),
468–80, 480.

a unified body of norms. Wehberg concluded that 'the hitherto legally regulated realm of economic relations' would have to be 'significantly extended' under the League.[45] Furthermore, he suggested that legal tools inherited from the nineteenth century must be adapted to manage the new political role that trade was called to play in international relations in the wake of the First World War.

Wehberg opened his article by reworking the classic nineteenth-century trope that free trade was the handmaiden of peace, remarking that 'it is not for nothing that the great champions of peace, such as Cobden, were also ardent supporters of free trade'.[46] Llewellyn Smith also claimed the legacy of Cobden, as a reformer who worked to construct open markets through international negotiation instead of following purer laissez-faire doctrine and relying on the free play of markets.[47] Wehberg looked beyond commercial treaties to sketch a broader and more muscular conception of Cobdenite 'free trade', based on a balanced distribution of territory, natural resources, and population:

Only when nations recognize one another as economically equal, when they do not aim to crush one another, but rather when each government has the necessary comprehension of the vital necessities of the other, only then is a peaceful association of states possible.[48]

Wehberg insisted that League trade policy could not be unlinked from outstanding territorial disputes. He hoped that a more robust system of international trade rules would generate reciprocal goodwill and thereby pave the way for an amicable revision of the post-war territorial settlement.[49] Wehberg's analysis reveals the heavy geopolitical burden placed on trade law in the 1920s by the conflicts over territory and security that were left unresolved after the Paris Peace Settlement. This context explains why a great deal of innovative energy was funnelled into League trade politics in the 1920s but only produced quite modest practical results. Many of the grander ideas that developed in the interwar crucible were not implemented until conflicts over defence and resources were offloaded onto more effectual institutions for collective security such as the North Atlantic Treaty Organization after 1945.[50] Wehberg devoted

[45] Wehberg, 'Verkehrsfreiheit und Völkerbund', 470–71.
[46] Wehberg, 'Verkehrsfreiheit und Völkerbund', 468.
[47] Llewellyn Smith, *The Board of Trade*, 63–4. On other interwar reinterpretations of Cobden's work that emphasized his internationalism, see Trentmann, *Free Trade Nation*, 265–6.
[48] Wehberg, 'Verkehrsfreiheit und Völkerbund', 468.
[49] Wehberg, 'Verkehrsfreiheit und Völkerbund', 468.
[50] K. K. Patel, *Project Europe: Myths and Realities of European Integration* (Cambridge University Press, 2020), 55–61.

particular attention to one fraught institutional issue – the intersection between multilateral trade policy and the League's regime of colonial mandates. Wehberg called for extensive League oversight of European colonial administration through the introduction of international standards for commercial access.[51]

Although there was relatively little economic discrimination against outside powers in British mandates, Llewellyn Smith insisted that the United Kingdom must retain the right to manage trade relations with mandates and all other imperial dependencies without interference from Geneva. He first affirmed this position at the Barcelona Conference and upheld it for the remainder of the 1920s. In practice, Britain ended up extending most League trade norms to most of its empire, but its insistence on preserving formal legal discretion in this matter precluded the creation of a fully universal system of commercial rights as demanded by Wehberg and Harms. The British legally partitioned international trade policy from disputes over colonial territory and natural resources. Yet at the same time, Llewellyn Smith and his British colleagues drew a direct link between League trade policy and the unresolved territorial conflicts in Central and Eastern Europe, in the other key area of League tutelage alongside the mandates. In the successor states, the British frequently claimed that freer trade would lower the stakes in border disputes.[52] Yet it was a delicate balancing act to promote trade cooperation in Europe while keeping a free hand in the British Empire. That balance was increasingly difficult to maintain as calls for exclusive systems of European and imperial commercial solidarity grew louder in the late 1920s, under pressure from a global agricultural crisis.[53]

Establishing a Multilateral Routine in League Trade Negotiations

Many of the Economic Committee's early projects for multilateral trade cooperation can be traced back to efforts to organize the post-imperial economies of Central and Eastern Europe at the Genoa Conference of 1922. Britain's prime minister, David Lloyd George, hoped to use the Genoa Conference to craft a sweeping economic, political, and military settlement that would bring Germany and Soviet Russia back into the international community. This strategy backfired when these two powers signed a separate side-agreement at Rapallo, which confirmed their

---

[51] Wehberg, 'Verkehrsfreiheit und Völkerbund', 478.

[52] G. Bátonyi, *Britain and Central Europe, 1918–1933* (Clarendon Press, 1999), 34–42.

[53] M. L. Dungy, 'The Global Agricultural Crisis and British Diplomacy in the League of Nations in 1931', *Agricultural History Review*, 65/2 (2017), 297–319.

wayward status.[54] Although the Genoa Conference failed in its diplomatic objectives, it did issue a long series of technical resolutions for freer trade in Central and Eastern Europe and passed this to-do list on to the League.[55] The Genoa Conference empowered the Economic Committee to facilitate administrative standardization in a range of areas, including customs formalities, quantitative restrictions, and commercial representation. Llewellyn Smith developed a new rule-making process to work through this list, beginning with customs formalities. In 1923 the League hosted the International Customs Conference in Geneva to produce an International Convention on the Simplification of Customs Formalities.[56] After Barcelona, this was the League's second major conference to negotiate formal economic conventions, and Llewellyn Smith deliberately used the occasion to create a multilateral routine. Point by point, the Economic Committee replicated the preparations for the Barcelona Conference: it gathered information about current practices and previous attempts to promote international cooperation; a small drafting committee used this material to sketch an international agreement and then circulated this draft text for review among technical experts, governments, and business leaders; finally the Economic Committee produced a final treaty for ratification through a formal diplomatic conference. This became the Economic Committee's standard operating procedure for writing trade rules.[57]

At the 1923 Customs Conference, Llewellyn Smith frequently referred to procedural precedents set in Barcelona. As he had done before, he intervened early to guide the conference towards the conclusion of a formal convention. He also used consultation with business leaders to build pressure for a binding outcome, declaring that 'the commercial world expected the Conference to arrive at a definite convention'. Étienne Clémentel confirmed this view at the conference, speaking on behalf of the 'commercial world' as the ICC's president.[58] Llewellyn Smith distributed copies of the Barcelona Convention on Freedom of

[54] Z. Steiner, *The Lights That Failed: European International History 1919–1933* (Oxford University Press, 2005), 162–8; Tooze, *The Deluge*, 428–36.
[55] *Papers Relating to International Economic Conference, Genoa, April–May, 1922* (H. M. G. Stationery Office, 1922), 70–74; C. Fink, *The Genoa Conference: European Diplomacy, 1921–1922* (University of North Carolina Press, 1984), 246–57; Clavin and Wessels, 'Transnationalism and the League of Nations', 23.
[56] League of Nations, *1. International Convention Relating to the Simplification of Customs Formalities 2. Protocol to the International Convention*, C. 678.M.241 (League of Nations, 1924).
[57] League of Nations, *International Conference on Customs and other Similar Formalities: Proceedings of the Conference*, vol. II, C.66.M.24.1924.II (League of Nations, 1924), 313–15.
[58] *International Conference on Customs and Other Similar Formalities: Proceedings of the Conference*, vol. I, C.66.M.24.1924.II (League of Nations, 1924), 65, 66.

Transit as a model for a binding convention and helped import its procedural articles on signature, ratification, and revision into the new convention on customs formalities. Over time, the Legal Section of the
Secretariat helped make these articles into a common legal core for all
multilateral trade conventions. This core included an important article
whereby signatories agreed to revise all previous treaty commitments,
multilateral and bilateral, to bring them in line with the agreement
under discussion. This made the League a central framework for integrating existing international economic law.[59]

Llewellyn Smith was able to carry nineteenth-century trade law into
the League though careful and determined innovation, but he was also
living proof that writing binding multilateral trade rules required
a tremendous political and institutional investment. Several delegates
at the Customs Conference who were members of the Economic
Committee underscored the importance of Llewellyn Smith's leadership. They emphasized that the project originated in his personal fiefdom, the Sub-Committee on Equitable Treatment, where he 'was at
once its chairman and its life and soul'.[60] Over the League's lifetime,
few, if any, other members of the Economic Committee were able to
match Llewellyn Smith's commanding influence over the multilateral
process, to shepherd agreements from conception to final ratification.
Indeed, he did not retain that influence long as competing voices quickly
emerged in the Economic Committee and beyond. Nevertheless, as
subsequent chapters will show, Llewellyn Smith's challengers continued to use the basic multilateral toolkit that he built during the
early 1920s to address new problems and objectives, adding their own
modifications in the process.

The 1923 Convention on Customs Formalities also attained a wide
geographic reach that was rarely achieved in subsequent agreements. It
was eventually ratified by thirty-five governments around the world
including all the Habsburg successor states as well as several British
Dominions and French protectorates.[61] Brazil also ratified the agreement
and advised other members of the Pan-American Union to align their
policies with it.[62] Debates over imperial preference at the 1923 Customs
Conference revealed how difficult it was to unite imperial, American, and

---

[59] International Conference on Customs and Other Similar Formalities: Proceedings of the
Conference, vol. I, 59, 64–6, 103.
[60] International Conference on Customs and Other Similar Formalities: Proceedings of the
Conference, vol. I, 130.
[61] League of Nations, Commercial Policy in the Interwar Period: International Proposals and
National Policies, II.A.6 (League of Nations, 1942), 91.
[62] International Conference on Customs and Other Similar Formalities: Proceedings of the
Conference, vol. I, 132.

European communities in a common commercial system. The Brazilian, Chilean, and Uruguayan delegates jointly submitted a motion to bar preferential customs treatment for intra-imperial trade, noting that their agricultural goods competed directly with Dominion exports on UK markets. Llewellyn Smith responded by dutifully defending *inter se* and reiterating that intra-imperial trade fell outside the purview of League conventions. He nevertheless gave the Latin American delegates verbal assurance that 'it was beyond question that Great Britain had every intention, if it signed this Convention, of conferring loyally all its advantages upon all the contracting States'.[63] Here we can see Llewellyn Smith straining to juggle national and imperial priorities. As a representative of the British Empire, he could not repudiate *inter se* outright. At the same time, as a representative of the UK Board of Trade, he was trying to use the League to keep Latin American markets open to British commerce. In 1923, Llewellyn Smith was able to unite European, Latin American, and Dominion partners partly because they were not actually discussing tariff levels and thus avoided the most contentious forms of imperial preference. The 1923 Convention on Customs Formalities only addressed administrative and procedural impediments to trade, such as discrimination in import and export licences, inspections for quality and hygiene, and certificates of origin. It also contained measures to facilitate the mobility of commercial travellers and their product samples, as part of the Economic Committee's long campaign to improve the 'treatment of foreigners' tied to trade.[64] It covered many of the same policy areas that were later included in the GATT and was a frequent reference point in the initial negotiations for that agreement.[65]

Llewellyn Smith saw the 1923 Convention on Customs Formalities as the template for a multilateral routine that could be applied to the list of other policy goals that the League inherited from the Genoa

---

[63] *International Conference on Customs and Other Similar Formalities: Proceedings of the Conference*, vol. I, 76–8.

[64] *International Convention Relating to the Simplification of Customs Formalities.*

[65] Preparatory Committee of the International Conference on Trade and Employment, Committee II. Technical Sub-Committee, Comments of the French Delegation on Articles 9 to 16 and 32 of the Proposed Charter of International Trade of the United Nations, 26 October 1946, WTO: GATT, E/PC/T/C.II/12; Preparatory Committee of the International Conference on Trade and Employment, Committee II. Technical Sub-Committee, Comments of the Delegations of the Netherlands and of the Belgian-Luxembourg Economic Union Concerning General Commercial Policy, 30 October 1946, WTO: GATT, E/PC/T/C.II/12; Preparatory Committee of the International Conference on Trade and Employment, A.6 (United States of America Article 13), Customs Formalities, 4 November 1946, WTO: GATT, E/PC/T/C.II/W.7/Add.; J. H. Jackson, *The World Trading System: Law and Policy of International Economic Relations*, 2nd ed. (MIT Press, 1997), 35.

Conference. In the end, he mainly advanced the standardization of business regulation. Working in concert with the ICC, Llewellyn Smith sponsored a series of initiatives on contract arbitration, intellectual property, commercial intermediaries, and bills of exchange, which will be discussed in more detail in Chapter Seven. Yet in the realm of public trade administration, Llewellyn Smith and the Economic Committee made little further concrete progress after 1923.

The Limits of Incremental Compromise in Trade Administration

Shortly after the 1923 Customs Conference, Llewellyn Smith sought to tackle a knottier area of trade policy: prohibitions. European governments had introduced prohibitions on imports and exports during and after the war to conserve raw materials and currency reserves, and to foster strategic industries. Traders could usually apply for a special licence to sell prohibited goods within a specified quota, but the approval process was often arbitrary and based on political criteria. Italian, Austrian, and German firms claimed that the other Habsburg successor states frequently denied them licences based on their nationality. The Genoa Conference had highlighted prohibitions as a source of rancour in Central and Eastern Europe, and in response the 1923 Convention on Customs Formalities included some provisions to try to ensure a more transparent allocation of licences.[66] In 1924, the Italian delegation prodded the Economic Committee to go further and eliminate prohibitions altogether through a new international convention. This was part of Italy's ongoing efforts to secure a stable supply of raw materials as a matter of national security. In the wake of the First World War, resource competition was frequently discussed as a threat to peace, but League collaborators offered several different solutions to this problem. Some, such as Clémentel, called for a direct international allocation of commodities according to need, on the model of the Allies' wartime administration. Yet in the 1920s, Salter and most other members of the EFO took the opposite tack, demanding full free trade in raw materials to prevent states from exerting geopolitical pressure by restricting supplies. The Prohibitions Convention was the most ambitious attempt to institutionalize that free trade approach. Alongside the more or less interventionist models of cooperation, there was also a third, more disruptive unilateral option: direct revision of territorial

---

[66] Article 3, *International Convention Relating to the Simplification of Customs Formalities.*

boundaries to secure a resource base.[67] The Fascists embraced this approach after international cooperation failed to address Italian concerns about the resource-population calculus, leading to increasingly assertive colonial claims that eventually culminated in the invasion of Ethiopia in 1935.[68]

In the Economic Committee, Llewellyn Smith gave strong backing to early Italian demands to ban prohibitions, but the scheme was ultimately undermined by Britain's own reluctance to loosen its grip on strategic supply chains. Llewellyn Smith linked the Prohibitions Convention with the League's mission to advance 'equitable' trade rather than full free trade. For, even if states substituted high tariffs for prohibitions, as was likely, he argued that progress would be made because tariffs were less likely to be applied in a discriminatory manner. The devil was in the details, however. There was broad support for the elimination of most prohibitions in League circles, but all governments demanded the right to preserve a few prohibitions to protect 'vital' commercial and security interests. Llewellyn Smith argued that such exemptions should be permitted but kept to a minimum.[69] Ironically, in the end the whole project was wrecked by a British demand to preserve a prohibition that Llewellyn Smith had helped to introduce. The crucial sticking point was synthetic dyes. As explained in Chapter Two, Llewellyn Smith had called for a prohibition on British imports of synthetic dyes to encourage the development of a secure domestic supply. Britain had been heavily reliant on German dye imports before 1914 and this had impeded wartime production of textiles and explosives (the latter depending on chemical processes linked to dye-making). Consequently, the Board of Trade singled out dyes for special protection after the war. While it 'safeguarded' other strategic industries using tariffs, it passed special legislation to protect synthetic dyes with an import prohibition, moderated by licences.[70] The Board of Trade was firmly committed to preserving this one prohibition, even as it backed the League's general efforts to eliminate the practice.[71] Britain's determination to protect dyes decisively undermined diplomatic negotiations for a final convention, which began just after Llewellyn Smith retired

---

[67] Ingulstad, 'Regulating the Regulators', 241.

[68] Tollardo, *Fascist Italy and the League of Nations, 1922–1935*, 26–7, 47, 164, 183.

[69] League of Nations. Economic Committee. Sub-Committee on the Equitable Treatment of Commerce. 13th Session, 1–5 March 1925, LON: R/308, 10/50616/6105.

[70] Position of the Dye-Making Industry, Memorandum by the President of the Board of Trade, 29 November 1920, TNA: CAB/24/115/92.

[71] Convention for the Abolition of Import and Export Prohibitions and Restrictions, Memorandum by the President of the Board of Trade, 10 October 1928, TNA: CAB 24/297/45.

from the Board of Trade in 1927. The Germans accurately perceived that the British dye prohibition was directed against them and responded by demanding an exemption to keep their own quantitative restrictions on coal, thus preserving an important weapon in an ongoing German–Polish trade war. These exemptions for highly politicized dye and coal prohibitions from Europe's commercial giants provoked an avalanche of special requests from other governments.[72]

The Convention on Prohibitions went through several further rounds of negotiations until it was more holes than cloth. The negotiations in 1927 produced a provisional agreement that listed many exemptions and allowed governments to demand more carve-outs. A second conference was held in 1928 to consider these additional requests and to finalize the convention. This gathering produced further side-agreements that laid out special provisions for trade in hides and bones. Even with these qualifications, the final convention did not reach the requisite threshold of ratifications. A third conference on prohibitions was held in December 1929 to try to salvage the project but once again failed to produce a workable compromise. It met in Paris immediately after a similarly fruitless conference to debate a draft convention protecting commercial intermediaries, which Richard Riedl had spearheaded. The back-to-back failure of these two treaty projects in November and December 1929 severely undermined confidence in the Economic Committee's procedure of incremental multilateral trade cooperation.[73]

The long saga of the Prohibitions Convention demonstrated the limits of Llewellyn Smith's strategy to use the League of Nations to reinforce general principles of open trade while allowing Britain to protect its own strategic interests. In multilateral negotiations, it was very difficult to secure a special exemption for one country's 'vital interests' without opening the floodgates to similar demands from other states. The politicization of foreign trade during the First World War made uniform multilateral rules more attractive to European leaders but also more difficult to achieve. Llewellyn Smith had hoped that compromise between conflicting national priorities could be hammered out gradually through successive rounds of consultation with political and economic stakeholders. The Prohibitions Convention demonstrated that this method could also simply lead to gridlock.

[72] D. Serruys to Commerce, Travaux Publics et Relations Commerciales, 29 October 1927, AMAE: Y/629.
[73] *Commercial Policy in the Interwar Period*, 32–5; League of Nations, *International Conference on the Abolition of Import and Export Prohibitions and Restrictions*, C. 559.M.201.1927.II (Geneva, 1927).

The 1927 World Economic Conference

Well before the final failure of the Prohibitions Convention, the World Economic Conference of 1927 had already presented a more direct challenge to Llewellyn Smith's model of incremental cooperation. The idea for the conference came from the French minister of finance, Louis Loucheur. Loucheur was an engineer who had made a fortune before the war in electricity. After serving as the wartime minister of munitions, he circulated through various ministerial posts in the 1920s and was a frequent presence in Geneva. Loucheur was an early advocate of Franco-German industrial cooperation through reparations-in-kind and cartels and hoped to build support in the League for those policies.[74] Llewellyn Smith firmly opposed Loucheur's conference as a threat to the ongoing work of the EFO. It risked undermining the League's fragile authority by suggesting that 'it was necessary to establish a new body to do in an effective way the work that the organisations of the League had failed to do'. Llewellyn Smith insisted that the 'slow progress' made by the young Economic and Financial Committees was 'due to the complicated and delicate nature of the problems with which they were dealing'. He advised that Loucheur's conference 'would do well to adopt the same cautious methods'.[75] Early in his tenure on the Economic Committee, Llewellyn Smith had mused that the proper function of an economic conference was to 'complete and endorse definite schemes of international action'. It should not 'explore fresh ground and exchange views of a more or less non-committal character on a wide variety of topics'.[76] The 1927 World Economic Conference violated every one of those principles, underscoring how thoroughly that event challenged Llewellyn Smith's approach.

The World Economic Conference was a massive gathering of roughly four hundred experts and delegates from fifty states who met for three weeks in May 1927.[77] Discussion ranged widely, covering agriculture, industry, and trade (though not finance). As Michele d'Alessandro and Quinn Slobodian explain, the conference helped foster more intensive

---

[74] E. Bussière, 'Les aspects économiques du projet Briand: essai de mise en perspective de l'Europe des producteurs aux tentatives régionales', in A. Fleury and L. Jílek (eds.), *The Briand Plan of European Federal Union: National and Transnational Perspectives, with Documents* (Peter Lang, 1998), pp. 75–92.
[75] 'Records of the Sixth Assembly. Meetings of the Committees. Minutes of the Second Committee', *League of Nations Official Journal, Special Supplement* (1925), 46–7.
[76] H. Llewellyn Smith, 'Draft Report on the Future Economic Organisation of the League of Nations', 31 January 1921, LON: Salter/S 134.
[77] *Actes de la Conférence Économique Internationale tenu à Genève du 4 au 23 Mai 1927*, vol. I, C.356.M.129.1927.II (League of Nations, 1927), 11; Clavin, *Securing the World Economy*, 42–3.

collaboration between League institutions and independent economic organizations, notably the ICC.[78] It was a pivotal event for Llewellyn Smith, Coquet, Harms, and Riedl, and they illustrate the diversity of actors and perspectives that the conference brought together. Llewellyn Smith attended the conference as a representative of the Economic Committee and fought a rearguard campaign to defend his early handiwork. The other three men offered programmes for reform that departed in new directions. Riedl was part of the Austrian delegation, representing the Austrian National Committee of the ICC. He outlined an ambitious scheme to shift European tariff negotiations from a bilateral to a regional footing. Lucien Coquet had helped develop a similar French plan for a European customs union in dialogue with Riedl, which he circulated in an unofficial memorandum to the conference. Neither Coquet nor Bernhard Harms was a formal conference delegate. Coquet did attend as an observer and made important diplomatic contacts that later served his outreach efforts. Bernhard Harms watched attentively from afar, staging a full re-enactment of the conference with his students in Kiel, complete with national delegations, committees, and a press corps.[79] In the years following the World Economic Conference, Harms helped sustain dialogue among the diverse actors and organizations that had gathered there and also strove to build new bridges with US partners. After Llewellyn Smith crafted the basic architecture of League trade policy in the early 1920s, Coquet, Harms, and Riedl constructed new networks of political activism and intellectual exchange around it, using the World Economic Conference as their springboard.

In the late 1920s, broader engagement with the League's trade policy also filtered through the Economic Consultative Committee, formed in 1928 to oversee the implementation of the resolutions from the World Economic Conference. The Economic Consultative Committee assumed the agenda-setting function that had been previously performed by Llewellyn Smith's Sub-Committee on Equitable Treatment of Commerce. The Consultative Committee was a much larger body. It had more than fifty members representing industry, agriculture, commerce, labour, and consumers. In contrast, the Sub-Committee on

[78] M. d'Alessandro, 'Global Economic Governance and the Private Sector: The League of Nations' Experiment in the 1920s', in C. Dejung and N. P. Petersson (eds.), *The Foundations of Worldwide Economic Integration: Power, Institutions, and Global Markets, 1850–1930* (Cambridge University Press, 2013), pp. 249–70, 260–61; Slobodian, *Globalists*, 37–41; Ridgeway, *Merchants of Peace*, 227–49; Boyce, *The Great Interwar Crisis*, 175–6.

[79] L. Coquet and A. Pawlowski to P. Berthelot, 26 October 1928, AMAE: RC/B27/30; F. Hoffmann, 'Die Geschichte des Instituts für Weltwirtschaft', 3 vols., unpublished manuscript, IfW (1943–5), vol. II, p. 253.

Equitable Treatment had only included eight members, and nearly all of them were public trade officials.[80] The Economic Consultative Committee overturned Llewellyn Smith's vision of League trade policy as a tightly controlled space for inter-ministerial consultation.

Trade Policy and Social Welfare

The influx of new actors and ideas into League trade policy that came with the World Economic Conference helped recentre discussion on social issues. As the main architect of Britain's unemployment insurance system, Llewellyn Smith backed national legislation to create a social safety net but did not see wide scope to advance that goal through international trade policy. He wrote an early memorandum for the Secretariat on cooperation between the Economic Committee and the ILO. He noted that trade policy influenced 'the increase or diminution of the production and consumption of commodities', and that these changes 'have direct and important reactions on the welfare of the workers which manifest themselves in such phenomena as fluctuations of employment, wages, and cost of living'. He suggested that the Economic Committee should bear these welfare consequences in mind and should also assess how trade performance was impacted by 'relief works, doles, unemployment insurance, etc'. To achieve these goals, Llewellyn Smith called for a regular exchange of information between the Economic Committee and the ILO.[81] He did not, however, propose to use trade regulation as a direct tool of social policy to promote full employment, as advocated in the 1930s and 1940s by later League collaborators such as James Meade.[82]

At the World Economic Conference, Daniel Serruys, France's top trade official, challenged the clear separation that Llewellyn Smith drew between social and trade policy. He proposed a common agreement to allow 'compensatory' tariffs that would equalize differences in wage rates and social protection as well as differential access to natural resources (Clémentel's old bugbear).[83] There was strong pushback against this proposal from many other conference delegates who argued that Serruys was simply providing cover for France's high tariffs. In the end,

[80] d'Alessandro, 'Global Economic Governance and the Private Sector', 262.
[81] H. Llewellyn Smith, Collaboration with the International Labour Office in the Enquiry on Unemployment, 11 May 1923, LON: 10/21233/21233.
[82] 'A Proposal for an International Commercial Union', in J. E. Meade, *The Collected Papers of James Meade* (Unwin Hyman, 1988), vol. III: International Economics, 27–35; Clavin, *Securing the World Economy*, 280–82.
[83] *Actes de la Conférence Économique Internationale*, vol. II, C.356.M.129.1927.II (League of Nations, 1927), 50.

the conference cut out explicit references to compensatory duties but agreed to expand the concept of 'equitable treatment of commerce' to include an explicit reference to wages and consumption. It was Walter Layton, the Liberal editor of *The Economist* newspaper, who preserved that language from Serruys's original proposal because, he argued it was important to acknowledge the importance of 'consumers' purchasing power' in some way.[84] Layton's intervention reflected the growing influence of the consumer cooperative movement in Britain and Europe during and after the First World War, led by an increasingly active corps of female voters and politicians.[85] However, in European economic policy, consumer interests were often superseded by the priorities of older capital-intensive sectors such as metallurgy, where there was a strong preoccupation with the dangers of overproduction in the wake of the war.[86]

In the preparations and proceedings of the World Economic Conference, consumers were primarily represented by Emmy Freundlich, a Social Democratic parliamentarian from Austria and the long-serving president of the International Co-operative Women's Guild. Freundlich forcefully denounced mounting trade barriers as a driver of consumer price rises but also insisted that more open markets would not be sufficient to ensure stable consumption and production. She suggested that household economy must be 'rationalized' in line with broader systems of production and distribution and demanded international supervision of cartels to defend consumer interests. While Llewellyn Smith had carefully avoided direct international intervention in market processes, Freundlich argued that open trade should be combined with a high level of organization at the local level.[87] She thus anticipated the evolution that the EFO later followed in the 1930s and 1940s. After the onset of the Great Depression, the EFO remained committed to reducing trade barriers but also began to try to support local systems of production and consumption more directly.[88]

Freundlich's presence on the world stage provoked considerable comment, revealing contemporary attitudes about women in international trade policy. The Austrian government protested vehemently when Freundlich was given the sole seat allocated to Austria on the preparatory committee for the World Economic Conference. Austrian leaders tried

[84] *Actes de la Conférence Économique Internationale*, vol. II, 72.
[85] Trentmann, *Free Trade Nation*, 191–240.
[86] Maier, *Recasting Bourgeois Europe*, 545.
[87] *Actes de la Conférence Économique Internationale*, vol. I, 77–8; *Actes de la Conférence Économique Internationale*, vol. II, 145, 175–6, 180–81.
[88] Clavin, *Securing the World Economy*, 159–92, 305–40.

hard, to no avail, to secure a second appointment for an official who more thoroughly 'mastered the problem of trade policy'. They suggested Richard Schüller, who was slated to take the new Austrian seat on the Economic Committee.[89] When the Economic Committee expanded in 1928 to include Austrian, German, and US seats, there was discussion about also adding a 'woman member'. Significantly, both the defenders and critics of this proposal took it for granted that a 'woman member' would not have general macroeconomic competence but instead would speak about 'domestic questions' from the viewpoint of the consumer. Gustav Stresemann underscored this point by noting that technically all governments were free to recommend a woman to serve as their primary trade representative on the Economic Committee, but, personally, he 'thought it would be better to confine the membership of that committee to men'.[90] In the end, there never was a female member of the Economic Committee. Freundlich served as an expert on consumer cooperatives in the auxiliary Economic Consultative Committee, alongside representatives from other organizations such as the ICC and the International Institute of Agriculture.

MFN As a Framework for International Trade Politics

Llewellyn Smith helped shift discussion at the World Economic Conference away from concrete concerns about consumption and production towards more abstract normative questions. His main intervention was to assert the primacy of MFN as the legal mainstay for global markets. After considerable debate on the matter, he wrote the final conference resolution that affirmed MFN in its 'widest and most liberal interpretation'.[91] Through this resolution, the conference empowered the League to define a standard definition of MFN and to prescribe its application in bilateral treaties. This was a pivotal moment when the trade treaty system inherited from the nineteenth century began to be reconfigured around a central institutional nucleus in Geneva.[92] The Economic Committee proceeded to spend two years conducting a thorough survey of previous treaty practice to produce a standard five-paragraph MFN clause in 1929. This text was

---

[89] Wildner to Duffek, 18 February 1925, ÖStA: AdR, AA/Handelspolitik/549.
[90] 'Second Meeting (Public, Then Private)', *League of Nations Official Journal*, 9/2 (1928), 133.
[91] *Actes de la Conférence Économique Internationale*, vol. II, 83; Members of the International Economic Conference to the President of the Board of Trade, 24 May 1927, TNA: FO 371/12659.
[92] *Actes de la Conférence Économique Internationale*, vol. I, 43 Economic Committee, Report to the Council on the Work of the Twenty-Seventh Session, 23 January 1929, LON: C.20.1929.II.

incorporated with minimal modifications into bilateral trade treaties around the world, including in those signed by non-League members such as the United States. This process established the League as the central guardian of a common legal system that linked together bilateral trade treaties in a standardized network.

Although it was Llewellyn Smith who intervened to enshrine MFN in League trade law, the German government was the most dogged champion of this norm in actual diplomatic practice. In the 1920s, German leaders considered it a top priority to reclaim the MFN rights that had been stripped from the country through the Treaty of Versailles.[93] In the process, Germany helped rally the commercial world around MFN. Soviet Russia concluded its first MFN agreement as part of the Russo-German Treaty of Rapallo signed during the 1922 Genoa Conference. Thereafter, it concluded a long series of MFN treaties to expand its commercial access to Western markets.[94] The United States also signed its very first unconditional MFN treaty with Germany in 1923, signalling its commitment to the country's economic recovery during the Franco-Belgian occupation of the German Ruhr. The US embrace of MFN in its treaty with Germany also marked the culmination of the gradual evolution initiated by Wilson away from the traditional US policy of reciprocal preferences towards 'equality of treatment'.[95] Patrick Cohrs explains that Wilson's Republican successors saw Germany as an important 'auxiliary power' that aided US efforts to pry open European markets for US exports under the banner of MFN.[96] Shortly after the World Economic Conference in 1927, France finally agreed to grant Germany unconditional MFN rights for most goods. This was an important agreement that consolidated lower rates on roughly two-thirds of France's tariff items. Thus, the treaty effectively formed the basis for a new French tariff.[97]

After 1927, the Franco-German agreement became the template for further treaties with other European partners, making the Franco-German pairing the nucleus of the European trade treaty system.[98]

---

[93] M. Schulz, *Deutschland, der Völkerbund und die Frage der europäischen Wirtschaftsordnung, 1925–1933* (Krämer, 1997), 47.

[94] E. Ustor, 'First Report on the Most-Favoured-Nation Clause', *United Nations Yearbook of the International Law Commission*, vol. II, 1969, 163–6; Steiner, *The Lights That Failed*, 166.

[95] Treaty between the United States of America and Germany, 8 December 1923, in J. V. Fuller (ed.), FRUS 1923, vol. II (United States Printing Office, 1938), doc. 28.

[96] Cohrs, *The Unfinished Peace*, 83.

[97] Guillen, 'La politique douanière de la France dans les années vingt'.

[98] Bussière, 'Les aspects économiques du projet Briand', 78–9; Bussière, *La France, la Belgique et l'organisation économique de l'Europe*, 281–5.

Germany had occupied that position alone from 1892 to 1914 after superseding France. The 1927 Franco-German trade agreement was thus a significant development which stimulated ambitions for European economic unity from Riedl, Coquet, and their partners. Well beyond the Franco-German network, the World Economic Conference helped initiate a treaty-making frenzy. Roughly seventy MFN treaties were signed in the two years following the conference.[99] In 1928, Salter affirmed that '1927 was prominently a year of commercial treaties', citing this trend as one of the main practical results of the conference.[100] Although the profusion of new trade law was generally seen as a positive trend in Geneva, many League collaborators argued that bilateral MFN treaties were not a sufficient basis for equitable and stable international markets.

MFN meant very different things in different national tariff systems, as Daniel Serruys emphasized at the 1927 conference. Serruys had entered France's Ministry of Commerce during the war as a protégé of Clémentel, and he inherited the gargantuan task of rebuilding France's treaty system after Clémentel's mass denunciation of MFN agreements in 1918. Serruys concluded over sixty new agreements as France's top trade nego-tiator in the 1920s.[101] In the process he gained a very thorough under-standing of different countries' treaty policies. At the World Economic Conference, Serruys outlined the wide diversity of 'contractual methods' that underpinned tariff agreements. Some states set their tariffs unilat-erally, based on internal production priorities and fiscal needs. This category included high-tariff countries such as the United States and low-tariff countries such as the United Kingdom. Other governments set 'conventional' tariffs at provisional rates that could then be negotiated downwards through treaties. This practice was followed in most of Continental Europe. A few governments used a 'double-column tariff', specifying high 'general' rates which were applied by default and a second set of 'minimum' rates to be accorded to treaty partners. France had followed this practice since 1892 before adopting conventional tariffs on most items through the Franco-German treaty of 1927. Within each of these tariff systems MFN rights could be *restricted* to certain products or certain kinds of regulations, and they could also be made *conditional*, meaning that benefits would only be transferred from one partner to the

---

[99] Boyce, *The Great Interwar Crisis*, 177.
[100] Speech by Sir Arthur Salter, 4 October 1928, LON: R 2663, 10A/3672/3672.
[101] Badel, *Un milieu libéral et européen*, 93. On Serruys's longer career trajectory, see Badel, *Un milieu libéral et européen*, 93–4, 131–92; Badel, *Diplomatie et grands contrats*, 92–4; L. Badel, 'Littéraires, libéraux et Européens: l'autre versant de la construction européenne', *Journal of European Integration History*, 3/2 (1997), 23–33.

next if both of them granted equivalent counter-concessions. Serruys argued that *unrestricted* and *unconditional* MFN – as advocated by Llewellyn Smith and many others – did not guarantee 'equitable treatment'. The United States was a case in point. The US government had adopted an unconditional and unrestricted interpretation of MFN in 1923, while simultaneously introducing very high tariffs. In the 1920s, the US government forcefully demanded full MFN rights in foreign markets – focusing especially on protectionist France – but in exchange it only gave partners equal access to a 'closed door' (a play on the 'open-door' concept that US leaders ballyhooed).[102]

The legal tangle resulting from the application of MFN rights in different tariff systems had already created considerable friction in the nineteenth century. Serruys emphasized that this complexity became more problematic in the 1920s because most governments (including France) signed treaties with a much shorter duration. At the World Economic Conference, Riedl illustrated this point in a vast survey of 248 European trade treaties that had been signed since 1918. Riedl found that only ninety treaties covered tariffs, and a mere fifteen had a fixed term, as had been the standard practice before 1914. All the others could be denounced on short notice, usually a few months.[103] Interwar governments were less willing to stabilize their trade policy through long-term trade treaties, and they also resorted to tariff hikes more frequently and for more diverse reasons. Factors including currency instability, corporatist political negotiations, and the enhanced security role of many industrial sectors had combined to drive up tariffs after the war.[104] In this complex and unpredictable environment, many delegates at the World Economic Conference demanded that the League provide more substantial multilateral guidance for trade policy, beyond the simple standardization of MFN. Riedl was the conference delegate who carried this logic the furthest.

Riedl called for a fundamentally different approach to tariff negotiations using the League's multilateral machinery. He demanded a wholesale shift away from 'the system of isolated and strictly bilateral negotiations' that had been used in the past towards a new regime based on 'joint negotiations between a group of states who have agreed beforehand to reduce their tariffs to the lowest degree possible'.[105] To manage

---

[102] D. Serruys, *Commercial Treaties: Tariff Systems and Contractual Methods* C.E.I.31 (League of Nations: 1927); *Actes de la Conférence Économique Internationale*, vol. II, 80–82; Cohrs, *The Unfinished Peace*, 83.

[103] Österreichisches Nationalkomitee der Internationalen Handelskammer, *Übersicht über die Europäischen Handelsverträge*, 1927, ÖStA, AVA/NL Riedl/82.

[104] James, *The End of Globalization*, 108–20.

[105] League of Nations, *Report and Proceedings of the World Economic Conference Held at Geneva, May 4th to 23rd, 1927*, vol. II, C.356.M129.1927.II (Geneva, 1927), 49.

this process, Riedl recommended the creation of a Permanent Conference on Tariff and Trade Questions.[106] This scheme appealed to Secretariat officials because it redefined multilateralism as continuous and open-ended dialogue and not a sequence of distinct treaty initiatives, as under Llewellyn Smith.[107] As a first step, Riedl proposed a temporary 'tariff truce' as well as a common upper limit on tariffs in order to create breathing space for a round of simultaneous bilateral tariff negotiations over a period of several years. Although the conference did not formally endorse these ideas, they permeated League trade debates and the surrounding associational networks, with considerable help from Coquet's UDE. In 1927 and 1928, Paul Elbel, one of Serruys's main collaborators who was then on leave from the Ministry of Commerce, worked with Coquet and his partners to develop a plan for a European customs union that borrowed many ideas from Riedl.[108] Their plan identified MFN as the broader superstructure that would anchor a regional customs union in the League of Nations.[109] Prevailing treaty norms exempted a full European customs union from outside MFN claims, without any need for legal or institutional innovation. Yet neither Riedl nor Coquet thought that European governments would be able to adopt a full customs union in one fell swoop. Both contemplated a gradual process of integration through progressive tariff reductions over many years. This would have to be covered by a novel exemption for free trade agreements that fell short of a full customs union. Thus, Riedl and Coquet's projects for promoting European unity fed into a broader debate about multilateral and global order in trade law.

MFN Rights and Multilateral Agreements: The General and the Particular

The World Economic Conference affirmed MFN as the core of the international treaty system and also endorsed 'collective action' to reduce tariffs through multilateral agreements, framing a central legal tension that has remained at the heart of international trade

---

[106] International Chamber of Commerce, *Report of the Trade Barriers Committee Presented to the Preparatory Committee of the Economic Conference of the League of Nations*, Brochure no. 44 (Herbert Clarke, 1927), 14–17, 28.

[107] R. Riedl to P. Stoppani, 11 November 1926, LON: R471, 10/55342/55342.

[108] Union Douanière Européenne, Comité Français d'Études, Rapports des Commissions, 1928, AN: F12/9416.

[109] Quoted in L. Coquet and A. Pawlowski, Union Douanière Européenne, Mémoire présenté à la Conférence Economique Internationale convoquée par l'Union Internationale des Associations pour la Société des Nations, October 1926, AMAE: RC/B27/47.

policy.[110] This was partly a conflict over the place of regional European unity in the League, but it also concerned a more fundamental question: was the new multilateral rule-making process that Llewellyn Smith helped craft in the Economic Committee compatible with the general treaty norms of non-discrimination handed down from the nineteenth century? Walter Stucki, the Swiss member of the Economic Committee was asked to prepare a report on this MFN-multilateral puzzle. He explained that according to current treaty practice 'a state may, on the basis of a bilateral treaty containing the most-favoured-nation clause, claim the advantages accorded under an international convention, even when it is not party to that convention, and has not assumed the obligations arising thereunder'. This requirement would 'constitute a serious obstacle' to cooperation in the League of Nations.[111] Salter concurred that 'the application of the [MFN] clause in its fullest sense and without any exception whatever, cuts away the very basis on which multilateral conventions are negotiated'.[112] At the same time, Salter insisted that MFN remained a valuable tool to combat tariff discrimination and thus should not be abandoned altogether. Stucki emphasized the novelty of the legal problems confronted, for they 'only arose, when, under the auspices of the League of Nations, the question of plurilateral economic conventions acquired practical importance'. Stucki suggested a method for the League to manage the new legal conundrum which it had created through its multilateralism. He recommended that the League outline a new MFN exemption for multilateral agreements to be inserted into bilateral treaties. To avoid endorsing protectionist blocks, he argued that this exemption should be reserved for 'conventions of a general character', which were 'intended to improve international economic relations as a whole', were 'open to the accession of all states', and were '*concluded under the auspices of the League of Nations*' [original emphasis].[113]

Stucki acted as the spokesman for a group of small, trade-dependent West European states – including the Netherlands, Switzerland, Belgium, and Austria – that all saw a strong advantage in multilateral trade

[110] Clavin, *Securing the World Economy*, 44; Boyce, *The Great Interwar Crisis*, 252.

[111] League of Nations. Economic Committee. The effect of the most-favoured-nation clause in bilateral treaties upon plurilateral Conventions, 28 March 1928, LON: R 2727, 10C/2383/578.

[112] Arthur Salter, The 'United States of Europe' Idea, LON: 2 September 1929, R2868 10D/14711/14711.

[113] League of Nations. Economic Committee. The effect of the most-favoured-nation clause in bilateral treaties upon plurilateral Conventions, 28 March 1928, LON: R 2727, 10C/2383/578.

negotiations. These countries had limited bargaining power in bilateral negotiations, but they were often able to exercise outsized influence over multilateral rules due to their strong traditions of international law and international administration. Madeleine Herren traces the emergence of this pattern of 'back-door' power politics in nineteenth-century internationalism.[114] In the 1920s, the Netherlands, Switzerland, Belgium, and Austria all endorsed Stucki's MFN exemption for multilateral treaties (the Netherlands had begun including a provision along these lines in its bilateral trade treaties in the early 1920s).[115] In the ICC, Riedl vocally supported solidarity among small states and backed Stucki's efforts to build legal space for multilateralism within the system of MFN treaties.[116] He collaborated with the League Secretariat to produce a lengthy survey of treaty practice that documented the numerous regional and imperial exemptions that were already permitted in current MFN treaties in order to build a case, by analogy, for Stucki's new multilateral exemption.[117]

At root, the debates about Stucki's proposed multilateral MFN exemption were about the League's authority over bilateral trade treaties. All members of the Economic Committee agreed that every national government had an individual right not to extend the benefits of a multilateral agreement to non-participating states that invoked a bilateral MFN claim. The central point of contention was whether the Economic Committee should officially endorse that course of action. Llewellyn Smith's successor, Sydney Chapman, argued that a formal 'declaration' from the League 'recommending a country to take measures of discrimination against another country if that country did not adhere to the convention' would violate the Economic Committee's core commitment to 'equitable treatment'. In contrast, Jules Brunet, the Belgian member of the Economic Committee, emphasized that the League was venturing into uncharted waters, and that the old rules of non-discrimination were no longer applicable. He reasoned that 'in all fairness' if 'a system had been established by numerous States in the interest of all' and one government 'for reasons peculiar to itself, remained outside this general agreement' it should not be able to claim those general benefits by

---

[114] Herren, *Hintertüren zur Macht*.

[115] A.-I. Richard, 'Colonialism and the European Movement in France and the Netherlands, 1925–1936', PhD thesis, University of Cambridge (2011), p. 199.

[116] R. Riedl, Gespräch über einheitliches Vorgehen der kleineren Staaten in der Internationalen Handelskammer höchst erfreute. Zustimmung, undated ÖStA: AVA, NL Riedl/82. R. Riedl, *Exceptions to the Most-Favoured Nation Treatment: Report Presented to the International Chamber of Commerce* (P. S. King, 1931).

[117] This survey was published in several instalments, which are collected in LON: R2732, 10C/1149/1149.

invoking bilateral MFN obligations, which had been 'established at a time when general agreements of this kind had not been foreseen'.[118] Brunet spoke with particular authority about the multilateral transition underway in the 1920s because he was the president of the Brussels-based International Customs Tariff Bureau, which had been closely tracking tariffs and treaties since 1890.

In the 1920s, not only was the legal architecture of international trade changing, so were the geopolitics, most notably due to the rise of the United States as a wayward commercial giant. When he first proposed his multilateral MFN exemption, Stucki explicitly argued that the League should use this tool to influence the construction of the new US treaty network that was developing around the norm of unconditional MFN. He led the way as Switzerland's trade negotiator. Shortly after he presented his initial report to the Economic Committee, Stucki attempted to insert a multilateral MFN exemption into a bilateral treaty that he was concluding between Switzerland and the United States. The US diplomatic representative in Switzerland highlighted this suggestion as 'a point of exceeding interest now that the nations of the world are beginning to negotiate multilateral economic treaties'. Yet the Hoover administration ultimately rejected Stucki's proposal, unwilling to participate in League-led tariff projects but also unwilling to be excluded from them.[119]

In the end, Chapman helped devise a middle way in which the Economic Committee neither endorsed nor condemned Stucki's new MFN exemption. The Economic Committee issued an ambiguous statement that it 'may in some cases appear legitimate' to exempt League trade treaties from outside MFN claims, but only 'in the case of plurilateral conventions of a general character and aiming at the improvement of economic relations between peoples'.[120] In order to give this recommendation, effect states would first have to insert an explicit reservation for multilateral conventions into their bilateral trade treaties. Several European states including Austria, Belgium, France, the Netherlands, and Switzerland did begin to do this, using language borrowed from the Economic Committee. However, Britain and the United States refused

---

[118] Economic Committee, Twenty-Fourth Session, Minutes, Eighth Meeting, 20 March 1928, LON: E/24th Session/P.V.8(1).

[119] The Minister in Switzerland (Wilson) to the Secretary of State, 18 July 1928, in J. V. Fuller (ed.) FRUS 1928, vol. III (United States Printing Office, 1943), doc. 765; The Acting Secretary of State to the Minister in Rumania (Wilson), 28 July 1930, in J. V. Fuller (ed.) FRUS 1930, vol. III (United States Printing Office, 1945), doc. 748; Economic Committee. Minutes of the Third Meeting, 16 January 1929, LON: E/27th Session/P.V.3.(1).

[120] 'Annex 1148. Work of the Economic Committee During Its Twenty-Eighth Session', *League of Nations Official Journal*, July 1929, 1228–9.

(though Cordell Hull later reversed the US policy in 1933).[121] As will be seen, this intransigence from the Anglo-Saxon heavyweights significantly impeded European trade cooperation within the League during the early years of the Great Depression.

The Institutional Legacy of a Cautious Innovator

The debates about the League's impact on the legal architecture of the MFN system in the second half of the 1920s were in fact debates about how to accommodate the new multilateral rule-making process that Llewellyn Smith had painstakingly constructed. During his time in the Economic Committee from 1920 to 1927, Llewellyn Smith had primarily focused on the production of multilateral treaties: his mission was to conduct policy research, write draft agreements, and prepare diplomatic conferences where final negotiations would take place. The diligence with which he undertook that work reflected his long-held belief in the value of treaties as a framework for commercial interdependence. Multilateral rules offered the possibility to manage trade policy in a more uniform way across a wider area of the globe under the watchful guidance of the League of Nations, but this approach raised new questions about just how far the League should innovate. For if the new multilateral treaties remained subject to outside MFN claims, in conformity with standard treaty practice handed down from the nineteenth century, there would be little incentive for governments to sign on to the full terms of a collective agreement. Llewellyn Smith and his colleagues in the Board of Trade were unwilling to close off opportunities for free riding by exempting multilateral treaties from outside MFN claims, a step that appeared logical to many other League collaborators.

Llewellyn Smith's reluctance to compromise unconditional MFN stemmed from fears that regional trade areas in East Asia and the Americas would pull apart Britain's global network of imperial and commercial relations. That fear was widely shared among British and also Dutch leaders, with the latter concerned that Japanese regional ambitions would undermine colonial rule in the Netherlands East Indies.[122] At the same time, the British system of imperial preference was arguably the most fully articulated regime of preferential trade – even before 1932 – and provided an important reference point for advocates of European

---

[121] See Draft Report Submitted to the Second Committee by Sub-Committee 'B'. Preliminary Conference with a View to Concerted Action, 27 February 1930, LON: R2763, 10C/18153/15298; H. Coit MacLean to E. Dolléans, 12 April 1929, LON: R2729, 10C/20810/578.
[122] Richard, 'Competition and Complementarity', 243.

unity and broader multilateral cooperation. It is noteworthy that Arthur Salter diverged from Britain's Board of Trade and advocated an MFN exemption for League-sponsored multilateral agreements. Salter had followed a similar career trajectory to Llewellyn Smith in the British civil service through the end of the First World War, but in the 1920s he landed in Geneva rather than in London and was thus more closely attuned to the institutional needs of the young League of Nations. Salter was deeply invested in building an international civil service in which Secretariat officials held allegiance to the League, and Eric Drummond, the secretary general, shared that view.[123] Thus, although the clutch of British nationals in the early Secretariat helped Llewellyn Smith gain influence, they did not form a united British front.

Llewellyn Smith and his compatriots did share an initial preference for cautious inter-governmental trade cooperation that would facilitate regulatory standardization through a series of circumscribed agreements. League collaborators quickly grew frustrated with this incrementalism. Critics were given a new platform to voice their complaints at the World Economic Conference of 1927. That event brought a changing of the guard. New collaborators came into League circles, demanding more radical innovation in the methods and substance of international trade policy, while continuing to use the basic organizational procedures developed by early innovators such as Llewellyn Smith. The World Economic Conference was Llewellyn Smith's last major engagement as a civil servant before he retired from the Board of Trade and the Economic Committee. His departure coincided with Britain's retreat from leadership on international trade policy, as protectionist pressure mounted from British industrialists who were being squeezed by a strong pound and by the high interest rates that were required to defend it.[124]

Llewellyn Smith created openings for other innovators to pick up on the work that he had begun by advocating an information-rich approach to international policy in Geneva. Indeed, the League was often criticized for engaging in endless study and debate. The impulse to conduct thorough analysis before acting was based on a clear understanding of the novel challenges posed by the First World War and its aftermath. The research-based approach to economic policy that developed in the League of Nations had important consequences for the long-run history

---

[123] Sluga, *Internationalism in the Age of Nationalism*, 60–62; Reinalda, 'Biographical Analysis: Insights and Perspectives from the IO BIO Dictionary Project', 26; Ikonomou, 'The Biography As Institutional Can-Opener: An Investigation of Core Bureaucratic Practices in the Early Years of the League of Nations Secretariat', 31.
[124] Boyce, *The Great Interwar Crisis*, 152–3.

of international economic governance. Today, think tanks that span academic research, business, and government form an essential substratum for formal multilateral institutions in Brussels, New York, and Geneva. That substratum was nourished in the 1920s by intellectually minded political insiders, such as Llewellyn Smith, and by politically engaged intellectuals, such as Bernhard Harms.

5   Studying the World Economy, from Kiel and from Geneva

In 1920, an article on German 'commercial intelligence' from Llewellyn Smith's Board of Trade gave pride of place to the 'well equipped organization for the collection and dissemination of information' that Harms had built up in Kiel. Harms's institute functioned as an international clearinghouse for information 'gathered from all sources', drawing both from 'foreign scientists' as well as 'technical and commercial experts'.[1] The value of the IfW and other similar think tanks lay in their capacity to bridge theory and practice and to foster open-ended, non-committal dialogue among a large group of collaborators. Although Llewellyn Smith and his colleagues admired the broad reach achieved by IfW, they were careful to restrict the outside expertise that fed into the early work of the League's Economic Committee. Llewellyn Smith supported an information-rich approach to policy, but he also feared that too much material coming from too many directions could overload the League's fledgling institutions and threaten efforts to craft a cohesive policy agenda. Salter and Loveday also shared these concerns during the League's early years. Yet Salter, Loveday, and Llewellyn Smith had limited influence beyond Geneva, and the creation of the League rapidly stimulated a wide-ranging debate about multilateralism in independent organizations such as the IfW. Many of these external conversations were integrated into League policy following the World Economic Conference of 1927. This trajectory can be seen most clearly in Germany, which did not join the League until 1926.

The long campaign for German accession helped create a large body of active League-watchers.[2] The IfW was an important part of the League's German shadow, providing a platform for debate among many of the League's most prominent critics and supporters. In the 1920s, Harms made substantial changes to the IfW's organization, which enabled it to engage more effectively with the League, developing its competence in

[1] Germany. The Government and Commercial Intelligence, 1920, IfW: Hs Allg./1.
[2] Wintzer, *Deutschland und der Völkerbund*.

152

international law and building links to US philanthropic societies. After operating on the periphery of the EFO for many years, Harms attempted to embed the IfW more firmly in official League structures in the late 1920s by spearheading a large economic bibliography for the International Committee on Intellectual Cooperation. Yet, in the end, Harms proved unable to balance conflicting agendas from US and European collaborators. He had hoped that intellectual exchange would be able to transcend transatlantic rifts more easily than formal policy but found that information flows were also constrained by geopolitical competition. This should not have come as a surprise for Harms, perhaps, since the link between international cooperation and rivalry was baked into the bricks of the IfW.

In 1920, Harms signalled his grand ambitions to make the IfW a world-renowned international centre of learning by relocating it to a storied luxury hotel on the Kiel Fjord, the *Seebade-Anstalt Dusternbrook*. Before the war, the hotel had been the base for the Kaiser's own yacht club and had gathered royals and socialites from across Europe every June for a weeklong regatta.[3] As the site for an international jamboree of sailing, dancing, parties, and fireworks, the *Seebade-Anstalt* was the backdrop for some of the more surreal episodes in the run-up to the First World War. The Kiel Regatta was always one of the biggest social events of the summer season, and there were added festivities in June 1914. The Kaiser began the week with a ceremony to reopen the newly enlarged Kiel Canal before welcoming a squadron of British dreadnoughts for a friendly naval review. He even dressed as a Vice-Admiral of the British Fleet for the occasion (as was his right as Queen Victoria's grandson). Thus, the Kaiser had been strutting around British battleships in a British uniform in Germany's main naval port just days before Franz Ferdinand was shot. The British ships were still moored in Kiel when news of the assassination broke, and they responded by lowering their flags to half mast and flying the Austrian ensign. One of the vessels, the HMS *Birmingham*, went on to sink the very first German U-boat of the war roughly one month later.[4] During the war the owner of the *Seebade-Anstalt*, Gustav Krupp, built many more U-boats from his Kiel shipyard. In a final plot twist, the mutiny of the German High Seas Fleet in Kiel, which sparked the German revolution in 1918, persuaded a panicked Krupp to offload his hotel as quickly as possible, fearing further socialist unrest as well as rising taxes on an

---

[3] Seebade-Anstalt Düsternbrook, Kiel, undated, IfW: Hs Allg./12.
[4] 'The Kiel Canal', *War Notes and Queries*, 22 August 1914, 44–5; H. White, 'Battleship View of the Days the World Changed Forever, and a Boy Went to War', *The Sydney Morning Herald*, 25 July 2014, www.smh.com.au/opinion/battleship-view-of-the-days-the -world-changed-forever-and-a-boy-went-to-war-20140725-zwu1q.html.

unprofitable relic of monarchy. He agreed to sell the whole property to the IfW for a bargain price in negotiations that reportedly lasted less than two hours.[5]

This property windfall helped Harms sustain the organizational momentum that he had built up during the war. The IfW managed to weather the initial moderate phase of German post-war inflation relatively well despite heavy investments in German war loans. More than one hundred workers spent a year and a half conducting a thorough renovation of the *Seebade-Anstalt*. Harms devoted particular attention to the design of the new reading room, installing tall windows and a state-of-the-art Zeiss 'light system' that minimized shadows.[6] It was a modern temple of learning. One student recalled that 'pin-drop silence prevails in the working hall. None is allowed to carry on any sort of conversation inside it. The student can bury himself in his work in absolute quiet'.[7] There were also female students at the IfW, although their social participation in the IfW's Scientific Club was somewhat constrained. Harms tried to give the club a 'casino' ambiance that would allow students, lecturers, and professors to mix freely on relatively equal footing, but female students had to leave before eight o'clock unless they were attending a planned event. The Scientific Club contributed to the IfW's intellectual life by hosting talks from business leaders and political dignitaries (including Riedl) in the former rooms of the Kaiser's Yacht Club. There were minimal renovations to the Yacht Club, so the space would have had a prelapsarian charm for visitors in the 1920s.[8] As in in the pre-war days when the *Seebade-Anstalt* hosted European royals for a friendly regatta, it continued to facilitate informal dialogue between rival factions who faced off in a more structured way in formal diplomatic channels. The *Seebade-Anstalt* offered a fitting base for Harms to engage with the young League of Nations, which also operated out of a converted belle époque hotel on Lake Geneva (shown on the cover of this book) before construction finally began on the Palace of Nations in 1929.

---

[5] Hoffmann, 'Die Geschichte des Instituts für Weltwirtschaft', vol. III, pp. 97–102.

[6] Hoffmann, 'Die Geschichte des Instituts für Weltwirtschaft', vol. I, pp. 102–8; Zur vorläufigen Vollendung des Kollegienhauses des Instituts für Weltwirtschaft und Seeverkehr an der Universität Kiel, 1926, IfW: Hs allg. 7.

[7] Zohadur Rahim, 'The Institute of World-Wide Economics and Ocean-Transport in the University of Kiel', 1934, IfW: HS Allg./1.

[8] Satzung des Wissenschaftlichen Klubs des Instituts für Weltwirtschaft und Seeverkehr, 8 July 1933, IfW: Hs Allg./20; Hoffmann, 'Die Geschichte des Instituts für Weltwirtschaft', vol. I, pp. 105–113.

Economic Intelligence in the League of Nations

The main hub for economic information in the League of Nations was the Secretariat's Economic Intelligence Service (EIS), run by the Scottish economist Alexander Loveday. Loveday spent much of the 1920s trying to produce standardized and comparable international economic statistics, and Llewellyn Smith gave him strong backing in that endeavour together with the head statistician in Britain's Board of Trade, Arthur Flux. Loveday crafted a more unified picture of the world economy just when it was disintegrating into competing blocs. The global markets of the nineteenth century had been charted through new numbers about supplies, prices, and flows, fed by a general enthusiasm for quantification. However, this early economic data was quite fragmented.[9] Before 1914, several organizations had tried to harmonize global economic statistics, chief among them the International Statistical Institute, but private bodies had little power to compel governments to align their counting methods with a uniform international programme.[10] The League's intergovernmental configuration made it possible for Loveday to enact formal and binding rules on the matter. He had to bridge some very wide gaps in national statistical methods.

The root problem was that governments simply used statistics for different practical functions and varied their methods of calculation accordingly. From country to country, the same product could be classified quite differently. Moreover, there were many possible ways to trace the trajectory of imports and exports. Some statistics were based on the location of production and final consumption, others monitored the point of purchase and the point of sale, while others counted outward and inbound shipments using customs data. States also had different ways to account for re-exports, which were excluded from 'special trade' but included in 'general trade'. This methodological diversity made it extremely hard to compare trade statistics issued by governments.[11] In the nineteenth century, there had been widespread interest among public officials, business leaders, and academics in making statistics more comparable, but this became a more urgent priority after the First World War.

---

[9] Q. Slobodian, 'How to See the World Economy: Statistics, Maps, and Schumpeter's Camera in the First Age of Globalization', *Journal of Global History*, 10/2 (2015), 307–32.

[10] R. Cussó, 'Building a Global Representation of Trade through International Quantification: The League of Nations' Unification of Methods in Economic Statistics', *The International History Review*, 42/4 (2020), 714–36, 717–18.

[11] M. Bemmann, 'Comparing Economic Activities on a Global Level in the 1920s and 1930s: Motives and Consequences', in W. Steinmetz (ed.), *The Force of Comparison: A New Perspective on Modern European History and the Contemporary World* (Berghahn Books, 2019), pp. 242–65, 245; Cussó, 'Building a Global Representation of Trade through International Quantification', 722–3.

The great shifts in economic fortunes brought by the war made it important to understand different countries' relative export positions in key markets and sectors. Moreover, the drive for reconstruction generated strong demand for specific raw materials, so an overview of global supplies was essential. Martin Bemmann explains that governments agreed to cooperate and pool their trade statistics using League machinery in the hopes of competing more effectively in a fluid post-war world economy where Europeans had lost ground. The ICC similarly favoured the standardization of trade statistics in order to create a level playing field for private commercial rivalry.[12]

The first interwar conference on economic statistics was held in summer 1919, before the League of Nations even officially began operations, reflecting the urgent demand for reliable numbers.[13] Shortly after the war, Llewellyn Smith had helped initiate the publication of a new *Monthly Bulletin of Statistics* under the authority of the Supreme Economic Council. The first issues were produced by Flux's statistical department in the Board of Trade until it could be transferred to the EIS in 1921–2. The *Monthly Bulletin of Statistics* defined a rough baseline against which post-war reconstruction could be measured by publishing economic statistics gathered from 'before, during, and since the war'. Crucially, this was not a one-off snapshot of the post-war world economy, but rather a periodical assessment that would help officials chart 'progress towards more normal conditions' over time.[14] The publication of international statistics at regular intervals was an important innovation that came with the League of Nations and supported sustained policy debate in Geneva. It also allowed for incremental improvement in methodological standards.[15]

Over the 1920s Loveday undertook a long standardization campaign that culminated in an International Convention Concerning Economic Statistics in 1928. This agreement specified that all imports and exports must be assigned a uniform 'declared value', defined as the value at the point of dispatch, plus shipping and insurance costs in the case of imports. Implementing this provision necessitated significant changes in many countries' border procedures. The convention also required signatories to distinguish between transit trade, which involved no intermediate transformation, and transnational production. It outlined rough standards concerning the level of processing required to count a given re-export

[12] Bemmann, 'Comparing Economic Activities on a Global Level', 244–8.
[13] Cussó, 'Building a Global Representation of Trade through International Quantification', 718.
[14] 'Introduction', *Monthly Bulletin of Statistics*, 1/1 (1919), 3.
[15] Bemmann, 'Comparing Economic Activities on a Global Level', 243.

in a country's foreign trade statistics (simply 'repacking, sorting or blending' was not sufficient). This significantly shifted valuations of many countries' 'general' and 'special' trade and anticipated the lengthy international debates about 'rules of origin' in the second half of the twentieth century.[16] Loveday's work had strong backing in the world's main commercial hubs (including in Britain's Board of Trade), but international statistical standards also held particular importance for many young states. Adopting the League's methods of counting was a way for the successor states of Central and Eastern Europe to claim their place in the commercial world. The long cycle of meetings to discuss statistical methods in the run-up to the final convention also gave non-European governments an opportunity to explain how and why they might diverge from economic models designed for highly industrialized commercial economies. For example, Indian delegates used the League's statistical conferences to present their country's ambitions for state-backed industrial policy after discovering deep ignorance about these plans among European statisticians.[17]

Loveday worked to bring greater uniformity to national economic statistics, and he also devised new methods to compare differences. The early issues of the *Monthly Bulletin of Statistics* began by compiling national trade statistics sequentially and the later issues offered more comparative tables charting different countries' economic performance side-by-side. These tables were riddled with methodological caveats, but they nevertheless brought an important perceptual shift. As observed in the 1930s by Arthur Sweetser, the influential US internationalist who eventually rose to the head of the Secretariat's Information Section, League statistics offered 'a perspective of the world looking down from above rather than the usual foreshortened view as seen horizontally from the window of a particular country'.[18] By that time some internationally minded liberals were beginning to abandon the premise that global markets could be comprehensively analysed and instead advocated a more abstract mode of international regulation, divorced from economic data.[19]

The fact that so many League collaborators were crunching numbers for different political and intellectual projects presented both opportunities and problems for Loveday. The fluid organizational structures

[16] '1. International Convention Concerning Economic Statistics', *International Conference Relating to Economic Statistics* (League of Nations, 1928), 9–11; Cussó, 'Building a Global Representation of Trade through International Quantification', 722–5.
[17] Bemmann, 'Comparing Economic Activities on a Global Level', 251–2.
[18] Quoted in Bemmann, 'Comparing Economic Activities on a Global Level', 246.
[19] Slobodian, *Globalists*, 55–90.

around the League threw up a massive flurry of data, and Loveday had to act as a stern gatekeeper to devise credible and rigorous international statistics. He also had to rebuff requests to provide statistical services for auxiliary associations. For example, when Coquet requested Loveday's assistance in analysing data on European economic integration, Stoppani wryly remarked, 'I hardly think that you feel inclined to correct their statistics?!' Loveday responded with a firm, 'No!'[20]

Experts in Early League Trade Policy

As Loveday strove to filter the information flowing through the EIS, Llewellyn Smith also tried to regulate the data that experts fed into the Economic Committee. He intervened most firmly to restrain the work of an Italian statistician, Corrado Gini, on raw material supplies. Italy's post-war government had demanded international cooperation on raw materials both at the ILO's annual conference and in the League Assembly, in continuity with Italian and French proposals at the Paris Peace Conference.[21] In response, the Economic Committee launched an inquiry into trade in raw materials, led by Gini. Elisabetta Tollardo highlights the political stakes of the Gini Inquiry for the Italian government. Italian Liberals argued that their country's security and prosperity depended on cooperation in raw materials because it had an insufficient resource base to support its population. The Fascist government later demanded more territory in lieu of international cooperation, using the Gini Inquiry to justify colonial claims.[22]

The British government opposed Italian plans for international management of raw materials as an invitation for international interference in imperial relations, as it had during the peace negotiations. In the Economic Committee, Llewellyn Smith sought to restrict Gini's remit and this brought him into conflict with Jean Monnet, who was then serving as a deputy secretary general in the League. Llewellyn Smith complained to Monnet that Gini was conducting his inquiry too independently, without sufficient oversight from the Secretariat or the Economic Committee. He demanded that Gini submit a 'detailed outline' of his planned report for preliminary review, 'so that we may know

---

[20] L. Coquet to A. Salter, 9 April 1929, LON: R 2716, 10C/2291/231; Minute from P. Stoppani to A. Loveday, undated, LON: R 2716, 10C/2291/231.
[21] League of Nations Provisional Economic and Financial Committee (Economic Committee), *Report on Certain Aspects of the Raw Materials Problem (with the Relevant Documents Submitted to the Committee by Professor Gini)* C.51.M.18.1922.II (League of Nations, 1921), 15–18.
[22] Tollardo, *Fascist Italy and the League of Nations, 1922–1935*, 26–7.

what he is about and be in a position to offer criticisms in good time'. For, he noted that finished drafts are 'notoriously difficult to re-shape', once written.[23] In sum, Gini was precisely the kind of rogue international expert beyond political control that Llewellyn Smith had warned against when discussing the EFO's original institutional design. Monnet dismissed Llewellyn Smith's concerns and argued that Gini's authority as an independent expert should be respected: 'he is a scientific statistician of high repute and was expressly engaged, not merely to classify material, but to assist as an expert in the conduct of the enquiry'.[24] Salter mediated, conceding that 'Professor Gini's work will produce a good scientific volume', while also declaring that 'the question has very little practical importance, either in Economics or Politics'. He agreed to intervene personally to try to rein in Gini.[25] In the end, Gini submitted his full draft report as a 'preliminary' document which the Secretariat and the Economic Committee then had to winnow down.[26] This was the messy *post-facto* clean-up that Llewellyn Smith had hoped to avoid.

Rather than thoroughly revising Gini's conclusions, Llewellyn Smith simply wrote a whole new report that firmly positioned the EFO against direct international intervention in commodity markets and then published Gini's original report as an annex, with some redactions.[27] Llewellyn Smith's report opened by declaring itself 'obsolete'. For, by the time Gini's data was published in December 1921, the concerns about raw material shortage that had originally motivated demands for post-war international cooperation were superseded by concerns about a global glut in commodity markets, as US-led deflationary policies drove down prices. Due to its focus on shortages, 'much of the material collected' by Gini had 'lost its significance except as an historical survey'.[28] Thus a long, elaborate, and expensive inquiry into global commodity markets produced a self-cancelling report that advertised the institutional inefficiency and indiscipline of the young EFO. The Gini Inquiry served

---

[23] H. Llewellyn Smith to J. Monnet, 11 July 1921, LON: Salter Papers, S134; J. Monnet to H. Llewellyn Smith, July 1, 1921, LON: Salter Papers, S134.

[24] J. Monnet to H. Llewellyn Smith, 1 July 1921, LON: Salter Papers, S134.

[25] A. Salter to J. Monnet, 26 August 1921, LON: Salter Papers, S123/73/20. The Secretary General, Eric Drummond also seems to have sided with Salter and Llewellyn Smith, evincing 'strong views' that Gini should not deliver 'too definitive a report to the Economic Committee'. See Miss Howard for Secretary General, Professor Gini's Report, 24 August 1921, LON: Salter Papers, S134, 8/5 (13).

[26] H. McKinnon Wood to H. Llewellyn Smith, 4 August 1921, LON: Salter Papers, S 134, 8/5(12).

[27] For the draft of the new report, initialled by Llewellyn Smith, see H Ll S, 'Report to the Council on Certain Aspects of the Raw Materials Problem', undated, LON: R369, 10/16034/16034.

[28] Economic Committee, *Report on Certain Aspects of the Raw Materials Problem*, 6.

as a cautionary tale in the Secretariat. Frank Nixon, one of Salter's main deputies, recommended that in the future, outside experts should be closely monitored by inside handlers 'with considerable knowledge of the administrative requirements of the Secretariat'. He explained, 'I do not want to repeat the Gini experience'.[29]

Procedural debates over Gini's role were tied to substantive disagreements over international cooperation in raw materials in the wake of the First World War. The divergence between French and British policies on raw materials can be traced back to the Allied Maritime Transport Council. Monnet served on this body alongside Salter and saw it as a model for permanent cooperative control of raw material flows (prefiguring his later approach to European integration in the European Coal and Steel Community). While some British internationalists such as Leonard Woolf shared Monnet's vision, Salter did not, nor did officials in the Board of Trade. Although Salter believed that some administrative principles could be transferred from the Inter-Allied bodies to the League, he was sceptical that the international management of commodity markets could be sustained in peacetime, as demonstrated by his rather dismissive response to the Gini Inquiry.[30] Instead, in the early 1920s Salter supported the free trade approach to raw material cooperation that Llewellyn Smith attempted to implement through the Prohibitions Convention. According to this logic, if commodities flowed freely, resource competition would cease to be a source of international conflict. When commodity prices plummeted during the Great Depression, Salter eventually became more open to direct market intervention through cartels and inter-governmental agreements. This was a new response to the economic dislocation of the 1920s and not a direct continuation of his wartime activity, however.[31]

The Ruhr Crisis and the German International Turn

Salter, Loveday, and Llewellyn Smith initially tried to keep trade policy in Geneva focused on a conventional model of free trade, but debates about multilateralism ranged more widely in private organizations. Because Germans were formally excluded from early League policy, they were

---

[29] F. Nixon to E. Drummond, 5 April 1922, LON: Salter Papers, S126, 76/3.
[30] Salter, *Allied Shipping Control*, 245.
[31] Frank Trentmann paints a neater picture, suggesting that Salter continued to support international coordination of commodity markets in the 1920s, based on his wartime experience See Trentmann, *Free Trade Nation*, 242–73. In fact, Salter (like Llewellyn Smith) initially advocated a fairly restrained and conventional trade policy, transposed onto the League's multilateral framework. In the early 1920s, they built out the League's institutional apparatus around that modest goal.

particularly vocal outside observers. Harms's IfW became an important base for monitoring the work of the League and its position in the larger international system, especially in relation to the United States. The Ruhr crisis of 1923 pushed the IfW and the German state towards more active engagement with the League and with the United States, in an uneasy combination. The Ruhr crisis stemmed from conflict over reparations, which Lloyd George had tried unsuccessfully to defuse at the 1922 Genoa Conference. He envisioned a grand bargain to fund reparations through German participation in Russian infrastructural development, with the capital coming from the United States and Western Europe. In the end, the Genoa Conference demonstrated Britain's incapacity to enforce a sweeping vision of international solidarity, inaugurating a piecemeal approach to European diplomacy that left the major sore spots of the 1919 Peace Settlement unresolved.[32] Harms concluded that only the United States had sufficient political and economic clout to sponsor a comprehensive international settlement, but he also recognized the institutional constraints that impeded US leadership, including its absence from the League of Nations.

After Genoa, conflict over reparations escalated rapidly with French and Belgian troops marching into the Ruhr industrial region in January 1923 to enforce German payments. The Ruhr occupation pushed the German economic and political system to the breaking point. The German government encouraged workers in the Ruhr to halt production in a concerted programme of 'passive resistance', fuelling runaway inflation that reached a peak of 4.2 billion marks to the dollar in November 1923.[33] The IfW's operating costs skyrocketed and it was forced to cut its staff by more than half.[34] Economic disorder provoked political challenges to the young Weimar Republic from the left and the right, as both the German Communist Party and the newly formed Nazi Party mobilized members. While the Ruhr crisis energized Germany's political extremes, it also propelled the ascent of the centrist Gustav Stresemann, who advocated a policy of reparations fulfilment and international engagement as foreign secretary from 1923 to 1929.

Stresemann's conciliatory strategy was a clear bid for treaty revision, as Manfred Berg demonstrated. Stresemann calculated that deepening international economic interdependence would gradually lead the United States and the Allies to accept a peaceful modification of the Treaty of

---

[32] Trachtenberg, *Reparation in World Politics*, 233, 243; Steiner, *The Lights That Failed*, 162–6; Tooze, *The Deluge*, 424–39.

[33] R. L. Carson, *Comparative Economic Systems* (Macmillan, 1973), 659; Trachtenberg, *Reparation in World Politics*, 292–335.

[34] Hoffmann, 'Die Geschichte des Instituts für Weltwirtschaft', vol. II, p. 38.

Versailles. In his view, Germany's chief source of leverage was its status as a large and productive economy that could drive European and global economic growth. He hoped that if Germany became an indispensable part of an integrated and well-ordered world economy, foreign leaders would see its revisionist ambitions as a force for economic prosperity and political stability.[35] Stresemann's plan depended on engagement with both the United States and the League, but this was a delicate balancing act. The restoration of German economic influence would require US capital and political backing as well as a regime of open markets policed from Geneva. Stresemann sympathized with regional plans to pry open Germany's main export markets in Western Europe but was wary of antagonizing US leaders who looked askance at European unity.[36] From the German perspective, the absence of the United States from the League was both a blessing and a curse. Because it never signed the Treaty of Versailles, the United States had more legal latitude to push for revision, but this also meant that it sat outside the main regulatory system that could be used to deepen commercial interdependence and create the political conditions for revision.[37]

The Ruhr crisis brought deeper German cooperation with the United States and the League. In 1924 an international commission led by the US banker Charles Dawes devised a new provisional reparations settlement that fixed a payment schedule through the end of the 1920s and secured international loans for Germany to promote economic stabilization. The 1925 Locarno Accords provided a political counterpart to the Dawes Plan by guaranteeing Germany's western borders with France and Belgium. Together these agreements helped pave the way for German accession to the League in 1926.[38] Harms enthusiastically endorsed the programme of international outreach pursued by Stresemann, with whom he had long-standing ties (Stresemann had been one of the IfW's founding members). Looking back from the vantage point of the World Economic Conference in 1927, Harms later concluded that 'the Ruhr conflict was a necessary link in the chain of events. It opened the path to all that followed'.[39] For him, the Ruhr demonstrated the decisive importance of 'Franco-German understanding'. He concluded that 'only on this basis might the European

---

[35] M. Berg, *Gustav Stresemann und die Vereinigten Staaten von Amerika: Weltwirtschaftliche Verflechtung und Revisionspolitik 1907–1929* (Nomos, 1990), 113–20, 383–5.
[36] Schulz, *Deutschland, der Völkerbund und die Frage der europäischen Wirtschaftsordnung*, 76–80.
[37] Berg, *Gustav Stresemann und die Vereinigten Staaten von Amerika*, 94–122, 383–5; Schulz, *Deutschland, der Völkerbund und die Frage der europäischen Wirtschaftsordnung*, 76–80.
[38] Steiner, *The Lights That Failed*, 236–50, 387–409; Cohrs, *The Unfinished Peace*, 129–219.
[39] B. Harms, 'Die Weltwirtschaftskonferenz', *Weltwirtschaftliches Archiv*, 25 (1927), 211–44, 216.

economy flourish anew and reach full bloom. But only then!'[40] Riedl and Coquet drew a similar conclusion from the Ruhr crisis, but they worked to unite France and Germany as a nucleus for regional European cooperation. In contrast, Harms, like Stresemann, sought to embed a bilateral partnership on the Rhine in a wider global framework that included the United States, by promoting Germany's image as a bastion of economic internationalism in the eyes of US partners.

Building a Network of Transatlantic Intellectual Cooperation from Kiel

From the nadir of the Ruhr crisis, Harms used the IfW to build a network of scientific cooperation that encompassed the United States and the League of Nations. He travelled to the United States in summer 1923 to try to encourage greater US involvement in Europe's troubles, touring the Midwest to lecture on 'Germany, Europe, and America' to large groups of German-Americans.[41] He also began to forge ties with US philanthropic organizations during the Ruhr crisis, when the IfW shifted its funding structure away from private business and towards public institutions and NGOs. By the end of hyperinflation, German state subsidies accounted for 70 per cent of the IfW budget. Harms also began to solicit funding from US philanthropic sources, including sizeable contributions from the Laura Spelman Rockefeller Memorial to support the IfW's library. In 1925, this donation amounted to roughly 10 per cent of the IfW's annual budget.[42]

The IfW's large staff cuts and funding changes during the Ruhr crisis accelerated its shift from high-volume, labour-intensive news towards more targeted, in-depth analysis. This evolution had already begun in 1922, when the IfW cut costs by handing over its news operations to the new German Economic Service. Over the course of the 1920s, the IfW focused its operations on research. This evolution aligned the IfW with US philanthropic bodies such as the Carnegie Endowment and Rockefeller Foundation, which both emphasized scientific inquiry over

---

[40] Harms, 'Die Weltwirtschaftskonferenz', 242.
[41] On the narrow limits of Dawes and Locarno as vehicles for US international engagement, see M. P. Leffler, *The Elusive Quest: America's Pursuit of European Stability and French Security, 1919–1933* (University of North Carolina Press, 1979), 158–93; Cohrs, *The Unfinished Peace*, 296–324; Tooze, *The Deluge*, 453–61.
[42] Institut für Weltwirtschaft to Minister für Wissenschaft, Kunst und Volksbildung, 6 September 1924, BArch/R 1501/116325; G. Take, '"One of the Bright Spots in German Economics": Die Förderung des Kieler Instituts für Weltwirtschaft durch die Rockefeller Foundation, 1925–1950', *Jahrbuch für Wirtschaftsgeschichte/Economic History Yearbook*, 59/1 (2018), 251–328, 257–8.

policy advocacy in their interwar European activities.[43] Through these organizations, the US elites who had originally favoured League membership redirected their efforts towards international education and research. In the process, they established important financial and institutional bonds with the League, especially its International Committee on Intellectual Cooperation.[44]

The IfW's new transnational intellectual linkages were reflected in its journal, the *Weltwirtschaftliches Archiv*. It provided extensive coverage of the Carnegie Endowment's publications, including more than one hundred announcements and reviews. The *Weltwirtschaftliches Archiv* also offered a mouthpiece for individual US internationalists with close links to the government. They included Frank Taussig, Wilson's top trade advisor who helped initiate the US shift towards unconditional MFN, Harry T. Collings, a US trade commissioner in Belgium, and Henry Chalmers, the long-serving chief of the Division of Foreign Tariffs in the US Department of Commerce. Chalmers followed the League's trade work closely, attending many conferences in person. He helped ensure the continuation of the League's multilateral methods after 1945, referring back to the 1923 Convention on Customs Formalities as an important precedent during the GATT negotiations.[45]

In the *Weltwirtschaftliches Archiv*, most of the direct reporting on League trade activities came from Louise Sommer, a Vienna-born economist who was a lecturer at the University of Geneva in the 1920s.[46] She acted as the IfW's eyes on the ground, and Harms intervened with the League Secretariat to ensure that they gave her access to the necessary documents.[47] Through her articles, Sommer sketched an expansive

---

[43] W. F. Kuehl and L. Dunn, *Keeping the Covenant: American Internationalists and the League of Nations, 1920–1939* (Kent State University Press, 1997), 83; K. Rietzler, 'From Peace Advocacy to International Relations Research: The Transformation of Transatlantic Philanthropic Networks, 1900–1930', in D. Rodogno, B. Struck, and J. Vogel (eds.), *Shaping the Transnational Sphere: Experts, Networks, and Issues from the 1840s to the 1930s* (Berghahn Books, 2015), pp. 173–96.

[44] Kuehl and Dunn, *Keeping the Covenant*, 64–75.

[45] Minutes of the Meeting of the Committee on Customs Procedures, ECEPF, 6 December 1946, USNA: RG 43/698, box 33; F. Grabb to W. Carr, 25 November 1933, USNA: RG 59, box 2532, 500.C1199/111.

[46] L. Sommer, 'Die Vorgeschichte der Weltwirtschaftskonferenz (Genf 1927)', *Weltwirtschaftliches Archiv*, 28 (1928), 340–418; L. Sommer, 'Vom Zollwaffenstillstand zur Handelskonvention. Bericht über die Genfer Zollkonferenz vom 17. Februar bis 24. März 1930', *Weltwirtschaftliches Archiv*, 32 (1930), 274–82; L. Sommer, 'Zweite Konferenz für ein vereintes wirtschaftliches Vorgehen vom 17. bis zum 28. November 1930', *Weltwirtschaftliches Archiv*, 34 (1931), 284–96. On Louise Sommer's biography see 'Dr. Louise Sommer, Economics Writer', *The New York Times*, 6 June 1964, 23.

[47] B. Harms to the Section Economique des Völkerbundes, 14 June 1927, LON: R444 10/49117/49117.

vision of League economic policy that encompassed scholarly institutions, business organizations, as well as quasi-diplomatic advocacy from actors such as Coquet and his partners.[48] Sommer contributed to the *Weltwirtschaftliches Archiv* as both an economist and as a journalist, by writing original pieces on monetary theory as well as reviews of academic research in English, French, German, and Italian.[49] The *Weltwirtschaftliches Archiv* gave Sommer and many other female contributors a vehicle to participate in the League multiverse. The wide scope of Sommer's articles for the IfW contrasts with the narrower role that Emmy Freundlich played in formal EFO committees, where she voiced consumers' concerns about household economy. In the 1920s women were often able to claim more extensive macroeconomic competence in the information sphere that developed around the League than in its internal decision-making bodies.

Sommer blended economic theory and practice freely in her writings for the *Weltwirtschaftliches Archiv*, and this was a characteristic feature of the journal in the 1920s. Contributors often reviewed texts that were rooted in a different intellectual orientation from their own, and the original scholarly papers also presented widely divergent viewpoints. On the left, the journal offered a platform for prominent defenders and critics of the Soviet Union, including Harold Laski and Wladimir Woytinsky. It also published numerous articles from the coterie of conservative liberals who worked alongside Riedl in the Vienna Chamber of Commerce, such as Friedrich Hayek, Gottfried Hablerer, and Ludwig von Mises, including one article from Mises that was simply entitled '*Antimarxismus*'.[50] An institutional commitment to the League of Nations was a central point of convergence for the diverse thinkers who gathered around the IfW in the 1920s.

The *Weltwirtschaftliches Archiv* showcased a wide variety of internationalisms, but it gave the ILO pride of place, reflecting the strong German ties to that organization. Germany was initially excluded from the League of Nations, but it joined the ILO right away in 1919. There were few Germans in the ILO secretariat, but they exercised outsized influence due to Germany's long history of state-funded welfare.[51] The

---

[48] L. Sommer, 'Die Mitteleuropäische Wasserstraßen-Konferenz (Budapest 1929)', *Weltwirtschaftliches Archiv*, 30 (1929), 447–57; L. Sommer, 'Sechste Mitteleuropäische Wirtschaftstagung am 18. und 19. März 1931', *Weltwirtschaftliches Archiv*, 35 (1932), 612–16; L. Sommer, 'Der VII. Kongreß der Internationalen Handelskammer (Wien 1933)', *Weltwirtschaftliches Archiv*, 38 (1933), 284–90.

[49] For example, L. Sommer, 'Freihandel und Schutzzoll in ihrem Zusammenhang mit Geldtheorie und Währungspolitik', *Weltwirtschaftliches Archiv*, 24 (1926), 33–72.

[50] L. Mises, 'Antimarxismus', *Weltwirtschaftliches Archiv*, 21 (1925), 266–93.

[51] S. Kott, 'Dynamiques de l'internationalisation: l'Allemagne et l'Organisation internationale du travail (1919–1940)', *Critique internationale*, 52/3 (2011), 69, 73–4.

Weltwirtschaftliches Archiv gave a detailed account of the ILO's activities, publishing summaries of its annual conference as well as in-depth studies of labour and migration issues in particular countries. These articles were often written by ILO officials and collaborators including Imre Ferenczi, Karl Přibram, and Ludwig Heyde. Ferenzci was a Hungarian housing official who served as the technical adviser on migration and population questions at the ILO, and Přibram was an Austrian economist who ran the ILO's statistical department. Both men gave guest lectures at the IfW in addition to writing for the *Weltwirtschaftliches Archiv*.[52] Heyde wrote a running 'Chronicle of Social Policy' for the *Weltwirtschaftliches Archiv* throughout the 1920s. He was an honorary professor at the IfW and the secretary of the German section of the International Association for Social Progress, which worked closely with the ILO. Heyde brought the ILO director, Albert Thomas, to Kiel in December 1926 to speak to IfW students about 'international social policy and peace among nations'.[53] Heyde also incorporated a two-day visit to the ILO secretariat into a series of study trips for IfW students to visit factories and meet with labour unions and business leaders.[54]

World Economic Law

Alongside international social policy, Harms also began to give international law more prominence in the activities of the IfW in the 1920s, and this facilitated engagement with the League system beyond the ILO. Following the Ruhr crisis, Harms outlined his own theory of 'world economic law' that emphasized the dynamic interplay between nationalism and internationalism in trade policy. He praised the 'significant advances' made through 'general international agreements', in the realm of trade and transit, referring to Llewellyn Smith's handiwork in

---

[52] Kieler Vorträge gehalten im Wissenschaftlichen Klub des Instituts für Weltwirtschaft an der Universität Kiel, undated, IfW: Hs; I. De Augustine Reid, Memorandum on Dr. Imre Ferenczi, 13 February 1941, University of Massachusetts–Amherst Libraries, Special Collections and University Archives: W. E. B. Du Bois Papers/MS 312.

[53] S. Kott, 'From Transnational Reformist Network to International Organization: The International Association of Labour Legislation and the International Labour Organization, 1900–1930', in D. Rodogno, B. Struck, and J. Vogel (eds.), *Shaping the Transnational Sphere: Experts, Networks, and Issues from the 1840s to the 1930s* (Berghahn Books, 2015), pp. 239–78, 239–54; 'Internationale Sozialpolitik und Völkerfrieden', 1927, IfW: Hs Harms/1.

[54] Kott, 'From Transnational Reformist Network to International Organization', 251–2; Bericht, erstattet dem Institut für Weltwirtschaft und Seeverkehr an der Universität Kiel und dem Büro für Sozialpolitik in Berlin über Exkursionen von Kieler Studierenden der Staatswissenschaften unter Leitung von Professor Dr. L. Heyde in den Jahren 1925 und 1926, January 1927, IfW: Hs. Allg./15.

Geneva. Alongside multilateral innovation, Harms also noted that a multitude of new bilateral trade treaties had been signed in the wake of the war, especially by the imperial successor states. He argued that the 'driving force' for this post-war proliferation of international economic law was 'not to be found in a growing "feeling of solidarity" among peoples' but rather in the essential 'nature' of trans-border economic interdependence, which 'leads to chaos without legal regulation'.[55] He conceded that 'undoubtedly we are heading for a period of more pronounced national economic policy' but predicted that this would be counterbalanced by a practical demand for stability and market integration, pushed by businessmen in organizations such as the ICC. Trade policy would be called upon to bridge the 'continual conflict between "national" and "international" interests', and this would entail a 'rapid development of world economic law'.[56] In other words, the war led to legal innovation because it brought more strident nationalism into a global economy that was already highly integrated.

Harms made international law more central to the programme of research and teaching at the IfW, in recognition of its growing importance in the post-war world. By this time, the University of Kiel had already become a hub for international law under the leadership Theodor Niemeyer. Harms and Niemeyer built parallel careers in Kiel. Before the war Harms had explored creating a joint Institute for the Science of World Trade with Niemeyer and a geographer.[57] In 1914, they parted ways when Harms created the IfW and Niemeyer founded a separate Institute for International Law. Both men published prestigious journals – the *Weltwirtschaftliches Archiv* and *Niemeyers Zeitschrift für internationales Recht*. During the war, as Harms was pursing research on the war economy, Niemeyer created a War Archive of International Law (Kriegsarchiv des Völkerrechts) and the German Society of International Law (Deutsche Gesellschaft für Internationales Recht), both with support from the German Foreign Office. Niemeyer helped the Foreign Office create a counter-narrative to Allied accounts of German wartime lawlessness, which focused on submarine warfare and the violent occupation of Belgium.[58] Niemeyer sought to demonstrate Germany's internationalism by coordinating the German drafts of the League Covenant discussed in

[55] B. Harms, 'Weltwirtschaftsrecht. Ein Beitrag zur sozialökonomisch-völkerrechtlichen Begriffsbildung', *Weltwirtschaftliches Archiv*, 20 (1924), 573–88, 586; Harms, 'Die Weltwirtschaftskonferenz', 238–9.
[56] Harms, 'Weltwirtschaftsrecht. Ein Beitrag zur sozialökonomisch-völkerrechtlichen Begriffsbildung', 586–8.
[57] Hoffmann, 'Die Geschichte des Instituts für Weltwirtschaft', vol. I, p. 30.
[58] M. Stolleis, *A History of Public Law in Germany, 1914–1945* (Oxford University Press, 2004), 63; Hull, *A Scrap of Paper*, 7.

Chapter Three, with help from Harms on the trade provisions.[59] In the 1920s, Harms and Niemeyer opened the doors of their respective institutes to one another's students.[60] Harms also personally supervised the doctoral dissertation of Niemeyer's daughter, Annemarie, together with an IfW economist.[61]

Harms relied on Niemeyer's protégés, Hermann Held and Hans Wehberg, to develop the IfW's work in international law. Held was responsible for building a legal studies programme at the IfW the 1920s.[62] His own research focused on proving the inequity of the Versailles Treaty, which placed him squarely in the mainstream of German international law.[63] Despite his critical stance towards the 1919 Peace Settlement, Held supported the League as a framework for treaty revision, as did Niemeyer and his successor as director of the Kiel Institute for International Law, Walther Schücking. Held introduced a new 'Chronicle of International Law' as a regular feature in the *Weltwirtschaftliches Archiv*. It provided a running account of happenings in Geneva and efforts to promote arbitration, disarmament, and legal codification beyond the League.[64] As Held implanted international law more firmly in the IfW's internal operations, Wehberg helped anchor the institute in broader legal networks that developed around the League.

Wehburg had worked for the IfW during the war, and his biography demonstrates the connection between the IfW's programme to document the world economy at war and its subsequent interest in peacetime multilateral regulation. During the war, Wehberg edited a monograph series on economic warfare at the IfW, *Der Wirtschaftskrieg*. He later recalled, 'in the long years of my activity in Germany, I never performed a task that filled me with as much gratification as my service as member of the scientific staff at Harms's institute in the years 1917–1919'.[65] In 1918, Wehberg also collaborated with Harms and Niemeyer to write the commercial provisions of the German draft League Covenant. He left the IfW in 1919 to work full time for the German League of Nations Union, where he served as the head of the international law department.

---

[59] Niemeyer, *Der Völkerbundsentwurf der Deutschen Gesellschaft für Völkerrecht.*
[60] Hoffmann, 'Die Geschichte des Instituts für Weltwirtschaft', vol. I, pp. 126–127.
[61] 'Dissertationen des Instituts für Weltwirtschaft und Seeverkehr an der Universität Kiel', *Weltwirtschaftliches Archiv*, 30 (1929), 254–6.
[62] Hoffmann, 'Die Geschichte des Instituts für Weltwirtschaft', vol. I, p. 125; H. Ibs, *Hermann J. Held (1890–1963): Ein Kieler Gelehrtenleben in den Fängen der Zeitläufe* (Peter Lang, 2000), 66–73.
[63] Hull, *A Scrap of Paper*, 5–12; Ibs, *Hermann J. Held (1890–1963)*, 75–6.
[64] H. Held, 'Chronik des Völkerrechts für die Jahre 1925 und 1926', *Weltwirtschaftliches Archiv*, 26 (1927), 193–4; Koskenniemi, *The Gentle Civilizer of Nations*, 237.
[65] H. Wehberg, 'Aus der Zeit, Bernhard Harms', *Friedens-Warte*, 33/10 (1933), 279–80, 279.

Edith Oske, who had directed the IfW's news archive during the war, also joined the Union to organize its information operations.[66] The Union quickly developed a strong relationship with the League Secretariat and served as a crucial backchannel of communication that enabled the German Foreign Office to discreetly explore prospects for accession.[67]

From his base in the League of Nations Union, Wehberg assumed a pivotal role in the associational networks that linked German international law to the League. He collaborated with Walther Schücking to write a massive three-volume commentary on the League, which became the standard reference in the German-speaking world for politicians and scholars.[68] In 1928, he moved to Geneva to join the international law faculty of the newly opened Graduate Institute of International Studies and remained in this position until his retirement in 1959. Founded with funding from the Rockefeller Foundation, the Graduate Institute became a central base for the study of international law and international relations, in active dialogue with the League.[69] Throughout the 1920s, Wehberg remained connected to the IfW as one of the most frequent contributors to the *Weltwirtschaftliches Archiv*.

Documentation and Policy-Research at the World Economic Conference

As Harms aligned the IfW more closely with the League by giving greater prominence to international law, he also plugged the IfW into broader networks of business-cycle research. Business-cycle theory had begun to emerge in the late nineteenth century. It gathered momentum in the 1920s as economists sought to identify the primary factors behind post-war economic volatility and to help firms and policymakers decide where to concentrate practical stabilization efforts.[70] In the League,

---

[66] E. Oske, *Die Informationsstelle der Deutschen Liga für Völkerbund* (Verlag Hans Robert Engelmann, 1921).

[67] Koskenniemi, *The Gentle Civilizer of Nations*, 236–8; Wintzer, *Deutschland und der Völkerbund*, 185–8.

[68] W. Schücking and H. Wehberg, *Die Satzung des Völkerbundes*, 3 vols (Franz Vahlen, 1921).

[69] C. Denfeld, *Hans Wehberg (1885–1962): Die Organisation der Staatengemeinschaft* (Nomos, 2008), 20–30; Koskenniemi, *The Gentle Civilizer of Nations*, 48–9; Kuehl and Dunn, *Keeping the Covenant*, 132.

[70] J. A. Tooze, *Statistics and the German State, 1900–1945: The Making of Modern Economic Knowledge* (Cambridge University Press, 2001), 106–9; A. M. Endres and G. A. Fleming, *International Organizations and the Analysis of Economic Policy, 1919–1950* (Cambridge University Press, 2002), 17–18; W. A. Friedman, *Fortune Tellers: The Story of America's First Economic Forecasters* (Princeton University Press, 2014), 7, 181–7.

Loveday coordinated a collaborative enquiry into business cycles between the ILO and the EFO, with participation from Llewellyn Smith. This enquiry had its roots in the post-war boom and bust in commodity markets. The inflationary spike in consumer prices following the war had put pressure on wages, bolstering organized labour. Conversely, the deflationary reaction led by the United States undercut the influence of unions by driving up unemployment and driving down commodity prices and government spending.[71] In 1921, the ILO responded by calling for a 'special Enquiry on the national and international aspects of the unemployment crisis and on the means of combating it'.[72] It formed a Joint Committee on Economic Crises with the EFO that met from 1921 to 1926. In the end, the Committee on Economic Crises gave minimal consideration to foreign trade as a factor in employment and general economic performance. Instead, it focused on price fluctuations resulting from monetary policy, in line with trends in formal macroeconomic theory in the 1920s. The main policy recommendation from the committee was to ensure that the international money supply increased at pace with production through the coordinated expansion of credit and physical gold. The League's Financial Committee established a special Gold Delegation at the end of the 1920s to discuss those objectives.[73]

Harms followed the work of the League's Committee on Economic Crises with interest and decided in 1927 to create the IfW's own Department of Statistical World-Economic Research and International Business-Cycle Research (Abteilung für Statistische Weltwirtschaftskunde und Internationale Konjunkturforschung, hereafter ASTWIK).[74] ASTWIK was directed by Adolf Löwe, who first came to the IfW as a young economist to use the library. Harms saw a fellow institutional entrepreneur in Löwe, telling him: 'I am ready to qualify you [habilitieren] immediately and the next day to make you a titular professor, under one condition, we conclude a ten-year contract for you to build a research department here'.[75] Löwe had been working in Berlin as the director of the international department at the Reich Statistical Office, under Ernst Wagemann. Wagemann created a massive Institute for Business-Cycle

---

[71] Tooze, *The Deluge*, 354–62; Maier, *Recasting Bourgeois Europe*, 135–232.

[72] Minutes of the 13th Session of the Governing Body of the International Labour Organization, Interlaken, July 1922 (International Labour Organization, 1922), 143.

[73] Endres and Fleming, *International Organizations and the Analysis of Economic Policy, 1919–1950*, 17–28; P. Clavin and J.-W. Wessels, 'Another Golden Idol? The League of Nations' Gold Delegation and the Great Depression, 1929–1932', *The International History Review*, 26/4 (2004), 765–95.

[74] Harms, 'Die Weltwirtschaftskonferenz', 238.

[75] Quoted in U. Beckmann, *Von Löwe bis Leontief: Pioniere der Konjunkturforschung am Kieler Institut für Weltwirtschaft* (Metropolis, 2000), 45.

Research within the Reich Statistical Office, with more than three hundred employees.[76] ASTWIK relied heavily on material from Wagemann, but Löwe was critical of some of his methods. Löwe accused Wagemann of amassing data and pursuing statistical innovation unguided by economic theory.[77] Löwe devised a comprehensive 'morphology of the world economy', designed to help researchers analyse the relative importance of different commodity supplies, transport flows, and capital movements.[78] ASTWIK was Harms's most far-reaching attempt to invest the IfW with a sustained research programme, yielding an output of several dozen books and articles.[79] Contemporary accounts suggest that ASTWIK's main achievements were organizational rather than intellectual, however.[80] It helped make the IfW a central gathering point for bright economists such as Hans Neisser, Gerhard Colm, and Wassily Leontief, facilitating the IfW's integration in transnational scholarly networks. Leaders in the Rockefeller Foundation noted that ASTWIK counted 'some of the best young economists in Germany'.[81] In the late 1920s, several IfW affiliates travelled in Anglo-Saxon countries as Rockefeller Fellows, and the foundation became an important source of funding for ASTWIK during the Great Depression.[82]

While ASTWIK helped the IfW forge international ties, it also housed a statistical department that focused on national trade policy, under a state-led Committee for the Investigation of the Production and Market Conditions of the German Economy.[83] This initiative was launched to define the parameters for German public trade policy following the restoration of tariff autonomy in 1925. In preparation for the World Economic Conference, it exchanged material with the League Secretariat and the network of collaborators who gathered around it, including Richard Riedl.[84] From 1927 to 1932, the committee prepared a sector-by-sector survey of 'German Foreign Trade under the Influence

---

[76] On Wagemann and his Institute for Business Cycle Research in Berlin, see Tooze, *Statistics and the German State, 1900–1945*, 103–76.
[77] Beckmann, *Von Löwe bis Leontief*, 50–51, 63, 101–6; Tooze, *Statistics and the German State, 1900–1945*, 110.
[78] Beckmann, *Von Löwe bis Leontief*, 51–3.
[79] Beckmann, *Von Löwe bis Leontief*, 55–61.
[80] Beckmann, *Von Löwe bis Leontief*, 71–80.
[81] Quoted in Beckmann, *Von Löwe bis Leontief*, 48. On the NBER's work in business-cycle research in the 1920s, see Friedman, *Fortune Tellers*, 176.
[82] Take, 'One of the Bright Spots in German Economics', 261–8.
[83] Take, 'One of the Bright Spots in German Economics', 262.
[84] S. Respondek to A. Salter, 9 August 1926, LON: R463, 10/53012/53012; B. Harms, Anregung zur Durchführung der Wirtschafts-Enquête [undated], ÖStA, AVA: NL Riedl/82.

of World-Economic Structural Transformations'.[85] Harms was charged with setting the intellectual goals for this enterprise, revealing his distinctive conception of policy research. He suggested that the enquiry and the League's World Economic Conference were responding to the same fundamental problem: 'in nearly all countries, economic legislation in the postwar period lacks a secure guide'.[86] Yet he emphasized that research must inform but not dictate policy. The enquiry should 'be limited to the investigation of facts and factual linkages, analysis and causal research, as well as the careful detection of developmental tendencies'. He warned that 'if beyond "what is", directives for what "should be" may be found, this must be done with the utmost caution and full separation from the real task of the committee: the production of foundational knowledge for those whose occupation it is to make policy'.[87] In keeping with his semi-detached stance towards policy, Harms followed the World Economic Conference attentively and published extensively on it, but did not directly participate in the proceedings.

Documenting Europe and the World in 1927

The World Economic Conference was an information-rich event. Loveday was responsible for coordinating the official documentation, which totalled fifty-six lengthy reports. The League staff wrote much of this text, and they also published documents submitted by auxiliary multilateral organizations such as the ICC or the International Institute of Agriculture. Harms celebrated the production of economic information within and around the League as one of the main achievements of the World Economic Conference and contributed by publishing more than three hundred pages of material in the *Weltwirtschaftliches Archiv*. Karl Přibram wrote a detailed summary of Loveday's collection of reports.[88] Louise Sommer wrote a one hundred page 'pre-history' of the conference, compiled with assistance from the

---

[85] Institut für Weltwirtschaft und Seeverkehr, *Der deutsche Außenhandel unter der Einwirkung der weltwirtschaftlicher Strukturwandlungen*, 2 (Mittler, 1932); Plehwe and Slobodian, 'Landscapes of Unrest', 196.

[86] 'Zusammentritt der Enquete-kommission', *Frankfurter Zeitung*, 8 July 1926, IfW: Hs/ Harms/6.

[87] B. Harms 'Anregung zur Durchführung der Wirtschafts-Enquête', 20 May 1926, GStA: I HA/ Rep. 120 C XIII 1/Nr. 80 adh. Bd. 1. On Harms's conception of scientific objectivity, see Beckmann, *Von Löwe bis Leontief*, 27–8; Take, '"Die Objektivität ist durch sein Wesen verbürgt": Bernhard Harms' Gründung des Kieler Instituts für Weltwirtschaft und sein Aufstieg im Ersten Weltkrieg'.

[88] K. Přibram, 'Die weltwirtschaftliche Lage im Spiegel des Schrifttums der Weltwirtschaftskonferenz', *Weltwirtschaftliches Archiv*, 26 (1927), 305–438.

League Secretariat.[89] Harms also marked the event by collecting his own wartime and post-war speeches in a single volume, which he published under the title 'From the Economic War to the World Economic Conference' (*Vom Wirtschaftskrieg zur Weltwirtschaftskonferenz*).[90] In it, he presented the 1927 conference as the culmination of a political cycle that began in 1916 with the Allies' economic conference in Paris. That event confirmed the transformation of the world economy into a tool of war, and the central objective of the League in 1927 was to turn the world economy back into a tool of peace. Harms declared: 'ten years ago the world stood in flames, today it stands under the sign of the League of Nations'.[91]

As Harms spread news about the World Economic Conference through the IfW's information channels, other private individuals and associations circulated unofficial documentation at the event itself, with varying levels of support from the Secretariat. For example, Loveday published his own comparison of tariff protection in different countries while also helping to disseminate similar measures prepared by Riedl and the British free trader Clive Morrison-Bell. Riedl analysed the tariff burden on several hundred kinds of Austrian exports in different countries. He then translated the data into a map, which he displayed at the conference alongside a more eye-catching three-dimensional map of European tariff walls from Morrison-Bell.[92] Morrison-Bell and Riedl corresponded with Loveday about the statistical methods behind comparative tariff measurements, most notably the use of 'index numbers'.[93] Index numbers were a technique to measure national tariff rates on a selection of key goods, weighted according to their importance in foreign trade. A single number indicating a country's level of protection could then be calculated based on the ratio of import values to customs revenues for the goods included in the index. As Loveday struggled to apply this approach to the League's trade data, he consulted Llewellyn Smith and the statisticians in the British Board of Trade. Their 1903–1904 'Blue Books' had been an important early application of the index-number method, charting the tariff burden on British exports in

---

[89] L. Sommer, 'Die Vorgeschichte der Weltwirtschaftskonferenz (Genf 1927): Chronik und Archivalien', *Weltwirtschaftliches Archiv*, 28 (1928), 180–92, 340–418. Note to Stoppani, Stencek, and Jacobsson, undated, LON: R444 10/49117/49117.

[90] Harms, *Vom Wirtschaftskrieg zur Weltwirtschaftskonferenz*.

[91] Harms, 'Strukturwandlungen der Weltwirtschaft', 57.

[92] C. Morrison-Bell, *Tariff Walls: A European Crusade* (J. Murray, 1930); Slobodian, *Globalists*, 40.

[93] Tariff Level Indices, May 1927, LON: R1821, 50/56098/51672.

different countries.[94] Llewellyn Smith expressed scepticism about the possibilities to internationalize the tariff-index method, however. For, it was relatively straightforward to construct an index that measured foreign tariffs on the most important goods in a single country's export profile (as he had done for Britain or as Riedl did for Austria). It was much harder to determine which goods were most important for world trade, as a whole. It was particularly difficult to craft a single international tariff index that had equal relevance for states that exported a variety of industrial goods and those that exported a small number of primary commodities.[95]

Indeed, raw material exporters from around the world complained about the bias towards industrial Europe at the World Economic Conference. European perspectives did predominate in the conference documentation. The general material that was written in the League Secretariat and the ILO had a broad geographic scope, but the sectoral assessments of the world economy only came from European economic organizations and public officials. The only channel through which non-European perspectives were directly communicated, was a set of national economic surveys that Loveday solicited from all League members ahead of the conference.[96] Moreover, Europe was the focal point for much of the unofficial material floating around at the conference alongside Loveday's curated documents. For example, Coquet and Riedl first pitched their plans for European economic unity in private memoranda for the conference.[97] Latin American delegates banded together to protest the marked Eurocentrism of the conference. Nine delegations from the region attended at great expense but felt decidedly unwelcome in an environment where the primacy of industrial Europe was quite explicit. In his opening remarks, the Belgian president of the conference, Georges Theunis, simply stated, 'it is obvious that many, perhaps even most, of the issues that will especially hold our attention will be more or less European'. The initial 'malaise' that such comments produced among the Latin American delegates did

[94] *British and Foreign Trade and Industry. Memoranda, Statistical Tables, and Charts Prepared in the Board of Trade in Reference to Various Matters Bearing on British and Foreign Trade and Industrial Conditions* (H. M. G. Stationery Office, 1903).

[95] H. Llewellyn Smith to A. Loveday, 16 February 1927, R1821 50/56098/51672; 'Discussion of Mr. Loveday's Paper' in A. Loveday, 'The Measurement of Tariff Levels', *Journal of the Royal Statistical Society*, 92/4, 487–529, 516–17. On further methodological problems related to the tariff-index method, see James, *The End of Globalization*, 108.

[96] See International Economic Conference, Guide to the Preparatory Documents of the Conference, May 1927, LON: R 531, 10C/59669/46431.

[97] R. Riedl, *Collective Treaties Facilitating International Commerce in Europe: Report of the Austrian National Committee to the Committee on Trade Barriers* (Vernay, 1926).

dissipate somewhat over the course of the conference as they found opportunities to debate Europe's place in the world and to draw inter-regional connections to the Pan-American Union.[98]

Perhaps most remarkably, Cuba used the conference to launch a long campaign to renegotiate its position in the world economy and its semi-colonial relationship to the United States through the conclusion of a League-backed international sugar agreement. Cuba had not fol-lowed the US defection from the League, and Geneva became an import-ant platform for the island nation to assert its formal sovereignty. In 1927, the Cuban delegation complained that the League's early engagement with commodity markets had mainly reflected the interests of European industrial importers who wanted secure access to cheap raw materials (this slant was evident both in the Gini Inquiry and the Prohibitions Convention). Cubans argued that the League must also consider com-modity exporters' demands for stable markets and remunerative prices. The price of tropical crops had recovered more slowly than other com-modities after the post-war boom and bust. In 1927, Cuba began to push for multilateral cooperation between sugar importers and exporters, eventually securing a League-sponsored International Sugar Agreement in 1937. This quota-based agreement not only confirmed Cuba's prefer-ential bond to the United States but also helped it cultivate other export markets.[99] If the inter-governmental commodity agreements of the 1930s refocused international attention on commodity exporters, they also brought new forms of administrative oversight that were resented in many producing countries.[100] In this context, League trade debates were still largely concerned with defining what kinds of rules governments could place on transnational business. It was a matter of 'regulating the regulators', as Mats Ingulstad aptly puts it.[101]

Harms discussed the changing position of primary commodity pro-ducers in global markets in his own commentary on the World Economic Conference. He noted that extractive economies around the world were building facilities to transform raw materials and directly export semi-processed goods such as oil, jute, or cotton, without passing through European entrepôts. The First World War accelerated this trend by expanding Europe's import needs while tying up its commer-cial and industrial capacity. Moreover, the war and its tumultuous

[98] C. Rodriguez, Memorandum sur la Conférence Économique de la Société des Nations au point de vue Latino-Américain, 24 May 1927, LON: 10C/59764/46431.

[99] M. Fakhri, 'The 1937 International Sugar Agreement: Neo-Colonial Cuba and Economic Aspects of the League of Nations', *Leiden Journal of International Law*, 24/4 (2011), 899–922.

[100] Martin, *The Meddlers*, 178–209.   [101] Ingulstad, 'Regulating the Regulators'.

aftermath had heightened awareness of economic vulnerabilities worldwide. Europeans fretted about securing supply lines for 'key goods', such as synthetic dyes, which were a choke point for many other industries. In contrast, countries that depended on exporting a few raw materials or 'hinge goods' could easily find their 'whole national economy shaken' when global commodity prices sank, as had happened in 1920.[102]

For Harms, the solution for most extractive economies lay in 'differentiation'. He acknowledged that past attempts to follow that strategy had produced mixed practical results, but 'the view that all the areas that produce hinge goods today are destined by nature to remain in this condition' was no longer tenable and required 'fundamental revision'.[103] He emphasized that differentiation did not mean walling off autarkic national economies but rather renegotiating the terms of their integration in a unified world economy. This could bring more and not less reliance on foreign investment and export markets. Harms was particularly interested in India's policies to expand manufacturing capacity, welcoming numerous Indian students and researchers to the IfW in the 1920s. One student from Calcutta wrote home about the 'many beautiful evenings' that he spent at the IfW's seminar dinners. He was left with the impression that 'if there is any country at all in this world where Indians are not only treated on equal footing but also regarded and respected, as being the descendants of a great nation possessing the oldest civilization, highest philosophy and finest culture, then it is Germany'.[104] This experience aligned with the German government's efforts to exploit the limited moves towards tariff autonomy in the colonial world to regain a foothold in global markets in the 1920s.

Harms was willing to support economic diversification in developing countries to reduce their exposure to global market shocks, but he was more sceptical of demands for strategic autonomy in the interest of national security. In the 1920s, many Habsburg successor states were pursuing industrial policies designed to reduce dependence on the export of primary products and shield strategic industries from potentially unfriendly neighbours (notably, Austria, Germany, and Italy). Harms complained that the political ideal of national self-determination often took precedence over commercial considerations in Central and Eastern

---

[102] Harms, 'Strukturwandlungen der Weltwirtschaft', 38–9.
[103] Harms, 'Strukturwandlungen der Weltwirtschaft', 40.
[104] Zohadur Rahim, 'The Institute of World-Wide Economics and Ocean-Transport in the University of Kiel', 1934, IfW: Hs Allg./1. These reflections come from Rahim's time at the IfW in 1931–2, just before the arrival of the Nazis transformed its operations.

Europe: 'the arbitrary and artificial division of the European economic space through the shredding of largely cohesive historic economic units is probably the basis for the structural changes in the European economy that are most disastrous and will have the longest-lasting effects'.[105] As will be seen in the next chapter, this same security logic motivated Coquet, Riedl, and many others to embrace pan-European solutions. Harms drew the opposite conclusion and looked towards the United States for global leadership.

Harms pointed to the First World War as proof that a comprehensive multilateral system was needed to manage relations between the world economy and its constituent parts. Within national borders, governments could intervene to settle conflicting economic interests. The absence of a world state meant that such conflicts had been settled at the international level by 'victory or defeat, hammer or anvil'.[106] This zero-sum logic had played out in the First World War and had brought massive economic losses to all European belligerents. From that conflict, only the United States emerged triumphant, 'nowhere else in the world'.[107] Yet pre-eminence in an impoverished world was a pyrrhic victory for the United States. Thus, Harms considered it to be a 'scientific necessity' for the United States to seek 'the economic solidarity of peoples and nations'.[108] Concretely, Harms recommended replacing bilateral trade treaties with a multi-party arrangement.[109] His enthusiasm for trade treaties aligned him with the Ministry of Economic Affairs and the Foreign Office, where leaders supported bilateral and multilateral negotiations as a means to counter the strong pressure for tariff protection after 1925 in the German parliament.[110] In Harms's view, an effective policy of freer trade would require the multilateral machinery of the League of Nations and US leadership.[111] He did not expect the World Economic Conference to produce that configuration, but it could help generate political will for a more comprehensive and durable economic settlement. In his view, the 'true mission' of the conference was to 'influence world opinion' by promoting 'international economic solidarity', and he suggested that the League could then continue that work by associating 'a larger number of leading personalities' with its economic work in the

---

[105] Harms, 'Strukturwandlungen der Weltwirtschaft', 35.
[106] Harms, 'Strukturwandlungen der Weltwirtschaft', 55.
[107] Harms, 'Strukturwandlungen der Weltwirtschaft', 56.
[108] Harms, 'Strukturwandlungen der Weltwirtschaft', 56.
[109] Harms, 'Strukturwandlungen der Weltwirtschaft', 57.
[110] Schulz, *Deutschland, der Völkerbund und die Frage der europäischen Wirtschaftsordnung*, 60–80.
[111] Schulz, *Deutschland, der Völkerbund und die Frage der europäischen Wirtschaftsordnung*, 76–9.

future.[112] Harms turned towards the League's International Committee on Intellectual Cooperation to coordinate public outreach.

An Economic Bibliography for the League

The International Committee on Intellectual Cooperation (ICIC) was the main branch of the League that was responsible for facilitating scientific and cultural exchange, serving as an anchor point for non-governmental intellectual organizations, such as the IfW.[113] It helped nurture the emerging discipline of international relations, and it also took up various practical issues that would later fall under the umbrella of the 'knowledge economy'. For example, it proposed labour standards for the growing ranks of university-educated 'intellectual workers' and sought to ease their transnational mobility by ensuring the equivalence of degrees.[114] Although the ICIC was founded on the basic premise that learning should transcend borders and serve as a force for peace, it was far from a cosmopolitan republic of letters. The League's intellectual activity mapped onto national, imperial, and regional cleavages, and Germany was a particular point of tension. Participation in the ICIC's staff and expert committees was not limited to League member countries. This allowed the United States to play a strong role in the in the ICIC from an early stage through a dedicated National Committee for Intellectual Cooperation. In contrast, German scholars were initially kept on the margins. Their absence was conspicuous because German universities had been the envy of the world before 1914 and retained considerable prestige in the 1920s. After the Locarno Accords paved the way for German accession to the League, there was a concerted push to integrate Germans more centrally into the ICIC.[115]

As part of the German rehabilitation effort, Harms assumed leadership for a large International Bibliography of Economic Sciences. This was a cooperative venture between five economic journals, each responsible for producing a regular survey of economic literature from specific regions and languages, according to standardized parameters. Participating journals came from Germany, Britain, France, Italy, and Spain but were also asked to include material in other languages. For example, the *Revue*

---

[112] Harms, 'Die Weltwirtschaftskonferenz', 240–41.

[113] D. Laqua, 'Internationalisme ou affirmation de la nation? La coopération intellectuelle transnationale dans l'entre-deux-guerres', *Critique internationale*, 52/3 (2011), 51–67, 53–4.

[114] D. Laqua, 'Transnational Intellectual Cooperation, the League of Nations, and the Problem of Order', *Journal of Global History*, 6/2 (2011), 223–47, 237–46.

[115] Laqua, 'Transnational Intellectual Cooperation', 229, 234–6.

d'Économie Politique would cover Romanian as well as French literature and the IfW's *Weltwirtschaftliches Archiv* would cover Scandinavian languages (non-European languages would not be covered, at least in the initial stages). Each journal would print special bibliographic supplements in its own language. The final goal was to publish all five supplements together as a stand-alone volume, available as a single running subscription.[116]

Although the economic bibliography was run out of the ICIC and the affiliated International Institute of Intellectual Cooperation, it enjoyed strong backing from the EFO as well. Salter declared that the economic bibliography 'would be of great value and that such a work is much needed'. Loveday concurred that the plan was 'an excellent one, and one which should receive our wholehearted support'. He stressed that it would be important to survey scholarly 'books and papers' as well as 'all official publications of all interest' and 'the sources of periodic statistical returns'. He noted that 'in the long run, it is the regular statements which are of the most value to the economist', but they were not widely reported. Thus, Loveday saw the bibliography project as a valuable contribution to his own efforts to create a running survey of the world economy. Both Loveday and Salter emphasized that the bibliography's practical value would hinge on its organization, a task that fell to Harms.[117]

As the 'General Manager' of the economic bibliography, Harms was responsible for drafting an overall implementation plan, setting a budget, and securing funding. The member of the ICIC who originally floated the idea for an economic bibliography, Friedrich von Gottl-Ottlilienfeld, was a professor of economic theory at the University of Kiel who was affiliated with the IfW, and he recommended Harms as a general manager based on the IfW's existing information services.[118] The *Weltwirtschaftliches Archiv* was already publishing extensive abstracts and reviews from a corps of regular contributors. Since the first volume in 1913, reviews had consistently made up one-third of each issue. Thus, by 1928, the journal was publishing more than three hundred pages of reviews twice per year. The IfW's reviews covered scholarship as well as official and commercial reports, in line with Loveday's vision. In addition to this published output, the IfW library was widely recognized as one of the leading

---

[116] *International Committee on Intellectual Cooperation. Minutes of the Ninth Session*, C. 424.M. 157.1927.XII (League of Nations, 1927), 106, 111–12.

[117] A. Loveday to A. Salter, 20 September 1928; A. Salter to G. Oprescu, 29 September 1928, LON: R 2191 5B/7355/377.

[118] 'Annex 15. Report on the Meeting of Experts, Held at Paris in January 1927 Submitted by Professor von Gottl-Ottlilienfeld', in *International Committee on Intellectual Cooperation. Minutes of the Ninth Session*, C. 424.M. 157.1927.XII (League of Nations, 1927), 105–114.

repositories for economic research in the world. The head librarian, Wilhelm Gülich, developed a sophisticated system of bibliographic classification and was considered as a candidate to run the League of Nations Library.[119]

Harms's relationship to US philanthropic bodies was another factor in his selection. Gottl-Ottlilienfeld reflected that, 'in the last resort, everything depends upon providing the enterprise with the necessary financial backing', with an eye to the United States. He hoped to 'induce the large philanthropic foundations in that country to add this important enterprise to the many which they have brought into being'.[120] Indeed, the Rockefeller Foundation already provided subsidies to many libraries in Europe, including at the IfW and the League. It also supported the ICIC's Committee on Bibliography, which oversaw Harms's project.[121] Through his prior contact with the Laura Spelman Rockefeller Memorial, Harms was familiar with the procedural norms that governed the increasingly professionalized world of US philanthropy.[122] He knew that the bibliography project must recruit influential backers before seeking US funding.[123] US collaborators emphasized Harms's value as a 'confidence-inspiring name' and endorsed a decision to extend his tenure as general manager to five years instead of the one-year rotation that was initially planned.[124]

Alongside Harms, the ICIC also enlisted its heavyweight transatlantic emissaries, Raymond Fosdick and Arthur Sweetser, to promote the economic bibliography. Both Americans had been involved in the Paris Peace Conference and the initial formation of the League and went on to play a pivotal role in securing private US financial support for the League's information work in the 1920s. Fosdick served briefly as an under-secretary general in the League Secretariat and then acted as an advisor to the Rockefeller Foundation before becoming its president in the 1930s. Sweetser stayed on in the Secretariat's Information Section and became a crucial backchannel to the United States.[125] Both men used a combination of professional and social levers to build support for the

---

[119] Take, 'One of the Bright Spots in German Economics', 260.

[120] 'Annex 15. Report on the Meeting of Experts, Held at Paris in January 1927 Submitted by Professor von Gottl-Ottlilienfeld', 113; See also letter from F. von Gottl-Ottlilienfeld, 25 June 1927, LON: R 1077, 13C/41587/60551.

[121] Kuehl and Dunn, *Keeping the Covenant*, 84–5, 131.

[122] Take, 'One of the Bright Spots in German Economics', 256–7, 265.

[123] Fleck to A. Dufour-Feronce, 1 September 1928, LON R2191, 5B/377/377.

[124] S. Chapin to A. Dufour-Feronce, 10 December 1928, LON: 5B/6114/377; G. Oprescu, Memorandum for M. Fosdick on the Coordination of Bibliography in Economics, 22 August 1928, LON: 5B/6114/377.

[125] Kuehl and Dunn, *Keeping the Covenant*, 5, 22, 83–7; Herren and Löhr, 'Being International in Times of War', 539–40.

League's economic bibliography. For example, Sweetser spent a transatlantic crossing extolling the merits of the economic bibliography to Isiah Bowman, a leader of the US Social Science Research Council (SSRC), after a visit to the United States that involved a Princeton hockey game with John D. Rockefeller and meetings with Fosdick. Salter also shared Bowman and Sweetser's dining table on the steamer back to Europe and added his own enthusiastic endorsement of the bibliography.[126] Bowmen was important as a potential friend or foe because the SSRC was preparing a competing bibliographic periodical, the *Social Science Abstracts*.

Without proper coordination, the *Social Science Abstracts* threatened to overshadow the League's economic bibliography and absorb its philanthropic funding. Gottl-Ottlilienfeld tried to avert this outcome by clearly differentiating the two projects. He described the *Social Science Abstracts* as 'a creation through which the active scientific life of a single, rich and powerful country seeks to establish its independence'. Surveying all branches of social science, it would have 'a far wider range of subject-matter' but would only cover scholarly publications. Its geographic scope would be 'adapted more particularly to American interests'. In contrast, the League's economic bibliography focused on 'a narrower but much more intensively cultivated field', and its 'strongly marked internationalism clearly reflects the lofty ideal of the League of Nations, upon whose patronage it relies'. Gottl-Ottlilienfeld argued that the two bibliographies must avoid duplication. By 1927, the Rockefeller Foundation had already agreed to finance the *Social Science Abstracts* for ten years and was unlikely to give the League money to 'do the same work twice over'.[127] There were several attempts to make the US and League projects compatible, but in the end the *Social Science Abstracts* wholly displaced the ICIC's economic bibliography.

Harms and Gottl-Ottlilienfeld first attempted to arrange a simple exchange of material. The London School of Economics, which was responsible for covering English-language publications for the League, would reprint the portion of the *Social Science Abstracts* that pertained to economics. The League would then provide early drafts of its five regional bibliographies, from which the SSRC could make selections to translate and reprint in its own section on economics.[128] The director of the *Social*

---

[126] A. Sweetser to W. Rose, 5 March 1929, LON: R2191, 5B/6114/377.
[127] 'Annex 15. Report on the Meeting of Experts, Held at Paris in January 1927 Submitted by Professor von Gottl-Ottlilienfeld', 113; Social Science Abstracts, 4 July 1928, LON R2191, 5B/6114/2191.
[128] 'Annex 15. Report on the Meeting of Experts, Held at Paris in January 1927 Submitted by Professor von Gottl-Ottlilienfeld', 113–14.

Science Abstracts, Stuart Chapin, pushed for deeper integration, however. He did not want Europeans merely to provide content but also to participate in the editorial process of the *Social Science Abstracts*. He aspired to make the publication 'broadly non-provincial and cosmopolitan'. To this end, he assembled a team of roughly two hundred 'consulting editors' from around the world to provide advice about what material to survey and to help recruit a multilingual pool of seven hundred abstractors. In Europe, Chapin grafted this editorial network onto the team that was working on League's economic bibliography.[129] Engagement with the ICIC helped Chapin to cultivate European collaborators, but the implementation of the *Social Science Abstracts* rapidly undercut support for the ICIC's own work. The *Social Science Abstracts* had a significant organizational and financial head start. The German under-secretary general in the League, Albert Dufour-Feronce, complained to Harms that 'thanks to the means at their disposal, the Americans were able to work faster than we poor Europeans'.[130] Chapin had begun to lay the groundwork for the *Social Science Abstracts* in 1923 when Europe was still in the depths of the Ruhr crisis. The SSRC began to raise funds in summer 1927, and by 1928 the *Social Science Abstracts* was 'a going concern', stripping the League's economic bibliography of much of its value.[131]

In March 1929, Harms and Dufour-Feronce gave up the fight. They met with Bowman to devise a pared-down plan in which the League would simply translate the *Social Science Abstracts* into French and German. Bowman made a valiant effort to implement this new arrangement, meeting repeatedly with the SSRC and the Rockefeller Foundation. He managed to persuade the Rockefeller Foundation to cover two-thirds of the cost for French and German editions of the *Social Science Abstracts* if the rest of the money needed could be raised in Europe, but even this modest goal was out of reach.[132] By summer 1929 the financial situation in Europe was already bleak, as high US interest rates intended to tame the runaway speculative frenzy on Wall Street sucked money across the Atlantic. Moreover, Harms concluded that the publication in 1929 of the first English edition of the *Social Science Abstracts*, 'which every learned person in Germany can read', made it hard to justify a German translation, confirming English as the academic *lingua franca* of the future.[133] He told Dufour-Feronce that

[129] Social Science Abstracts, 4 July 1928, LON: R2191, 5B/6114/2191.
[130] A. Dufour-Feronce to B. Harms, 10 July 1929, LON,: R2192, 5B/6114/377.
[131] S. Chapin to A. Dufour-Feronce, 10 December 1928, LON: R2191, 5B/6114/377.
[132] I. Bowman to A. Dufour-Feronce, 23 May 1929, LON: R2191, 5B/6114/377; I. Bowman to G. Oprescu, 14 June 1929, LON R2191, 5B/6114/377.
[133] B. Harms to A. Dufour-Feronce, 23 September 1929, LON: R2191, 5B/6114/377.

the SSRC had simply 'pre-empted' the League's economic bibliography and concluded that 'never in my life have I participated in such a fruitless endeavour!'[134] This episode reveals the United States as a clumsy giant that was still learning its own strength, even in the realm of private internationalism. Despite strong interest in transatlantic engagement on all sides, from the League and from the SSRC and Rockefeller Foundation, the Americans still managed to undermine their European partners' slower and more sprawling collaborative efforts. Harms and Gottl-Ottlilienfeld had hoped that there would be room in the world for both projects, but the version in American English ultimately won out. The story of the League's failed economic bibliography also invites reflection about how League trade politics were shaped by the US absence in the 1920s. The US withdrawal did preclude discussion of some of the most fundamental imbalances in the interwar world economy, notably related to US tariffs and sovereign lending. Yet, it also left Europeans more space to be slow and quarrelsome in Geneva, generating a multi-centric, multi-level approach to trade policy that left a durable imprint in international institutions even after the United States assumed a more prominent global role in the 1940s.

Through the economic bibliography, Harms confronted the limits of his own worldview. He came out of the 1923 Ruhr crisis with a firm belief that European cooperation was an essential prerequisite for the recovery of the world economy. At the same time, he insisted that this process of recovery could not be 'purely European and must include outside powers, especially the United States'. He thought that Europe and the United States must be brought under the same umbrella of 'world economic law', based in the League, and saw economic information as a tool to orient leaders on both sides of the Atlantic towards that goal. His attempts to consolidate the League's bonds to US organizations such as the SSRC and the Rockefeller Foundation aligned with efforts to expand formal League trade policy across the Atlantic following the World Economic Conference, with the addition of a US member on the Economic Committee. The economic bibliography demonstrated how difficult it was to engage US internationalists in European-led multilateralism, however. Cooperation quickly became outright domination due to the massive imbalance in resources between the United States and Europe. Yet Harms saw no alternative. He argued that multilateral projects that were limited to Europe simply would not work, declaring in 1927 that 'structures between national economy and world economy are destined to

---

[134] B. Harms to A. Dufour-Feronce, 24 July 1929, LON: R2191, 5B/6114/377.

regression if not death'. This negative judgement applied to British imperial preference as well as the movement to create a 'United States of Europe'.[135]

The same sequence of events that led Harms to reject European unity brought Lucien Coquet and Richard Riedl to embrace it. Both Coquet and Riedl initially outlined their plans for a 'United States of Europe' in response to the Ruhr crisis and then gave those plans a more precise institutional formulation in the run-up to the World Economic Conference. Coquet and Riedl both adopted a narrower regional vision of multilateral order and they also worked through a more limited set of organizational channels. Like Harms, Coquet built a broad coalition of academics, politicians, and business leaders, but he did not use this network to facilitate general information exchange. Instead, Coquet mustered support for one specific policy goal: a European customs union. Riedl engaged with the League through the intermediary of the ICC, and his interventions privileged practical business priorities over politics. Notably, he went to great lengths to close the gap between the ICC's general commitment to open markets guaranteed by MFN and his personal determination to pursue regional unity around an Austro-German core. Coquet and Riedl shared Harms's ambition to weld the disparate regulatory initiatives that Llewellyn Smith began in the early 1920s into a more coherent system. Yet greater institutional coherence also brought underlying conflicts over geopolitics into sharper relief; a total worldview raised difficult questions about how the different parts of the world fit together.

[135] Harms, 'Die Weltwirtschaftskonferenz', 243–4.

6   European Unity and Security

While Bernhard Harms was a well-known figure in interwar internationalist circles as the IfW's leader, Lucien Coquet was
a workhorse who operated in the shadows, exerting influence as an
intermediary between more prestigious partners. Harms and Coquet
shared many collaborators, but the two men had very different
methods and underlying political motives. Through the IfW,
Harms gathered a dizzying kaleidoscope of perspectives around
a very general set of multilateral principles. In contrast, Coquet
advanced a more precise political objective, the formation of
a European customs union. Coquet built out a vast association in
the service of this cause, the European Customs Union (Union
Douanière Européenne, UDE). The UDE encompassed numerous
national committees and sectoral study groups and aggregated many
other non-governmental associations. Coquet went to great lengths
to forge ties with the policy associations that orbited around the
League of Nations, such as the Federation of League of Nations
Societies and the Inter-Parliamentary Union. He also cultivated
close relations with the French Ministry of Commerce and
Ministry of Foreign Affairs, making the UDE into a central interface
between public and private internationalist activity. Coquet intervened in lots of different public and private forums but did so in
a quite repetitive way; indeed, repetition was the point. He kept up
a steady drumbeat to build consensus around a defined set of
options for regional trade cooperation: a tariff truce, a tariff ceiling,
percentage-based tariff reductions, and cartels, all gradually leading
to a full customs union. The UDE helped ensure that this basic
policy menu framed debates about European trade cooperation in
the League of Nations.

The UDE already has an established place in the long history of
European integration. Among the flurry of Europeanist associations
that emerged in the 1920s, the UDE is generally seen as the most
broadly influential organization that promoted regional economic

unity. The leadership role played by the UDE's French Committee in relation to the other national branches is also widely recognized.[1] Laurence Badel has provided a particularly valuable account of the UDE French Committee's evolution from the 1920s to the 1940s.[2] Thus, the goal of this chapter is not to rewrite the fundamental history of the UDE, but rather to analyse the role that it played in the legal and organizational context of League trade politics. Coquet's personal trajectory illustrates the changes in European diplomatic practice that facilitated League engagement with private policy advocacy organizations such as the UDE. His similar but less successful pre-war initiative, the Franco-German Commercial Committee, offers a useful baseline. Coquet's perspective also underscores the tight links between European cooperation and conflicts over Franco-German security. His interactions with Richard Riedl reveal how the complex dynamics of geopolitical rivalry and cooperation around 'the German problem' helped propel the movement for European unity in the 1920s. Coquet hoped that introducing a system of Europe-wide multilateral policy constraints would reduce Germany's capacity to use trade as a lever for political pressure over its neighbours, to the east and the west. This approach first began to crystallize during the Franco-Belgian occupation of the Ruhr in 1923.

The Rhineland, the Ruhr, and French Security in the 1920s

During the Ruhr crisis, Coquet developed his ideas about a European customs union in dialogue with his former brother-in-law, Otto Wolff, who had become one of Cologne's biggest steel magnates.[3] Coquet welcomed the Ruhr occupation as an opportunity to secure greater autonomy for that region as well as the neighbouring Rhineland, where Allied troops had been stationed since 1918. Only ten days after the

---

[1] E. Stern-Rubarth, *Aus zuverlässiger Quelle verlautet . . .* (W. Kohlhammer Verlag, 1964), 122; C. H. Pegg, *Evolution of the European Idea, 1914–1932* (University of North Carolina Press, 1983), 77–8; J.-L. Chabot, *Aux origines intellectuelles de l'Union européenne: L'idée d'Europe unie de 1919 à 1939* (Presses Universitaires de Grenoble, 2005), 78–87; J.-M. Guieu, *Le rameau et le glaive: les militants français pour la Société des Nations* (Presses de la fondation nationale des sciences politiques, 2008), 151; Richard, 'Colonialism and the European Movement', pp. 191–205.

[2] L. Badel, 'Les promoteurs français d'une union économique et douanière de l'Europe dans l'entre-deux-guerres', in A. Fleury and L. Jilek (eds.), *The Briand Plan of European Federal Union: National and Transnational Perspectives, with Documents* (Peter Lang, 1998), pp. 17–30; Badel, *Un milieu libéral et européen*, 131–474.

[3] L. Coquet, Mémoire de défense, 10 October 1945, AN: F12/9640; Visite de M. Coquet à M. de Peretti, 3 January 1923, AMAE: RC/B 81–82/334.

French and Belgian armies arrived in the Ruhr, Coquet sent France's prime minister, Raymond Poincaré, a detailed plan to promote Rhenish autonomy by dividing responsibility for German reparations among the country's individual regions. Coquet also offered to serve as a liaison to Wolff, who supported regional decentralization within Germany as a path to cooperation with France. Coquet and Wolff highlighted the broader geopolitical implications of this plan in a conversation with one of France's delegates to the League, Georges Reynald. They explained that 'the experiment of a customs union might first be attempted with the Rhineland and then with all of Germany'.[4] Wolff reiterated this point in his direct exchanges with French leaders, declaring that a new Rheno-Westphalian state within Germany, separated from Prussia, could serve as a 'bridge' to France that would lead to the formation of a 'true customs union' between the two countries.[5] He emphasized that Rhenish autonomy could facilitate federal devolution away from Prussia across Germany, a goal that many French officials shared.[6]

Wolff came to play a pivotal role in the Ruhr occupation, and his reputation as an advocate of Franco-German cooperation was an important factor in his agency. In the early months of the Ruhr occupation, he repeatedly reached out to French officials with offers of collaboration, on his own and through Coquet. Poincaré initially rebuffed these overtures, only willing to negotiate directly with the German government. Poincaré abruptly changed tack in August 1923 and authorized French occupation officials to begin discussions with Wolff

---

[4] Résumé de l'entretien du 2 Janvier entre M. le Sénateur Reynald, M. Otto Wolff, M. Charles Stein, et M. Lucien Coquet, 3 January 1923, AMAE: RC/B 81–82/334.

[5] 'Le Général Denvignes à Monsieur le Général Commandant l'Armée', 17 August 1923 [Pièce Annexe 786], in J. Degoutte, L'Occupation de la Ruhr, Rapport d'ensemble (Imprimerie de l'Armée du Rhin, 1924), 2018; D. Dahlmann, 'Das Unternehmen Otto Wolff: vom Alteisenhandel zum Weltkonzern (1904–1929)', in P. Danylow and U. S. Soénius (eds.), Otto Wolff: Ein Unternehmen zwischen Wirtschaft und Politik (Siedler, 2005), 69.

[6] J. Degoutte, L'Occupation de la Ruhr, Texte (Imprimerie de l'Armée du Rhin, 1924), 22–3; S. Jeannesson, Poincaré, la France et la Ruhr, 1922–1924: histoire d'une occupation (Presses universitaires de Strasbourg, 1998), 227–9, 312; Jackson, Beyond the Balance of Power, 410. Coquet and his collaborator Michel Klecker de Balazuc surpassed Wolff in their enthusiasm for Rhineland independence, however. They supported the separatist leader Hans Dorten in his scheme for a Rhenish Republic. In contrast, Wolff favoured regional autonomy but not independence. A Rhenish Republic, he averred, would 'create a new Alsace-Lorraine' that would durably sour Franco-German relations. 'Le Général Denvignes à Monsieur le Général Commandant l'Armée', 17 August 1923 [Pièce Annexe 786], in Degoutte, L'Occupation de la Ruhr, Rapport d'ensemble, 2017; E. Conze, '"Titane der modernen Wirtschaft" Otto Wolff (1881–1940)', in P. Danylow and U. S. Soénius (eds.), Otto Wolff: Ein Unternehmen zwischen Wirtschaft und Politik (Siedler, 2005), 119; Dahlmann, 'Das Unternehmen Otto Wolff: vom Alteisenhandel zum Weltkonzern (1904–1929)', 58–9.

and his associates.[7] Wolff broke ranks with other German industrialists to end their common policy of passive resistance by signing an agreement to resume reparations deliveries on terms that were very favourable to France. This placed France in a position of strength vis-à-vis the German government and the other industrialists in the Ruhr, who all signed agreements modelled on Wolff's.[8] The success of these private negotiations emboldened Poincaré to spurn opportunities to consolidate France's territorial and economic influence in the Ruhr and the Rhineland through formal dialogue with German officials in autumn 1923.[9] Instead, Poincaré held out hope that worsening political turmoil would give him more leverage in negotiations over Rhenish autonomy and reparations. He agreed to begin the Dawes negotiations from a position of apparent strength but rapidly lost ground as the French franc plummeted in winter 1923–4, forcing him to plead for assistance from US banks.[10]

Coquet does not seem to have been directly involved in Wolff's crucial negotiations with French occupation officials in autumn 1923, but he did help establish Wolff's reputation as a politically reliable partner by repeatedly affirming the latter's credentials as a partisan of Franco-German cooperation. Indeed, he had already started touting Wolff's value as a political asset before the Ruhr occupation began. In 1922, Coquet had tried to help Wolff secure coal deliveries from the French-controlled Saar by presenting him as an advocate of Rhineland autonomy who favoured rapprochement with France.[11] Stanislas Jeannesson argues that Wolff's political orientation helped persuade French leaders to work with him. Many other industrialists in the Ruhr and Rhineland reached

---

[7] L. Coquet to R. Poincaré, 22 January 1923, AN: AJ/9/6047; R. Poincaré to L. Coquet, 9 March 1923, AN: AJ/9/6047; Le Ministre des Affaires Étrangères to the Consul Français, Dusseldorf, 10 March 1923, AMAE: RC/B 81–82/334.

[8] J. Bariéty, *Les relations franco-allemandes après la Première-Guerre mondiale: 10 novembre 1918–10 janvier 1925, de l'exécution à la négociation* (Pédone, 1977), 243–4; Jeannesson, *Poincaré, la France et la Ruhr*, 313–14; C. Fischer, *The Ruhr Crisis, 1923–1924* (Oxford University Press, 2003), 231, 260–61; Dahlmann, 'Das Unternehmen Otto Wolff: vom Alteisenhandel zum Weltkonzern (1904–1929)', 63–67.

[9] M. Trachtenberg, 'Poincaré's Deaf Ear: The Otto Wolff Affair and French Ruhr Policy, August–September 1923', *The Historical Journal*, 24/3 (1981), 699–707; Bariety, *Les relations franco-allemandes après la Première-Guerre mondiale*, 232, 249, 261; Fischer, *The Ruhr Crisis, 1923–1924*, 218–19.

[10] Jeannesson, *Poincaré, la France et la Ruhr*, 379–99; Jackson, *Beyond the Balance of Power*, 410–13.

[11] Exposé relative à une importante demande de charbons de la Sarre formulé par l'industrie rhénane, 16 November 1922, AN: AJ/9/5906/A; M. Klecker de Balazuc to Haut Commissaire de la République française dans les territoires rhénans, 20 November 1922, AN: AJ/9/5906/A. Ottmar Strauss, Wolff's main business partner, was also a strong advocate of Franco-German cooperation. See Conze, "Titane der modernen Wirtschaft' Otto Wolff (1881–1940)', 117.

out to French officials, hoping to steal a march on their local competitors, but Wolff was the only major player who was known to French leaders as a politically committed proponent of regional autonomy.[12] Indeed, when the French high commissioner in the Rhineland recommended that Poincaré collaborate with Wolff, he emphasized that Wolff and his coterie of 'moderate industrialists' had been 'waiting with impatience and for a long time for the *decisive* opportunity that now seems to present itself' (original emphasis).[13] They knew that Wolff was as self-interested as any other businessman, but his private political and material ambitions favoured France. It was rumoured that Wolff hoped to claim a leadership position in a new system of local corporatist governance in the occupied territories.[14]

In the French elite, the Ruhr occupation helped consolidate two distinct but complementary approaches to European unity: one emphasizing direct coordination of industrial resources through private cartels and one emphasizing joint market regulation through a customs union. Both strategies had an important afterlife in the history of European integration, in the European Coal and Steel Community and the Common Market. In the 1920s, as in the 1950s, projects for tariff cooperation and cartels focused heavily on a strategic triangle of coal and steel production that linked France, Belgium, Luxembourg, and Germany. When Georges Reynald demanded assurance that the industrial riches of the Ruhr and Rhineland would not be turned against France in the event of a war, Wolff proposed to orient the whole region towards peaceful economic collaboration through 'a loyal and sincere entente between France and Germany based on economic conventions which, with time, could reach the stage of a customs union'. He argued that only this type of legal framework could 'provide a real guarantee of security to France'. Coquet admitted to Reynald that some branches of French heavy industry would face stiff competition in an enlarged Franco-German market but argued that those branches had recovered sufficiently under the shelter of steep unilateral protection against Germany to withstand more open trade between the neighbours.[15]

---

[12] Jeannesson, *Poincaré, la France et la Ruhr*, 313; C. Fischer, 'Scoundrels without a Fatherland? Heavy Industry and Transnationalism in Post-First World War Germany', *Contemporary European History*, 14/4 (2005), 441–64, 453.

[13] M. Klecker de Balazuc, *La République Rhénane* (La Revue d'Alsace et de Lorraine, 1924); 'Le Général Denvignes à Monsieur le Général Commandant l'Armée', 13 August 1923 [Pièce Annexe 768], in Degoutte, *L'Occupation de la Ruhr, Rapport d'ensemble*, 1974.

[14] Bariety, *Les relations franco-allemandes après la Première-Guerre mondiale*, 242; Fischer, 'Scoundrels without a Fatherland?' 453.

[15] Résumé de l'entretien du 2 Janvier entre M. le Sénateur Reynald, M. Otto Wolff, M. Charles Stein, et M. Lucien Coquet, 3 January 1923, AMAE: RC/B81-82/334.

Many other French leaders argued that the country's industrial security could not be analysed merely in terms of markets and productivity. France's long-serving minister of public works, Yves Le Trocquer, concluded that the country's basic natural resource endowments left its steel sector fundamentally vulnerable. He complained that French blast furnaces simply could not operate without German coking coal, but Germany 'can do without our iron ore' after cultivating alternative Scandinavian sources during the war.[16] Le Trocquer declared bluntly, 'this situation must end. The twentieth century is essentially the century of steel, and any country that is dependent on another for the production of steel is inevitably dominated by it, not merely from an economic standpoint, but also from the standpoint of national security'.[17] Le Trocquer recommended that France use the Ruhr occupation as an opportunity to secure permanent French ownership stakes in German coal mines as well as Allied control of the railways that served those mines. Furthermore, he demanded that Germany participate in the development of French industrial infrastructure through reparations-in-kind.[18] His proposals for reparations-in-kind were later incorporated into the Dawes Plan, but without the reciprocal French participation in German mines and railways. In the second half of the 1920s, he tried to compensate for the gaps in the Dawes Plan by combining Franco-German industrial cooperation with a wider regime of international legal guarantees as the president of the UDE French Committee.

In his work for the UDE, Le Trocquer embraced the idea of a Franco-German customs union, but he remained committed to direct cartels between producers to secure strategic production capacity and supply lines. On this point, he endorsed the views of Louis Loucheur, France's leading advocate of cartels, who warned against the dangers posed to the French steel industry by a pure customs union:

Supposing that tomorrow the United States of Europe were created, that you would have made your nations understand that tariff barriers must be eliminated. Where would the steel industry go? Naturally to the very place where it would find coal deposits, facilities to produce coke, and the possibility to obtain iron ore; it would go to the place where it would be the most economically efficient, consequently in one country, perhaps one sole

---

[16] Y. Le Trocquer to Ministère des Affaires Étrangères, 31 March 1923, AMAE: RC/B 81–82/334;Jackson, *Beyond the Balance of Power*, 396.
[17] Y. Le Trocquer to Ministère des Affaires Étrangères, 31 March 1923, AMAE: RC/B 81–82/334; also quoted in Jeannesson, *Poincaré, la France et la Ruhr*, 334.
[18] Jeannesson, *Poincaré, la France et la Ruhr*, 334.

country, best situated economically to exploit opportunities for production. It would thus concentrate in a single point the most powerful weapon from a political standpoint.[19]

This comment from Loucheur demonstrates the extent to which trade and industrial policy were seen as tools of European security in the 1920s, a linkage that must be understood against the backdrop of the League's own mixed record on disarmament. In the 1920s the League's work on disarmament was stuck in an impasse between French views that substantive security guarantees were a precondition for reducing military capacity and British views that disarmament would produce an environment of greater security by reducing the risk of war. There was little prospect of bridging these differences in the League, which drove French leaders to pursue security priorities through alternative channels of trade and industrial policy.[20] After 1945, European economic integration arguably proceeded more smoothly because it focused more squarely on trade, while security cooperation was handled through separate institutions.[21] More generally, Robert Boyce suggests that the tendency for economic cooperation to run far ahead of security cooperation was an important source of instability in interwar international politics.[22]

Cartels in Interwar Europe, between Security and 'Rationalization'

Louis Loucheur had begun to promote direct Franco-German industrial cooperation through cartels as a solution to France's security vulnerabilities after British and American leaders rebuffed Clémentel's broader plans for a transatlantic commodity organization at the Paris Peace Conference. Loucheur hoped to use cartels to consolidate continental Europe's industrial core along the Rhine and counterbalance the market dominance of British and US manufacturing.[23] After Loucheur's early projects failed to transform reparations-in-kind into a platform for Franco-German industrial cooperation, he took advantage of the provisional calm following the Locarno Accords and Dawes Plan to relaunch his plans. He proposed the World Economic Conference in 1925 with the goal to use private business agreements to construct what Eric Bussière

---

[19] Quoted in Y. Le Trocquer, l'Union Douanière Européenne, Comité National d'Études Sociales et Politiques, 27 January 1930, AMAE: Y/636.
[20] Steiner, *The Lights That Failed*, 565–82. [21] Patel, *Project Europe*, 55–61.
[22] Boyce, *The Great Interwar Crisis*.
[23] Bussière, *La France, la Belgique et l'organisation économique de l'Europe*, 131–3.

has called a 'Europe of producers'.[24] The British Foreign Office complained that Loucheur's plan was 'was designed with the object of forming a European economic bloc for the discomfiture of America'.[25] Llewellyn Smith's effort to reorient the conference towards more abstract principles of free trade was, in part, an attempt to keep the door ajar for the United States to engage with the League as it began to align its treaty policy with European norms based on unconditional MFN. Clémentel also never thought that France could realistically hope to restrain German economic dominance in Europe without Anglo-Saxon backing and continued to pursue engagement with Britain and the United States through private business channels in the ICC.[26] As Clémentel well understood from his wartime multilateralism, it was politically difficult to exclude Britain from the European trade system partly because doing so would place Belgium in a very difficult position due to the two countries' deep commercial links.[27]

A European Steel Cartel was established in 1926 with Belgian participation shortly before the League's World Economic Conference convened the following year. It offered a powerful example of Continental industrial cooperation by coordinating steel markets along the Rhine through production quotas. In the early years, the steel cartel was not a terribly effective scheme (Germany routinely overran its quota). It nevertheless had powerful symbolism at the World Economic Conference when these weaknesses were not yet evident. The steel cartel offered an alternative model for European unity alongside Coquet's treaty-based, law-driven proposal for a regional customs union. Cartels could proceed largely through business channels without substantial state intervention. In the 1920s, the cartel movement drew momentum from a private Franco-German Information and Documentation Committee led by a steel magnate from Luxembourg, Émile Mayrisch.[28]

The 'Mayrisch Committee' registered wide interest in cartels among European industrial elites during the interwar period, with many sectoral and national variations. There was considerable interest in the idea that cartels could serve as a vehicle for rationalization in the League Secretariat and in the ICC, but few interwar cartels actually functioned in that way. Charles Maier argues that in the 1920s,

[24] Bussière, 'Les aspects économiques du projet Briand', 77.
[25] The International Economic Conference, 2 February 1926, TNA: FO 371/11900; Clavin, *Securing the World Economy*, 41.
[26] International Chamber of Commerce, *Proceedings Organization Meeting, Paris France* (International Chamber of Commerce, 1920), 15–17, 49–52.
[27] Bussière, *La France, la Belgique et l'organisation économique de l'Europe*, 131–3.
[28] Kaiser and Schot, *Writing the Rules for Europe*, 191.

anxiety about overproduction (and attendant social strains) was a more powerful incentive for cooperation through cartels than ambitions for higher productivity.[29] The approach that Loucheur favoured, and which dominated in practice, allocated market share among members for production and distribution through quotas. Loucheur and other French leaders were particularly concerned about managing a potential surplus of iron ore in the newly annexed Lorraine. Germany had been forced to buy Lorraine ore on favourable terms until 1925 under the Treaty of Versailles, but French producers needed to find stable long-term markets to sustain their operations thereafter.[30] In political terms, Loucheur offered a form of limited industrial disarmament; he aimed to reduce surplus output resulting from the war but ensure that Europe's main military powers preserved some production capacity in strategic sectors. An alternative approach sought to expand market share instead of cutting output, by making European producers more competitive through gains in efficiency. This 'rationalization' strategy had strong backing in Germany, where more firms stood to benefit from it, but was less popular in France. For, rationalization meant eliminating the weakest competitors, precisely the outcome that Loucheur was trying to avoid.[31]

It was not Loucheur but Clemens Lammers, a German enthusiast of rationalization, who was asked to prepare the documentation on cartels for the World Economic Conference. Lammers was also the head of the ICC's sub-committee on cartels.[32] He had ties to the globally competitive German chemical industry and was working with Bernhard Harms to coordinate the official enquiry in to Germany's export capacity that was run through the IfW in the late 1920s. Lammers declared that the 'highest purpose of all cartels' was 'to support the rationalization of production in the name of cheaper and better products'.[33] He warned that Loucheur's model had a strong potential to lead to inefficient monopolies that would undermine European competitiveness over the long term. Lammers did not think that the League should try to regulate against anti-competitive tendencies in industrial agreements because there was not sufficient consensus on the goals and functions of cartels to allow for unified international rules. This diversity of opinion could

---

[29] Maier, *Recasting Bourgeois Europe*, 481–578.
[30] Maier, *Recasting Bourgeois Europe*, 517–45.
[31] Schulz, *Deutschland, der Völkerbund und die Frage der europäischen Wirtschaftsordnung*, 101–5.
[32] Kaiser and Schot, *Writing the Rules for Europe*, 197.
[33] Quoted in Schulz, *Deutschland, der Völkerbund und die Frage der europäischen Wirtschaftsordnung*, 104.

be seen across Europe but also within Germany, where leaders in many capital-intensive industries such as steel favoured the quota-based approach.[34]

At the World Economic Conference in 1927, Lammers helped craft a compromise position. He recognized the value of some market-sharing agreements that had already been concluded, such as the steel cartel, but also affirmed the importance of rationalization. The conference neither endorsed nor condemned cartels, but rather urged the public to judge each agreement on its own merits.[35] Debates over cartels continued in the League for several years following the World Economic Conference. Ultimately, the Economic Committee did not define any clear international rules on the matter but simply worked with the ICC to collect and disseminate information about their activities, relying on the discipline of public opinion.[36] Salter became more open to private cartels and inter-governmental commodity agreements as tools to manage the sharp drop in prices that came with the Great Depression, while warning against the dangers of monopoly.[37] Although the League's engagement with the cartel issue produced limited concrete results in the 1920s, it helped initiate a transition away from abstract models of trade liberalization (as favoured by Llewellyn Smith) towards more direct intervention in relations of production.

Initially, Loucheur and other advocates of industrial cooperation predicted that their approach would lead to tariff reduction by eliminating opportunities for surplus production to be 'dumped' at cut-rate prices on export markets (defence against 'dumping' was a common justification for tariff protection in the 1920s).[38] The many cartels that were established in the 1920s did not lead to tariff reduction, however. It is true that the steel cartel did pave the way for the Franco-German tariff agreement of 1927 by eliminating key points of conflict. Yet the basic institutional mechanics of interwar cartels, in which market-sharing arrangements were based on tariff rates at the time of negotiation, tended to consolidate protection. This was true for the cartels covering cement, potash, wire, gas,

---

[34] Schulz, *Deutschland, der Völkerbund und die Frage der europäischen Wirtschaftsordnung*, 105.
[35] Schulz, *Deutschland, der Völkerbund und die Frage der europäischen Wirtschaftsordnung*, 106; Kaiser and Schot, *Writing the Rules for Europe*, 195–9.
[36] d'Alessandro, 'Global Economic Governance and the Private Sector', 267–8; M. Bertilorenzi, 'Legitimising Cartels: The Joint Roles of the League of Nations and of the International Chamber of Commerce', in S. Fellmann and M. Shanahan (eds.), *Regulating Competition: Cartel Registers in the Twentieth-Century World* (Routledge, 2019).
[37] A. Salter, *Recovery: The Second Effort* (G. Bell and Sons, 1933), 202–7.
[38] Bussière, *La France, la Belgique et l'organisation économique de l'Europe*, 257–9.

coke, and aniline.[39] In the late 1920s, Daniel Serruys tried unsuccessfully to circle back and coordinate tariff reductions on cartelized
commodities in the Economic Committee.

A Legal and Political Framework for European Economic Unity

Cartels between producers were often cited as a means to forge
private economic solidarities that transcended inter-state rivalry, but
this 'depoliticization' also limited the extent to which cartels could
serve as an institutional matrix for a wider programme of European
unity.[40] Even Lammers conceded that cartels 'could never constitute
the only, or even the decisive factor for the union of nations'.[41] In
contrast, Coquet's advocacy of a European customs union was based
on a belief that regional market regulation had legal and political
importance above and beyond any immediate material impact. The
UDE's memorandum for the World Economic Conference explained
that 'arrangements concluded in the private economy can attenuate
existing international antagonisms', but ultimately, 'the power and
means to end the economic anarchy that reigns among the states of
Europe belongs exclusively to sovereign states, in the form of collective contracts'.[42] This view was consonant with a law-led approach to
foreign policy that gained ascendency in France following the Ruhr
occupation.

France's turn towards international law and multilateralism is com-
monly associated with Aristide Briand's long stint as France's foreign
minister from 1926 to 1932. Peter Jackson shows that the key turning
point came earlier with the government of Édouard Herriot, who
served as both prime minister and foreign minister in the aftermath
of the Ruhr occupation. The concerns about French security that had
motivated Poincaré's more confrontational policy in the Ruhr did not
dissipate with his departure as prime minister in 1924. His successors
simply worked to safeguard French security through normative and
institutional mechanisms rather than by claiming direct territorial and

---

[39] Schulz, *Deutschland, der Völkerbund und die Frage der europäischen Wirtschaftsordnung*,
103–4; Bussière, *La France, la Belgique et l'organisation économique de l'Europe*, 287–93;
Maier, *Recasting Bourgeois Europe*, 516–45.
[40] Salter, *Recovery: The Second Effort*, 207; d'Alessandro, 'Global Economic Governance
and the Private Sector', 257; Kaiser and Schot, *Writing the Rules for Europe*, 191, 194.
[41] Quoted in Kaiser and Schot, *Writing the Rules for Europe*, 203.
[42] Quoted in Comité International de l'Union Douanière Européenne, Mémorandum
présenté à la XXIVe Conférence de l'Union Interparlementaire, August 1927, AMAE:
SDN/2495.

industrial guarantees or *gages*.[43] Herriot's legalist ethos grew out of the well-established arbitration movement in France, where Coquet had also begun his career before the war and where he drew support for the UDE in the 1920s.

After winning an election in May 1924 on an internationalist platform, Herriot concluded the Dawes Plan and initiated negotiations for a more general agreement that would strengthen the mechanisms for political arbitration within the League and pave the way for a regime of collective security through disarmament. These efforts culminated in a Protocol for the Pacific Settlement of International Disputes, which was to serve as a framework for a series of bilateral security pacts. A change of government in Britain undermined this 'Geneva Protocol', but the agreement continued to serve as a matrix for French foreign policy for the remainder of the 1920s.[44] Elements of the Geneva Protocol's juridical multilateralism were incorporated into the more modest Locarno Accords of 1925. French leaders signalled their faith in the League's security capacity by entrusting it to enforce the permanent demilitarization of Rhineland. They also favoured German accession to the League as a corollary to the Locarno Accords, on the grounds that League membership would facilitate the imposition of legal restraints on German power. At Locarno, Germany agreed to submit disputes concerning its western and eastern borders to political arbitration through the League (though arbitration was the *only* form of security that Germany's eastern neighbours received, while France and Belgium also obtained a clearer affirmation of their territorial sovereignty).[45]

Herriot used arbitration to address the security concerns relating to French dependence on German coking coal and other strategic resources, which Le Trocquer had flagged during the Ruhr occupation. The Dawes Plan ensured a steady supply of such resources as German reparations-in-kind, and France had recourse to new arbitration mechanisms if Germany tried to exert political pressure by withholding deliveries.[46] Coquet embraced these arrangements as the foundation for a programme of Franco-German cooperation, interceding with French officials on behalf of Otto Wolff to facilitate his participation in reparations-in-kind.[47]

---

[43] Jackson, *Beyond the Balance of Power*, 427–68.
[44] Jackson, *Beyond the Balance of Power*, 427–68.
[45] Jackson, *Beyond the Balance of Power*, 469–513.
[46] Bariéty, *Les relations franco-allemandes après la Première-Guerre mondiale*, 582–5.
[47] L. Coquet to M. Hermant, 8 September 1924, AN: AJ/9/6090; L. Coquet to Haut Commissariat Français dans les Provinces du Rhin, 26 May 1925, AN: AJ/9/6090; P. Tirard to A. Briand, 27 May 1925, AN: AJ/9/6090; Bariety, *Les relations franco-allemandes après la Première-Guerre mondiale*, 302.

Like Herriot, Coquet placed his faith in law and in the League of Nations to constrain national animosities. An early UDE memorandum to the Inter-Parliamentary Union drew an explicit analogy between a European customs union and military disarmament:

to intervene effectively against protectionist measures that ruin the European economy, it is necessary to begin by uniting, through a collective contract, the sovereign powers of European states to fix protectionist armaments to which they have access.[48]

On this reasoning, the 'most urgent necessity' was not to seek freer trade through tariff reductions but rather to prevent governments from using the 'threat' of further tariff hikes as a political bludgeon. The UDE's main recommendation was that European governments agree on a common tariff ceiling so as 'to eliminate the reciprocal threat posed by the possibility of tightening, at any moment, the protectionist vice'. This was an idea that the UDE borrowed from Richard Riedl.[49] Once European states agreed to tie their hands and renounce punitive tariff hikes under the 'Riedl system', they could then begin to wind down existing protection gradually by committing to automatic annual tariff reductions (the UDE suggested reductions of 2.5 per cent). The UDE calculated that this plan would eventually create a full European customs union over a period of forty years.[50] Proposals for incremental tariff reductions were circulating in different Europeanist associations in the 1920s. The UDE likely drew this idea from the French economist Francis Delaisi, who had submitted a plan for percentage-based tariff reductions to the inaugural conference of the Pan-European Union in 1926.[51] Delaisi briefly served as a member of the UDE French Committee before leaving to work for the Pan-European Union but remained an important intellectual influence on Coquet and other UDE leaders.[52] As Laurence Badel has shown, the UDE was a very porous structure whose significance

---

[48] Comité International de l'Union Douanière Européenne, Mémorandum présenté à la XXIVe Conférence de l'Union Interparlementaire, August 1927, AMAE: SD/2495.

[49] Comité International de l'Union Douanière Européenne, Mémorandum présenté à la XXIVe Conférence de l'Union Interparlementaire, August 1927, AMAE: SDN 2495; Union Douanière Européenne, Comité Français d'Études, Rapports des Commissions, 1928, AN: F12/9416.

[50] Comité international de l'Union Douanière Européenne, Mémorandum présenté à la XXIVe Conférence de l'Union Interparlementaire, August 1927, AMAE: SDN/2495.

[51] F. Delaisi, *L'Union économique européenne est-elle possible? Rapport présenté au 1er Congrès Paneuropéen, Vienne* (Le Monde Nouveau, 1926).

[52] On Delaisi's early departure from UDE, see Rapport de Monsieur Lucien Coquet, Délégué Général de L'Union Douanière Européenne sur son voyage à Bruxelles, 14–15 February 1929, AMAE: RC/B47/47.

lay less in its original conceptual innovation and more in its capacity to give vague ideas organizational heft.[53] Plans for a European customs union had already been floating in trade debates before 1914 (Coquet and Riedl both dallied with these schemes in their youth). The UDE institutionally anchored the customs union concept in the League, in government policy, and in the private associational networks that bridged national and international institutions. A general summary of interwar plans for European economic unity that the League Secretariat drafted for the US State Department in the run-up to the GATT negotiations credited the UDE with ensuring that the ideal of a regional customs union was 'widely publicized as a possible solution for the political and economic problems of Continental Europe' and noted that among the UDE's various branches, the French Committee had been the 'most active'.[54] As the general delegate of the French Committee, Lucien Coquet was the UDE's most energetic organizational beaver.

The UDE's Base of Support in France

Coquet was asked to gather members for a French Committee of the UDE in January 1927 after the parent organization had already begun to coalesce. The UDE grew out of a 'Call to Europeans' which advocated 'concerted tariff reduction' as an existential imperative to prevent renewed warfare in Europe:

> If you do not want us to be engulfed in economic anarchy and to fight without hope until our territory – which offers all of nature's bounty but is disorganized – is completely transformed into chaos under a regime where peoples massacre one another without end, support the 'European customs union'.[55]

A small and motley group of intellectuals issued this manifesto in 1924 and then began to form a string of national committees that were collectively known as the European Customs Union (Europäischer Zoll-Verein, Union Douanière Européenne or UDE). The first national committees formed in Germany and Hungary under the leadership of the journalist Edgar Stern-Rubarth and the businessman Ernö

---

[53] Badel, 'Les promoteurs français d'une union économique et douanière de l'Europe dans l'entre-deux-guerres'.
[54] League of Nations, Economic Aspects of Customs Unions: Some Historical Illustrations, May 1944, USNA: RG 43/698, International Trade Organization Files/box 103.
[55] Cited in E. Blier, 'Rapport sommaire sur l'activité et les travaux du Comité International et des quinze premiers Comités Nationaux de l'U.D.E', in Premier Congrès d'Union Douanière Européenne Section de Documentation et de Propagande, August 1930, AMAE: Y/636.

Blier.[56] Stern-Rubarth asked Coquet to organize a French branch after reading his articles on European unity in *La Revue d'Alsace et de Lorraine*.[57] Coquet formed the UDE French Committee by following the same playbook he had used to create the Franco-German Commercial Committee before the war. He began by recruiting few influential patrons, including Yves Le Trocquer as president, and then exploited their personal networks to compile a roster of well-connected board members.[58]

As Laurence Badel has demonstrated, the French Committee of the UDE served as a central meeting ground for French internationalists. It included the leaders of France's nebulous pro-League associations as well as the president of the Inter-Parliamentary Union. The international law community was represented by Georges Scelle and Henri Truchy. Scelle was deeply involved in formal debates about European legal sub-structures within the League.[59] There were members from all the major branches of French industry as well as the expanding retail sector. The UDE recruited heavily from France's corps of Foreign Trade Advisors (to which Coquet belonged). Coquet had already cultivated relations with many of these groups before the First World War when he began to operate as a liaison between political and business associations. He was able to perform this intermediary function more effectively in the 1920s due to the general bureaucratization of organizational activity. The prevalence of secretaries, delegates, presidents, vice-presidents, and directors from other private associations in the UDE French Committee is striking. The overwhelming majority of its board-members were officers in other organizations.[60] Coquet's associational outreach also grew easier in the 1920s because he enjoyed stronger diplomatic backing.

The French Ministry of Foreign Affairs gave the UDE French Committee more support than Coquet's earlier Franco-German Commercial Committee. Aristide Briand himself intervened as foreign

---

[56] J. Cristu, *L'Union douanière européenne: ses conditions et ses difficultés* (L. Chauny & L. Quinsac, 1928), 137–8; Stern-Rubarth, *Aus zuverlässiger Quelle verlautet . . .*, 121–2; Pegg, *Evolution of the European Idea*, 77; Badel, *Un milieu libéral et européen*, 136; Chabot, *Aux origines intellectuelles de l'Union européenne*, 78–9.

[57] L. Coquet to J. Seydoux, 28 December 1926, AMAE: RC/B47/30.

[58] A list of the UDE's founding board members can be found in Comité International de l'Union Douanière Européenne, Memorandum présenté à la XXIVe Conférence de l'Union Interparlementaire, August 1927, AMAE: SDN 2495.

[59] J.-M. Guieu, 'The Debate about a European Institutional Order among International Legal Scholars in the 1920s and Its Legacy', *Contemporary European History*, 21/3 (2012), 319–37.

[60] Badel, 'Les promoteurs français d'une union économique et douanière de l'Europe dans l'entre-deux-guerres'; Badel, *Un milieu libéral et européen*, 139–45.

minister in the group's founding. Yves Le Trocquer asked Briand for approval before accepting the presidency, which prompted the ministry to conduct a thorough review of the UDE's early activities across Europe.[61] From local reports on UDE activism in Austria, Czechoslovakia, Germany, Hungary, and the Netherlands, French officials concluded that the organization's other budding branches were dominated by Germans and Germanophiles, but these were not 'first-rate figures'.[62] Briand and his colleagues saw an opening to seize momentum in the UDE by creating a French Committee with prominent leaders such as Le Trocquer.[63] French diplomats helped the French Committee assume leadership over the UDE's operations, notably by intervening directly on Coquet's behalf with French and foreign diplomats (a privilege that the ministry had been less willing to extend to him before the war). French diplomatic backing enabled Coquet to cooperate with foreign governments and business leaders to build a wide network of national UDE branches (there were fifteen by 1930).[64] Coquet also enjoyed easy access to the foreign policy establishment in Paris through the French Service of the League of Nations. This department was created within the Ministry of Foreign Affairs in 1919 to coordinate France's official representation in the League. One of its main tasks was to manage relations with the army of private internationalists who worked to shape France's foreign policy through the new organizational platforms that opened in and around Geneva.[65]

Coquet and the UDE French Committee also developed a close relationship with the Ministry of Commerce, in continuity with Coquet's prewar Franco-German Commercial Committee. Both before and after the war, Coquet recruited heavily from the Foreign Trade Advisors attached to the Ministry of Commerce through its National Office of Foreign Trade. Coquet was himself an honorary Trade Advisor in the 1920s ('honorary' because he retained his affiliation after his active service in the corps formally ended). The general secretary and president of the National Committee of Foreign Trade Advisors, Armand Megglé and

---

[61] Y. Le Trocquer to A. Briand, 13 April 1927; Ministre des Affaires Étrangères to Budapest, Vienna, the Hague, London, 15 April 1927, AMAE: RC/B47/30.
[62] P. de Margerie to A. Briand, 20 April 1927, AMAE: RC/B47/30.
[63] Ministre des Affaires Étrangères to Y. le Trocquer, 6 May 1927 AMAE: RC/B47/30; Boyce, *The Great Interwar Crisis*, 173.
[64] E. Blier, 'Rapport sommaire sur l'activité et les travaux du Comité International et des quinze premiers Comités Nationaux de l'U.D.E', in Premier Congrès d'Union Douanière Européenne Section de Documentation et de Propagande, August 1930, AMAE: Y/636; L. Badel, *Un milieu libéral et européen* (Comité pour l'Histoire économique et financière de la France, 1999), 159–60.
[65] Guieu, *Le rameau et le glaive*, 124–6.

Étienne Clémentel, were both members of the UDE French Committee. Coquet also forged ties to Clémentel's ICC and to the latter's protégés in the Ministry of Commerce, most notably Paul Elbel. Elbel had come into the Ministry to work for Clémentel during the war and went on to serve as the assistant director of trade agreements under Daniel Serruys. Elbel left the Ministry of Commerce in 1925 to become the director of a new association that advocated a simpler and more moderate French tariff, the Committee of Economic and Customs Action (Comité d'action économique et douanière, hereafter CAED).[66] Elbel was a founding member of the UDE French Committee, which held its meetings in the headquarters of the CAED from 1927 to 1930. Elbel took the lead in developing the UDE's core tariff-reduction programme, borrowing heavily from Riedl.[67] With support from Clémentel, Elbel returned to the Ministry of Commerce in summer 1928 to succeed Serruys as director of trade agreements, although he did not take over Serruys's seat on the League Economic Committee until 1930.

For his part, Serruys initially expressed scepticism about plans for concerted tariff reduction at the World Economic Conference, but he showed more openness in the Economic Committee.[68] Shortly after the close of the conference, Serruys was elected to the rotating presidency of the Economic Committee and thus assumed responsibility for planning the implementation of the conference resolutions. To mark his election, he issued a press statement announcing that he hoped to refocus League-led economic cooperation on multilateral agreements:

The League of Nations has arrived at a turning point in its history, for we now know that Europe is nothing other than a single economic unit in the world. Previously, we too often applied the principle of state sovereignty to economic matters and today we are finally beginning to realize that the task at hand is organizing collective government action for the demobilization of customs tariffs.

Lucien Coquet declared that this statement from Serruys 'exactly defines our programme'.[69]

After assessing the legal and political obstacles that impeded a comprehensive programme of multilateral tariff reduction, the Economic Committee decided to proceed product-by-product. Serruys explained that 'in the case of each product it will be possible to choose between the system of maximum duties and that of percentages'. He

[66] Badel, *Un milieu libéral et européen*, 94–105.
[67] P. Elbel 'Abaissement progressif des tariffs douaniers (Voies et Moyens)', *Union Douanière Europénne. Rapports des Commissions*, AN: F12/ 9416.
[68] On Serruys's initial scepticism, see *Actes de la Conférence Économique Internationale*, vol. II, 63, 74.
[69] *Union Douanière Européenne. Rapports des Commissions*, AN: F12/ 9416.

proposed to focus on commodities that were already covered by cartels. This effort would begin with raw materials such as cement, aluminium, and iron ore, which were generally protected by fairly low and uniform tariffs, before tackling more finished products, which were covered by higher and more complex tariffs.[70] Since the mid-1920s, Belgian leaders had been advocating this kind of product-based tariff reduction, as an intermediary option between customs unions and cartels.[71] In practice, this compromise strategy met with strong opposition from producers and governments, partly because focusing on individual commodities precluded the horse-trading that balanced concessions between different sectors in traditional trade negotiations.[72] These early experiments nevertheless helped Serruys and other League collaborators begin to flesh out the legal and institutional mechanics of collective tariff reduction and prepared them to launch more ambitious multilateral projects in response to the Great Depression. Although Serruys did not endorse a full customs union, he did use the two core UDE principles – a tariff ceiling and incremental percentage-based rate reductions – to frame debate about tariff reduction in the Economic Committee after the World Economic Conference. The UDE did not invent those principles but did disseminate them widely through its publications and branch committees, helping to define a common horizon of multilateral innovation.[73]

The UDE within the Broader Interwar Movement for European Unity

Two main organizational features enabled the UDE to mobilize support for League-led tariff cooperation across Europe: its friendly collaboration with other policy-advocacy groups and its decision to privilege technical economic solutions and avoid political flashpoints. These features differentiated the UDE from the Pan-European Union, which was the most publicly visible organization promoting European

---

[70] Economic Committee, Twenty-Fourth Session, Minutes, 18 March 1928, LON: E/24th Session/P.V.6.(1); Bussière, *La France, la Belgique et l'organisation économique de l'Europe*, 328.

[71] Bussière, *La France, la Belgique et l'organisation économique de l'Europe*, 261.

[72] *Commercial Policy in the Interwar Period*, 44–5.

[73] Economic Committee, Twenty-Fourth Session, Minutes, 18 March 1928, LON: E/24th Session/P.V.6.(1); Economic Committee. Commercial Policy. Collective Action in Tariff Matters, 31 March 1928, LON: R2734, 10C/1229/1229. In its retrospective summary of interwar trade policy from 1944, the League Secretariat later noted the general consensus that formed around the two dominant approaches to tariff cooperation through a general ceiling or a percentage-based reduction. See *Commercial Policy in the Interwar Period*, 44.

solidarity in the 1920s. The Pan-European Union was led by the Bohemian count Richard Coudenhove-Kalergi from offices in the old Habsburg palace in Vienna. He began by publishing a manifesto in 1923 and then rapidly rallied adherents to his cause, gathering 2,000 people for the Pan-European Union's first conference in 1926. Coudenhove-Kalergi sought to drum up enthusiasm for general principles of regional cooperation, whereas Coquet worked to advance more specific institutional changes. Both men focused on elites, but Coquet recruited from a narrow band of economic and political decision-makers, while Coudenhove-Kalergi had a more colourful following of novelists and aristocrats.[74] Officials in the League Secretariat preferred Coquet's technocratic backroom dealing. Stoppani sympathized with the goal of European unity but warned that 'the confused and passionate controversies around an idea which is vague and which everyone interprets in his own way are liable to compromise from the outset any possibility of practical results'.[75] Coudenhove-Kalergi did endorse concrete plans for a European customs union, but he gave clear precedence to political conciliation over economic integration.[76] In contrast, both Coquet and Riedl argued that cooperation must begin in the economic sphere, hoping that this would eventually open a path for Europeans to resolve their political disputes.

The French Ministry of Foreign Affairs initially preferred Coquet's economics-first strategy and saw Coudenhove-Kalergi's plans for political cooperation as a veiled bid for dangerous treaty revision.[77] Coudenhove-Kalergi's statement on 'War and Peace' that prefaced the first issue of his journal, *Paneuropa*, prompted the Ministry to send an alarmed circular to its European embassies. In the name of peace, Coudenhove-Kalergi proposed far-reaching territorial changes including the redistribution of African colonies to Italy and Germany as well as the transfer of the Danzig corridor to Germany. The Ministry wrote, 'it must be hoped for the future of the new association that it is not committed to pursuing goals that are so extravagant and so distant from those that inspire French policy'.[78] Briand and his colleagues tried unsuccessfully to persuade Coudenhove-Kalergi to shift his focus from politics to

---

[74] Badel, *Un milieu libéral et européen*, 163–7; Patel, *Project Europe*, 118.

[75] P. Stoppani, Memorandum, 21 September 1921, LON: R2868 10D/14711/14711.

[76] R. Coudenhove-Kalergi, *Pan-Europa* (Pan-Europa Verlag, 1923), 68–9; A. Ziegerhofer-Prettenthaler, *Botschafter Europas: Richard Nikolaus Coudenhove-Kalergi und die Paneuropa-Bewegung in den zwanziger und dreißiger Jahren* (Böhlau, 2004), 131–56, 273–5; Chabot, *Aux origines intellectuelles de l'Union européenne*, 45–50.

[77] Badel, *Un milieu libéral et européen*, 133–4.

[78] Ministre des Affaires Étrangères to Rome, Prague, Brussels, Berlin, London, Bern, Vienna, 16 March 1927, AMAE: SDN/2495.

economics, working through Louis Loucheur, the president of French branch of Pan-European Union, and Francis Delaisi, its general secretary.[79]

Coudenhove-Kalergi rapidly clashed with Loucheur and Delaisi. They both expressed frustration with Coudenhove-Kalergi's unwillingness to cooperate with other international and European organizations, including the UDE, the Inter-Parliamentary Union (IPU), and the International Federation of League of Nations Societies (IFLNS). Delaisi told Coudenhove-Kalergi, 'it would seem that you have taken out a patent for the promotion of European unity and you believe that any other group or leader that pursues the same goal is a plagiarist, a counterfeiter, or even a "traitor"'.[80] He noted that Briand took a broader view. As a matter of course, Briand agreed to serve as an honorary president in most pro-European groupings, and he also tried to plant loyal leaders with close ties to the French ministerial elite. This strategy worked most effectively in the case of the UDE where the French Committee under Le Trocquer assumed a commanding position in the general organization and was deeply loyal to Briand's foreign policy. In contrast, Loucheur had limited interest in the Pan-European Union, which remained firmly under the sway of Coudenhove-Kalergi.[81]

If Coudenhove-Kalergi resisted alignment with the French government and avoided organizational intermingling, Coquet considered such outreach to be a top priority. He thus helped enmesh goals of European economic unity in the web of organizations that surrounded the League in the 1920s such as the ICC, the IPU, and the IFLNS. Anne-Isabelle Richard indicates that the IFLNS was an important interface between the League Secretariat and private associational networks and a forum for discussions about the relationship between regional and international order.[82] Participating in the IFLNS and the IPU brought Coquet and Le Trocquer into regular contact with League officials such as Stoppani, enabling them to exert influence over trade debates in the League despite having only limited access to its formal bodies. For example, Coquet helped persuade both the IPU and the IFLNS to pass resolutions endorsing collective negotiations to reduce tariffs by fixed percentages.[83] These

[79] Badel, *Un milieu libéral et européen*, 165–7, 184–5.
[80] Quoted in Badel, *Un milieu libéral et européen*, 168; See also Richard, 'Colonialism and the European Movement', p. 173 n. 753.
[81] Badel, *Un milieu libéral et européen*, 164–9; Ziegerhofer-Prettenthaler, *Botschafter Europas*, 281–5.
[82] Richard, 'Competition and Complementarity', 245–7.
[83] League of Nations Societies, International Economic Conference, Prague, 4–6 October 1928, Text of Resolutions adopted by the Conference at its concluding session, 6 October 1928; Comité International de l'Union Douanière Européenne,

organizations helped forge a consensus about the institutional toolkit for economic cooperation, but they also exposed the divergent geopolitical ends that those common methods advanced.

Dynamics of Cooperation and Rivalry between Riedl and Coquet

A 1928 meeting of the IFLNS in Prague produced a revealing debate over the question of *Anschluss* between French and Austrian delegates. Both Coquet and Riedl attached particular significance to this exchange, though they each interpreted it quite differently. Coquet attended the Prague conference himself, and the Austrian delegate to the conference, Robert Breza, was Riedl's close associate as the head of the trade policy department in the Vienna Chamber of Commerce. Riedl briefed Breza ahead of the conference and received his report after the event.[84] Breza boasted to Riedl that he had obtained an 'explicit commitment' from the 'leading figures' associated with the UDE French Committee to the effect that 'France would withdraw its opposition to *Anschluss* if the political objections to an Austro-German economic union were eliminated through a customs union between France and Germany or a similarly comprehensive economic rapprochement'. He noted, however, that 'to motivate them, it was necessary that the question of *Anschluss* be raised in some form on the Austrian side'. Breza did this obliquely by telling the conference that Austria would only be able to implement the goals of trade liberalization that had been outlined at the World Economic Conference if it were incorporated into a 'larger area' with neighbouring states.[85]

Breza hit his mark. A member of the UDE French Committee responded, 'we object most strenuously to the assertion of Mr. Dr. Breza ... The word "Anschluss" was not pronounced, I must admit, but it was in the mind of Mr. Breza and that of his audience'. The

Mémorandum au Congrès Économique International de l'Union Internationale des Associations pour la Société des Nation; Report on the Economic Conference of the International Federation of League of Nations Societies (Prague, October 4th to 6th 1928), 5 November 1928, LON: R2663, 10A/3672/3672; Cristu, *L'Union douanière européenne*, 205–6.

[84] R. Breza, Bericht über die Fühlungnahme mit den Vertretern der europäischen Zollunion anlässlich der Prager Wirtschaftskonferenz im Oktober 1928, ÖStA, AVA: NL Riedl/121. Correspondence between Riedl and Breza concerning the latter's participation in the Economic Sub-Committee of the International Federation of League of Nations Societies can be found in WKW: NL Riedl//2.735.

[85] R. Breza, Bericht über die Fühlungnahme mit den Vertretern der europäischen Zollunion anlässlich der Prager Wirtschaftskonferenz im Oktober 1928, ÖStA, AVA: NL Riedl/121.

French delegate insisted that a European economic union 'must be established in tiers, through the progressive aggregation of diverse states around a central core. This core, we see it necessarily in an association of France, Germany, Belgium, and Luxembourg'. He suggested that other states could later join this nucleus, affirming that 'we quite naturally accept that Austria could link its tariff with Germany' once Germany was 'already attached to France, Belgium, and Luxembourg'. This was exactly the response that Breza was hoping to elicit from the UDE. Significantly, Breza interpreted that statement as evidence that French leaders might eventually be willing to accept *Anschluss* within a wider European framework, but Coquet drew the opposite conclusion. Coquet later quoted the Prague exchange to show 'the very clear orientation of our propaganda against *Anschluss*', when he was trying to allay Belgian concerns that the UDE might be opening a path for Austro-German rapprochement.[86] French scholarship on the UDE has generally followed Coquet's interpretation of the Prague debate with Breza.[87] Yet it is precisely the ambiguity of that interaction that is noteworthy. This useful ambiguity lasted until 1931, when the proposal for an Austro-German customs union compelled Riedl, Coquet, and other advocates of European unity to take a more concrete and explicit position on the issue of German regional power.

In the late 1920s, the UDE French Committee developed a close but complex relationship with Riedl, and the French Ministry of Foreign Affairs did not look askance at this alliance. Indeed, an internal ministerial report suggested that Riedl was valuable in French eyes because he was a credible German nationalist and was thus in a position to rally the large segment of the Vienna business community that favoured *Anschluss* around a relatively moderate, legalistic, pro-League course. Riedl assured a French member of the ICC that 'while among his followers there might be known partisans of *Anschluss*, they will not use underhand methods to achieve their goal'.[88] According to a similar logic, the UDE was diplomatically useful because it could help direct Riedl and other advocates of a German-dominated Mitteleuropa towards a broader arrangement in which France could exercise legal oversight via the League. During a visit that Le Trocquer and Coquet made to Vienna, the local ambassador

---

[86] L. Coquet to P. Berthelot, 10 January 1929, AMAE: RC/B47/47.
[87] Badel, *Un milieu libéral et européen*, 175–6; Chabot, *Aux origines intellectuelles de l'Union européenne*, 81.
[88] M. Beaumarchais to A. Briand, 8 July 1926, AMAE: SDN/1197. The French Ministry of Foreign Affairs generally had a policy of engaging with Europeanists who were suspected of pro-*Anschluss* leanings in order to try to restrain them (Boyce, *Great Interwar Crisis*, 173).

noted approvingly that Riedl's 'clear tendencies in favour of *Anschluss*'
were 'well known' to the UDE French Committee. Le Trocquer
responded by making a speech to the Vienna Chamber of Commerce
that underscored the strong links between European unity and the
League, as the main legal bulwark against *Anschluss*.[89]

The UDE French Committee cultivated relations with Riedl but also
with his rival, the Hungarian economist Elemér Hantos. Hantos had been
one of the signatories of the UDE's foundational 'call to Europeans', which
was co-written by his close associate Ernö Blier. Hantos and Blier were
largely responsible for building the UDE's initial committee network in
Central Europe, with Blier providing much of the funding.[90] Hantos and
Blier tried to link the UDE to a parallel organization, the Central European
Economic Conference (Mitteuropäische Wirtschaftstagung, hereafter
MWT). Hantos hosted the MWT's first meeting in 1925 where he clashed
sharply with German delegates over the geopolitical architecture of
regional cooperation. Hantos advocated a 'Danubian' union that would
be limited to the Habsburg successor states, but German delegates refused
to be excluded from any planned regional grouping.[91] Riedl shared the
Germans' hostility to Hantos's 'Danubian federation', which 'in reality'
meant walling off Austria from Germany'.[92] During the MWT's early
years, Hantos's Danubian approach predominated, and consequently
Riedl distanced himself from the organization and repeatedly refused to
speak at MWT meetings. However, when the MWT encountered financial
trouble in 1929, Riedl and the Vienna Chamber seized the opportunity to
claim leadership and force a course change. The Vienna Chamber became
the main organizational and financial base for the MWT, with German
backing, and Hantos split away from the organization to form a new
network of Central European Institutes.[93] This rift between Riedl and
Hantos impeded the formation of an effective Austrian Committee within

---

[89] B. Clauzel to A. Briand, 30 November 1930, AMAE: RC/B47/47.
[90] L. M. de Vienne to A. Briand, 9 May 1927, AMAE: RC/B47/30; C. de Chambrun to
A. Briand, 9 June 1927, AMAE: RC/B47/30; Stern-Rubarth, *Aus zuverlässiger Quelle
verlautet . . .*, 121; Pegg, *Evolution of the European Idea*, 77–8.
[91] P. M. R. Stirk, 'Ideas of Economic Integration in Interwar Mitteleuropa', in
P. M. R. Stirk (ed.), *Mitteleuropa: History and Prospects* (Edinburgh University Press,
1994), pp. 86–112, 92.
[92] Enderes to Riedl, 13 April 1927, ÖStA, AVA, NL Riedl/5.
[93] Enderes to Riedl, 15 February 1927, ÖStA, AVA, NL Riedl/5; P. Fischer, 'Die
österreichischen Handelskammern und der Anschluß an Deutschland. Zur Strategie
der "Politik der kleinen Mittel" 1925 bis 1934', in Wissenschaftliche Kommission des
Theodor-Körner-Stiftungsfonds und des Leopold-Kunschak-Preises (ed.), *Das
Juliabkommen von 1936: Vorgeschichte, Hintergründe und Folgen* (Oldenbourg, 1977), pp.
299–314, 306–9; D. Jančik and H. Matis, '"Eine neue Wirtschaftsordnung für
Mitteleuropa . . ." Mitteleuropäische Wirtschaftskonzeption in der Zwischenkriegszeit',
in A. Teichova and H. Matis (eds.), *Österreich und die Tschechoslowakei 1919–1938: die*

the UDE because the organization maintained close ties to both men. Coquet and Le Trocquer tried without success to bring the two sides together during a visit to Vienna in 1930.[94] Although their efforts at conciliation did not bear fruit, Coquet and Le Trocquer were well placed to serve as peacemakers in Vienna because one point that Hantos and Riedl agreed upon was the importance of Franco-German rapprochement. Riedl declared that 'the first and highest condition' for the 'organization of Europe' was 'reconciliation and absolute entente between France and Germany'. For, 'if those great nations reach agreement, they form the natural core around which the new European organization will form'.[95] In similar language, Hantos affirmed that 'the pivot of European economic unity is the solution of the Franco-German question. No organization of Europe is possible without first resolving that old conflict'.[96] Hantos and Riedl disagreed about whether to place Austria in Western Europe alongside France and Germany (in a form of supervised *Anschluss*) or to place in a separate ex-Habsburg Danubian bloc alongside Hungary. Coquet and Le Trocquer did not definitively take sides on this question, discussing both configurations in different contexts. The extent to which European unity hinged on the Austrian question was later revealed in the debacle of the Austro-German customs union in 1931.

Forging Unity in Western Europe: Between Regional and Imperial Solidarity

While conflict over German power relations to the east impeded European unity, so too did tensions among the countries of North-Western Europe over competing commercial and colonial priorities. The UDE network was less robust and slower to form in Western Europe than in Eastern Europe. The UDE French Committee was particularly frustrated by halting progress in Belgium and Luxembourg, which had formed a bilateral customs union in 1921.

---

wirtschaftliche Neuordnung in Zentraleuropa in der Zwischenkriegszeit (Böhlau, 1996), pp. 329–87, 348–50.

[94] L. Coquet to B. Clauzel, 17 November 1930, AMAE: RC/IE/47. Laurence Badel has also noted that the tension between Riedl and Hantos impeded the UDE's outreach in Vienna, but she places Coquet and Le Trocquer firmly on the side of Hantos. In contrast, I see the French UDE leaders engaged in a dynamic balancing act between Riedl and Hantos, which continued even after the the Austro-German customs union was announced. See Badel, *Un milieu libéral et européen*, 175–6.

[95] R. Riedl, La politique des alliances et la stabilisation de l'Europe, undated, ÖStA: AVA, NL Riedl/82.

[96] Quoted in Badel, *Un milieu libéral et européen*, 175.

Belgium had been central to Coquet's initial conception of European unity. In 1924, after the French and Belgian governments failed to settle on a common response to the upcoming restoration of German tariff autonomy, Coquet called for a revival of Clémentel's wartime plans for a customs union between France, Belgium, and Luxembourg.[97] The French and Belgian governments decided to pursue separate bilateral trade negotiations with Germany, but relations with Belgium remained a central preoccupation for the UDE. In January 1929, Coquet took pains 'to affirm most solemnly' to Philippe Bertholet, Briand's main deputy, that 'this whole movement is destined for failure' unless a national UDE committee was 'established without delay' in Belgium.[98] Bertholet responded by placing the French diplomatic apparatus at Coquet's disposal. The formation of the UDE Belgian Committee reveals the new mechanics of diplomacy-by-committee in the 1920s. It also highlights a fundamental tension between geopolitical solidarity within Western Europe based on shared concerns about security vis-à-vis Germany and divergent commercial and colonial orientations in the wider world.

In his northern outreach, Coquet initially attempted to avoid formal diplomacy and work through private channels such as the Belgian Chamber of Commerce in Paris, but his interlocutors demanded official approval at the ambassadorial level before proceeding.[99] Coquet had confronted a similar situation in 1907–8 when he was trying to set up the Franco-German Commercial Committee and was rebuffed by French officials. He received much stronger backing from the French and Belgian governments for his work with the UDE. In 1929 Bertholet told the UDE French Committee that the Ministry of Foreign Affairs 'carefully followed the work and efforts of your committee since its founding and will spare nothing to support your action insofar as it seeks to improve economic relations among the countries of Europe'.[100] He wrote to the French Ambassador in Brussels to ensure a warm welcome when Coquet arrived. The Ambassador gathered information about possible sources of hostility to the UDE in Belgium and then met with Coquet to help him devise a strategy. The Ambassador highlighted Belgian fears that the UDE would cut Belgium off from Anglo-Saxon export markets, finance,

---

[97] É. Bussière, *La France, la Belgique et l'organisation économique de l'Europe, 1918–1935* (Institut de la gestion publique et du développement économique, 1992), 202–16; Bussière, 'Les aspects économiques du projet Briand', 79; L. Coquet, 'Si nous parlions un peu d'économie ... politique', *La Revue d'Alsace et de Lorraine* 7/63 (1924), 57.

[98] L. Coquet to P. Bertholet, 10 January 1929, AMAE: RC/B27/47.

[99] L. Coquet to P. Bertholet, 10 January 1929, AMAE: RC/B2747.

[100] P. Bertholet to Y. Le Trocquer, 9 February 1929, AMAE: RC/IC/47.

and commercial services. A Belgian Association for International Economic Cooperation (Association belge de coopération économique internationale, hereafter ABCEI) had already formed to promote a more universalist model of free trade in the wake of the World Economic Conference, working under the conference president, Georges Theunis. At the time of the conference Theunis had met with Coquet and agreed to help him create a Belgian UDE committee, but other members of the ABCEI feared that a regional customs union would function as a protectionist bloc. In 1929 Theunis helped Coquet find a compromise. The ABCEI would create a new sub-committee focused on European tariff relations, which could then serve as the Belgian contact point for the UDE.[101] After founding the Belgian branch, Coquet tried to extend the UDE's network in the Netherlands and Britain using similar techniques, calling on local French diplomatic officials to help consolidate relations with existing pro-trade associations: the Dutch Free Trade Association and the Cobden Club in Britain. In the free-trading states along the Channel, he had trouble implanting durable committees, however.[102]

The UDE's outreach in Britain was an important point of divergence with Coudenhove-Kalergi, who defined Russia and the British Empire as distinct economic and civilizational units alongside 'Pan-Europa'. Coudenhove-Kalergi extended his plans for continental cooperation southward to encompass French, Belgian, Italian, Spanish, and Portuguese colonies in a vast 'Eurafrica' that would counterbalance the British Empire and other large territorial blocs.[103] Similar schemes circulated in European colonial circles in the 1920s, especially in

[101] P. Bertholet to Y. Le Trocquer, 9 February 1929, AMAE: RC/IC/47; Ministre des Affaires Étrangères to J. Herbette, 11 February 1929, AMAE: RC/IC/47; J. Herbette to Ministre des Affaires Étrangères, 15 February 1929, AMAE: RC/IC/47; Rapport de Monsieur Lucien Coquet, Délégué Général de l'Union Douanière Européenne sur son voyage à Bruxelles, 16 February 1929, AMAE: RC/IC/47; L. Coquet, 'Trois années de propagande en faveur de l'Union Douanière Européenne', in Documentation présentée au Congrès d'Amsterdam de la Chambre de Commerce Internationale, 8–13 July 1929, AMAE: Y/636; Badel, *Un milieu libéral et européen*, 159; G. Duchenne, *Esquisses d'une Europe nouvelle: L'européisme dans la Belgique de l'entre-deux-guerres (1919–1939)* (Peter Lang, 2008), 80–84.

[102] L. Coquet to R. Massigli, 23 January 1930, AMAE: SDN/2495; R. Massigli to F. J. Shaw, 8 February 1930, AMAE: SDN/2495; L. Coquet to R. Massigli, 20 May 1930, AMAE: SDN/2495; Richard, 'Colonialism and the European Movement', p. 200; A.-I. Richard, 'Les Pays-Bas entre l'Europe et le monde. L'européisme hésitant aux Pays-Bas durant l'entre-deux-guerres', *siècles*, 41 (2015).

[103] Ziegerhofer-Prettenthaler, *Botschafter Europas*, 338–9; A. Fleury, 'Paneurope et l'Afrique', in M.-T. Bitsch and G. Bossuat (eds.), *L' Europe unie et l'Afrique: de l'idée d'Eurafrique à la convention de Lomé I; actes du colloque international de Paris, 1er et 2 avril 2004* (Bruylant, 2005), pp. 35–58; Richard, 'Colonialism and the European Movement', pp. 46–83.

France.[104] Interwar visions of Eurafrica have attracted much interest from historians, with some even arguing that inter-imperial cooperation was the driving force for European unity.[105] This work offers a useful counterpoint to narratives that present European integration after 1945 as a compensatory substitute for the loss of empire.[106] Although European integration and colonial empire were not distinct, successive processes, they also were not identical. Anne-Isabelle Richard and Joseph Bohling warn that an excessive focus on Eurafrica can lead historians to overlook the structural tension between regional unity and imperial consolidation from the 1920s to the 1950s, as Europeans struggled to confront their marginalization in global markets. While Eurafrica did eventually gain some support in the 1950s as a practical policy option, it had limited traction among interwar officials, who usually tried to partition regional and imperial relations.[107]

The general preference for separate European and imperial policy tracks reflected the architecture of high diplomacy. Coudenhove-Kalergi's plans for Eurafrica alarmed leaders in the French Ministry of Foreign Affairs. They feared that cooperation in Africa would encourage German challenges to French control over former German colonies that were being administered as League mandates.[108] They also opposed his plans to separate Europe from the British Empire because on the Continent 'one would necessarily end up with a power structure dominated by Germany'.[109] Although Coquet had briefly considered Coudenhove-Kalergi's geopolitical model, he and other UDE leaders quickly concluded that Britain must somehow be associated with any Continental trade system, as a counterweight to

---

[104] C.-R. Ageron, 'L'idée d'Eurafrique et le débat colonial franco- allemand de l'entre-deux -guerres', *Revue d'histoire moderne et contemporaine*, 22/3 (1975), 446–75; Y. Montarsolo, 'Albert Sarraut et l'idée d'Eurafrique', in M.-T. Bitsch and G. Bossuat (eds.), *L' Europe unie et l'Afrique: de l'idée d'Eurafrique à la convention de Lomé I; actes du colloque international de Paris, 1er et 2 avril 2004* (Bruylant, 2005), pp. 77–96.

[105] Ageron, 'L'idée d'Eurafrique et le débat colonial franco-allemand de l'entre-deux-guerres'; P. Hansen and S. Jonsson, *Eurafrica: The Untold History of European Integration and Colonialism* (Bloomsbury, 2014); Beckert, 'American Danger'.

[106] J. Marseille, *Empire colonial et capitalisme français: histoire d'un divorce* (Seuil, 1984); More recently, G. Garavini, *After Empires: European Integration, Decolonization, and the Challenge from the Global South 1957–1986* (Oxford University Press, 2012).

[107] Richard, 'Colonialism and the European Movement'; J. Bohling, 'Colonial or Continental Power? The Debate over Economic Expansion in Interwar France, 1925– 1932', *Contemporary European History*, 26/2 (2017), 217–41.

[108] Ministre des Affaires Étrangères to Rome, Prague, Brussels, Berlin, London, Bern, Vienna, 16 March 1927, AMAE: SDN/2495; Bohling, 'Colonial or Continental Power?' 230. Pedersen, *The Guardians*, 195–286.

[109] Visite du Comte Coudenhove-Kalergi à M. Seydoux, 4 March 1927, AMAE: SDN/ 2945.

Germany.[110] In order to facilitate rapprochement with Britain and other colonial powers such as Belgium and the Netherlands, Coquet and the UDE French Committee made open-ended statements about European unity and imperial order. A 1931 memorandum suggested that 'closely associating England with efforts to unite France and Germany' would 'lay the groundwork for a customs agreement which could be extended bit by bit to colonial Europe'. As the world's foremost colonial powers, France and Britain had 'a common interest in the enlargement of the European market that is in formation, as a prelude to a wider agreement between this great European market and the universal market'.[111] The studied vagueness in these statements reflects the primacy that the UDE assigned to Continental security and its desire to avoid politically sensitive subjects that might jeopardize cooperation there.[112]

The UDE's proposals for inter-imperial cooperation also remained fuzzy due to the sheer legal complexity of bridging regional and colonial tariff relations. European colonies fell under diverse tariff arrangements that ranged from full customs unions (as between Algeria and France) to full tariff autonomy (as in the British Dominions) to full free trade (as in the Dutch East Indies), with many variations in between. Mounting demands for economic and political autonomy across the colonial world, buoyed by Wilson's ideal of national self-determination, added further uncertainty about future tariff relations.[113] Colonial powers did not want to invite multilateral scrutiny of their interactions with increasingly assertive nationalist leaders. The UDE French Committee responded to these challenges by bracketing imperial from regional trade using MFN. They endorsed a standard clause in French trade treaties that exempted intra-imperial trade relations from outside trade treaties. A French expert invited to speak to the UDE on this matter stated, 'it does not seem that the legitimacy of this exception can be questioned'. It was a question of principle, 'based in the right possessed by all countries to regulate exchange between different areas of the national territory (metropolitan and colonial) as they see fit and in full sovereignty'. This was 'a matter of internal policy in which foreign

---

[110] L. Coquet, 'Les États-Unis d'Europe et l'Union douanière franco-allemande', *La Revue d'Alsace et de Lorraine* 9/91 (1926), 127–9; L. Coquet to R. Massigli, 23 January 1930, AMAE: SDN/2495. On Coudenhove-Kalergi's own ambivalence about the thorny 'British question', see Ziegerhofer-Prettenthaler, *Botschafter Europas*, 76–7.

[111] Comité français de l'U.D.E. to A. Briand, 12 January 1931, AMAE: SDN/2495.

[112] Richard, 'Colonialism and the European Movement', p. 40.

[113] Richard, 'Colonialism and the European Movement', pp. 19–21; Bohling, 'Colonial or Continental Power?' 237; On the complex ramifications of Wilsonian self-determination in the imperial world, see Manela, *The Wilsonian Moment*.

countries, in principle, do not participate'. In other words, colonial trade relations fell outside the purview of any multilateral arrangements that might be made through the League or through a smaller regional framework.[114] In short, there was a strong default assumption in the 1920s that any European or international cooperative scheme would not cover the preference regimes that regulated trade with protectorates, mandates, and colonies. In the 1920s, Llewellyn Smith and Serruys joined forces to confirm this principle in League trade law. They ensured that League trade treaties included a 'colonial clause' exempting imperial relations. The UDE then imported this provision in its own plans for further League tariff conventions.[115] Thus, the basic UDE strategy to focus on tariff cooperation in continental Europe and bracket off imperial entanglements aligned with standard bilateral and multilateral treaty norms during the interwar period. In 1929, the onset of the Great Depression made this strategy increasingly difficult to sustain. European leaders were forced to define their global, imperial, and regional trade policies more explicitly as they confronted mounting demands for protection from all sides. This resulted in a process of stock-taking as Europeans tried to use the full toolkit of League trade policy to reconcile competing priorities in a series of complex multilateral schemes. These projects failed to stem the tide of the depression or contain the centrifugal political forces that it unleashed in the world economy, but they did establish important legal and institutional precedents while affirming trade policy as a central arena for geopolitics.

The Great Depression and Mounting Tensions over European Unity

The years 1928 and 1929 brought the first signs of the Great Depression, with a shift towards deflationary monetary policy led by the United States and a steep decline in global commodity prices. The League reported that from September 1929 to March 1930, the world price for maize declined by roughly 34 per cent and the price for wheat declined by 15 per cent.[116] The result was growing protectionist pressure worldwide. Of particular

---

[114] Paul Naudin, Restrictions à apporter à l'application inconditionnelle de la 'clause de la nation la plus favorisée', in Premier Congrès d'Union Douanière Européenne: Le Problème Douanier Européenne, October 1930, AMAE: SDN/2495. Also quoted in Richard, 'Colonialism and the European Movement', p. 196.

[115] Richard, 'Colonialism and the European Movement', p. 196.

[116] Commission of Enquiry for European Union, Report on Enquiry into the Course and Phases of the Present Economic Depression, 14 May 1931, LON: R2882, 10D/29531/22556.

concern for Europeans was the US Smoot-Hawley Tariff, which was proposed in early 1929 and ultimately raised US rates by an average of 15 per cent, above rates that were already quite high.[117] Amidst mounting fears of a generalized shift towards protection, 1929 also brought new plans for multilateral trade cooperation in Europe. In a cryptic speech to the League Assembly that has now gained a hallowed status in the lore of European integration, Briand called for 'some kind of federal bond' among European nations, noting that 'obviously this association will be primarily economic, for that is the most urgent aspect of the question'.[118] The 'Briand Plan' grew out of negotiations in 1929 to set the final terms for German reparations and the end of the Rhineland occupation. The definitive resolution of these questions stripped away France's diplomatic levers over Germany. In compensation, Briand tried to embed Germany in a broader institutional framework that would facilitate political arbitration and economic cooperation. He was also hoping to capitalize on European anxieties about US protectionism to foster regional commercial solidarity. Briand's precise intentions remain obscure. He seems to have made an open-ended pitch for European federation to the League Assembly to test the waters and see what type of regional cooperation the other members might be willing to support.[119]

He received a fairly clear signal from the Belgian delegate, Paul Hymans, who proposed his own plan for a tariff truce at the 1929 League Assembly, just before Briand took the rostrum. Belgian leaders were trying to take advantage of the recent election of a new Labour government in Britain that favoured free trade, in order to restrain mounting demands for imperial preference. Britain's Board of Trade backed the tariff truce but insisted that it be universal and not limited to Europe.[120] European leaders nevertheless sought to give the scheme a regional cast, as Briand prepared a more precise formulation of his

---

[117] Irwin, *Clashing over Commerce*, 389–90.

[118] Quoted in P. M. R. Stirk, 'Introduction: Crisis and Continuity in Interwar Europe', in P. M. R. Stirk (ed.), *European Unity in Context: The Interwar Period* (Bloomsbury, 2016), pp. 1–22, 17.

[119] C. Navari, 'Origins of the Briand plan', *Diplomacy & Statecraft*, 3/1 (1992), 74–104, 88–9; A. Fleury and J. Bariety, 'Le plan Briand d'Union fédérale européenne: les dimensions diplomatiques, 1929–1932', *La Société des Nations et l'Europe, 1929–1932* (Presses universitaires de Strasbourg, 2007); Cohrs, *The Unfinished Peace*, 566–71; C. Schwarte, *Le Plan Briand d'Union Européenne: De sa genèse au Quai d'Orsay à son échec dans la diplomatie des Grandes Puissances Européennes (1929–1931)* (Presses Académiques Francophone, 2014), 126–63.

[120] Comité néerlandais pour l'Entente douanière européenne, Communiqué paru dans la presse, 29 November 1929, AMAE, Y/635; Bussière, *La France, la Belgique et l'organisation économique de l'Europe*, 330; Duchenne, *Esquisses d'une Europe nouvelle*, 86–100; Boyce, *The Great Interwar Crisis*, 252–3.

own plan. The League Assembly endorsed the tariff truce as the first part of a two-step process. Participating states would agree to freeze their rates for a period of two or three years and would use that provisional stability to negotiate agreements to reduce tariffs. The tariff truce thus embodied the package of institutional innovations that both Coquet and Riedl had long advocated: a preliminary agreement to engage in sustained and concerted tariff negotiations with assistance from the League bureaucracy. This principle was also at the heart of plans for European unity that Salter and Stoppani devised in autumn 1929 to inform discussions about the Briand Plan and the tariff truce.

Stoppani and Salter's proposals for a 'United States of Europe' were some of the most detailed plans for multilateral trade policy that were produced in the interwar period and highlight the institutional significance of regionalism for the League. European unity offered a comprehensive framework that connected disparate projects for regulatory standardization, tariff cooperation (and also economic migration).[121] Yet many officials in the Secretariat, especially the secretary general, Eric Drummond, perceived regionalism to be an existential threat to the League of Nations. As Anne-Isabelle Richard has highlighted, European unity held special risks due to the League's de facto Eurocentrism. Creating an explicit European pole might simply reinforce the Continent's dominance within international organizations and, conversely, removing European concerns from the League would strip away most of its practical activity.[122] This was the beginning of an uneasy relationship between European integration and global governance that has persisted through to the present. On the one hand, European unity has provided a space for exceptionally thorough regimes of trans-border economic integration, acting as an institutional buttress and a normative wellspring for wider systems of multilateral cooperation. On the other hand, European integration inevitably entails discriminatory preferences that favour neighbours over more distant trade partners and can thus also undermine global trade norms. This tension continued in the close but uneasy relations between the GATT and the European Economic Community after 1945.[123]

---

[121] A. Salter, The 'United States of Europe' Idea, 2 September 1929, LON: R2868, 10D/14711/14711; P. Stoppani, Memorandum on the Idea of a Collective Agreement to Improve the Organisation of International Economic Relations in Europe, 21 September 1921, LON: R2868, 10D/14711/14711.
[122] Richard, 'Competition and Complementarity', 238–9.
[123] Slobodian, *Globalists*, 183–217; F. McKenzie, *GATT and Global Order in the Postwar Era* (Cambridge University Press, 2020), 141–73.

The complex organizational relationship between regional and international cooperation was vividly illustrated in the UDE French Committee's proposal to create a physical European sub-structure within the League by establishing a network of 'Houses of Europe'. In 1930, Coquet devised detailed plans for a House of Europe in Paris that would serve as a model for corresponding buildings in other cities. He originally planned to call his edifice the 'Palace of Europe and of Nations'. This appellation highlighted the connection between Coquet's project and the League of Nations, which had recently begun construction on its new headquarters, the Palace of Nations, in Geneva.[124] Coquet adopted the more modest title, 'House of Europe', to avoid any appearance of competition with the League while continuing to link the two construction projects. Coquet explained that his building would 'accommodate, under one roof, the offices of diverse European and international associations. We indeed say European and international, for it is a question of organizing a federated Europe, but within the framework of the League of Nations and not a cloistered Europe, in conflict with the rest of the world'.[125] Coquet's House of Europe would contain offices for private Europeanist associations such as the UDE, for foreign and French commercial attachés, and for the French Service of the League of Nations, which was a department of the Ministry of Foreign Affairs. It would include an old-fashioned trade museum displaying product samples from 'metropolitan' and 'colonial' Europe. Its library would gather private publications on European unity as well as official documents from the League of Nations. It would have physically aggregated the worlds of formal diplomacy, information, and private commerce around an interlocking European and international apparatus. This was also an attempt to turn projects for multilateral trade cooperation outward to respond to growing concerns that the general public felt detached from the highly technical policy debates in the UDE and the Economic Committee. Coquet's planned House of Europe included a movie theatre and a tourist office.[126]

Although they made gestures towards greater public engagement, the UDE leaders continued to define the fundamental relationship between European and international order through the esoteric language of MFN. In 1929 Riedl, Coquet, and many other advocates of European unity enthusiastically seized upon the tariff truce as a platform for regional cooperation, exempt from outside MFN claims.[127] Stoppani and Salter

---

[124] L. Coquet, Palais de l'Europe et des Nations à Paris, 15 April 1930, AMAE: SDN/2495.
[125] Premier Congrès d'Union Douanière Européenne, Paris 30 Juin–1er Juillet: Résolutions et Vœux du Congrès, AMAE: SDN/2495.
[126] L. Coquet, Palais de l'Europe et des Nations à Paris, 15 April 1930, AMAE: SDN/2495.
[127] R. Riedl to P. Stoppani, 10 October 1929, LON: R2868, 10D/15378/14711.

agreed that the tariff truce should be exempt from MFN, but also insisted that it must not be explicitly confined to Europe. If at first tariff cooperation only attracted European governments, Stoppani and Salter hoped that the United States might eventually agree to join.[128] Thus, they anticipated the later GATT practice to allow preferential relations within nebulous 'free-trade areas' of variable geometry and not only within territorially defined regional or imperial blocs. The US Secretary of State Cordell Hull later embraced that approach in 1933, when he tried to revive the idea of a League-led tariff truce and also sponsored a pact exempting collective agreements from MFN.[129] Yet by the time Hull came to the table in 1933, European multilateralism was already deeply fractured. That process of fragmentation began with the increasingly tense negotiations surrounding the tariff truce and the Briand Plan.

The Tariff-Truce Debacle

In autumn 1929 the Economic Committee moved quickly to implement the Belgian proposal for a tariff truce, preparing an initial draft agreement for a conference the following spring. In the intervening months, enthusiasm for the project quickly waned, however. In France, the UDE enthusiastically backed the tariff truce, but most economic groups aligned against it, citing the uncertain effects of the American stock market crash and declining commodity prices. The French government responded to these anxieties by passing a steep tariff increase in January 1930 and withdrawing support for the truce.[130] Coquet travelled to Geneva to observe tariff truce negotiations in March 1930 and watched from the sidelines as the project disintegrated.[131] In order to counter strong protectionist headwinds in France and abroad, Serruys tried to persuade the conference to adopt a more open-ended programme of multilateral cooperation in lieu of a fixed truce.[132] His efforts to devise a programme for 'concerted economic action' were cut short by the new French prime minister, André Tardieu,

---

[128] A. Salter, The 'United States of Europe' Idea, 2 September 1929, LON: R2868, 10D/14711/14711; Richard, 'Competition and Complementarity', 244.

[129] The Chairman of the American Delegation (Hull) to the Acting Secretary of State, 6 July 1933, in R. P. Churchill, G. V. Blue, and S. F. Landau (eds.) FRUS, Diplomatic Papers, 1933, General, vol. I (United States Printing Office, 1950), doc. 524; Clavin, Securing the World Economy, 101–23.

[130] L. Badel, 'Trêve douanière, libéralisme et conjoncture (septembre 1929–mars 1930)', Relations Internationales, 82 (1995), 141–61, 149–51; Boyce, The Great Interwar Crisis, 255.

[131] L. Coquet to A. Salter, 16 February 1930, LON: R2716, 10C/2291/231.

[132] Part C, Annex 5: 'Memorandum Submitted by the French Delegation', Proceedings of the Preliminary Conference with a View to Concerted Economic Action (League of Nations, 1930), 423–5.

who was elected in in the middle of the conference. Tardieu intervened to hollow-out the negotiations, bowing to pressure from the French agricultural lobby.[133] The final truce that was concluded in March 1930 was a meagre agreement. It bound states with autonomous tariffs (Britain, Denmark, Norway, the Netherlands, and Portugal) not to raise rates for one year and bound states with conventional tariffs (the rest of Europe) not to withdraw from the bilateral treaties that consolidated their current rates. Crucially, there was a blanket exemption for agricultural tariffs, which were climbing rapidly and stimulating demands for protection in other sectors.[134] Eighteen states signed this modest pledge, but it still faced steep resistance for ratification.[135] Coquet lamented that the tariff truce was 'not as substantial as one could have hoped' but nevertheless celebrated it as a 'historic event' because it was the first multi-party tariff agreement sponsored by the League.[136] He vowed that the UDE would engage in a 'very active' propaganda campaign to try to secure the required ratifications. In summer 1930 he held a large conference on European economic unity in the French Ministry of Foreign Affairs to drum up support for the tariff truce as the starting point for a more thorough programme of European trade cooperation.[137]

Because only European countries had opted to sign the tariff truce, Coquet hoped that this agreement could become the foundation for a regional sub-unit within the League, fulfilling the Briand Plan. Yet, in May 1930 Briand issued a memorandum that distanced his own vision of European unity from the tariff truce. He now insisted on the 'subordination of economic to political questions', explaining that 'all possibility of progress toward economic union' was 'strictly determined by the question of security'. He concluded: 'it is therefore on the political field that the best efforts of organizers to create for Europe an organic structure must be concentrated'.[138] This shift in emphasis from economics to politics reflected declining enthusiasm for trade cooperation across Europe as well as the geopolitics of the agricultural crisis that accompanied the onset of the Great

---

[133] Badel, 'Trêve douanière', 157–9; Boyce, *The Great Interwar Crisis*, 252–6.

[134] League of Nations, *Proceedings of the Preliminary Conference with a View to Concerted Economic Action* (League of Nations, 1930).

[135] *Commercial Policy in the Interwar Period*, 53–4; *Proceedings of the Preliminary Conference with a View to Concerted Economic Action*, C.222.M.109.1930.II (League of Nations, 1930).

[136] L. Coquet to A. Salter, 19 March 1930, LON: R2716, 10C/2291/231; L. Coquet to A. Salter, 1 April 1930, LON: R2716, 10C/2291/231.

[137] Premier Congrès d'Union Douanière Européenne, 30 June–1 July 1930, AMAE: SDN/2495.

[138] 'Briand Plan for the Federation of Europe', *Advocate of Peace through Justice*, 92/3 (1930), 195.

Depression in Europe. Notably, Briand and his colleagues feared that Germany would exploit allowances made for regional trade preferences to exert political influence over agricultural exporters to the East.[139]

The Agricultural Crisis Shifts European Geopolitics

A sharp global decline in crop prices starting in 1928 gave Germany – as Europe's biggest food importer – a powerful new source of leverage over its Eastern neighbours. At the same time, discontent in France's powerful farm lobby left the government little scope to offer meaningful trade concessions to strategic allies. German leaders who favoured a more aggressive foreign policy believed this circumstance must be fully exploited.[140] In 1931, the Chancellor Heinrich Brüning told his cabinet that 'the strongest weapon at the disposition of Germany in its foreign relations is the fact that we are an importer of agricultural products. This weapon must be kept sharpened'.[141] German trade officials had begun to explore possible bilateral preferences on food imports as part of a strategy of power projection in Central and Eastern Europe.[142] The First World War had shown that dependence on foreign food could be a strategic vulnerability, but it could also become a source of power when commodity prices plunged. Starting in 1929, the UDE's programme evolved in response to the agricultural crisis and the resulting changes to Europe's geopolitical landscape.

The UDE French Committee advocated a two-tiered arrangement to separate Germany from the agricultural states to the east.[143] From the outset, the UDE French Committee had advocated a compartmentalized arrangement that would bind Germany tightly to France and Belgium.[144] In 1930, they started to place greater emphasis on creating an eastern counterweight to this western grouping by backing movements for solidarity among farmers in the Habsburg successor states. Danubian leaders met repeatedly in summer of 1930, forming a loose 'agrarian bloc' to

[139] Boyce, *The Great Interwar Crisis*, 254–6.
[140] H. Sundhaussen, 'Die Weltwirtschaftskrise im Donau-Balkan-Raum und ihre Bedeutung für den Wandel der deutschen Außenpolitik unter Brüning', in W. Benz and H. Graml (eds), 'Aspekte deutscher Aussenpolitik im 20. Jahrhundert', special issue, *Schriftenreihe der Vierteljahrsheft für Zeitgeschichte* (1976), pp. 121–64.
[141] Quoted in Sundhaussen, 'Die Weltwirtschaftskrise im Donau-Balkan-Raum', p. 137.
[142] D. E. Kaiser, *Economic Diplomacy and the Origins of the Second World War: Germany, Britain, France, and Eastern Europe, 1930–1939* (Princeton University Press, 1981), pp. 17–56; Schulz, *Deutschland, der Völkerbund und die Frage der europäischen Wirtschaftsordnung*, pp. 174–306; Dungy, 'The Global Agricultural Crisis'.
[143] Badel, *Diplomatie et grands contrats*, 186–7; Richard, 'Colonialism and the European Movement', pp. 194–5.
[144] Badel, *Un milieu libéral et européen*, 187.

lobby for European farm aid through the League.[145] They invoked
a bifurcated vision of 'two Europes' that Francis Delaisi had outlined in
a popular book by this title in 1929.[146] Delaisi argued that 'industrial'
Europe should intensively promote trade, investment, and infrastructural
development in 'agricultural Europe'. This strategy would raise purchasing
power across the Continent, expanding the rural market for manufactured
goods.

In 1930 Yves Le Trocquer enthusiastically endorsed the 'two
Europes' paradigm, but other UDE collaborators urged caution.[147]
Michel Augé-Laribé, the general secretary of France's National
Confederation of Agricultural Associations gave a speech to the UDE
in summer 1930 that forcefully contested the 'two Europes' concept as
a threat to France's own large agricultural sector. Augé-Laribé did
concede that French farmers might be willing to cooperate in regional
cartels or commodity agreements that would safeguard their own position in domestic markets.[148] The UDE French Committee began to
explore more interventionist policy options along these lines. It proposed to differentiate 'complementary' areas production, in which tariffs could be lowered without risk, from 'competitive' areas of
production, which would have to be managed through cartels or other
cooperative arrangements to allocate market share.[149] Over the course
of 1931, the UDE French Committee developed this scheme into a fully
fledged 'Five-Year Plan' that also included infrastructural investment in
Europe and in overseas colonies.[150]

Even as the UDE French Committee began to embrace more direct
coordination of production in response to the agricultural depression, it

---

[145] *Proceedings of the Preliminary Conference with a View to Concerted Economic Action*, C.222.
M.109.1930.II (League of Nations, 1930), 41–45; 'The International Wheat
Conferences during 1930–1931', *Wheat Studies of the Food Research Institute*, 7 (1931),
441–3; D. G. H., 'The European agrarian bloc', *Bulletin of International News*, 7 (1930),
3–11; Badel, 'Trêve douanière', 156; S. Schirmann, *Crise, coopération économique et
financière entre États européens, 1929–1933* (Comité pour l'histoire économique et
financière de la France, 2000), 109–13.

[146] F. Delaisi, *Les deux Europes: Europe industrielle et Europe agricole* (Payot, 1929). 'Report of
the sub-committee appointed to examine the question of the negotiations concerning
the trade of agricultural states of central and eastern Europe', in *Second International
Conference with a View to Concerted Economic Action* C.655.M.270 (Geneva: League of
Nations, 1930).

[147] Yves Le Trocquer, 'Les Deux Europes: Pour L'Union Douanière Européenne', *Les
Documents Politiques, Diplomatiques et Financiers*, 11/7–8 (1930), 440–4, in AMAE:
Y/636.

[148] Premier Congrès d'Union Douanière Européenne. Le Problème Douanier
Européenne sous ses Trois Aspects: Commercial – Industriel – Agricole, Rapports –
Discours – Documents, October 1930, AMAE: SDN/2495.

[149] Comité français de l'U.D.E. to A. Briand, 12 January 1931, AMAE: SDN, 2495.

[150] Richard, 'Colonialism and the European Movement', pp. 203–4.

continued to support conventional proposals for regional free trade. In 1932, Belgium, Luxembourg, and the Netherlands concluded an agreement for percentage-based tariff reduction at Ouchy, on Lake Geneva. In neighbouring Lausanne, Coquet met with leaders from European chambers of commerce to sing the praises of the Ouchy Convention as the first multilateral agreement for tariff reduction under League auspices.[151] He presented it as the paradigmatic test case for the League's proposal to exempt multilateral agreements from outside MFN claims because it scrupulously conformed to the Economic Committee's recommendations. Firstly, Ouchy was a free trade agreement; it did not raise new barriers against outside powers but only lowered the (already low) tariffs between the three signatories. Secondly, it was an open agreement, meaning that any country willing to accept the terms could join.

Ouchy was an irreproachable free trade agreement, but under League rules, it could not proceed unless all outside partners voluntarily assented to waive their MFN rights. Britain refused, even as it laid plans to extend its own exclusive regime of imperial preference through the Ottawa Agreements. This reflected the Board of Trade's long-held position that MFN was sacrosanct but did not apply to imperial preference.[152] Although the United States had previously sided with Britain in opposing an exception from MFN for multilateral treaties, the two countries diverged in their response to the Ouchy Convention. On the occasion of the League's World Economic and Financial Conference in 1933, the new US Secretary of State, Cordell Hull, made a case that conventions 'such as the type of the Ouchy agreement' should be exempt from outside MFN claims.[153] This was an important reversal of formal US policy, although it had limited immediate practical effects. The British veto continued to block Ouchy and other similar arrangements, and Hull went on to pursue his own trade agreements programme through bilateral rather than multilateral channels.

By 1933, Hull found few willing partners for multilateral cooperation in League circles because European trade policy had already begun to split down political lines. The decisive turning point came in spring 1931 with the announcement of an Austro-German customs union. This scheme

[151] Pour l'extension européenne de la Convention d'Ouchy, 1932, LON: R2716/10C/2291/231.
[152] Bussière, *La France, la Belgique et l'organisation économique de l'Europe*, 411–13; Boyce, *The Great Interwar Crisis*, 372–4; Duchenne, *Esquisses d'une Europe nouvelle*, 105–6, 546.
[153] The Chairman of the American Delegation (Hull) to the Acting Secretary of State, 6 July 1933, in R.P. Churchill, G.V. Blue, and S.F. Landau (eds.) FRUS, Diplomatic Papers, 1933, General, vol. I (United States Printing Office, 1950), doc. 524.

was widely seen as the first step towards *Anschluss*, and it unleashed a diplomatic firestorm in Europe. The uproar over the Austro-German customs union exposed conflicts over 'the German problem' that cut across the interwar movement for European unity, exemplified by Coquet and Riedl. In essence, Riedl aimed to secure German domination of Europe while Coquet sought collective European domination of Germany. They both turned towards Geneva to pursue these strategies but followed different organizational paths. While Coquet engaged with the League through the UDE's semi-diplomatic networks, Riedl operated through the ICC.

Riedl's preference for an indirect, business-led approach to trade diplomacy stemmed from his more radical ambitions. Coquet was trying to consolidate the territorial status quo established in 1919. In contrast, Riedl was challenging that status quo at one of its most sensitive points, the Austro-German border. Working through the ICC, Riedl tried to recast the German problem as a business proposition, arguing that ethnic Germans were simply Europe's best managers. The relatively favourable responses to the Austro-German customs union in the commercial press demonstrated that this view had significant resonance in the 1920s, as does the fact that Riedl was able to gain wide influence in the ICC and the League as an avowed German nationalist.[154]

---

[154] 'Germany and Austria', *The Economist*, 28 March 1931, 659–60.

7 The International Chamber of Commerce and the Politics of Business

The International Chamber of Commerce (ICC) formed in 1920 as trans-border business was facing mounting national restrictions. States were imposing capital controls in order to preserve hard currency and were placing limits on foreign ownership of strategic economic assets of all kinds. The bonds of international trade and investment loosened as subsidiaries expanded their local roots.[1] The ICC worked closely with the Economic Committee to try to devise new international business rules for this more assertively nationalist environment. The ICC comprised a central secretariat in Paris as well as a confederal network of national committees. It grew out of the pre-war International Congress of Chambers of Commerce and took over many initiatives from that earlier body, including the standardization of bills of exchange, the protection of foreign commercial agents, the codification of intellectual property rights, and the promotion of commercial arbitration.[2] By collaborating with the League in these areas, the ICC became a central interface between public and private business regulation, a position that it still occupies today.

The ICC was a sprawling organization and had many points of contact with the League's Economic and Financial Organization (EFO). The Economic Committee consulted the ICC on nearly all projects and even allowed it to take the lead in some instances. Arthur Salter regularly attended the ICC's biannual conference during his time at the helm of the EFO, and his trade deputy, Pietro Stoppani, participated in many smaller committee meetings at the ICC headquarters.[3] In 1927, Salter reflected on the deep practical interdependence that had developed between the EFO and the ICC: 'we divide and time our work so as to correspond; we interchange our documents, we are represented at each other's meetings;

---

[1] Jones, *Multinationals and Global Capitalism*, 27–32, 173–4, 203–4.
[2] Ridgeway, *Merchants of Peace*, 21–8.
[3] On relations between the ICC and the EFO in the 1920s, see dossier 10/24789 in LON: R389 and R390. See also Druelle-Korn, 'Étienne Clémentel président-fondateur de la Chambre de commerce internationale', 428–9.

we take the other's drafts and resolutions as the basis of our discussions'. He emphasized that the EFO and the ICC performed distinct political functions, telling an ICC gathering, 'if the League can offer the machinery for achieving administrative reform, it must look to you for much of the motive force'. The Economic Committee had to strive for unanimity and follow the policy roadmap agreed by governments in the League Council. In contrast, the ICC's private national committees could run ahead of local governments and encourage them to pursue bold reform. Salter declared: 'above all we ask you to push us and to push the other official forces without which we cannot advance'.[4] Thus, Salter saw the ICC as an essential complement to the inter-ministerial conclave in the Economic Committee.

Although the ICC exerted considerable influence over the League's operations, it did so largely behind the scenes. It became an important channel for economic diplomacy with non-League members, especially the United States. Members of the US Chamber of Commerce had supported the decision to locate the ICC headquarters relatively near Geneva in Paris for this reason.[5] There were practical limits to US transatlantic engagement due to the idiosyncrasies of the United States as a federal system as well as its ambitions for hemispheric hegemony. Notably, in commercial arbitration, an important sphere of activity for the ICC, the United States only partially aligned with European norms. Moreover, although the ICC could help preserve the transatlantic ties that the Allies had forged through the war, it could also provide a platform for revisionist ambitions from the defeated powers. In sum, the new multilateral tools offered by the ICC could be used to pursue quite disparate ends, as in the League itself.

It is significant that Richard Riedl, who openly professed his determination to pursue *Anschluss*, was the ICC's primary point of contact with League trade policy in the crucial years following the 1927 World Economic Conference. Riedl's commitment to *Anschluss* was not exceptional in interwar Austria but did make him an outlier in internationalist circles, for many Europeans (especially the Czechoslovaks and the French) believed that one of the League's main functions was to prevent *Anschluss*. This mission was legally enshrined in the Austrian and German peace treaties and in a subsequent agreement that accompanied a League-backed currency stabilization loan to Austria in 1922. Riedl chose to work through business channels to evade the legal fetters

---

[4] A. Salter, The World Economic Conference of May 1927: How to Secure Practical Results, 1 July 1927, LON: R 390, 10/58999/24789.
[5] On Clémentel's Atlanticist vision for the ICC, see Druelle-Korn, 'Étienne Clémentel président-fondateur de la Chambre de commerce internationale', 420–25.

that bound the Austrian and German governments. He told colleagues in the Vienna Chamber of Commerce that 'no constraint prevents commercial associations from taking the economic destiny of their country in their hands and pursuing negotiations among themselves, which are impossible for states to pursue under the present treaty conditions'.[6] He facilitated ongoing efforts by Austrian and German business organizations to harmonize economic regulation between the two countries, and he strove to embed this bilateral integration in the broader multilateral work of the ICC and the League. Indeed, by the end of the decade he had earned a reputation as one of the foremost champions of multilateral trade law.[7] Pierre Vasseur, a top official in the ICC, described Riedl in 1930 as 'the legislator of the new Europe' to a gathering of French internationalists.[8] Yet, less than one year after this statement was made, Riedl embraced divisive plans for an Austro-German customs union that laid bare the fundamental tensions in his international strategy. This scheme used the tools of League-sanctioned trade law to contest the territorial settlement of 1919. It highlighted the central role assumed by trade policy in the League system as a framework for security and geopolitics but also demonstrated that the conflicts over markets and territory that came out of the First World War could not be reduced to purely commercial terms.

Riedl's story is a useful reminder that business leaders in the ICC were not neutral actors; the way that they conceptualized markets and efficiency had a distinct political cast.[9] Riedl's vision of post-Habsburg economic space was fundamentally rooted in his belief that ethnic

[6] Protokoll über die Sitzung in Salzburg am 18 Mai 1926 über Fragen europäischer Handelspolitisk, 18 May 1926, ÖStA: AVA, NL Riedl/80.
[7] Fischer, 'Die österreichischen Handelskammern und der Anschluß an Deutschland'; J. Nautz, 'Tarifvertragsrecht und "Anschluss". Das Projekt einer gemeinsamen Tarifrechtsreform in Deutschland und Österreich 1919–1931', *Archiv für Sozialgeschichte*, 31 (1991), 123–35.
[8] 'Allocution de M. Pierre Vasseur', in R. Riedl, *La Réorganisation économique de l'Europe* (Le Foyer de la nouvelle Europe, 1930), 8. Lucien Coquet's own copy of this pamphlet is preserved at the *Bibliothèque nationale de France* (FOL-V PIÈCE-2332).
[9] On this point, I am in agreement with much of the recent scholarship on the ICC and business internationalism more generally. See M. Herren, '"They Already Exist": Don't They? Conjuring Global Networks along the Flow of Money', in I. Löhr and R. Wenzlhuemer (eds.), *The Nation State and Beyond* (Springer Berlin Heidelberg, 2013), pp. 43–62; R. Hoffer, 'Is the Business of Business Business Alone? The International Chamber of Commerce and the Origins of Global Business Diplomacy, 1920–1931', *LSE Economic History Student Working Papers*, 004 (2021); T. David and P. Eichenberger, 'Business and Diplomacy in the Twentieth Century: A Corporatist View', *Diplomatica*, 2/1 (2020), 48–56; P. Müller, 'Coordonner le capitalisme européen. Les délégués français et allemands de la Chambre de commerce internationale des années 1930', in P. Müller and H. Joly (eds.), *Les espaces d'interaction des élites françaises et allemandes: 1920–1950* (Presses universitaires de Rennes, 2021), pp. 111–26.

Germans had a mission to lead Europe as naturally gifted economic organizers. For Riedl, the Austrian problem and the German problem were inextricably linked. In *The Globalists*, Quinn Slobodian emphasizes the pivotal role played by Riedl and the Vienna Chamber of Commerce in transposing post-imperial regional hierarchies onto the ICC and the League, but Slobodian does not address the question of German regional power, which loomed very large in interwar Austria.[10] Helen Thompson, in contrast, has highlighted the central importance of the Austro-German relationship for the long-term legacy of the Habsburg Empire in European political economy.[11] Riedl's pan-German nationalism is significant in the history of the ICC because it complicates the idea that deepening trans-border business ties promotes peace, as ICC leaders liked to claim frequently and grandiloquently. Rivalry and cooperation were intertwined in the ICC, as they were in the League.[12] Even before Riedl's arrival on the scene in 1926, a dynamic tension between friends and foes was already evident in the ICC's early movement to forge transatlantic norms for commercial arbitration.

International Commercial Arbitration: Bringing States into a Private Legal Order

Commercial arbitration was arguably the single most consequential area of collaboration between the League and the ICC. In the 1920s the League helped the ICC develop a standardized procedure for international commercial arbitration. Today, commercial arbitration has become an important part of the business environment and the ICC stands as the primary guardian of this shadowy legal realm. The ICC sets standards that other arbitration bodies follow, and it also defines norms for governments in their interactions with private arbitrators.[13]

The significance of the collaboration between the League and the ICC in the 1920s can be seen clearly when set against the pre-war baseline.

---

[10] Slobodian, *Globalists*.

[11] H. Thompson, 'The Habsburg Myth and the European Union', in F. Duina and F. Merand (eds.), *Europe's Malaise: The Long View* (Emerald Publishing Limited, 2020), pp. 45–66.

[12] My analysis of the ICC contrasts with that of Michele d'Alessandro, who presents private multilateralism as a repudiation of inter-state rivalry, in the context of the 1927 World Economic Conference. See d'Alessandro, 'Global Economic Governance and the Private Sector'. I build on Gerald Horst Brettner-Messler's biography of Riedl, which focuses on the tension between his pan-German and internationalist aspirations but provides limited analysis of Riedl's institutional interventions in the ICC and the League. See Brettner-Messler, 'Richard Riedl'.

[13] A. Stone Sweet and F. Grisel, *The Evolution of International Arbitration: Judicialization, Governance, Legitimacy* (Oxford University Press, 2017), 45–66.

Commercial arbitration had emerged as a relatively autonomous system of self-regulation among businessmen in the late nineteenth century. Before 1914, wholesale organizations such as the London Corn Trade Association provided dispute-resolution services to their members as part of standardized contracts. Such arbitration decisions were enforced through reputational sanctions, with the threat of commercial banishment from the wholesale community ensuring compliance. Britain was the hub for wholesale trade, and so it was also the seat for most arbitration proceedings. British legal practice concerning contracts and arbitration spread throughout commodity trading networks, covering transactions that did not involve a British partner. These practices came under pressure during and after the war. A broader range of firms began to resort to private arbitration in a shifting commercial environment where currency instability and rapidly evolving national regulation made it hard to define stable contract terms. Moreover, the instrumentalization of foreign trade for national security led many firms to distrust foreign courts and prefer private dispute resolution. Thus, many traders began to seek arbitration even when they were not members of a merchant association that offered this service.[14]

The ICC stepped in to help meet these new demands by providing a more versatile arbitration mechanism which could be used by traders in any sector and from any country, reviving pre-war proposals that had been floated in the International Congress of Chambers of Commerce. In 1923, the ICC established its own Court of Commercial Arbitration, although this was not a court in any ordinary sense. Rather, it was a panel of experts who helped designate arbitrators and define common decision-making procedures. The ICC issued a standard clause that traders could insert into their contracts to refer eventual disputes to this 'court'. Meanwhile, the ICC had to rely more heavily on formal national courts to enforce its arbitration clause than private merchant associations had done in the nineteenth century. The ICC did briefly consider trying to name and shame non-compliant parties but quickly abandoned this approach because it was not sufficiently cohesive to use that type of community enforcement. Thus, the ICC brought what had been a largely private transnational legal order into closer contact with national legal systems, and it relied on the League to do this.[15]

---

[14] Petersson, 'Legal Institutions and the World Economy', 31–6; Lemercier and Sgard, *Arbitrage privé international*, 14–17; C. J. W. Baaij, 'Hiding in Plain Sight: The Power of Public Governance in International Arbitration', *Harvard International Law Journal*, 60/1 (2019), 135–80, 164–6.

[15] International Chamber of Commerce, *Inauguration of the Court of Commercial Arbitration*, brochure no. 22 (International Chamber of Commerce, 1923); Petersson, 'Legal

It was Llewellyn Smith who first pushed the League to reinforce judicial support for private arbitration in 1922, responding to debate on this issue in the ICC and to direct complaints from British merchant associations. The core problem was that courts in many countries simply did not recognize private arbitration clauses as binding. This meant that when foreign firms were unhappy with a private arbitration decision, they could ask their home court to overrule it, initiating the long and costly legal proceedings that an arbitration clause was supposed to preclude.[16] Fear of reputational sanctions had previously prevented members of the organized wholesale trade from using such legal recourse, but the many unaffiliated merchants who were demanding arbitration proceedings in the 1920s were less inhibited. To address this issue, Llewellyn Smith convened an international committee of jurists and businessmen in Britain's Board of Trade, including one member of the ICC's newly formed Court of Commercial Arbitration.[17] They devised a common Protocol on Arbitration Clauses for the League, which bound signatory governments to recognize the legal validity of private arbitration clauses.[18] The Economic Committee sponsored this protocol in 1923 as well as a further agreement in 1927, which enjoined national courts to carry out arbitration decisions that had been taken in foreign countries.[19] In sum, the League was asking national courts to defer to decisions made through the ICC and other private bodies, while also helping to enforce those decisions. This remains the basic regulatory framework for commercial arbitration today. Over time, the ICC has worked to strengthen both forms of judicial support using the levers of formal international governance.

The procedure for commercial arbitration under League norms remained rather cumbersome, however. Enforcing the delivery of awards from foreign arbitration decisions required formal approval

Institutions and the World Economy', 33–7; Lemercier and Sgard, *Arbitrage privé international*, 18–21; Stone Sweet and Grisel, *The Evolution of International Arbitration*, 41–2; Baaij, 'Hiding in Plain Sight', 167–77.

[16] International Chamber of Commerce, *Commercial Arbitration*, brochure no. 13 (International Chamber of Commerce, 1921), 10–14; H. Llewellyn Smith, Recognition of Arbitration Clauses in Commercial Contracts, 21 March 1922, LON: Economic Committee, Papers, 1920–22, B. 65; Provisional Economic and Financial Committee. (Economic Committee). Fourth Session, Second Meeting, 21 March 1922, LON: E&F/Economic/4th Session/P.V.2.

[17] League of Nations. Provisional Economic and Financial Committee. Economic Section. Sub-Committee on Arbitration Clauses. 1st Meeting, London, 3 July 1922, LON: Economic Committee, Papers, 1920–22, B. 78.

[18] League of Nations, *Protocol on Arbitration Clauses*, A.83.1923.II (Geneva: League of Nations, 1923).

[19] *Convention on the Execution of Foreign Arbitral Awards*, C.659.M.220.1927.II (League of Nations, 1928).

from judges in the country where the arbitration took place and the country where it was implemented. Additionally, national regulations concerning arbitration procedures trumped any private code that the parties might voluntarily adopt (such as ICC rules). These issues were not ironed out until the 1950s when the ICC pushed hard for a further arbitration convention from the United Nations. The new convention made it easier to enforce foreign arbitral awards and gave parties full latitude to choose the applicable procedure. Only after these innovations took effect did trans-border commercial arbitration begin to expand dramatically in the 1960s and 1970s. The number of new cases filed with the ICC did not consistently exceed 100 per year until the 1970s (it now exceeds 800).[20]

Although international commercial arbitration did not become a pervasive feature of the business environment in the interwar period, the League and the ICC helped bring about important changes to national legal institutions and practice that prefigured later trends. At first, the ICC handled only a small number of low-value cases that were fairly similar to those previously addressed by sectoral merchant associations, for example, complaints from dissatisfied traders about the quality of a particular delivery. By the 1930s, the ICC began to handle more legally complex disputes concerning patents, variations in exchange rates, and contracts for commercial representation abroad. The parties were often large corporations in engineering or chemicals, and the financial stakes were high. These big-ticket cases were increasingly arbitrated by professional lawyers who were familiar with the relevant regulation rather than by traders who knew the practical technicalities of the sector, as had been the standard practice up to that point. The ICC Secretariat became a central repository for legal competence in contract arbitration and provided substantial guidance.[21] Today, the ICC still specializes in handling high-value, legally complex disputes. It offers close supervision of the arbitration process to ensure that final awards will be legally enforceable.[22] The development of this legal capacity in the ICC was rooted in the basic principle that private arbitration must be upheld by national courts – a principle that the League first generalized through its arbitration agreements of 1923 and 1927.

As collaboration with the League shaped the ICC's internal arbitration practices, both institutions also worked to encourage reform in national

---

[20] Petersson, 'Legal Institutions and the World Economy', 36; Lemercier and Sgard, *Arbitrage privé international*, 21–2; Stone Sweet and Grisel, *The Evolution of International Arbitration*, 45–6, 61–3; Baaij, 'Hiding in Plain Sight', 176–7.

[21] Lemercier and Sgard, *Arbitrage privé international*, 30–42.

[22] Stone Sweet and Grisel, *The Evolution of International Arbitration*, 48–9, 58–9.

judicial systems. They notably facilitated a long process of legal innovation in France, which hosted the ICC's headquarters. Before the 1920s,
French courts did not recognize arbitration clauses as valid. The ICC's
founding president, Étienne Clémentel, helped sponsor national legislation that finally made private arbitration clauses legally binding in France
in 1925. Yet it was not until the 1930s that French higher courts established a jurisprudence supportive of ICC procedures, laying the groundwork for the country to become a central venue for arbitration.[23] From
the outset, both the League and the ICC highlighted France's wayward
position as a crucial obstacle to the broader development of international
commercial arbitration, given the country's central economic and institutional importance.[24] Clémentel, in turn, invoked the authority of the
League and the ICC to overcome internal resistance in French courts to
private arbitration. In this as in other areas, the Economic Committee and
the ICC very deliberately exerted joint political pressure on national
governments to advance business-friendly policies. Llewellyn Smith
described the 1923 Protocol as 'a focussing point for all the appeals
made by the national chambers of commerce to their governments' to
promote private arbitration.[25] ICC engagement helped France catapult
from being a laggard in commercial arbitration in 1920 into a global
leader today. In comparison with France, the ICC's outreach operated
more imperfectly in the United States due to the idiosyncrasies of US
federalism.

Transatlantic Cooperation and Rivalry in Commercial Arbitration and Beyond

In the 1920s, there was strong backing for commercial arbitration in the
US business community but only limited engagement with the ICC's
work on it. The US Chamber of Commerce lobbied aggressively for new
legislation to facilitate private arbitration, leading to the American
Arbitration Act of 1925. This law brought significant changes by establishing the primacy of the federal government in the regulation of international and inter-state private arbitration and confirming the legal

---

[23] Lemercier and Sgard, *Arbitrage privé international*, 12–13.
[24] League of Nations. Provisional Economic and Financial Committee. Economic Section.
Sub-Committee on Arbitration Clauses. Report on the Session Held in London,
24 August 1922, LON: Economic Committee, Papers, 1920–22, B. 78; International
Chamber of Commerce, *Règlement de Conciliation et d'Arbitrage, Deuxième Édition*, brochure no. 21 (International Chamber of Commerce, 1921), 41; Lemercier and Sgard,
Arbitrage privé international, 13.
[25] Economic and Financial Commission. Economic Committee, 7th Session. Minutes of
the 5th and last meeting, 1 March 1923, LON: E.F.S./E/7th. Session/P.V.5(1).

validity of private arbitration clauses for such disputes. The ICC declared that this law 'really amounts to a ratification of the Protocol of the League of Nations, as it makes the same principles legally valid in America as those established under the Protocol'.[26] Formal legal alignment did not bring institutional rapprochement but rather facilitated the development of a separate American Arbitration Association (AAA). Founded in 1926, the AAA was based on similar principles to the ICC's own Court of Commercial Arbitration. It issued a standard contract clause that referred disputes to the AAA for settlement and offered to appoint arbitrators from a panel of 7,000 prominent business leaders across the country. As in the ICC, access to this service did not require associational membership and so it also depended on courts and not on reputational sanctions for enforcement. Judicial enforcement was especially complex in the US federal system, however. One of the primary objectives of the AAA was to persuade states to align their procedures for local disputes with federal law, which could only cover inter-state and international commerce.[27] More generally, the AAA claimed specialized expertise concerning state-federal dynamics in US business law.

Over time, the ICC and the AAA established a geographic division of labour, formalized in 1939. They devised a common contract clause, which specified that AAA procedure would be used for disputes that included a US party, and ICC procedure would be used for all other cases.[28] Significantly, Lucius Eastman, the first US member to sit on the League Economic Committee in 1928, was the founder and long-serving president of the AAA and also a prominent leader in the US National Committee of the ICC. He symbolized the arms-length cooperation that the ICC sustained between the United States and the League in the 1920s. The unevenness of US engagement with multilateral business regulation during this period was also evident in the other areas of collaboration between the League and the ICC, intellectual property and trade credit.

While the United States engaged with the League and the ICC's work on arbitration at a distance, it participated more directly in cooperation on intellectual property but did so outside the confines of the League. To facilitate US adoption of rules on intellectual property, the Economic Committee worked with another ancillary organization alongside the

[26] The International Chamber of Commerce, 'Arbitration Report No. 4', Supplement to *Journal of the International Chamber of Commerce*, April 1925, 5; Stone Sweet and Grisel, *The Evolution of International Arbitration*, 177; Baaij, 'Hiding in Plain Sight', 43–6.

[27] 'Arbitration Open to All Sections', *The New York Times*, 26 January 1930, 5; Lemercier and Sgard, *Arbitrage privé international*, 17.

[28] Lemercier and Sgard, *Arbitrage privé international*, 28.

ICC, the Industrial Property Union in Bern.[29] As part of its effort to combat 'unfair competition' through the improper use of trademarks, the Economic Committee gathered experts to prepare a revision in 1925 of the International Convention for the Protection of Industrial Property.[30] This was a longstanding agreement from 1883 to standardize patents and trademarks that the Bern Union administered (Lucien Coquet was an enthusiastic supporter during his early career as a trademark lawyer).[31] The Economic Committee drafted a text to revise the 1883 Convention, but it allowed the Bern Union to lead negotiations in 1925 in order to facilitate the participation of non-League members, notably the United States and Germany.[32] This strategy worked, and both countries signed on to the 1925 revision.[33]

In contrast, both the United States and Britain remained aloof from the League's work on trade credit, which was rooted in the Continental tradition of civil law. Cooperation on bills of exchange had begun before the First World War and continued after 1918 in both the ICC and the League. The initial demand for international codification came from France, Germany, and the Netherlands, where civil law prescribed the content and the procedures for bills of exchange much more precisely than British common law. Britain's looser rules governed bills of exchange and promissory notes in its empire and most of the non-colonial world, reflecting London's historically dominant position in trade credit. New York banks were starting to claim more business in this sector, but they also used British-inflected common law. Llewellyn Smith and his colleagues in the Board of Trade were unwilling to accept any constraints on British bills of exchange but nevertheless supported codification in order to 'reduce the existing large number of laws on Bills of Exchange to two great systems, the continental and the English'. That is, roughly, what happened (although the 'English' system became increasingly American).[34] The Economic Committee debated international standards on bills of exchange for many years before issuing a series of

---

[29] 'Conference of the International Union for the Protection of Industrial Property', *Journal of the International Chamber of Commerce*, December 1925, 9–14.
[30] Economic Committee. Report to the Council on the Twelfth Session, 12 June 1924, LON: A.9.1924.II; *Commercial Policy in the Interwar Period*, 27–8.
[31] Gorman, *The Emergence of International Society in the 1920s*, 205–6.
[32] H. Llewellyn Smith, Unfair competition: Note on the replies received to the questionnaire, 3 September 1921, LON: Economic Committee, Papers, 1920–22, B. 40.
[33] *WIPO-Administered Treaties, Contracting Parties Paris Convention, The Hague Act (1925)*, WIPO IP Portal, https://wipolex.wipo.int/en/treaties/ShowResults?search_what=A&act_id=27.
[34] Report on the Unification of the Laws of Different Countries Relating to Bills of Exchange, LON: Economic Committee, Papers, 1920–22, B 17.

conventions in 1930.[35] From that point on, most civil law countries began to base trade credit on the 'Geneva Uniform Law on Bills of Exchange', while common law countries continued to refer to British and US legislation from the 1880s and 1890s.[36] The Economic Committee encountered more difficulties in its attempt to clarify another area of messy nineteenth-century commercial practice: business travel. In the 1920s, that issue gained political salience in post-imperial Central and Eastern Europe.

The New Politics of Foreigners and Foreign Trade

Prior to the First World War, international commercial conferences had already begun to demand more standardized regulations on business travel.[37] Trade intermediaries often had to pay fees and register with a local chamber of commerce before they could import product samples, sign and execute contracts, use exhibition space or warehouses, and access transportation infrastructure. Moreover, those regulations varied considerably from country to country. In Europe the war brought more onerous border controls as well as many new borders to be controlled, and the League responded on several fronts.[38] The Transit Organization standardized passport and visa procedures. The Economic Committee worked to streamline border controls related to samples and business travel and also outlined a more ambitious commercial code governing the general 'treatment of foreigners'. Riedl became the standard-bearer for League efforts to facilitate multinational business mobility following the 1927 World Economic Conference, and cooperation in this area had focused heavily on the post-Habsburg context from the outset. Passports had been an early priority for the League Transit Committee because they were an obstacle to the resumption of rail travel and trade in Central Europe.[39] After falling

---

[35] League of Nations Economic, Financial and Transit Department, *Commercial Policy in the Interwar Period: International Proposals and National Policies* (League of Nations, 1942), 29–30.

[36] C. Pejovic, 'Civil Law and Common Law: Two Different Paths Leading to the Same Goal', *Victoria University of Wellington Law Review*, 32/3 (2001), 817–42, 829–30; Petersson, 'Legal Institutions and the World Economy', 26–31.

[37] J. Hayem (ed.), *Congrès international du commerce et de l'industrie tenu à Paris du 23 au 28 septembre 1889: Rapports, discussions, travaux et résolutions du congrès* (Librairie Guillaumin et Cie., 1890), 110–18.

[38] For a survey of pre-war regulations, see *Commercial Travellers: Memorandum Summarizing the Regulations in Force in Foreign Countries with Regard to British Commercial Travellers* (H. M. G. Stationery Office, 1904).

[39] For a discussion of League-led passport cooperation in the Central European context, see P. Becker, 'Remaking Mobility: International Conferences and the Emergence of the

out of use in most of Europe in the nineteenth century, passports were reintroduced during the war, in neutral and belligerent countries alike. In the 1920s, moving around on a passport required securing exit and entry visas from the state of departure and arrival as well as transit visas for all the countries crossed in between. The League of Nations offered a central framework to streamline and standardize these document procedures, sponsoring a widely adopted template for an 'international type' of passport.[40]

ICC leaders enthusiastically supported the League's work on passports, and some of them also demanded further action to reopen labour markets, arguing that the restoration of free movement and free trade must proceed hand in hand: 'it is in the interests of all countries, including those who have an excess of working men, as well as those who have a deficiency, that working men should be able to circulate as freely as possible in the world so as to bring an equilibrium between demand and supply'.[41] League bodies adopted a narrower approach that privileged foreign trade over broad labour mobility. They selectively focused on helping the members of the trading community move around and conduct business rather than pursuing open labour markets as factor in macroeconomic stabilization. In his opening speech at the Transit Committee's 1920 Passport Conference, Yves Le Trocquer, speaking as the French minister of public works, declared that 'anything which hinders personal relations between producers of all countries, creates a grave obstacle, preventing the resumption of commercial exchanges'.[42] He enjoined the assembled experts to use their status 'as technical people', to rise above political tensions to achieve pragmatic solutions. This meant that the League's passport norms would cover only procedural questions, such as the format, price, and method of delivery for travel documents, but would not cover admission to labour markets.[43] Within the League multiverse, only the ILO claimed an explicit mandate to weigh in on labour migration, but it also avoided the contentious question of admission and focused instead on promoting

Modern Passport System', in P. Becker, N. Wheatley (eds.), *Remaking Central Europe: The League of Nations and the Former Habsburg Lands* (Oxford University Press, 2020), pp. 193–211.

[40] Becker, 'Remaking Mobility', 193–200.

[41] International Chamber of Commerce, *Proceedings of the First Congress*, brochure no. 18 (International Chamber of Commerce, 1921), 107–8.

[42] League of Nations Conference on Passports, Customs Formalities, and Through Tickets, 15 October 1920, LON: R1092, 14/7612/5097.

[43] Conférence spéciale des passeports, formalités douanières & billets directs (transit), 4ème séance, 16 October 1920, LON: R1092, 14/7612 /5097.

workers' access to social protection after they had already been admitted to work in a foreign country.[44] The Economic Committee similarly skirted admission policy, while working to facilitate the movement of commercial intermediaries and their product samples. In interwar Europe, commercial rights often depended on immigration status, on possession of an economic visa or a residence permit. The Economic Committee made a first attempt to address these issues through its 1923 Convention on Customs Formalities, which proposed a model Identity Card for Commercial Travellers that functioned as a complement to the League's international passport.[45] Signatory governments also submitted periodic reports to the League explaining national procedures for obtaining passports and commercial identity cards, which the League disseminated in regular instalments.[46] Thus, fittingly, it was at borders that European traders would have been most immediately aware of the new forms of multilateral regulation emanating from the Geneva. Most of them would have carried a League-standardized passport and commercial identity card, and they would have followed a series of routinized procedures concerning samples, product analyses, indications of origin, and customs declarations that had been defined by the League.

The Economic Committee also undertook a more ambitious effort to standardize the 'treatment of foreigners' behind borders, aiming to facilitate commercial representation and foreign direct investment. It began by issuing a series of non-binding recommendations in 1923 and 1924 concerning foreign nationals' fiscal treatment, property rights, judicial protection, and access to certified professions.[47] Daniel Serruys and Hubert Llewellyn Smith were the main sponsors for this initiative, but they also intervened to limit its reach. They firmly excluded questions of admission and residency to avoid international interference in imperial immigration policies. Llewellyn Smith was particularly concerned about the British Dominions. Successive Japanese members prodded the Economic Committee to take up the question of migrant admission, in

---

[44] P.-A. Rosental, 'Géopolitique et État-providence. Le BIT et la politique mondiale des migrations dans l'entre-deux-guerres', *Annales. Histoire, Sciences Sociales*, 61/1 (2006), 99–134.

[45] League of Nations, *1. International Convention Relating to the Simplification of Customs Formalities 2. Protocol to the International Convention*, C. 678.M.241 (League of Nations, 1924).

[46] See, for example: League of Nations Advisory and Technical Committee on Communications and Transit, *Replies of the Governments to the Questionnaire Regarding Passport Regulations*, C.405.M.143.1925.VIII (League of Nations, 1925), 5–7, 12–15.

[47] Traitement des ressortissants étrangers et des entreprises étrangères, rapport du Comité Économique, 15 May 1923, PA AA, Rechtsabteilung/R 54262; Rapport du Comité Économique au Conseil, PA AA, 10 June 1925, Rechtsabteilung/R 54262, 4–8.

the hope that even soft international norms might provide leverage to contest racial restrictions on migrant selection in the Dominions, most prominently the 'white Australia' policy.[48] The Japanese thus tried to use the Covenant's clause on the 'equitable treatment' of commerce to revive their demands for racial equality that had been sidelined at the Paris Peace Conference.[49] Japanese leaders pushed for ambitious League action on the 'treatment of foreigners' in form as well as content, demanding a binding multilateral treaty. Daniel Serruys responded that the unsettled political conditions of the Habsburg successor states made it impossible to implement 'super-laws over-riding national legislation'. Consequently, the Economic Committee issued a modest set of non-binding recommendations in 1923 and 1924 that applied only to firms and individuals who had already been legally admitted to a foreign country.[50]

A few years later, Serruys and Llewellyn Smith agreed to revise the form but not the substance of the League's work on the 'treatment of foreigners'. They both endorsed a push from the ICC led by Richard Riedl to transform the initial advisory recommendations into a binding treaty, during the World Economic Conference, but they still refused to address the issue of admission. At the conference, Llewellyn Smith was the rapporteur responsible for Riedl's draft proposals, and he recommended that they be transferred from the ICC to the League to serve as the basis for a new multilateral treaty.[51] This handover was fitting because Riedl had explicitly modelled his own draft agreements on the multilateral treaties that Llewellyn Smith had sponsored to standardize other areas of commercial administration, such as transit and customs formalities.[52] For his part, Llewellyn Smith had worked hard to incorporate the ICC as a partner in those early agreements. Although both men drew from the same multilateral toolkit, Riedl used his foothold in the ICC to push the Economic Committee away from Llewellyn Smith's universalist vision and towards a more explicit programme

---

[48] A. McKeown, *Melancholy Order: Asian Migration and the Globalization of Borders* (Columbia University Press, 2008), 185–216.

[49] The Japanese had linked racial equality to demands for free trade in the colonial world at the Paris Peace Conference, see T. W. Burkman, *Japan and the League of Nations: Empire and World Order, 1914–1938* (University of Hawaii Press, 2007), 52–8.

[50] Traitement des ressortissants étrangers et des entreprises étrangères, rapport du Comité Économique, 15 May 1923, PA AA: Rechtsabteilung/R 54262; Rapport du Comité Économique au Conseil, 10 June 1925, Rechtsabteilung/R 54262, 4–8.

[51] Société des Nations, *Actes de la Conférence Économique Internationale tenue à Genève du 4 au 23 mai 1927*, vol. 2 (League of Nations, 1927), 42.

[52] *Collective Treaties Facilitating International Commerce in Europe.*

of regional European integration. Moreover, Riedl's general commitment to European unity and his specific interest in the 'treatment of foreigners' remained deeply rooted in his pan-German nationalism.

Internationalizing *Anschluss*: Richard Riedl's Winding Path to Geneva

Riedl started to engage intensively in trade debates in the League of Nations only after he retired from his state functions and returned to his home base in the Vienna Chamber of Commerce in 1926. By that time, the Vienna Chamber was already well known in internationalist circles as a centre for high-level debates about economic theory due to the activities of Ludwig von Mises, who had served as a secretary in the Chamber since 1910. Mises used the Chamber's headquarters to host a legendary 'private seminar' as well as an Institute for Business-Cycle Research, which he founded with Friedrich Hayek. Mises was involved in the Austrian Reparation Commission, where he helped establish an international image of the Vienna Chamber as a competent, liberal organ of policy formulation.[53] Stoppani, who had also served on the Commission, praised the Vienna Chamber as an 'institution remarkable for its organization and its seriousness'.[54] In 1922, Mises collaborated with the League's Financial Committee to organize an international currency stabilization loan to the Austrian government. The 1922 Austrian loan was a crucial early triumph that helped consolidate the fledging EFO. From the standpoint of monetary policy, this intervention was successful, but it was followed by high unemployment and weak growth rates. League officials and collaborators were sensitive to allegations that the intrusive austerity policies tied to the 1922 loan had contributed to the sluggish performance of the Austrian economy.[55] They agreed with the economists at the Vienna Chamber that the solution to Austria's economic woes should not be sought in the relaxation of

[53] F. Geißler, *Österreichs Handelskammer-Organisation in der Zwischenkriegszeit: Ein Idee auf dem Prüfstand* (Österreichischer Wirtschaftsverlag, 1977), 27; A. Hörtlehner, 'Ludwig von Mises und die österreichische Handelskammerorganisation', *Wirtschaftspolitische Blätter*, 28/4 (1981), 140–46; R. M. Ebeling, *Political Economy, Public Policy and Monetary Economics: Ludwig von Mises and the Austrian Tradition* (Routledge, 2010), 23, 90.

[54] P. Stoppani, Notes pour Sir Arthur Salter, 19 March 1925, AMAE: Papiers Joseph Avenol/19.

[55] N. Piétri, *La société des nations et la reconstruction financière de l'Autriche, 1921–1926* (Centre européen de la Dotation Carnegie pour la paix internationale, 1970); Clavin, *Securing the World Economy*, 25–33; N. Marcus, *Austrian Reconstruction and the Collapse of Global Finance, 1921–1931* (Harvard University Press, 2018); Martin, *The Meddlers*, 76-90.

fiscal austerity but rather in the elimination of barriers to Austrian exports, particularly in the successor states.[56]

In the 1920s, the Vienna Chamber's policy interventions and economic theory connected internal fiscal restraint and external free trade, as Quinn Slobodian emphasizes, but this was not a straightforward attempt to recreate the Habsburg economic space.[57] Trade policy in the Vienna Chamber of Commerce was strongly influenced by pan-German nationalism in the 1920s, especially after 1926 when Friedrich Tilgner arrived as president and recruited Riedl.[58] Riedl was the main spokesman for German nationalism in the Vienna Chamber, but the liberal economists backed him at crucial junctures. For example, at an ICC conference in May 1931, Mises spoke as Riedl's alternate to defend the controversial plan for an Austro-German customs union as a legitimate exception to general MFN rules.[59] As a stridently and famously liberal organization, the Vienna Chamber was a powerful voice in favour of regional free trade areas precisely because no one suspected that it was advocating autarky.

The internal structures of the Vienna Chamber firmly linked commitments to freer international trade and *Anschluss*, and Riedl assumed a prominent role in both areas. He was the general secretary of the Austrian National Committee of the ICC, which was based in the Vienna Chamber. At the same time, he served as the Delegate to the Austrian Chambers of Commerce for the Extension of the Economic Area, a position specifically dedicated to promoting *Anschluss*. In this latter role, Riedl was responsible for coordinating efforts by other private associations to facilitate legal and administrative rapprochement with Germany and for preparing semi-annual joint meetings of the Austrian and German chambers of commerce.[60] Riedl's collaboration with the League and the ICC was, in part, an attempt to safeguard this bilateral harmonization effort by linking it to broader multilateral structures.[61]

---

[56] Jürgen Nautz notes that Austrian exports faced higher barriers in the mid-1920s partly because the other successor states were facing their own stabilization crises and responding with tariff hikes. See J. Nautz, *Die österreichische Handelspolitik der Nachkriegszeit 1918 bis 1923: Die Handelsvertragsbeziehungen zu den Nachfolgestaaten* (Böhlau, 1994), 531–8.

[57] Slobodian, *Globalists*, 27–54.

[58] Fischer, 'Die österreichischen Handelskammern und der Anschluß an Deutschland'.

[59] Chambre de commerce internationale, *Compte-rendu du Congrès de Washington, Mai 1931* (ICC, 1931), 68.

[60] Fischer, 'Die österreichischen Handelskammern und der Anschluß an Deutschland'; Brettner-Messler, 'Richard Riedl', p. 350.

[61] Nautz, 'Tarifvertragsrecht und "Anschluss". Das Projekt einer gemeinsamen Tarifrechtsreform in Deutschland und Österreich 1919–1931'.

When Riedl hosted his first joint meeting of the German and Austrian chambers of commerce in 1926, he explained that business organizations would have to take the lead in pursing *Anschluss*, because they were less constrained than governments by the terms of the 1919 Peace Settlement. He suggested that there were many areas of regulatory policy in which Austrian and German business leaders could 'reach an agreement without colliding with international commitments'. The main example that he cited was legislation on the treatment of foreign nationals, including regulations governing the operation of foreign subsidiaries, the right to conduct commercial transactions, and the recognition of diplomas.[62] This type of 'foreigners' law' (*Fremdenrecht*) held particular interest for both Austrian and German business leaders. Regulatory rapprochement in this area would facilitate bilateral integration between the two economies and would also make it easier for each of them to project influence abroad. Austrian trading houses were eager to regain access to their former markets in Habsburg successor states, while German banks and industrial firms were looking to roll back restrictions on foreign direct investment that had been introduced across Europe after the war.

Riedl's vision of European solidarity projected imperial hierarchy onto the rest of the continent. He proposed that Austria and Germany band together with the industrialized states of Western Europe to set trade norms for their Eastern neighbours. He lamented 'the endeavours of the new States in Eastern and South Eastern Europe to develop as extensively as possible their home production and to become self-supporting through shutting out foreign competition'.[63] To shield his plans from the successor states' anticipated objections, Riedl argued that multilateral negotiations should be limited, in the first instance, to 'states which in a certain sense form a geographical unit and which in regard to their cultural and economic development stand closer to one another'. He suggested that this grouping might include France, Belgium, Switzerland, Italy, Austria, Germany, and Czechoslovakia.[64] In Riedl's plan, these states would first agree on a common rulebook for their own foreign trade and then extend those norms eastward.

Riedl was able to persuade the leaders of the Vienna Chamber of Commerce to subsume their ambitions for *Anschluss* under his hierarchical vision of trade liberalization. As soon as he returned to the Chamber in 1926, he drafted a fifty-page 'Action Plan' outlining an elaborate

---

[62] Protokoll über die Sitzung in Salzburg am 18 Mai 1926 über Fragen europäischer Handelspolitik, 18 May 1926, ÖSta: AVA, NL Riedl/80.
[63] *Collective Treaties Facilitating International Commerce in Europe*, 3.
[64] R. Riedl, *A Collective Treaty Relating to a Common Upper Limit of Customs Charges and to Reciprocal Most-Favoured Nation Treatment* (Vernay, 1927), 8.

scheme to promote bilateral Austro-German integration within a multilateral framework. In it, he clearly identified *Anschluss* as the long-term objective of Austrian trade policy. This was a mainstream position in interwar Austria, where *Anschluss* had backers across the political spectrum. Important segments of the Austrian elite also favoured a Danubian orientation that prioritized cooperation with the other Habsburg successor states.[65] Riedl doubted that Austria could assert itself in a Danubian grouping without German backing, but his approach to *Anschluss* was cautious. The peace treaties prohibited *Anschluss* without the consent of the League Council. Riedl suggested that Austria might earn that consent through sustained international engagement, and, in the meantime, he advocated limited Austro-German administrative rapprochement within the bounds of the treaties. He argued that Austrian leaders should begin by pursuing general pan-European cooperation and simply take care not to foreclose a future Austro-German union. In his internal 'Action Plan', he told his colleagues in Vienna:

Our approach must not appear to be a threat to European interests but rather must serve to advance them. It should not be limited to reciprocal relations between Austria and Germany, but rather must organically incorporate efforts in favour of an economic rapprochement of European countries with the goal of establishing a preferably *large economic area in Europe*. This is by no means camouflage, but rather an earnest attempt to end the present state of economic fragmentation and incoherence, in which the whole of Europe, but perhaps Austria most of all, suffers. [original emphasis][66]

Riedl was able to secure strong backing in Germany for his trade projects precisely because he was not advocating exclusive Austro-German rapprochement.[67]

Gustav Stresemann was committed to a peaceful revision of the territorial terms of the 1919 Peace Settlement over the long term, but he was ambivalent about *Anschluss*. There was much popular enthusiasm for *Anschluss* in both Germany and Austria, so he could not foreswear it altogether. Privately he held deep doubts that a full union between Austria and Germany was desirable or feasible because it would complicate Germany's internal confessional and party politics. In the 1920s, the idea of an eastward-oriented

---

[65] Suppan, 'Mitteleuropa Konzeptionen zwischen Restauration und Anschluss'; J. Thorpe, *Pan-Germanism and the Austrofascist State, 1933–38* (Manchester University Press, 2011), 16–44; E. R. Hochman, *Imagining a Greater Germany: Republican Nationalism and the Idea of Anschluss* (Cornell University Press, 2016).

[66] R. Riedl, Denkschrift über die Möglichkeiten einer Erweiterung des Österreichischen Wirtschaftsgebietes, April 1926, ÖStA, AVA/NL Riedl/80.

[67] Protokoll über die Sitzung in Salzburg am 18. Mai 1926 über Fragen europäischer Handelspolitik, ÖStA: AVA/NL Riedl/80.

Mitteleuropa held limited appeal for most German officials and business leaders, who were more focused on regaining access to richer West European and overseas markets, especially in the Americas and the British Empire.[68] Yet they did not want to see Austria join a Danubian grouping that would block German access to the east. Riedl worked hard to stymie all initiatives along these lines, but he also accepted that Austro-German rapprochement could only be pursued peacefully and gradually, through the League of Nations, with French and British acquiescence. As a result, Riedl was considered a valuable ally in Berlin and continued to receive support from German leaders after he returned to Vienna. He remained in regular contact with Stresemann, with Ernst Trendelenburg, who held the German seat on the Economic Committee, and with Eduard Hamm, who led the German chambers of commerce.

Riedl was useful to German leaders because his position in the Vienna Chamber of Commerce gave him a base of power outside the ministerial apparatus, which allowed him to act independently to counteract government policies that were inimical to German interests. Riedl notably offered a counterweight to Richard Schüller. Schüller was the most senior public trade official in interwar Austria, and he prioritized cooperation with Italy over Germany.[69] Riedl categorically rejected Schüller's Austro-Italian plans; he had long viewed Italian expansionary ambitions in the Adriatic as one of the greatest threats to Austrian regional influence.[70] Riedl and Schüller also had a longstanding professional rivalry. In 1909, Riedl had been appointed to serve as a department head in the Austrian Ministry of Commerce over Schüller. At the time, Schüller had been the most technically qualified candidate for the position within the ministerial staff, but he was not promoted partly because he was a Jew.[71] The tables turned during the war, when Riedl was marginalized due to his links to divisive German nationalists as Schüller rose to prominence.[72] In the interwar period, Schüller became Austria's top trade negotiator.[73] In 1926, Schüller was

[68] Schulz, *Deutschland, der Völkerbund und die Frage der europäischen Wirtschaftsordnung*, 71–6; Berg, *Gustav Stresemann und die Vereinigten Staaten von Amerika*, 405–8.

[69] J. Nautz, 'Historische Einführung', in R. Schüller, *Unterhändler des Vertrauens: Aus den nachgelassenen Schriften von Sektionschef Dr. Richard Schüller*, J. Nautz (ed.), (R. Oldenbourg Verlag, 1990), pp. 9–70, 45.

[70] Brettner-Messler, 'Richard Riedl', pp. 53–4, 220. R. Riedl, Denkschrift über die Möglichkeiten einer Erweiterung des Österreichischen Wirtschaftsgebietes, April 1926, ÖStA, AVA/NL Riedl/80.

[71] Brettner-Messler, 'Richard Riedl', pp. 59–60.

[72] '22.7.16'; '6.12.16', in Wildner, Agstner (ed.), *1915/1916. Das etwas andere Lesebuch zum 1. Weltkrieg. Heinrich Wildner: Tagebuch.*

[73] On Schüller's career as Austria's trade negotiator, see R. Schüller, *Unterhändler des Vertrauens: Aus den nachgelassenen Schriften von Sektionschef Dr. Richard Schüller*, J. Nautz (ed.), (R. Oldenbourg Verlag, 1990).

given the Austrian seat in the League Economic Committee. According reports in Berlin, Riedl sought this appointment himself and would have been preferred over Schüller by German leaders.[74] Despite the fact that Riedl was not a formal member of the Economic Committee, he was able to advance his own agenda by cultivating ties to the League through the ICC, with strong support from German officials and business circles. In their prosopography of ICC presidents across the twentieth century, Thomas David and Pierre Eichenberger found that many of them had a hybrid career profile similar to Riedl's, split between business and government. This gave them influence in both spheres while enabling them to pursue independent policy initiatives.[75]

The ICC and the 1927 World Economic Conference

Riedl joined the ICC at a propitious moment when it was strengthening its bonds with the League in the run-up to the World Economic Conference.[76] The conference's sprawling preparatory committee helped facilitate this collaboration. Salter later recalled that the preparatory committee 'was itself a small international conference', specifically noting that the ICC 'took a very positive and active part' in its activities.[77] Within the ICC, engagement with the conference was handled through Étienne Clémentel's Trade Barriers Committee. In 1926 this body gathered suggestions from the ICC's national committees and then formed a series of seven sub-committees to compile these proposals into a forty-page report for the World Economic Conference.[78] Among the many documents prepared for the conference, the ICC report held particular significance both for active delegates and outside observers. In Kiel, Bernhard Harms described this report as the basis for a 'Magna Carta guaranteeing the freedom of world commerce' and insisted that the 'the first and highest task' of the conference was to develop the ICC's

---

[74] Hemmen to Trendelenburg, 5 December 1926, BArch: R 3101/1951.

[75] T. David and P. Eichenberger, '"A World Parliament of Business"? The International Chamber of Commerce and Its Presidents in the Twentieth Century', *Business History* (2022), 1–24.

[76] Ridgeway, *Merchants of Peace*, 83–106; d'Alessandro, 'Global Economic Governance and the Private Sector'; Slobodian, *Globalists*, 37–41; Hoffer, 'Is the Business of Business Business Alone?' 27–32.

[77] A. Salter, 'The Contribution of the League of Nations to the Economic Recovery of Europe', *The Annals of the American Academy of Political and Social Science*, 134/1 (1927), 132–9, 134, 137; A. Salter, 'The Economic Conference: Prospects of Practical Results', *Journal of the Royal Institute of International Affairs*, 6/6 (1927), 350–67, 351.

[78] Ridgeway, *Merchants of Peace*, 86–8; M. Rosengarten, *Die Internationale Handelskammer: wirtschaftspolitische Empfehlungen in der Zeit der Weltwirtschaftskrise 1929–1939* (Duncker & Humblot, 2001), 123.

proposals into a full commercial code.[79] In Geneva, Salter declared that the ICC report was 'in some respects the most important which is before the Conference'. Salter stressed that the ICC wrote its report in direct consultation with active business leaders, and so it provided 'a picture of trade barriers as seen by those who have daily experience of their consequences'. This gave the report a practical orientation; Salter noted that 'unlike almost all the rest of the documentation' it included 'specific recommendations and proposals'.[80] It was Riedl who had supplied three of the most concrete suggestions in the ICC's report: two draft conventions and a scheme for an ongoing international trade conference.

Remarkably, the proposals that Riedl fed through the ICC to the World Economic Conference can be traced directly back to the internal 'Action Plan' for *Anschluss* that he prepared for the Vienna Chamber of Commerce upon arrival in 1926. Riedl gave the ICC's Trade Barriers Committee an abridged version of his Action Plan, stripped of the baldest references to *Anschluss*.[81] The sanitized version that he presented to the ICC laid out a three-phase programme of European integration: firstly, the League should promote international norms governing a wide range of regulatory questions, including the treatment of foreigners; secondly, it should establish a multilateral framework for tariff reduction; and finally, it should create a common system of ongoing policy coordination among treaty members. Stoppani, who was responsible for organizing the World Economic Conference, singled out Riedl's memorandum for high praise. He sent it to national trade officials as recommended reading and told the ICC leaders that among the various proposals that the Trade Barriers Committee had received, 'the one that contains very definite seeds for future development is the Austrian report'.[82] ICC leaders responded by appointing Riedl to lead a Sub-Committee on the Treatment of Foreigners and on Legal and Social Discrimination. He used this perch to prepare two draft conventions on the legal treatment of commercial agents for the 1927 conference, along with a plan for a Permanent Conference on Tariff and Trade Questions.[83]

[79] Harms, 'Die Weltwirtschaftskonferenz', 228.
[80] League of Nations Economic, Financial and Transit Department, *International Economic Conference. Geneva, May 1927. Guide to the Preparatory Documents of the Conference* (League of Nations, 1927), 6, 12; Also quoted in Ridgeway, *Merchants of Peace*, 88–9.
[81] Compare R. Riedl, *Kollektivverträge zur Erleichterung des internationalen Handels in Europa* (Vernay, 1926) and R. Riedl, Denkschrift über die Möglichkeiten einer Erweiterung des Österreichischen Wirtschaftsgebietes, April 1926, ÖStA, AVA/NL Riedl/80.
[82] P. Stoppani to E. Dolléans, 1 July 1926, LON: R529, 10C/51057/46431; P. Stoppani to E. Trendelenburg, 24 August 1926, BArch: R 3101/3008.
[83] International Chamber of Commerce, *Report of the Trade Barriers Committee Presented to the Preparatory Committee of the Economic Conference of the League of Nations*, brochure no. 44 (Herbert Clarke, 1927), 14–17, 28.

After Llewellyn Smith prodded the World Economic Conference to accept Riedl's texts as the basis for a new multilateral agreement, the ICC appointed Riedl and the Economic Committee appointed Serruys to serve as the authors for a new Draft Convention on the Treatment of Foreigners (hereafter, Draft Convention). Stoppani ensured that Riedl was the primary author by dispatching a Secretariat official to the Vienna Chamber of Commerce to help write an initial text before finalizing the draft with Serruys in Geneva.[84] Riedl and Serruys produced an agreement to eliminate many of the legal obstacles and tax penalties that placed foreign nationals at a disadvantage in the negotiation and execution of contracts, the use of transport infrastructure, the creation of subsidiaries, the selection of personnel, and the acquisition and management of property.[85] The resulting Draft Convention closely followed the original proposals that Riedl wrote for the ICC.[86]

This was an agreement written for and by businessmen. In 1926 Riedl had prepared his initial plans by sending ICC national committees a detailed, twelve-page questionnaire about legislation governing the commercial activities of foreign nationals and firms.[87] He adopted a problem-oriented approach and paid little heed to jurisdictional boundaries. One bemused international lawyer remarked that the Draft Convention was:

in part a codification of international law relating to the protection of aliens, and in part a unification of municipal legislation relating to trade and commerce. It represents the labors of economists and business men rather than of lawyers and jurists. This fact may account for its comprehensive scope and its tendency to embrace various subjects ordinarily considered unrelated by those accustomed to view only the legal scene.[88]

The Draft Convention was divided into three main sections. The first, 'Safeguards for International Trade', asserted traders' fundamental rights to buy, sell, and deliver goods. The second section covered the freedom of movement, freedom of establishment, property rights, and fiscal

---

[84] P. Stoppani to R. Riedl, 20 October 1927, LON: R405, 10/60780/29200; C. Smets to R. Riedl, 1 December 1927, ÖStA: AVA, NL Riedl/115.

[85] Avant-Projet de Convention concernant le Traitement des Étrangers présenté par MM. Serruys et Riedl, 15 December 1927, PA AA: Rechtsabteilung/R 54262.

[86] Internationale Handelskammer. Komitee für Fremdenrecht. Bericht des Präsidenten über den Gang der Verhandlungen betreffend die Internationale Konvention über Fremdenrecht, 4 January 1928, ÖStA: AVA, NL Riedl/115.

[87] Société des Nations. Comité preparatoire de la conférence économique international. Documentation pour la deuxième Session (Novembre 1926). C. Problèmes relatifs au commerce et aux marches, 26 October 1926, ÖStA: AVA, NL Riedl 79.

[88] A. K. Kuhn, 'The International Conference on the Treatment of Foreigners', *American Journal of International Law*, 24/3 (1930), 570–73, 573.

treatment of people who had already been admitted to live and work in a foreign country. The third section covered the treatment of legally admitted foreign subsidiaries. These provisions covered a wide swath of public and private commercial administration, from port associations to chambers of commerce. They thus raised fundamental questions about the League's authority to mediate between public administration and transnational business.

International Law, National Governments, and Transnational Business

Although it was never directly implemented, the Draft Convention became a focal point for broader discussions about the relative merits of bilateral and multilateral treaties and helped crystallize disagreements about the role of the League as a locus of regulatory authority and an agent of economic change. It addressed an issue that was at the heart of both national sovereignty and international order, the legal rights of foreign nationals, and thus intersected with heated population politics in post-imperial Central and Eastern Europe.[89] Riedl specifically designed the Draft Convention to facilitate Austrian commercial activity in former Habsburg territory. After the collapse of the Austro-Hungarian Empire, many of the other successor states introduced new licensing and registration requirements that forced Vienna trading houses to operate through local intermediaries in order to perform routine operations such as signing contracts.[90] The 'Safeguards for International Trade' would have allowed Austrians to bypass many of those local registration requirements; they did not make it easier to migrate but rather extended the range of activities foreign traders could perform without formal admission. Riedl's bid to facilitate Austrian economic penetration in the former Habsburg space gave a post-imperial cast to broader legal hierarchies.

Riedl, Serruys, and many other League collaborators assumed as a matter of course that international trade law should reflect the priorities

---

[89] J. T. Kauth, 'Fremdenrecht und Völkerbund: Das Scheitern der International Conference on the Treatment of Foreigners 1929', *Archiv des Völkerrechts*, 56/2 (2018), 202–28, 216–17; Dungy, 'Writing Multilateral Trade Rules', 60–75.

[90] 'Die Zentrale zur Frage der Behandlung fremder Angehöriger', *Mitteilungen der Zentrale der tschechoslowakischen Handels und Gewerbekammern*, 1 April 1926; 'Gegen die Besteuerung der österreichischen Geschäftsreisenden in Polen', *Der Reisende Kaufmann*, 1 May 1928, 3; 'Die ungarischen Handelskammern gegen die österreichischen Reisenden', *Der Reisende Kaufmann*, 1 August 1928; Sub-Committee on the Equitable Treatment of Commerce. Second Session. Sixth Meeting, 6 September 1922, LON: R307, 10/23134/6105; Christian Meyer, *Exportförderungspolitik in Österreich*, 94–5, 133.

of the most commercially developed states. Riedl declared that the Draft Convention offered 'a codification and a stabilization of the legal principles that usually govern the treatment of foreigners in civilized countries'.[91] Interwar international lawyers widely accepted the notion that the basic legal rights that West European states usually accorded to one another's citizens constituted a common 'minimum standard of treatment'.[92] That concept dovetailed with a more general theoretical proposition that international order entailed a fundamental obligation for governments to grant 'hospitality' to foreign traders. This principle could be traced back to Immanuel Kant, who had included it as one of the 'Definitive Articles' in his 1795 essay on perpetual peace.[93] A League report on the 'Economic Tendencies Affecting the Peace of the World' by the eminent social scientists Moritz Bonn and André Siegfried highlighted this lineage, praising the Draft Convention as the basis for 'a code of international economic hospitality'.[94]

Riedl and Serruys saw the Draft Convention as part of a more general progression from bilateral treaties to uniform multilateral trade law. Serruys announced that they were witnessing 'a form of revolution whose importance only appeared to the experienced'. Reflecting upon his own work as a trade negotiator, he observed that 'economic relations between peoples were until now established on the basis of bilateral treaties, including *relative* legal guarantees' [original emphasis]. The League of Nations opened new possibilities for 'the substitution of

---

[91] Notes additionnelles présentées au Comité Économique par le co-rapporteur M. Riedl en annexe au rapport de M. Serruys, 16 January 1929, ÖStA: AVA, NL Riedl/115.

[92] During the interwar years, there was an effort among international lawyers affiliated with the League to codify the minimum standard of treatment. See M. Paparinskis, *The International Minimum Standard and Fair and Equitable Treatment* (Oxford University Press, 2014), 39–46. Jasper Kauth emphasizes that the minimum standard emerged in the nineteenth century as a tool to support Euro-American commercial activity. See Kauth, 'Fremdenrecht und Völkerbund', 210. Theodore Kill suggests that League norms on the treatment of foreign nationals went beyond the customary definition of the minimum standard of treatment at the time, however. Riedl's Draft Convention was nevertheless based on the same general principle that international law concerning the treatment of foreign nationals need only take account of the West European context. See T. Kill, 'Don't Cross the Streams: Past and Present Overstatement of Customary International Law in Connection with Conventional Fair and Equitable Treatment Obligations', *Michigan Law Review*, 106/5 (2008), 853–80, 870–71.

[93] I. Kant, *Perpetual Peace: A Philosophical Essay* (George Allen and Unwin, 1917), 137–42. Isaac Nakhimovsky emphasizes the central role played by commerce – undergirded by republican constitutionalism – in Kant's vision of perpetual peace. He also notes, however, that Kant did endorse some restrictions on trade intended to guard against exploitation by the most commercially developed states. See I. Nakhimovsky, *The Closed Commercial State: Perpetual Peace and Commercial Society from Rousseau to Fichte* (Princeton University Press, 2011), 66–9.

[94] M. Bonn and A. Siegfried, 'Economic Tendencies Affecting the Peace of the World', *The Annals of the American Academy of Political and Social Science*, 50 (1930), 192–219, 198.

plurilateral conventions for these bilateral treaties'. This required 'the acceptance, in common, of a *positive* law and the introduction of a regime, which, as a general proposition, abstracts from the specific economic conditions of each one of the parties' [original emphasis].[95] Thus, for Serruys, the value and the novelty of multilateral norms lay precisely in the fact that they accommodated the demands of individual national governments less easily than bilateral treaties had done.

If Riedl and Serruys believed that the treatment of foreign nationals should be regulated through uniform international law, other League collaborators insisted that national governments must retain undivided authority in this domain, as an essential attribute of their sovereignty. Institutional questions about international law and state power overlay a deeper debate about whether the League should work to restore relations of commercial interdependence that had existed before the war, along with the underlying power hierarchies, or whether it should support the autonomous economic development of young nation states. That debate played out in the ICC as well as the Economic Committee. The Czechoslovak chambers of commerce warned the ICC that 'the implementation of the whole liberal system as concerns the treatment of foreign nationals must be done in such a way that freedom of trade and free development proceed hand in hand with the freedom and security of states. The previous development and the particular relations of individual states must also be considered'.[96] Czechoslovak leaders were deeply invested in cooperation with the League and with Western Europe, but they also had to manage strategic vulnerabilities associated with the large manufacturing sector that they inherited from the Habsburg Empire.[97] In the early 1920s, Czechoslovakia had introduced extensive restrictions on multinational trade networks and also pursued a programme of 'nostrification' that transferred industrial and financial assets to local hands. Foreign capital and expertise nevertheless continued to play an important role in Czechoslovakia's economy, and officials there wanted to retain wide discretion to regulate this outside involvement.[98]

---

[95] D. Serruys, 'L'Oeuvre économique de la S.D.N.', *La Revue des Vivants*, 3 (1929), 1213. Note that in League trade debates, 'plurilateral' was used in much the same way that 'multilateral' is used today. It did not necessarily refer to a smaller sub-group within a larger multilateral system, as it does in current WTO parlance.

[96] 'Die Zentrale zur Frage der Behandlungen der fremder Angehöriger', *Mitteilungen der Zentrale der tschechsl. Handels- und Gewerbekammer*, March 1926, PA AA: Sonderreferat Wirtschaft/R 118543.

[97] A. Orzoff, *Battle for the Castle: The Myth of Czechoslovakia in Europe, 1914–1948* (Oxford University Press, 2009), 57–93.

[98] A. Teichova, *An Economic Background to Munich: International Business and Czechoslovakia, 1918–1938* (Cambridge University Press, 1974), 97–8, 119–21, 339–40.

Poles similarly argued that the legal rights of foreign commercial agents were not yet 'ripe' for international codification because national legislation on this topic was still in a state of flux. In the 1920s, Poland was in the process of integrating legal systems inherited from three different empires into a unified national framework. It would be very difficult to implement the wide-ranging provisions of the Draft Convention in this fragmented legal landscape. Moreover, doing so would transfer the locus of national legislative integration from the Polish government to the League and could thereby undermine the process of Polish state-building.[99] Both Czechoslovak and Polish leaders recommended that the Draft Convention be substantially weakened or abandoned in favour of bilateral treaties, but they initially met with strong resistance in the Economic Committee.[100]

Serruys and Riedl were able to restrict debate within the confines of the Economic Committee, but they lost control of their treaty when it passed to a sprawling international conference for final diplomatic negotiations in 1929.[101] Serruys and Riedl attended the 1929 International Conference on the Treatment of Foreigners as non-voting consultative delegates representing the Economic Committee and the ICC, respectively. Thus, they could do little to counter decisions by the forty-seven official delegations to weaken the Draft Convention. Over three weeks of negotiations, the conference considered roughly four hundred amendments and produced a series of elaborate compromises. While discussions about the Draft Convention in in the Economic Committee had focused on the Danubian basin, the final international conference in 1929 opened debate about a much wider array of imperial, post-imperial, and semi-imperial relationships.

The Egyptian and Chinese governments claimed a particular interest in the League's work on the treatment of foreign nationals. They used the 1929 conference to challenge treaty commitments obligating them to grant Europeans and North Americans more extensive legal protections than they gave their own nationals. They did not secure meaningful concessions concerning Egyptian 'capitulations' or Chinese 'unequal treaties'. They nevertheless were able to use the international stage to highlight the extent to which their regimes of attenuated sovereignty

[99] Comité Économique. Observations sur le projet de convention concernant le traitement des étrangers, Observations communiquées par M. Dolezal (Pologne), 2 April 1928, LON: R2776, 10D/295/338.
[100] League of Nations. Economic Committee. Twenty-Seventh Session. Minutes of the Fifth Meeting, 17 January 1929, LON: E/27th Session/P.V.5(1), 22–3.
[101] Observations du Comité National Polonais sur le Projet de Convention relative au Traitement des Étrangers, 13 June 1929, PA AA: Rechtsabteilung/R 54265.

diverged from the League's core norm of 'equitable treatment' in trade, while also demanding wider legal latitude to intervene in trade relations on national soil.[102] For example, Egypt joined a coalition of young countries including Czechoslovakia, Estonia, India, the Irish Free State, Latvia, Poland, and Turkey, to oppose a contentious provision that would help foreign subsidiaries transplant their own managers and technical staff, instead of hiring locals.[103] In the end, the article in question was significantly watered down but not wholly scrapped.

After three weeks of these hard-fought compromises, the Belgian and Dutch delegates abruptly shut down negotiations by announcing that they would not sign a convention that incorporated the proposed amendments. The president of the conference, the Belgian jurist Albert Devèze, complained that the conference had attempted to accommodate too many country-specific reservations resulting in 'restrictive texts which would be appropriate to the worst possible situation which could be contemplated'. He argued that the delegates were on-track to produce a set of international norms that offered less protection to traders than the status quo obtained through bilateral treaties.[104] In a radical move, Devèze recommended that the final decisions which had been approved by the majority of the conference delegates be wholly discarded and that the original draft text prepared by Riedl and Serruys be adopted with minimal modifications. A second conference could then meet to consider whether individual countries might be granted special, temporary exemptions from specific articles. These exemptions would be phased out over time under the supervision of the Economic Committee. Riedl and Serruys sided with the Belgian, Dutch, and German delegations to endorse Devèze's proposal as a path to 'liberal progress'.[105] As Serruys saw clearly, continuing down that path would transform the Economic Committee from a platform for negotiating treaties into a system of sustained tutelage:

There were certain countries whose geographical situation and history was such that they could not for the moment, nor perhaps within less than fifteen years, join in the effort which certain other countries were prepared to make or had already made. The second Conference would consider their reservations. Taking as its doctrine that of the most liberal States, it would be able, in greater security, to try to bring within the fold those States which might still need to adapt themselves to

---

[102] G. Martius, Schlußbericht über der Konferenz über die Behandlung der Ausländer, 6 December 1929, PA AA: Referat Völkerbund, R 96707.
[103] League of Nations, *Proceedings of the International Conference on the Treatment of Foreigners*, C.97.M.23.1930.II (League of Nations, 1930), 41–153.
[104] *Proceedings of the International Conference on the Treatment of Foreigners*, 67.
[105] *Proceedings of the International Conference on the Treatment of Foreigners*, 67–9, 84–5.

this more liberal doctrine in five or even ten years, when certain conditions had been removed. This would be the work of the League.[106]

Riedl had long favoured this type of two-speed rule-making process in the League as a means for Austria and Germany to reassert their commercial influence in the Habsburg successor states.[107] Thus, through the Draft Convention, the commercial powers of Western Europe converged with Riedl's pan-German imperialism to support a more sharply hierarchical regime of international economic regulation.

Significantly, it was Giuseppe De Michelis, an Italian delegate, who intervened to overturn this vision. He offered a different assessment of the conference from Devèze and also a very different solution. He contested Devèze's claim that 'the Conference was in a difficult situation owing to the fact that it had not been able to achieve a satisfactory Convention'. He demanded, 'what was a satisfactory Convention? The President thought that it was one inspired by the most liberal principles. There were, however, perhaps some members of the Conference who thought that, on the contrary, a good Convention was one which respected the interests of each State, while not injuring the interests of the others'.[108] In the end, De Michelis rallied the majority of the assembled delegates, including Austria's official representatives, around a more limited consensus-based procedure. Governments would prepare an exhaustive list of objections to the Draft Convention, which would then be circulated in preparation for a second conference. This would bury the project in amendments and counter-amendments indefinitely, but most conference participants preferred a more inclusive if slower negotiating process.[109] The 1929 conference officially endorsed the Italian proposal, but Devèze then used his discretion as the conference president to pursue the two-stage negotiating process that he preferred. In 1930–1, he met five times in Geneva with representatives from six other West European states to try to negotiate a new treaty text, which he hoped to present to the wider League membership as a fait accompli.[110] This new round of smaller negotiations

---

[106] *Proceedings of the International Conference on the Treatment of Foreigners*, 78.
[107] Riedl explicitly outlined this strategy in his 1926 'Action Plan' presented to the Vienna Chamber of commerce (in ÖStA/AVA/NL Riedl/80). He presented it in more neutral language of multilateral cooperation in R. Riedl, *Rapport sur le Projet d'une Convention Internationale relative au Traitement des Étrangers* (International Chamber of Commerce, 1929), 17.
[108] *Proceedings of the International Conference on the Treatment of Foreigners*, 72.
[109] *Proceedings of the International Conference on the Treatment of Foreigners*, 67–91.
[110] The meeting minutes and working papers related to Devèze's second round of negotiations in 1930–31 can be found in PA AA: Rechtsabteilung/R 54269–54279 and in LON: R 2885, dossier 10D/23109.

received strong support from the League Secretariat but once again failed to produce a final treaty text for ratification.[111] The Draft Convention on the Treatment of Foreigners was never implemented directly as a multilateral agreement, but key portions of it were transferred to Dutch and Belgian bilateral agreements.[112] The Draft Convention thus fit into a broader evolution towards a more indirect rule-making procedure in the League. Starting in the late 1920s, League economic norms increasingly operated as 'soft' guidelines for national and bilateral policy. For example, a set of model agreements on double taxation served as the basis for roughly one hundred bilateral treaties in the 1930s, laying the foundations for modern international tax law.[113] By adopting a more flexible approach to regulation, the League was able to define more ambitious multilateral standards aligned with the current practice of the most commercially developed states and then allow governments to implement those norms gradually at their own pace. Writing in 1938, Alexander Loveday reflected that the EFO was, 'gradually moving from a system of general conventions to the system of applying to each problem the procedure which seems most likely to result in business being done'. In many instances, this meant pursuing negotiations 'not universally' but only 'between those States where there is a desire to do business'.[114] In the second half of the twentieth century, indirect norm-setting became an important part of international economic governance, as seen in the OECD's Fair and Equitable Treatment Standard and the WTO's General Agreement

[111] Riedl privately supported Devèze's second round of negotiations, but the Austrian government refused to participate due to concerns that employment provisions would impede its internal labour-market controls. On the conflict between Riedl and his government on this question, see M. L. Dungy, 'International Commerce in the Wake of Empire: Central European Economic Integration between National and Imperial Sovereignty', in P. Becker and N. Wheatley (eds.), *Remaking Central Europe: The League of Nations and the Former Habsburg Lands* (Oxford University Press, 2021), pp. 213–40.

[112] Convention d'établissement et de travail entre la Belgique et les Pays-Bas (signed 20 February 1933), no. 3824, *League of Nations Treaty Series*, vol. 165 (League of Nations, 1936), 383–413. Luxembourg et Pays-Bas; Convention d'établissement et de travail entre le Grand-Duché de Luxembourg et le Royaume des Pays Bas (signed 1 April 1933), no. 4130, *League of Nations Treaty Series*, vol. 179 (League of Nations, 1936), 11–40.; League of Nations Economic, Financial and Transit Department, *Commercial Policy in the Interwar Period*, 27; Economic, Financial Committees, *Commercial Policy in the Post-war World* (League of Nations, 1945), 41; M. Pinchis, 'The Ancestry of "Equitable Treatment" in Trade', *The Journal of World Investment & Trade* (2014), 13–72, 29 n. 93.

[113] Loveday, 'The Economic and Financial Activities of the League', 788–90; S. Jogarajan, *Double Taxation and the League of Nations* (Cambridge University Press, 2018).

[114] Loveday, 'The Economic and Financial Activities of the League', 789; Clavin, *Securing the World Economy*, 231.

on Trade in Services. Like the Draft Convention, both sets of norms were first defined multilaterally and then shifted to a more flexible bilateral basis.[115] The ICC has continued to participate in the operation of soft law mechanisms, by supplying expertise during the rule-making process and exerting pressure on governments to implement non-binding international norms.

The Austro-German Customs Union and the Politics of International Business

Although the ICC played an increasingly important role in new forms of soft law emanating from Geneva, Riedl, was not able to use business channels to shape the formal architecture of international trade politics. While Riedl was in Paris in 1929 for the League's International Conference on the Treatment of Foreigners, he met with Stoppani and ICC leaders on the side to discuss a more comprehensive proposal for European tariff cooperation, and Lucien Coquet also brought him to present this plan to the head of the League of Nations Service in the French Ministry of Foreign Affairs.[116] Riedl demanded bold action from the ICC at a juncture when it briefly appeared that the onset of the Great Depression could spur multilateral cooperation through the Briand Plan and the tariff truce. Riedl saw this as 'an entirely new situation' and urged the ICC to seize the opportunity to press for a dramatic transformation of League economic institutions. If the ICC wished to 'reserve for itself a definite influence over the course of events', Riedl counselled that it 'must present concrete and clear proposals, if possible before the Economic Committee has the time to submit its own'.[117] As evidence that this strategy could work, he cited his own involvement in writing the Draft Convention on the Treatment of Foreigners, when the Economic Committee had simply adopted his blueprints wholesale. Hoping to replicate this process on a larger scale, he wrote a detailed protocol for an 'Economic Union of European States', to be negotiated alongside the tariff truce. It chimed with Stoppani and Salter's own proposals for a 'United States of Europe', and they gave Riedl

---

[115] S. Lavenex and F. Jurje, 'The Migration-Trade Nexus: Migration Provisions in Trade Agreements', in L. S. Talani and S. McMahon (eds.), *Handbook of the International Political Economy of Migration* (Edward Elgar, 2015), pp. 259–81; Kill, 'Don't Cross the Streams', 874–9.

[116] Note. Entente douanière européenne. Visite de M. Riedl, 3 December 1929, AMAE: SDN 2495.

[117] F. Tilgner and R. Riedl, Mémoire du Comité National Autrichien de la C.C.I. à la Chambre de Commerce Internationale, 10 October 1929, AMAE: SDN/2495.

access to the League translation service to help produce French and English versions of his text.[118] Although Riedl's plan sparked interest in the League and the ICC, it proved too ambitious as European trade policy was shifting towards protectionism and was being burdened with new security concerns about Germany's growing influence in the agricultural economies of Central and Eastern Europe. By May 1930, Riedl told Eduard Hamm, the head of the German chambers of commerce, 'I must sincerely confess that the International Chamber of Commerce is becoming an ever-greater disappointment'. He complained that his 'repeated proposals for a new organization of Europe have not yet been seriously discussed'. The ICC had 'abandoned the League of Nations, rather than leading it in the discussion of difficult questions and presenting it with recommendations for their solution'. It was 'assuming more and more the role of a choir that accompanies the operations in Geneva with hymns and harps'.[119] Disappointed with the slow pace of progress in the ICC, Riedl began to focus more narrowly on Austro-German cooperation. This activism became more concrete in March 1931 when formal plans for a bilateral customs union were announced. Richard Schüller excluded Riedl from the secretive official negotiations that led to the customs union, but Riedl's policy studies were an important part of the scheme's legal foundation.[120]

The political initiative for an Austro-German customs union came from German leaders, and they invoked Riedl's ideas to overcome Schüller's reticence. The German foreign minister, Julius Curtius was trying to undercut proposals to facilitate the exchange of grain surpluses for manufactures in the former Habsburg Empire, which threatened to block German influence to the south-east. He also hoped that a gesture towards *Anschluss* would placate nationalist outcry over the final reparations settlement, which committed Germans to pay the Allies through 1988 just as the German government was beginning to demand deep domestic fiscal austerity.[121] Schüller and other Austrian officials were initially sceptical that Curtius's proposal for an Austro-German customs union would be judged compatible with the anti-*Anschluss* provisions in League

---

[118] The working drafts and final version of Riedl's 'Preliminary Draft Protocol Concerning the Convening of a Conference for the Conclusion of an Economic Union of European States' are in LON: 2868 10D/15378/14711.
[119] R. Riedl to E. Hamm, 10 June 1930, WKW/NL Riedl/31001–31700.
[120] R. Riedl, Österreichisch Deutsch Zollunion Vorbereitende Arbeiten, 1930, ÖStA, AVA/ NL Riedl/86.
[121] A. Orde, 'The Origins of the German-Austrian Customs Union Affair of 1931', *Central European History*, 13/1 (1980), 34–59, 45; Cohrs, *The Unfinished Peace*, 568–9.

treaties.[122] Curtius countered with policy studies from Riedl that outlined a customs union model that would purportedly conform to treaty constraints and insisted that Riedl's work be used a basis for Austro-German negotiations. Thus, obliquely, Riedl's work in the Vienna Chamber and the ICC helped undermine the official line taken by his government, in what became one of the most spectacularly catastrophic diplomatic moves of the interwar period, the Austro-German customs union.[123]

For his part, Riedl warmly praised the Austro-German customs union after it was announced, presenting it as a direct outgrowth of League-led cooperation. The plan was a frontal challenge to the territorial settlement of 1919, but it was carefully articulated through League norms on international trade. A full customs union was proposed, in lieu of reciprocal tariff preferences, because customs unions were widely recognized to be exempt from MFN claims, and the Economic Committee had explicitly confirmed that norm in 1929. In contrast, preferential trade agreements remained more contentious.[124] Austrian and German leaders also attempted to conform with the 1922 Geneva Protocol that bound Austria not to give another state 'exclusive economic advantages'.[125] They insisted that their customs union was not an exclusive bilateral project; rather, it was the basis for a broader multilateral organization, open to all willing participants. This was diplomatic window dressing for Curtius, but Riedl told his colleagues in Vienna that it was 'entirely serious for us'.[126] Riedl hoped to shock the ICC and the League into renewed multilateral action:

What Austria needs is to be incorporated into a large economic area that enables the development of our economic capacities, our application of modern economic methods, and our rational insertion into the structure of a viable economy.

---

[122] Auszug aus der Niederschrift über die politischen Besprechungen am 22 Februar 1930 in der Reichskanzlei anlässlich des Besuches des Herrn Bundeskanzler Dr. Schober in Berlin, 22 February 1930, PA AA, Politische Abteilung II/Österreich/R 30368.

[123] Orde, 'The Origins of the German-Austrian Customs Union Affair of 1931', 44. Auszug aus der Niederschrift über die politischen Besprechungen am 24. Februar 1930 in der Reichskanzlei anlässlich des Besuches des Herren Bundeskanzlers Dr. Schober in Berlin, 24 February 1930, PA AA: Politische Abteilung II, Österreich/R 30368.

[124] E. Emminger, Memorandum über die Herstellung eines engen Wirtschaftsbündnisses zwischen Deutschland und Österreich, 26 November 1930, PA AA: Politische Abteilung II, Österreich/R 30368; Orde, 'The Origins of the German-Austrian Customs Union Affair of 1931', 42.

[125] 'Protocol No. I', in League of Nations, The Restoration of Austria: Agreements Arranged by the League of Nations and Signed at Geneva on October 4th, 1922, C.716.M.428.1922.X (League of Nations, 1922), 39.

[126] R. Riedl, Vertrag gehalten in der Urania in Wien über eine Zollunion zwischen Österreich und den Deutschen Reich, 24 April 1931, ÖStA: AVA, NL Riedl/109.

We have to this end earnestly collaborated in European solutions. The result was failed attempts, empty resolutions, in the best case, conventions that did not take effect. After five years of this Sisyphean labour we have the right to lose patience and to break out of the cage of paper terms, in which one has tried to enclose us. We have taken our destiny into our own hands by concluding the union agreement. We are, however, always ready, together with the German Reich, to integrate into a larger whole or a united Europe. We are also ready to contribute to such a solution, and perhaps even the criticism directed at our own project will help to show the way.[127]

Many prominent League collaborators shared Riedl's views. *The Economist*, a newspaper with strong Austrian links, published a quite favourable assessment of the customs union plan.[128] Its emphasized that Austria had been 'a protagonist of lower tariffs and commercial treaties' in the 1920s, specifically citing Riedl's recent proposal to the ICC for European tariff cooperation. *The Economist* argued that the meagre results of Austria's multilateral efforts justified radical action: 'finding herself blocked at every turn ... she has every inducement to present Europe with a *fait accompli* and to compel the nations of Europe to do something to relieve the situation in which she is placed'.[129] The German economist Moritz Bonn used similar arguments in a lengthy defence of the Austro-German customs union at Chatham House, a prestigious London forum for debates over international politics.[130] In spring 1931, there was some reason to hope that the Austro-German customs union might rekindle League multilateralism by spurring critics in France and Britain to react. Lucien Coquet's UDE roundly condemned the customs union, arguing that Austria and Germany were 'too disproportionate in size' to collaborate as equal and independent partners, but it also cited 'the Austro-German project and the responses it provoked' as evidence that 'the idea of a customs union is starting to pass from the domain of theoretical discussion to that of realization'.[131] In particular, Coquet hoped that the Austro-German customs union would

---

[127] R. Riedl, Vortrag über die deutsch-Österreichische Zollunion gehalten im Verein für Handel und Industrie in Wien, 12 June 1931, ÖStA, AVA N Riedl/109; also quoted in Brettner-Messler, 'Richard Riedl', 366.

[128] The editor of *The Economist* was Walter Layton, who had conducted the League's 1925 survey of the Austrian economy, and its chairman was Henry Strakosch, a London-based but Austrian-born financier who retained close ties in Vienna. Both men were heavily involved in the League's economic work in different forums.

[129] 'Germany and Austria', *The Economist*, 28 March 1931, 659–60.

[130] M. Bonn, 'The Austro-German Customs Union', *International Affairs*, 10/4 (1931), 460–76.

[131] Mémoire et Documents présentés à la Commission d'Étude Pour l'Union Européenne, 15–18 May 1931, AMAE: SDN/2495.

persuade the ICC and the League to endorse Riedl's proposed multilateral exemption from MFN in order to allow for regional cooperation and open a path to absorb the Austro-German customs union into a larger bloc.[132] There were official counter-proposals along these lines in London and Paris. The French government initially told British diplomats that the Austro-German plan could simply be transformed into a European customs union before embracing a more elaborate 'constructive plan' that included cartels alongside tariff preferences and credits.[133] Philip Noel-Baker, a former League official linked to the Foreign Office, pushed Britain to offer a liberal alternative, warning that the state of diplomatic turmoil resulting from the Austro-German bombshell was a grave danger for the League's work on disarmament.[134] Noel-Baker called for a sweeping programme of European tariff reduction but he got caught in the spiderweb of British MFN policy. He proposed to freeze Britain's low tariffs in order to persuade Continental Europeans to engage in a programme of regional tariff reduction. Yet this meant that Britain would have to allow the Dominions to be hit with regional tariff preferences in Europe while also reinforcing its own free trade posture as demands for imperial protectionism mounted. The Dominions Office rejected this double blow to imperial partners. The Board of Trade stuck to its standard position and refused, on principle, to support a multilateral exemption to MFN that would allow for European tariff cooperation but continued to place imperial preference outside the purview of MFN.[135]

---

[132] Riedl, *Exceptions to the Most-Favoured Nation Treatment: Report Presented to the International Chamber of Commerce*; L. Coquet, Documentation présentée au VIe congrès de la Chambre de Commerce Internationale, Washington 4–9 Mai 1931, Les États-Unis et l'Union Européenne, AMAE: B47/47.

[133] 'Annex 5. Proposals for Remedying the Present European Crisis. Memorandum from the French Government', in League of Nations *Commission of Enquiry for European Union. Minutes of the Third Session of the Commission*, C.395.M.158.1931 (Geneva, 1931), 79–88; Schirmann, *Crise, coopération économique et financière entre États européens, 1929–1933*, 141–58.

[134] Anonymous (attributable to Philip Noel-Baker), Proposals for a possible solution of the present conflict concerning the Austro-German Union, 18 April 1931, TNA: T 188/19; Boyce, *British Capitalism at the Crossroads*, 314–19. Joseph Maiolo shows that fiscal pressures tied to the onset of the Great Depression made disarmament vital for Britain's economy. See J. Maiolo, 'Naval Armaments Competition between the Two World Wars', in T. Mahnken, J. Maiolo, D. Stevenson (eds.), *Arms Races in International Politics: From the Nineteenth to the Twenty-first Century* (Oxford University Press, 2016), pp. 93–114, 101–2.

[135] Anonymous (Philip Noel-Baker), Proposals for a possible solution of the present conflict concerning the Austro-German Union, 18 April 1931, TNA: T 188/19; Record of an interdepartmental meeting held at the Foreign Office on April 23rd to Consider the proposed Austro-German Customs Union, 23 April 1931, TNA: T188/19; Boyce, *British Capitalism at the Crossroads*, 313–18.

Bowing to pressure within the Cabinet, the Foreign Office agreed to register a purely legal challenge to the Austro-German customs union, without committing to any concrete alternatives.[136] The customs union finally ended in the League's Permanent Court of International Justice. In July 1931, the Court narrowly ruled that the customs union violated the anti-*Anschluss* clause in the agreement covering Austria's 1922 currency-stabilization loan. The lengthy dissenting opinion insisted that, in formal legal terms, the planned customs union was compliant with all the countries' treaty commitments, and the majority opinion openly admitted that their negative decision was based primarily on extraneous political factors, namely a presumed evolution towards full *Anschluss*.[137] This outcome demonstrated the deep interpenetration of security and trade in the legal sinews of the League. The Austro-German customs union was a watershed moment for the League. It was one of the most provocative challenges to the 1919 Peace Settlement, but it was simultaneously a strong affirmation of the League's authority. It was widely seen as a decisive step towards *Anschluss*, but it was also very carefully designed to conform to League trade norms. The Austro-German customs union contributed to the breakdown of international order, even though many of its defenders pledged fealty to the League. The announcement in spring 1931 shook already unstable financial markets in Central Europe and then impeded diplomatic efforts to address the ensuing banking crisis. The Austro-German customs union thus helped accelerate a cycle of political radicalization and economic collapse that fragmented Europe into competing regional and imperial blocs.[138]

Although the fragile foundations for European multilateral cooperation began to crumble in 1931, the organizational bonds that the ICC had forged in the 1920s with the Genevan international bureaucracy endured. ICC leaders had turned to the League to help reconfigure the legal relationship between business and government. It is important to recognize that the ICC did not act as a buffer between political and economic forces, mediating between bounded national communities and a nebulous global market. Rather, Riedl and other business leaders used

---

[136] Record of an interdepartmental meeting held at the Foreign Office on April 23rd to Consider the proposed Austro-German Customs Union, 23 April 1931, TNA, T188/19.

[137] E. M. Borchard, 'The Customs Union Advisory Opinion', *American Journal of International Law*, 25/4 (1931), 711–16, 711–16. *Permanent Court of International Justice, Twenty-Second Session, Customs Régime between Germany and Austria (Protocol of March 19th, 1931), Advisory Opinion*, World Courts International Case Law Database, www.worldcourts.com/pcij/eng/decisions/1931.09.05_customs.htm.

[138] H. James, *The German Slump: Politics and Economics, 1924–1936* (Clarendon Press of Oxford University Press, 1986), 285–319; Boyce, *The Great Interwar Crisis*, 381–421.

the ICC to try to shape the geopolitical structures of the world economy, by intervening in the relationship between Europe and the United States and in the transition from empires to nation states in Central and Eastern Europe. In doing so, they established patterns of business diplomacy that became an important feature of the modern international landscape.[139]

[139] David and Eichenberger, 'Business and Diplomacy'.

Conclusion

In the long history of international trade politics, the League era was a complex period of transformation. Export growth slowed in the 1920s, especially in Europe, but this was not a straightforward rollback of pre-war globalization. Many functional relations of trans-border economic interdependence remained and many intellectuals, business leaders, and public officials were deeply committed to expanding those linkages even as they embraced more assertive national, regional, and imperial programmes. League collaborators used convergent multilateral methods to pursue sharply divergent visions of international order. Much of their conflict stemmed from the inconclusive 1919 Peace Settlement, which left openings for competing institutional programmes to develop. The regulation of foreign trade became a central platform for world-ordering impulses, but no single individual or government was strong enough to impose a unified vision of the world economy on the League. Llewellyn Smith arguably came closest during his brief period of dominance in the early Economic Committee. Yet, from the outset, Llewellyn Smith had to contend with demands for greater tariff autonomy within the British Empire as well as bourgeoning movements for regional solidarity in Europe and the Americas. He achieved only limited practical results but did help craft new multilateral machinery which other reformers – including Coquet, Harms, and Riedl – later repurposed to push the League in different directions.

Both Llewellyn Smith and Harms came out of the First World War with plans to use the League to implement a global regime of trade rules. Llewellyn Smith aimed to prevent the formation of regional trade blocs that would splinter Britain's sprawling commercial networks but also insisted that the British Empire must remain a legally cohesive unit, sheltered from outside interference. In contrast, Bernhard Harms initially hoped that the League would enforce a strict 'open-door' policy in all European colonies. The US withdrawal from the League project removed an influential advocate for the open-door principle (although US leaders were less categorical in their commitment to this norm than Harms and still left plenty of room for the United States' existing regional and imperial preferences). Harms had only a brief window to try to implement his own vision once Germany finally joined the League in 1926. After shadowing the League from afar for many years, Harms attempted to anchor the IfW more firmly in Geneva by spearheading an international economic bibliography. He adopted a transatlantic approach, drawing support from both the League and from US philanthropic bodies, but he ended up falling between two stools.

Like Harms, Coquet and Riedl both used the League's 1927 World Economic Conference as an opportunity to move beyond Llewellyn Smith's cautious incrementalism, but they also drew on many of his innovations. Coquet and Riedl both proposed programmes for League-led European unity that offered a more confrontational response to the rise of the United States than the Atlanticist programme favoured by Harms. The crucial difference between Coquet's and Riedl's European plans lay in their treatment of Germany. Riedl embraced multilateralism as a means to extend ethnic Germans' influence over their neighbours, whereas Coquet saw it as a strategy to place legal fetters on German power. Both men understood the League as the central organizing structure for European unity and worked together to try to carve out legal space for regionalism by advocating an exemption from general MFN norms for multilateral trade blocs. After several years of uneasy collaboration, the Austro-German customs union of 1931 brought the underlying geopolitical conflict between Coquet and Riedl into sharp relief and overwhelmed the mechanisms of multilateral cooperation that had begun to develop in the early League of Nations.

In the 1920s, Europeans had used the League to devise short-term procedural compromises while pushing deeper conflicts over the disposition of territory and resources into an indefinite future. European governments had been willing to submit their conflicting ambitions for national, regional, and imperial power to multilateral mediation as long as they could see a gradual path to attain those ambitions over the long term. Riedl was initially prepared to wait decades to achieve League-sanctioned *Anschluss*, but he lost patience by 1931. The onset of the Great Depression undercut multilateralism by simultaneously compressing time horizons and political room for manoeuvre. The fundamental economic problems to be solved became more urgent, and national and imperial political demands grew more strident. Starting in 1928, rising nationalism, sharply declining commodity prices, and tighter monetary and financial constraints made advocates of multilateralism more desperate to achieve concrete results but also undermined political support for their endeavours. The depression hit just as several important multilateral projects were coming to fruition, notably Riedl's Convention on the Treatment of Foreigners as well as the Prohibitions Convention. The Depression also stimulated ambitious new multilateral initiatives, such as the Tariff Truce and the Briand Plan. In 1929–30, those projects all collapsed in rapid succession against a backdrop of generalized economic and political crisis, causing many internationalists and many European governments to back away from the League.

Restrictive systems of imperial and regional commercial solidarity developed rapidly outside the League, as combative authoritarian politics engulfed much of Europe. The Nazi regime began to construct a commercial sphere of influence to the east by locking neighbours into a series of bilateral clearing agreements. This eastward thrust was part of a broader strategy to reorient German supply lines and export relationships; German trade with Scandinavia and Latin America also expanded significantly, as ties to the United States were sharply curtailed. As Adam Tooze demonstrated, this was not 'autarky'; it was a geopolitical recalibration of German trade relationships, which reversed the Atlanticist economic strategy that Gustav Stresemann had spearheaded (and Harms had backed) in the 1920s.[1] At the same time, France and Britain also turned away from outside trade partners to reinforce preferential links to colonial producers. Britain made a striking pivot by finally agreeing in 1932 to apply imperial preference to core staple goods, as Dominion leaders had long demanded. In both Britain and France, imperial solidarity became an important question of prestige, although it brought only very limited practical advantages.[2]

In the 1930s, many members of the UDE French Committee began to view European and imperial economic solidarity as divergent alternatives. This was notably true of Armand Megglé, the director of the National Committee of French Foreign Trade Advisors, a corps that included Coquet and many other members of the UDE French Committee. In 1931, Megglé reflected that France had 'already travelled down two paths: the first, the International Path, the second, the European Path'. He counselled that, 'while regretting that the first two methods have not yet succeeded', the French must 'resolutely turn towards the third method that is available to us, the Colonial Path'.[3]

---

[1] Feinstein, Temin, and Toniolo, *The European Economy between the Wars*, 163–5; A. Tooze, *The Wages of Destruction: The Making and Breaking of the Nazi Economy* (Allen Lane, 2006), 86–9.

[2] Marseille, *Empire colonial et capitalisme français*, 162–284; Clavin, *The Great Depression in Europe, 1929–1939*, 136–40, 179–88; McKenzie, *Redefining the Bonds of Commonwealth*, 20–27.

[3] A. Megglé, *'Terres Françaises': Nos Vielles Colonies d'Asie d'Océanie et d'Amerique* (Société Française d'Éditions, 1931), 12.

Coquet and the rest of the UDE followed a similar strategy in the 1930s; they held out hope for League-led trade liberalization but also made more space in their plans for imperial solidarity and for the complex system of clearing agreements that the French government devised to keep the franc on the gold standard. During the Second World War, Coquet embraced principles of planned economy more fully as he, Megglé, and many other French Europeanists tried in vain to claim a place for France in Hitler's New Order.[4]

Coquet and Megglé's embrace of Nazi-inflected models of regional cooperation was not an about-face. Throughout the interwar period, the links between European unity and democratic norms had been tenuous. The UDE did include many parliamentarians and forged strong ties to the Inter-Parliamentary Union, but external concerns about geopolitics and security were uppermost for Coquet and for most of his collaborators. Moreover, Coquet had already shown an openness to cooperation with anti-democratic forces well before the war. In the late 1920s, he secured backing from the Fascist government for a UDE Italian Committee. Mussolini provided both funding and office space as a sign of official patronage.[5] In 1937, Coquet joined forces with Otto Wolff to try to help Nazi Germany secure raw materials from France's African colonies (by then, Wolff had made his peace with the Nazi regime and had taken over the shares of his long-time Jewish business partner, Ottmar Strauss).[6] The shift in the 1930s towards a more confrontational logic of trade blocs foreclosed some kinds of League-led cooperation but also invigorated efforts to overcome national conflict through common intellectual and cultural projects that remained open to German, Italian, and Japanese participants. Across Europe and the United States, the elaboration of more closed and interventionist national economic models drew on trans-border networks of expertise that spanned communism and capitalism, democracy, and dictatorship.[7] By the same token, Fascist and Nazi dictators borrowed many functional components from the League's multilateral practice, even though they were ideologically oriented against liberal internationalism. During the war, when Nazi leaders contemplated how to incorporate occupied territories into a new world system, they

---

[4] Badel, *Un milieu libéral et européen*; B. Bruneteau, *'L'Europe nouvelle' de Hitler: Une illusion des intellectuels de la France de Vichy* (Rocher, 2003).
[5] L. Coquet to P. Bertholet, 10 January 1928, AMAE: B27/47.
[6] S. Schirmann, *Les relations économiques et financières franco-allemandes, 1932–1939* (Institut de gestion publique et du développement économique, 1995), 200.
[7] Sluga, *Internationalism in the Age of Nationalism*, 62–79; S. Kott and K. K. Patel (eds.), *Nazism across Borders: The Social Policies of the Third Reich and Their Global Appeal* (Oxford University Press, 2018); Tworek, *News from Germany*, 170–95.

painstakingly catalogued the vast array of internationalist associations that had composed the League multiverse, in order to identify those that could serve as tools of political discipline and propaganda in their imagined post-war future.[8]

Gunnar Take reveals that in the run-up to the Second World War, the IfW preserved its links to the Rockefeller Foundation, even as it began to support Nazi ambitions for commercial expansion to the east. A former Rockefeller Fellow, Andreas Predöhl, took the helm of the IfW in the 1930s and secured funding from the Foundation to conduct studies on agriculture and trade, in close coordination with the Nazi officials who were preparing the war economy. For example, the IfW used Rockefeller funds to research the regulation of grain and livestock markets in Europe as well as methods for Germany to pursue greater agricultural self-sufficiency without adversely affecting the country's exports. Raymond Fosdick, who had collaborated with Harms's bibliography at the end of the 1920s and had since become the president of the Rockefeller Foundation, opposed further collaboration with the IfW because he doubted its scope for intellectual freedom. However, the head of the Rockefeller Foundation's Paris Office held Predöhl in high esteem and argued that the IfW should continue to participate in the League's work on intellectual cooperation even after Germany formally left the League in 1933. Fittingly, the final payment that the Rockefeller Foundation made to the IfW in 1938 was earmarked for a collaborative venture with the League-backed International Institute for Intellectual Cooperation, the same body that had sponsored Harms's economic bibliography.[9]

In the 1930s Predöhl operated with a substantially new research team because the Nazis' arrival forced a rapid and violent departure of the IfW's Jewish economists. The University of Kiel was one of the main strongholds of the National Socialist German Student Association (Nationalsozialistische Deutsche Studentenbund, hereafter NSDStB). In April 1933, when the Nazis declared a national boycott of Jewish businesses, four Jewish economists affiliated with the IfW's business cycle research programme were 'advised' by the NSDStB 'to disappear'. They initially refused and faced a series of violent raids before finally deciding to emigrate, mostly to the United States. Harms privately

---

[8] M. Herren, 'Fascist Internationalism', in G. Sluga and P. Clavin (eds.), *Internationalisms: A Twentieth-Century History* (2016), pp. 191–212.

[9] Take, 'One of the Bright Spots in German Economics', 277–326; G. Take, *Forschen für den Wirtschaftskrieg: Das Kieler Institut für Weltwirtschaft im Nationalsozialismus* (De Gruyter, 2019).

disapproved of the Nazis' anti-Semitism but told the Ministry of Education that he would not oppose the 'enforcement of the "people's will"'. He tried unsuccessfully to save his own teaching position in Kiel and to obtain a new professorship in Berlin.[10]

After Harms relinquished leadership of the IfW in 1933, the Rockefeller Foundation gave him a final grant to undertake a seven-month trip in Europe and the Middle East, with a special mission to study Jewish emigration to Palestine. Harms coordinated this work with the German Foreign Office and with the Jewish banker Max Warburg. Warburg had long been one of the IfW's main private backers and began to provide substantial funding for Jewish emigration after the Nazis came to power. Based on his visit to Palestine, Harms reported that Jewish refugees there could form a substantial market for German exports (Riedl later tried to make a similar argument concerning Jewish emigration from Austria). Such attempts to connect foreign trade and asylum were based on an assumption that Jews would be able to leave with part of their assets, converted into some type of purchasing credit for German exports. Warburg did help operate a scheme along these lines, the 'Haavara Agreement', which facilitated the emigration of tens of thousands of Jews from Germany to Palestine from 1933 to 1939. This was a central channel for asylum, but it was also a system of extortion that squeezed desperate Jews to offset Germany's massive shortage of hard currency. The Nazis eventually adopted a strategy of direct expropriation. In 1938 Warburg had to hand over nearly all his assets before he could leave Germany.[11]

In the 1930s, Harms fell under suspicion from the Nazis despite his protestations of loyalty and Riedl fell out of favour with Austria's new anti-Nazi dictatorship despite his insistence that he was not actually aligned with the Nazi party. Riedl resigned from the Austrian National Committee of the ICC in 1934 shortly after the new Austrian Chancellor, Engelbert Dollfuss, consolidated dictatorial power by vio-lently suppressing the Social Democratic Party and the affiliated trade unions. Dollfuss's brand of ultra-Catholic 'Austro-fascism' firmly

---

[10] F. Hoffmann, 'Die Geschichte des Instituts für Weltwirtschaft', vol. II, 287–92; Ibs, *Hermann J. Held (1890–1963)*, 65–8; Beckmann, *Von Löwe bis Leontief*, 81–7; Take, 'One of the Bright Spots in German Economics', 14, 25.

[11] F. Bajor, 'Beneficiaries of Aryanization: Hamburg as a Case Study', *Yad Vashem Studies*, XXVI (1998), 173–2011; Brettner-Messler, 'Richard Riedl', pp. 378–9; Tooze, *The Wages of Destruction*, 89–90; Take, 'One of the Bright Spots in German Economics', 286–90; S. Friedlander, *Nazi Germany and the Jews: The Years of Persecution, 1933–1939* (Harper Collins, 1997), 170, 62–3, 237–8. For an interesting reflection on the moral ambiguities of trade-linked asylum routes out of Germany in the 1930s, see L. Ahamed, *Lords of Finance: The Bankers Who Broke the World* (Penguin Press, 2009), 483.

barred rapprochement with Protestant Germany, leading to a crackdown on Austria's two largest pro-*Anschluss* political parties, the Social Democrats and the Nazis. Riedl had never joined either grouping; he seems to have been uncomfortable with socialist elements in both. More generally, he believed that German nationalism should transcend party politics. Riedl was, however, a pragmatist. He had tried to help the post-war Social Democratic government unite with Weimar Germany, travelling to Berlin with the Foreign Minister Otto Bauer in 1919. At the World Economic Conference of 1927, he made common cause with Emmy Freundlich, who, as a Social Democrat, was the only other 'Anschluss-friendly' Austrian delegate.[12] After Hitler came to power, Riedl accepted that union with Germany would mean cooperation with the Nazis. He continued to argue that Nazi-led *Anschluss* should remain rooted in the League's multilateral framework, with growing implausibility.

In his last major engagement with the ICC, Riedl helped host the organization's biannual conference in Vienna in summer 1933, just as the League was convening its own World Economic and Financial Conference. He began his speech to the ICC by declaring solemnly that 'the League of Nations Covenant constitutes the starting-point of all the attempts made towards the regulation of the economic relations between peoples by international agreements'.[13] He went on to publish a detailed fifty-five-page plan for League-led European cooperation in the IfW's *Weltwirtschaftliches Archiv* in spring 1934, just after he and Harms withdrew from active political life and the Nazis pulled Germany out of the League.[14]

Riedl finally joined the Austrian Nazi Party as member 6,220,702 shortly before the *Anschluss* in March 1938. The Austrian Nazis accepted Riedl as a minimally reliable man of competence. Their personnel office reported that 'Riedl has always been a nationalist, but due to his age he can only embrace National Socialism within certain limits'. The Nazis called him out of retirement only briefly to coordinate the wholesale absorption of the Austrian Ministry of Commerce and the Vienna Chamber of Commerce into German structures. It is difficult to gauge the depth of Riedl's personal commitment to the Nazis, but it can be said with certainty that this was not the model of *Anschluss* that he had worked towards for most of his career. His vision of a treaty-based Germanic

---

[12] Enderes to Riedl, 13 April 1927, ÖStA: AVA, NL Riedl/5.
[13] R. Riedl, Efforts towards the Economic Organization of Europe, 1 June 1933, ÖStA: AVA/NL Riedl 143.
[14] R. Riedl, 'Innereuropäische Handelspolitik', *Weltwirtschaftliches Archiv*, 39 (1934), 13–66; Brettner-Messler, 'Richard Riedl', pp. 296–300, 370–75.

partnership at the heart of a liberal pan-European system remained impossible even after the Nazis fell from power, as the architecture of Cold War diplomacy split Austria away from Germany and from the rest of the Habsburg successor states.[15]

As Harms, Riedl, and Coquet struggled to reconfigure their multilateral plans for a new European landscape dominated by dictatorships, Llewellyn Smith was participating in Britain's transition from a free trade regime towards a more interventionist mode of economic policy based on a firmer commitment to welfare and full employment. After he retired from the Board of Trade in 1927, Llewellyn Smith returned to his roots as a social investigator. He was invited to direct a repetition of the original Booth Survey of poverty in London by his friend and protégé William Beveridge, who had become the head of the London School of Economics. Llewellyn Smith worked meticulously to replicate Booth's methods in his *New Survey of Life and Labour in London*. His obsessive zeal to ensure comparability between the two sets of results reflected an urgent desire to evaluate the recent past. Llewellyn Smith explained that the original Booth Survey had been a 'static' snapshot. The *New Survey* was a more ambitious attempt to evaluate historical change and answer the fundamental economic question: 'is poverty growing or diminishing? Are conditions becoming better or worse?'[16] The response would be a judgement on Britain's nascent social welfare programmes as well as the effects of the war economy and the international response to it. Given Llewellyn Smith's central involvement in all those policy areas, the *New Survey* was, to some extent, also a critical assessment of his own handiwork as a civil servant.

The main changes that the *New Survey* highlighted were higher wages and a massive expansion in unemployment. On the eve of the Great Depression in 1928, real income in London had increased by roughly 30 per cent, compared against the baseline of 1886, but long-term unemployment had also become endemic.[17] Llewellyn Smith and his collaborators determined that a family was likely to fall below the poverty line if the principal wage-earner spent at least 25 per cent of a six-month period out of a job.[18] Extraordinarily, they found that half of the adults living in working-class East London fell into this category at

---

[15] Brettner-Messler, 'Richard Riedl', pp. 296–300, 370–75.

[16] H. Llewellyn Smith, 'The New Survey of London Life and Labour', *Journal of the Royal Statistical Society*, 92/4 (1929), 530.

[17] H. Llewellyn Smith, 'Wages, Hours of Labour and Earnings', *The New Survey of London Life and Labour*, 9 vols (P. S. King, 1930), vol. I, pp. 111–42, 130.

[18] H. Llewellyn Smith, 'Unemployment and Poverty', *The New Survey of London Life and Labour*, 9 vols (P. S. King, 1932), vol. III, pp. 153–87, 158–9.

the beginning of 1929. 'Tramping for work' brought material hardship and, Llewellyn Smith noted, it was also simply a 'wearisome, disheartening and wasteful experience'.[19] In-person interviews indicated that many of London's jobless were spending twenty hours or more each week walking around the city asking for work and being turned down.[20] Llewellyn Smith explained that the unemployment insurance regime that he and Beveridge had crafted in 1911 was designed only to cover brief 'ins and outs'. However, 'it cannot and was never intended to meet the case of the victims of long[-]period unemployment who have practically lost all hope of regaining their job'. In other words, the chronic unemployment that set in after the stabilization of the pound at a high rate simply could not be managed through compensatory transfers. It was a macroeconomic problem that could be solved by 'nothing but a revival of industrial demand'.[21] This view led the next generation of reformers, including William Beveridge, to argue that full employment must become an explicit objective of trade and monetary policy at the national and international levels.

The transition towards welfare-oriented trade policy was also evident in the League's work in the 1930s, as expressed most clearly by James Meade. Meade was a British economist who was a member of the Economic Committee of the League of Nations Union from 1934 to 1937 before joining the EFO to lead a massive analytical survey of the Great Depression.[22] He left the Secretariat during the war to work for the British government and wrote an influential 'Proposal for an International Commercial Union' in 1942, which is generally considered to be the first sketch of the GATT.[23] Meade's vision of international order after 1945 was based on his assessment of the League's record in the 1920s. He had already reached a quite negative initial verdict by the time the League held its World Economic and Financial Conference in 1933. He complained that the EFO's policies had been based on an overly rigid commitment to the gold standard and free trade, which 'can only work smoothly if there is a very large degree of laissez-faire within every nation'.[24] In the 1920s more political pressure on policymakers and more organized labour markets and production processes had impeded the rather brutal adjustment mechanisms that economists would normally expect to correct imbalances in trade and monetary reserves, and

---

[19] Llewellyn Smith, 'Unemployment and Poverty', 172.
[20] Llewellyn Smith, 'Unemployment and Poverty', 176.
[21] H. Llewellyn Smith, 'Introduction', *The New Survey of London Life and Labour*, 9 vols (P. S. King, 1932), vol. III, pp. 1–28, 14.
[22] Clavin, *Securing the World Economy*, 253–4.
[23] Irwin, Mavroidis, and Sykes, *The Genesis of the GATT*, 28.
[24] J. Meade, 'International Economic Cooperation', in S. Howson (ed.), *The Collected Papers of James Meade* (Unwin Hyman, 1988), pp. 1–10, 7.

those imbalances had been amplified by the heavy burden of sovereign debt coming out of the war.

In a world that was fundamentally lopsided, Meade argued that the EFO had also erred in trying to impose uniform economic rules on all parties. This was Meade's second crucial insight: the obligations to sustain international economic growth and stability did not fall evenly on every country. He argued that 'perhaps the most important principle of all' for 'international economic cooperation' was that 'creditor countries must lead the way in a depression by an easy money policy, by a policy of public works and by lowering their tariffs in favour of the countries in a weak exchange position'.[25] This comment was largely directed against the United States, which had blocked transatlantic imports that would have helped Europeans repay their debts and had put further pressure on European currency reserves by raising interest rates in 1928 and sucking up gold. Those policies had been quite intelligible from a domestic standpoint – the US government was trying to rein in a runaway speculative boom on Wall Street in the late 1920s and tried to use tariffs to boost declining farm incomes. In the wartime discussions leading up to the GATT, Meade and other League collaborators argued that greater flexibility must be built into the international economic system to allow all governments to respond to domestic political demands, but big creditor economies such as the United States must still be willing to shoulder a larger adjustment burden when the world economy got off kilter.

In the 1930s, the US government did begin to move fitfully towards a more internationalist trade policy, starting with the League's World Economic and Financial Conference of 1933. That event opened opportunities for transatlantic dialogue with the incoming US president, Franklin Roosevelt, but also revealed the limits of that cooperation. Roosevelt's Secretary of State, Cordell Hull, arrived in spring 1933 with a strong commitment to tariff reduction, but this was initially overshadowed by Roosevelt's own ambitious agenda for the domestic economy. Hull attempted to make trade liberalization a top priority in US preparations for the 1933 conference, working closely with the League Secretariat. He agreed to sponsor a plan from Pietro Stoppani for a renewed tariff truce and hoped to extend this arrangement as a basis for sustained multilateral trade negotiations.[26] Hull met stiff resistance at

---

[25] Meade, 'International Economic Cooperation', 10.
[26] P. Clavin, *The Failure of Economic Diplomacy: Britain, Germany, France and the United States, 1931–36* (Macmillan Press, 1996), 143–50; Clavin, *Securing the World Economy*, 111–14.

home, where New Dealers insisted on protective measures to safeguard national recovery, and foreign governments were similarly unwilling to relinquish new national and imperial trade controls. Hull and Roosevelt concluded that tariff negotiations must be handled on a bilateral rather than a multilateral basis. Prospects for international trade cooperation were further hindered by conflict over the British and US departure from the gold standard.[27] At the 1933 conference, Roosevelt strongly objected to the secretive way that central bankers handled monetary negotiations and made his displeasure known with an infamous 'bombshell message' renouncing concerted currency stabilization and condemning 'the old fetishes of so-called international bankers'.[28] Roosevelt's missive sapped momentum for further cooperation on trade at the 1933 conference, but political support was already low on all sides.[29] The 1933 conference dashed hopes that Roosevelt would lead a coordinated international response to the Great Depression, but it nevertheless signalled Hull's new willingness to participate in League trade debates. The conference was the starting point for substantive bonds to develop between the new national trade bureaucracy that formed under Hull and the League's EFO.

Hull combined League engagement with a programme of hemispheric cooperation, the 'Good-Neighbor Policy'. He had used the League's World Economic and Financial Conference to begin trade negotiations with partners in Latin America, which he then continued the following winter at the Seventh Pan-American Conference in Montevideo.[30] The US State Department treated the League and the Pan-American Union as complementary frameworks, interweaving institutional and legal precedents from both in the preparatory documents for Montevideo.[31] The Montevideo Conference passed a landmark convention that recast the US Monroe Doctrine as a collective commitment to mutual defence,

---

[27] The Chairman of the American Delegation (Hull) to the Acting Secretary of State, 11 July 1933, in R. P. Churchill, G. V. Blue, and S. F. Landau (eds.) FRUS, Diplomatic Papers, 1933, General, vol. I (United States Printing Office, 1950), doc. 535; Clavin, *The Failure of Economic Diplomacy*, 147; Clavin, *Securing the World Economy*, 114–21; K. K. Patel, *The New Deal: A Global History* (Princeton University Press, 2016), 122–4; Irwin, *Clashing over Commerce*, 424.

[28] Quoted in Clavin, *Securing the World Economy*, 120.

[29] Clavin, *The Failure of Economic Diplomacy*, 147.

[30] Clavin, *Securing the World Economy*, 135.

[31] Instructions to the Delegates to the Seventh International Conference of American States, Montevideo, Uruguay, 10 November 1933, in V. J. Farrar and H. P. Beers (eds.) FRUS, Diplomatic Papers, 1933, The American Republics, vol. IV (United States Printing Office, 1950), doc. 56; The Chairman of the American Delegation (Hull) to the Acting Secretary of State, 11 July 1933, in V. J. Farrar and H. P. Beers (eds.) FRUS, Diplomatic Papers, 1933, The American Republics, vol. IV (United States Printing Office, 1950), doc. 54.C.

underpinned by equal sovereign rights. This agreement consolidated the Pan-American Union as an independent regional structure rather than a sub-unit in the League, as most Latin American states backed away from the League in the 1930s to avoid getting embroiled in the looming European war.[32] The Montevideo Conference did establish new legal links between the Pan-American Union and League trade policy. The conference endorsed bilateral treaties as the main channel for trade liberalization but it left an opening for future multilateral cooperation by resolving to 'revive and revise' the League's 1927 Prohibitions Convention, which the United States had been one of the few countries to ratify.[33] The conference also empowered the Pan-American Union to sponsor a new multilateral agreement in 1934 that enjoined signatory governments not to use MFN to claim the benefit of multilateral treaties.[34] Hull borrowed both the wording and the idea for this pact directly from the League.[35] Wallace McClure, one of Hull's main collaborators, remarked:

> the League of Nations realized that so long as the application of the most-favored-nation clause to multilateral treaties continued, the building up of its desired program of multilateral treaties would be retarded on two grounds (1) the hesitancy of countries to enter into them because of their most-favored-nation promises and (2) the temptation of countries to abstain and to stand on their most-favored-nation rights.

McClure explained that it was 'in view of these facts' that the Montevideo Conference had sponsored an agreement to exempt multilateral treaties

[32] M. Ingulstad and Lixinski, Lucas, 'Pan-American Exceptionalism: Regional International Law As a Challenge to International Institutions', in S. Jackson and A. O'Malley (Eds.), *The Institution of International Order: From the League of Nations to the United Nations* (Routledge, 2018), pp. 65–89, 71–9.

[33] Patel, *The New Deal*, 148; Irwin, *Clashing over Commerce*, 424. Economic Committee. Resolutions V and LXXXI adopted by the Seventh Pan-American Conference, 17 September 1934, LON: R 4421,10A/11630/11630. On the ratification history of the Prohibitions Convention, see *Commercial Policy in the Interwar Period*, 32–5, 93.

[34] Economic Committee. Most-Favoured-Nation Clause and Multilateral Treaties. Note by the Secretariat, 18 September 1934, LON: R 4421, 10A/11630/11630; Agreement to Refrain from Invoking the Obligations of the Most-Favoured-Nation Clause for the Purpose of Obtaining the Advantages or Benefits Established by Certain Economic Multilateral Conventions, no. 3801, *League of Nations Treaty Series*, vol. 165 (League of Nations, 1936), 9–18.

[35] Economic, Financial Committees, *Commercial Policy in the Post-war World*, 50. The Chairman of the American Delegation (Hull) to the Acting Secretary of State, 20 July 1933, in R. P. Churchill, G. V. Blue, and S. F. Landau (eds.) FRUS, Diplomatic Papers, 1933, General, vol. I (United States Printing Office, 1950), doc. 554; The Chairman of the American Delegation (Hull) to the Acting Secretary of State, 6 July 1933, in R. P. Churchill, G. V. Blue, and S. F. Landau (eds.) FRUS, Diplomatic Papers, 1933, General, vol. I (United States Printing Office, 1950), doc. 524.

from MFN claims.[36] This legal innovation prefigured the GATT, which later developed as a closed club whose rules and benefits were limited to members. It also anticipated the formation of smaller free trade areas within the GATT. The decision to exempt multilateral agreements from outside MFN claims was a significant turning point in US policy. The US government had refused to grant this provision in US bilateral treaties when asked to do so by European partners and had been following League debates on the topic since 1928. The Hoover administration objected to 'the comprehensive nature of the exemption' and 'the uncertainty as to the circumstances in which exception from the obligation to grant most-favoured-nation treatment might be claimed'.[37] After 1933, the United States no longer needed to rely on MFN as a safeguard to avoid being dragged along by European multilateral projects because Hull's State Department quickly became the main governmental base of support for trade cooperation in the League. As the 1933 conference came to a close, Hull told Roosevelt: 'the question whether the Economic Committee can continue to operate effectively remains in the balance, and our ability to put forward [a] positive programme may be a decisive factor'.[38] In the 1920s, European governments and private activists had inundated the Economic Committee with ambitious trade projects, but in the 1930s they shifted their focus away from Geneva towards national and imperial forums. This significantly reduced the scope for effective intergovernmental trade cooperation in Geneva, but it also meant there was less danger that League economic policy would develop its own momentum that would escape Hull's control. Hull used that low-risk environment to cultivate closer ties to Geneva and to adapt the multilateral innovations that had been handed down from the 1920s to fit his own vision of national and international tariff policy.

The legislative framework for Hull's international outreach was the 1934 Reciprocal Trade Agreements Act (RTAA), a programme to negotiate down tariffs and other trade barriers through bilateral agreements. The RTAA led to the signature of twenty-one trade treaties over the course of

---

[36] League of Nations Economic Committee, Development of the Commercial Policy of the United States since June 1934, 8 March 1935, USNA: RG 59, box 2532, 500. C.1199/137.

[37] The Minister in Switzerland (Wilson) to the Secretary of State, 18 July 1928, in J. V. Fuller (ed.) FRUS 1928, vol. III (United States Printing Office, 1943), doc. 765; The Acting Secretary of State to the Minister in Rumania (Wilson) 28 July 1930, in J. V. Fuller (ed.), FRUS 1930, vol. III (United States Printing Office, 1945), doc. 748.

[38] The Chairman of the American Delegation (Hull) to the Acting Secretary of State, 11 July 1933, in R. P Churchill, G. V. Blue, and S. F. Landau (eds.), FRUS, Diplomatic Papers 1933, General, vol. I (United States Printing Office, 1950), doc. 535.

the 1930s, but this was not a free trade bonanza, as Douglas Irwin has explained. Taken together, Hull's treaties simply brought average US tariffs back to the baseline before Smoot-Hawley, which was already quite high. These modest results reflected the clear priority that the Roosevelt administration assigned to domestic recovery. The institutional significance of the RTAA far outweighed its practical impact because it fundamentally transformed the machinery of US trade policy. Within the State Department, Hull built up a large staff of trade experts to write and implement treaties and he also coordinated closely though discreetly with the League. The RTAA facilitated these institutional changes by transferring authority for trade negotiations to the executive branch by giving the president and his cabinet the authority to reduce tariffs by up to 50 per cent through bilateral treaties. These were 'reciprocal' agreements in the sense that they entailed negotiated concessions from both parties, but the benefits were generalized to all other trade US partners through the operation of unconditional MFN, another key component of the RTAA.[39]

Hull used the League's standard MFN clause as the legal anchor for most of the trade agreements that he negotiated, firmly linking the RTAA to Geneva.[40] With a few wording changes, the League's MFN clause became the very first article in a model treaty that Hull compiled to guide RTAA negotiations, which also later framed US preparations for the GATT.[41] Hull thereby consolidated the League's authority as a central arbiter of bilateral trade law. The League Secretariat, in turn, presented Hull's trade agreements programme as the model for other governments to follow, as a virtuous counter example to the barter-based clearing agreements that proliferated across Europe in the 1930s. In 1935, the Secretariat published a long survey of Hull's policies that highlighted the US commitment to unconditional MFN and its closer ties to the League.[42] It worth noting that, in practice, Hull mostly used Leaguenorms to cultivate regional trade relations. As part of Roosevelt's 'Good Neighbor Policy', he constructed a network of trade agreements that was heavily concentrated in Latin America. This can be understood as part of a broader centrifugal movement

---

[39] Irwin, *Clashing over Commerce*, 413–47; Patel, *The New Deal*, 137–8, 159.
[40] Preparatory Committee of the International Conference on Trade and Employment, Committee II, Sub-Committee on Procedures, 29 October 1946, WTO: GATT, E/PC/T/C.II/25.
[41] Compare: 'Wording of the Clause' in Economic Committee, Report to the Council on the Work of the Twenty-Seventh Session, 23 January 1929, LON: C.20.1929.II. to 'General Provisions for Inclusion in Trade Agreements' (Annex A), Irwin, Mavroidis, and Sykes, *The Genesis of the GATT*, 204–5; Irwin, *Clashing over Commerce*, 436.
[42] League of Nations Economic Committee, Development of the Commercial Policy of the United States since June 1934, 8 March 1935, USNA: RG 59, box 2532, 500.C.1199/137; Clavin, *Securing the World Economy*, 127–8, 140–41; Patel, *The New Deal*, 187.

towards regional segmentation in the world economy during the depression, alongside Japan's Greater East-Asia Co-prosperity Sphere and Hitler's commercial penetration of agrarian Eastern Europe. In terms of legal architecture and ideology, Hull's regionalism was by far the most internationalist variety on offer in the 1930s.[43] It thus crystalized the dynamic tension between universal economic law and trade blocs that was already evident in the League trade debates of the 1920s.

Hull affirmed the League's architectonic role in the international trade system by establishing stronger organizational ties to the Economic Committee. As discussed in Chapter 7, Lucius Eastman, the first US member of the Economic Committee from 1927 to 1933, had been a private businessman and a leader in the ICC. Eastman frequently emphasized his status as an independent expert and often communicated the views of the US business community more than those of the US government. In 1933, Hull decided that Eastman was not 'up to the full potentialities of the job' and declared that it was 'highly important that the American member be able in that influential body to present the American outlook and ideas'. He chose James Harvey Rogers, a Yale professor of economics who served as an advisor to Roosevelt.[44] Rogers coordinated much more closely with the State Department and the US Consul in Geneva than Eastman had done, participating in long briefings before and after every meeting of the Economic Committee.[45] The State Department also sent its own staff to the Economic Committee when important issues were on the agenda. For example, Hull sent Leo Pasvolsky in 1936 to discuss MFN as well as multilateral plans to link tariff cooperation and currency stabilization. Pasvolsky had covered the League as a journalist for the Brookings Institution in the 1920s and then moved into the State Department's trade agreements programme in the 1930s. He went on to help craft the international settlement after the Second World War as one of the main authors of the UN Charter.[46]

In 1937, Hull signalled a higher level of commitment to the Economic Committee and a stronger desire to use it to engage with Europe by replacing Rogers with someone who had an even closer

---

[43] Patel, *The New Deal*, 150–60.
[44] C. Hull to President, 5 October 1933, USNA: RG 59, box 2532, 500.C1199/104B; American Membership on the Economic Committee, 20 September 1933, USNA: RG 59, box 2532, 500.C1199/106.
[45] American Consulate in Geneva to Secretary of State, 14 December 1933, USNA: RG 59, box 2532, 500.C1199/114.
[46] F. Livesey to P. Gilbert, 12 June 1936, USNA: RG 59, box 2532, 500.C1199/195A; C. Hull to L. Pasvolsky, 4 September 1936, USNA: RG 59, box 2533, 500.C1199/222A; Clavin, *Securing the World Economy*, 151–2.

relationship to the State Department, Henry Grady. Grady was the vice-chairman of the US Tariff Commission and had also served as a top official in the trade agreements programme.[47] Hull's commercial strategy was 'more and more dependent on the support of Europe'. Consequently 'effective representation on the Economic Committee at Geneva, the membership of which includes very influential officials of the European Governments is extremely essential'.[48] Grady shouldered ever greater political weight as Europe edged towards war. His appointment in 1937 coincided with a pivot towards cooperation with Europe in the Roosevelt administration, driven by concern about increasingly concrete German, Japanese, and Italian plans for expansion.[49] For the same reasons, Britain also became more open to trade negotiations with the United States. The two countries finally signed a modest bilateral trade agreement in 1938, without resolving their underlying conflicts over imperial preference.[50]

In 1939, Grady tried to ground this limited US–British partnership in a wider multilateral system.[51] In effect, he proposed to generalize Hull's trade agreements programme to form a united front of 'free countries' against 'totalitarian' rivals. The US Consul in Geneva captured the Manichean, logic behind the plan, quoting a statement from Grady that 'two diametrically opposed economic systems could not be maintained in the same world over any extended period'.[52] MFN was Grady's main weapon to secure the victory of 'free' principles. Concretely, he proposed a collective agreement to withhold MFN rights from the 'totalitarian' states in order to put pressure on them to abandon their discriminatory quotas, clearing arrangements, and other forms of trade control. This was a return to the logic of the Paris Peace Settlement, making MFN the legal gateway to the commercial world, with the League of Nations standing guard. The Secretariat supported Grady by devising a detailed programme to translate the core tenets of Hull's trade agreements programme into international policy. Yet most members of the Economic Committee feared that putting 'economic pressure on Germany' would only hasten war, at a time when Britain and many other states were still

---

[47] Gilbert to Secretary of State, 25 January 1937, USNA: RG 59, box 2534, 500.C1199/260; on Grady's institutional role, see Irwin, *Clashing over Commerce*, 437.

[48] R. W. Moore to C. Hull, 10 December 1936, USNA: RG 59, box 2533, 500.C1199/249.

[49] Clavin, *The Failure of Economic Diplomacy*, 190; Patel, *The New Deal*, 188; D. Ekbladh, *Plowshares into Swords: Weaponized Knowledge, Liberal Order, and the League of Nations* (University of Chicago Press, 2022), 101–105.

[50] Clavin, *The Failure of Economic Diplomacy*, 193; Irwin, *Clashing over Commerce*, 438.

[51] Clavin, *Securing the World Economy*, 239.

[52] Report on the Forty-ninth Session of the Economic Committee, 5 April 1939, USNA: RG 59, box 2535, 500.C1199/381; also quoted in Ekbladh, *Plowshares into Swords*, 102.

seeking appeasement.[53] Ultimately, the Economic Committee refused to act on Grady's plan in 1939, but it nevertheless stands as a testament to the new level of legal and institutional integration that developed between the League and the US State Department over the course of the 1930s. By the end of the 1930s, both the Secretariat and the State Department had reached the point where they wanted to multilateralize Hull's trade agreements programme through League channels. They had begun to work out the mechanics of this process, building on the League's multi-lateral experiments of the 1920s. Although Hull borrowed many components from early League trade cooperation, he was operating in a fundamentally different political environment. In the 1920s, the Economic Committee had been a field of active competition among many different models of freer trade, inflected by diverse national and organizational perspectives. In contrast, by 1938 the Secretariat very openly endorsed Hull's RTAA as the only remaining model of economic progress.[54] At the same time, Hull gave trade cooperation a more categorical ideological cast by counterposing 'freedom' against 'totalitarian' tyranny.[55]

After the war began, Alexander Loveday confirmed the new position of the United States as the standard-bearer for international economic cooperation by transferring the EFO to Princeton, where it was hosted by the Institute for Advanced Study.[56] The goal of the Princeton Mission was not institutional preservation. On the contrary, Loveday and his staff were looking forward to a fresh start after the war, when the world would have an opportunity to innovate. The transition from the League of Nations to the United Nations entailed a long and complex dialogue between the two systems, as recent historiography has emphasized.[57] The 1940s and 1950s brought a large 'stock-take' of interwar multilateral legacies. From its new base in Princeton, the EFO helped guide that

---

[53] Report on the Forty-ninth Session of the Economic Committee, 5 April 1939, USNA: RG 59, box 2535, 500.C1199/381; League of Nations Economic Committee, Draft Report, 20 May 1939, USNA: RG 59, box 2535, 500.C1199/388.

[54] H. Bucknell to Secretary of State, 12 July 1938, USNA: RG 59, box 2534, 500. C1199/347.

[55] Mazower, *Governing the World*, 181; Clavin, *Securing the World Economy*, 303.

[56] Clavin, *Securing the World Economy*, 261–6; D. Ekbladh, 'American Asylum: The United States and the Campaign to Transplant the Technical League, 1939–1940', *Diplomatic History*, 39/4 (2015), 629–60; Ekbladh, *Plowshares into Swords*, 127–169.

[57] P. Jackson and A. O'Malley, 'Rocking on Its Hinges? The League of Nations, the United Nations and the New History of Internationalism in the Twentieth Century', in S. Jackson and A. O'Malley (eds.), *The Institution of International Order: From the League of Nations to the United Nations* (Routledge, 2018), pp. 1–21; G. F. Sinclair, 'A Bridge and a Pivot: The ILO and International Organizations Law in Times of Crisis', in G. Politakis (ed.), *ILO 100: Law for Social Justice* (International Labour Organization, 2019), pp. 123–34.

process by producing a series of publications that summarized the League's experience and offered advice for future policy.[58] These documents help clarify what was carried over from the League trade policy after 1945 and what was changed.

The League's most concrete legacy was its institutional toolkit. An EFO report published in 1943 under the chairmanship of Henry Grady noted that the League had developed a new 'machinery for international action' through its committee structures, its negotiation processes, its legal precedents, and its administrative apparatus.[59] It offered a forum for regular dialogue among national officials, a framework to promulgate new international rules, and a central hub to coordinate the actions of other organizational partners who were active in trade policy such as the UDE, the IfW, or the ICC. The EFO report reflected that 'whatever difficulties there may be in the restoration of a freer system of trade, the foundations of the legal structure within which trade can be conducted have been laid in a number of international conventions elaborated by the League Committees'. Some conventions had been implemented directly, such as those related to customs formalities, intellectual property, arbitration, and bills of exchange. Many other draft norms were 'used as models in the conclusion of bilateral treaties', for example the rules on the treatment of foreigners, on double taxation, and on customs nomenclature.[60] Although the EFO bequeathed a large store of legal and institutional precedent, the difficulties that it encountered also highlighted the scope for further innovation.

James Meade and many other internationalists concluded that League trade policy had focused too narrowly on trade, on the trans-border exchange of goods and services. Another EFO report lamented 'the assumption that trade policy could be separated from economic policy as a whole and that, since a general reduction in tariffs was in the economic interest of all countries, governments, when brought to realise this fact, would draw the necessary consequences'. In the 1920s, free trade boosterism in League circles had sometimes been very strident (recall Clive Morrison-Bell carting around his giant diorama of European tariff barriers). Many League collaborators had stubbornly believed that 'given good will and understanding, trade barriers would fall like the walls of Jericho'.[61] Although such positivism appeared naïve in

[58] Clavin, *Securing the World Economy*, 269–72.
[59] Economic and Financial Committees, Report to the Council on the Work of the 1943 Joint Session, December 1943, LON: R4384, 10A/42227/1778.
[60] Economic and Financial Committees, Report to the Council on the Work of the 1943 Joint Session, December 1943, LON: R4384, 10A/42227/1778.
[61] *Commercial Policy in the Interwar Period*, 152.

retrospect, in the 1920s it helped drive the development of the League's information-rich multilateral apparatus, with help from auxiliaries such as Bernhard Harms. Moreover, Harms and other peripheral collaborators began to turn League trade policy outwards and embed it in broader analyses of consumption and production, anticipating the more comprehensive approach to economic development that emerged from the ashes of the Great Depression and the Second World War.

In the 1930s, the EFO tried harder to address the practical experience of welfare through a series of studies and cooperative initiatives. With commodity prices plummeting, the EFO began to advocate more direct management of raw materials, moving away from the free trade approach it had tried to implement through the Prohibitions Convention. The League sponsored commodity agreements to organize markets in wheat and sugar. As similar private agreements spread throughout the world economy, a League Committee on Raw Materials fostered dialogue about trade intervention among consumers, producers, governments, and business actors.[62] At the same time, a growing interest in the science of nutrition linked commodity production to health and welfare and led the EFO to forge new bonds with the League Health Organization and the ILO. The League's statistical and sociological work highlighted distinctly European modes of 'rural life' that were rooted in family farming, while the science of nutrition offered a common framework to compare European and non-European contexts.[63] During this period, the EFO's documentation, methods of inquiry, and expert networks helped make rural economy and global wealth disparities central problems of international order, contributing to the emerging field of economic development.[64] In 1945, an EFO report emphasized that the League's shift towards practical economic issues in the 1930s had profound implications for trade policy:

a multilateral trading system could only be restored if there was a real popular demand for it and that demand would only arise if the average consumer was brought to realize to what an extent his own standard of living was adversely affected by his inability to buy in the cheaper market. The League, therefore, concerned itself more and more with the general problem of how to raise living

---

[62] Ingulstad, 'Regulating the Regulators', 243–4; Martin, *The Meddlers*, 178–209.

[63] P. Clavin and K. K. Patel, 'The Role of International Organizations in Europeanization: The Case of the League of Nations and the European Economic Community', in M. Conway and K. K. Patel (eds.), *Europeanization in the Twentieth Century: Historical Approaches* (Palgrave Macmillan, 2010); S. Amrith and P. Clavin, 'Feeding the World: Connecting Europe and Asia, 1930–1945', *Past & Present*, 218/Special Supplement: Transnationalism and Global Contemporary History (2013), 29–50.

[64] Clavin, *Securing the World Economy*, 159–97.

standards. This approach to the international problem of commercial policy is a heritage of the Great Depression that should not be lost.[65]

The EFO continued to advocate the reduction of import barriers and the elimination of discrimination as the primary means to secure welfare gains through trade policy, but it also demanded more responsiveness to consumer needs and greater flexibility to allow governments to pursue full employment.

In line with the EFO's critical self-assessment, raising living standards did become a more explicit goal of trade policy in the GATT. Yet as participation in international trade politics expanded rapidly beyond the North Atlantic in the 1950s, this led to somewhat contradictory policies to promote wage growth in industrialized states and to facilitate 'development' in the rest of the world. Article XIX of the GATT offered a general 'safeguard' to allow governments to introduce tariffs when a spike in imports might 'cause or threaten serious injury to domestic producers'.[66] In practice, this provision was mainly used by industrialized states to protect sectors that faced competition from lower-cost producers abroad, including heavy industry, apparel, and agriculture. Such carve-outs were combined with 'Voluntary Export Restraints' such as the Multifibre Arrangement that long sheltered textile manufacturing in the rich world. Many developing countries complained that these special protections impeded their own efforts to diversify exports. After an ambitious bid to address development concerns through a stand-alone International Trade Organization failed, the GATT offered a more limited regime of 'special and differential treatment' for imports from developing countries. Most scholars now agree that this rather cumbersome machinery did not significantly improve developing countries' trade position, however.[67] In practice, industrialized economies dominated GATT negotiations. This outcome may partly reflect a conscious model of liberal progress grounded in the European experience of empire.[68] Yet, there were also powerful latent institutional pressures at work. Developed economies that were undergirded by complex tariffs and regulations simply had more points of leverage in international negotiations. Moreover, industrialized states

---

[65] Economic, Financial Committees, *Commercial Policy in the Post-war World*, 18.

[66] Article XIX, No. 814. *General Agreement on Tariffs and Trade* (1947); Irwin, Mavroidis, and Sykes, *The Genesis of the GATT*, 161–2. A. O. Sykes, 'Protectionism As a "Safeguard": A Positive Analysis of the GATT "Escape Clause" with Normative Speculations', *The University of Chicago Law Review*, 58/1 (1991), 255.

[67] Sykes, 'Protectionism As a "Safeguard"', 256–7; D. Rodrik, *The Globalization Paradox: Democracy and the Future of the World Economy* (Oxford University Press, 2011), 71–4; P. C. Mavroidis, *The Regulation of International Trade, GATT*, 2 (MIT Press, 2016), vol. I, 246–76, 399–412; McKenzie, *GATT and Global Order*, 174–231.

[68] Slobodian, *Globalists*, 218–62.

could exert pressure on trade partners because they controlled access to large markets.[69] Those asymmetries were already evident in the League of Nations and became more pronounced when international trade policy shifted from general rulemaking towards concrete tariff bargaining in the GATT and as the international community expanded to include many new post-colonial states.

As the GATT struggled to mediate trade relations between developed and developing countries, it also opened new lines of solidarity in the industrialized world through the formation of 'free trade areas'. The wartime planning documents from the League's EFO discussed the potential advantages of such arrangements at length, as well as the institutional conditions necessary to make them viable. Looking back on the League's experience, 'the absence was felt of an agreed body of principles concerning admissible exceptions to the m.f.n. clause and of an international body to which the proposals could have been referred'.[70] In 1929, the Economic Committee had outlined a 'body of principles' that were subsequently incorporated into European and American trade treaties over the course of the 1930s. Yet the League did not have a clear mandate to supervise this process, and key holdouts (notably Britain) continued to oppose any form of regionalism. The EFO lamented this state of affairs and recommended that provision for free trade areas and customs unions be included as an integral part of the post-war international economic order. Such groupings must be based on a set of agreed guidelines and submitted to an 'international economic authority' for approval and supervision.[71] Thus, the paradoxical lesson from the interwar period was that smaller free trade areas could only operate smoothly under a more robustly centralized international institutional framework.

The GATT created this architecture by affirming a universal commitment to MFN rights for all members while also allowing them to form smaller customs unions and free trade areas. The Secretariat of the preparatory conference for the GATT made a direct link back to the League's standardization of MFN and its exemption for multilateral treaties, also citing Riedl's work for the ICC on these topics.[72] Yet, the Second World

---

[69] P. Collier, *The Bottom Billion: Why the Poorest Countries Are Failing and What Can Be Done about It* (Oxford University Press, 2007), 170–72; McKenzie, *GATT and Global Order*, 195–217.

[70] Economic, Financial Committees, *Commercial Policy in the Post-war World*, 52.

[71] *Commercial Policy in the Interwar Period*, 53.

[72] General Agreement on Tariffs and Trade, no. 814, *United Nations Treaty Series*, vol. LV (United Nations, 1950); Preparatory Committee of the International Conference on Trade and Employment. Committee II. Sub-Committee on Tariffs and Tariff Preferences (presented by the Secretariat), 1 November 1946, WTO: GATT, E/PC/T/ C.II/W.10; Second Session of the Preparatory Committee of the United Nations

War brought important changes, most notably in the relationship between imperial and regional order. The GATT did not eliminate imperial prefer-ences altogether but did bring them under the purview of international trade law, a move that Wilson's team had tried unsuccessfully to make in 1919 through a general agreement on 'equality of trade conditions'. The GATT allowed imperial preferences up to a cut-off date of April 1947, but they had to be explicitly enumerated. This solution did not satisfy staunch advocates of 'non-discrimination'. Nevertheless, the GATT did place a closing bracket around the regime of imperial preference while simultaneously creating new space for 'free trade areas'.[73] On these terms, British imperial preference would be frozen and gradually phased out, and former imperial territories would move into new regional groupings. This was the outcome that the Board of Trade had been fighting to prevent since 1897.

Conceptually, the GATT's allowance for free trade areas can be traced back to the Economic Committee, but substantively it differed in import-ant ways. The Economic Committee's MFN exemption for multilateral groupings had covered 'collective conventions' that were concluded 'under the auspices of the League of Nations or registered by it' and were 'open to the accession of all states'.[74] In contrast, free trade areas concluded under Article 24 of the GATT did not have to be open to all comers – narrower bilateral arrangements also counted. This new formu-lation better fit US regional policy. It was the US government that pushed to add free trade areas to Article 24 at a late stage to create space for a planned bilateral preferential agreement with Canada.[75] Although the GATT allowed for smaller and more restrictive groupings, it imposed more precise conditions upon them than the Economic Committee had done. Under Article 24, free trade areas can only reduce restrictions between participants but cannot raise new barriers against outsiders. Moreover, these reductions must cover 'substantially all the trade between the constituent territories'.[76] The GATT also had greater

Conference on Trade and Employment. Report from the International Chamber of Commerce, 14 April 1947, WTO: GATT, E/PC/T/44.

[73] Article 1, General Agreement on Tariffs and Trade, no. 814, *United Nations Treaty Series*, vol. LV (United Nations, 1950); Article 15, Havana Charter for an International Trade Organization, *Final Act of the United Nations Conference on Trade and Employment* (Interim Commission for the International Trade Organization, 1948); McKenzie, *Redefining the Bonds of Commonwealth*, 239–42.

[74] Preparatory Committee of the International Conference on Trade and Employment. Committee II. Sub-Committee on Tariffs and Tariff Preferences (presented by the Secretariat), 1 November 1946, WTO: GATT, E/PC/T/C.II/W.10.

[75] Chase, 'Multilateralism Compromised'; Irwin, Mavroidis, and Sykes, *The Genesis of the GATT*, 167–8.

[76] General Agreement on Tariffs and Trade, no. 814, *United Nations Treaty Series*, vol. 55 (United Nations, 1950).

powers of supervision than the League to ensure compliance with these conditions. In practice, however, the GATT and the WTO have rarely denied applications for free trade areas.[77] As WTO negotiations have stalled, these applications have multiplied. Many commenters argue that Article 24 is the Achilles heel of the WTO because its operation undermines the 'unconditional' character of MFN.[78] Today, the WTO recognizes over three hundred preferential free trade agreements based on Article 24.[79] The proliferation of such arrangements in recent decades puts states with mere MFN status at a marked disadvantage in the WTO.

The early genesis of the European Union (EU) in the 1950s brought the first major test case for Article 24, exposing broader tensions between regional and global order. Neither the European Coal and Steel Community of 1951 nor the European Economic Community of 1957 fit the formal criteria for a free trade area, and it quickly became clear that the GATT had little power to compel Europeans to align their regional plans with international norms. Europeans did have to come to Geneva to justify their deviations from GATT rules and to hear complaints from countries that stood to lose. Thus, much like the Economic Committee, the force of the GATT lay in its capacity to make governments explain their policies in an open international forum. In 1958, one Geneva watcher remarked that 'this process of public laundering of policy has been one of the most useful quiet processes through which GATT has been effective for years'.[80] Francine McKenzie notes, however, that the collegial atmosphere of the GATT masked persistent power hierarchies between different subgroups within the organization.[81]

McKenzie's comprehensive history of the GATT shows that the relationship between universal MFN norms and less-than-universal free trade areas could not be settled definitively, and this ambiguity invested foreign trade with considerable geopolitical heft.[82] As a fragment of a larger whole, a free trade area is a normative statement about how

---

[77] McKenzie, *GATT and Global Order*, 145–52.
[78] C. B. Picker, 'Regional Trade Agreements v. The WTO: A Proposal for Reform of Article XXIV to Counter This Institutional Threat', *University of Pennsylvania Journal of International Law*, 26/2 (2005), 267–319; J. N. Bhagwati, *Termites in the Trading System: How Preferential Agreements Undermine Free Trade* (Oxford University Press, 2008); R. Leal-Arcas, 'Proliferation of Regional Trade Agreements: Complementing or Supplanting Multilateralism?' *Chicago Journal of International Law*, 11/2, 597–629. For wider context and debate, see Mavroidis, *The Regulation of International Trade, GATT*, 295–334.
[79] *RTA Tracker*, WTO/OMC Regional Trade Agreements Database, https://rtais.wto.org /UI/PublicMaintainRTAHome.aspx.
[80] Quoted in McKenzie, *GATT and Global Order*, 140.
[81] McKenzie, *GATT and Global Order*, 191–2.
[82] McKenzie, *GATT and Global Order*, 141–73.

a group of states should collectively relate to one another and to the rest of the world economy. Such arrangements can also significantly redefine regulatory bonds between governments and private business. Sophie Meunier has traced the EU's complex efforts to regulate globalization, first by promulgating universal rules through the WTO and then by consolidating market power through smaller free trade agreements.[83] The tension between free trade areas and global order means that foreign trade policy is never simply about recalibrating bilateral relations between two countries. It is also a bid to rewrite the general rules of play for governments and business in the wider multilateral system, and that is particularly true when economic heavyweights are involved. The potential for conflict and cooperation in a multilateral trade system was already evident in the League era, most visibly in the 1931 plan for an Austro-German customs union. It remains evident today, as the United States and China compete for global influence through rival projects for economic cooperation.

Through their participation in the League of Nations, interwar advocates of European unity such as Riedl and Coquet helped carve out space for regionalism within the wider regime of international trade rules, but their direct contribution to the process of European integration that gathered steam after 1945 is more difficult to assess. In the 1950s, the formal diplomatic process of European integration filtered through many different multilateral institutions with varying levels of contact with private Europeanist networks. It is evident that early European bodies drew heavily on organizational practice, legal precedent, and networks of expertise from the League of Nations, but the debt to private interwar Europeanists is less clear. While the handover from the Economic Committee to the GATT was relatively straightforward, there was a much more complicated transition from the nebulous pan-European groupings of the interwar period towards the larger and even more nebulous European Movement after 1945.[84]

Lucien Coquet briefly tried to insert himself and the UDE (renamed the European Economic and Federal Union) into the postwar European Movement but found himself out of step. His experience illustrates how significantly the political context for European cooperation changed after the Second World War, even though much of the basic institutional framing remained in place. Coquet published a European peace plan in

[83] S. Meunier, 'Managing Globalization? The EU in International Trade Negotiations', *JCMS: Journal of Common Market Studies*, 45/4 (2007), 905–26.
[84] Clavin and Patel, 'The Role of International Organizations in Europeanization: The Case of the League of Nations and the European Economic Community'; Patel, *Project Europe*, 11–38, 119–34.

1947 that outlined possible institutional configurations that would lock the Nordic countries and the Soviet Union into a common framework with the rest of Europe. In effect, Coquet was trying to use trade law to address the looming geopolitical conflicts of the early Cold War, as he had previously tried to use a customs union to resolve the Franco-German security tensions coming out of the First World War.[85] In the 1920s, Coquet had been able to secure official backing in Paris for his strategy to pursue French security through trade because there were few other good options, given the weak support for collective security from United States, Britain, and the League itself. Kiran Klaus Patel has shown that European economic integration after 1945 was greatly eased by the fact that security burdens were offloaded onto robust new structures such as the North Atlantic Treaty Organization. The European Common Market succeeded in part because it was merely a customs union and did not have to be more.[86]

Today, the institutional arrangements crafted after the Second World War are under tremendous strain, and, as in the 1920s, many high-stakes conflicts over security and economic development are being channelled through foreign trade policy. It would be a mistake to think that we are reliving the interwar crisis, however. The WTO has accumulated tremendous institutional capacity and is now morphing into something new along an unpredictable course that has no direct precedent. If anything, interwar history reveals the limited ability of any single individual, government, or organization to control the politics of transition according to a clear design. In the 1920s, Coquet, Harms, Llewellyn Smith, and Riedl groped towards a new multilateral order, in dialogue with the numerous other reformers who gathered in Geneva. Together they produced an unwieldy set of trade rules that no one intended but that proved remarkably durable.

---

[85] Badel, *Un milieu libéral et européen*, 418–20; L. Coquet, *La paix monétaire et le problème européen-rhénan* (J. Vrin, 1947).
[86] Patel, *Project Europe*, 32–3, 49–58.

Bibliography

Archives

Austria
Archiv der Wirtschaftskammer Wien [WKW]
    Nachlass Richard Riedl [NL Riedl]
Österreichisches Staatsarchiv, Vienna [ÖSta]
    Allgemeines Verwaltungsarchiv [AVA]
        k.k. Handelsministerium, Allgemeine Registratur
        Nachlass Richard Riedl [NL Riedl]
    Archiv der Republik [AdR]
        Handelspolitik
    Haus-, Hof-, und Staatsarchiv [HHSta]
        Nachlass [NL] Joseph Baernreither

France
Archives de Paris
    Chambre de commerce et d'industrie de Paris
Archives départementales des Yvelines, Montigny-le-Bretonneux
    Bureau de recrutement militaire de Versailles, Registre matricule
Archives du Ministère des Affaires Étrangères, La Courneuve [AMAE]
    Affaires diverses commerciales, 1798–1901
    Guerre 1914–1918
    Correspondance politique et commerciale, Nouvelle Série
    Relations commerciales, 1918–1940 [RC]
        B 27: Informations économiques
        B 81–82: Délibérations internationales
    Société des Nations [SDN]
    Y Internationale
    Papiers d'Agent
        Papiers Joseph Avenol

Archives Nationales, Pierrefitte sur Seine [AN]
 F 12: Commerce et Industrie
 AJ/9: Haute Commission Interalliée des Territoires Rhénans

Germany
Bundesarchiv, Lichterfelde [BArch]
 R 1501: Reichsministerium des Innern
 R 3101: Reichswirtschaftsministerium
Geheimes Staatsarchiv Preußischer Kulturbesitz [GStA]
 Ministerium für Handel und Gewerbe
Institut für Weltwirtschaft, Kiel, Hausarchiv [IfW Hs]
 Harms
 Allg.
 K.N. W.N. u. Wi.D.
 N.A.
 Friedrich Hoffmann, 'Die Geschichte des Instituts Für
  Weltwirtschaft', 3 vols., unpublished manuscript (1943–5).
Politisches Archiv des Auswärtigen Amts, Berlin [PA AA]
 Paris Gesandtschaft
 Nachlass Gustav Stresemann [NL Stresemann]
 Rechtsabteilung
 Sonderreferat Wirtschaft
 Referat Völkerbund
 Politische Abteilung II, Österreich
Stadtarchiv Kiel
 32983: Institut für Seeverkehr und Weltwirtschaft, 1914–1929

Switzerland
League of Nations Archive, Geneva [LON]
 Registry Files [R]
  10: Economic and Financial
  10A: General
  10 C: Customs
  10 D: Economic
  5B Intellectual Cooperation
  14: Communications and Transit Section
  Economic Committee, Papers, 1920–1922 [B]
  Economic Committee, Papers, 1923–1940 [E]
  Economic Committee, Minutes, 1920–1940 [P.V.]

Section Files [S]
Arthur Salter Papers
Personnel Files
World Trade Organization [WTO]
[GATT] Documents, 1946–50

United Kingdom
[Bodleian Library] Department of Special Collections, Oxford
Herbert Henry [Asquith Papers]
The National Archives, Kew [TNA]
Board of Trade Papers [BT]
Cabinet Papers [CAB]
Foreign Office Papers [FO]
Treasury Papers [T]

United States
University of Massachusetts-Amherst Libraries,
Special Collections and University Archives: W. E. B. Du Bois
Papers
United States National Archive, College Park [USNA]
RG 256: American Commission to Negotiate Peace
RG 43/698: International Trade Organization Files
RG 59: Department of State Central File

Published Works

Abbenhuis, M. M., *An Age of Neutrals: Great Power Politics, 1815–1914* (Cambridge University Press, 2014)

Abbenhuis, M., *The Hague Conferences and International Politics, 1898–1915* (Bloomsbury Academic, 2019)

Accominotti, O. and M. Flandreau, 'Bilateral Treaties and the Most-Favored-Nation Clause: The Myth of Trade Liberalization in the Nineteenth Century', *World Politics*, 60/2 (2008), 147–88

Ageron, C.-R., *France coloniale ou parti colonial?* (Presses universitaires de France, 1978)

Ageron, C.-R., 'L'idée d'Eurafrique et le débat colonial franco-allemand de l'entre-deux-guerres', *Revue d'histoire moderne et contemporaine*, 22/3 (1975), 446–75

Ahamed, L., *Lords of Finance: The Bankers Who Broke the World* (Penguin Press, 2009)

Albert, B. and P. Henderson, *South America and the First World War: The Impact of the War on Brazil, Argentina, Peru, and Chile* (Cambridge University Press, 1988)

Aldous, M., 'Trading Companies', in T. da S. Lopes, C. Lubinski, and H. J. S. Tworek (eds.), *The Routledge Companion to the Makers of Global Business* (Routledge, 2021)

Aldous, M. and C. Coyle, 'Examining the Role of a Private-Order Institution in Global Trade: The Liverpool Cotton Brokers' Association and the Crowning of King Cotton, 1811–1900', *Business History Review*, 95/4 (2021), 671–702

Amrith, S. and P. Clavin, 'Feeding the World: Connecting Europe and Asia, 1930–1945', *Past & Present*, 218/Special Supplement: Transnationalism and Global Contemporary History (2013), 29–50

Angell, N., *The Great Illusion: A Study of the Relation of Military Power to National Advantage* (William Heinemann, 1909)

Angell, N., 'Weltwirtschaft und territoriale Machtpolitik. Eine Erwiderung', *Weltwirtschaftliches Archiv*, 3 (1914), 367–82

Anghie, A., *Imperialism, Sovereignty, and the Making of International Law* (Cambridge University Press, 2005)

Baaij, C. J. W., 'Hiding in Plain Sight: The Power of Public Governance in International Arbitration', *Harvard International Law Journal*, 60/1 (2019), 135–80

Badel, L., *Diplomatie et grands contrats: l'État français et les marchés extérieurs au XXe siècle* (Publcations de la Sorbonne, 2010)

Badel, L., 'Les promoteurs français d'une union économique et douanière de l'Europe dans l'entre-deux-guerres', in A. Fleury and L. Jílek (eds.), *The Briand Plan of European Federal Union: National and Transnational Perspectives, with Documents* (Peter Lang, 1998), pp. 17–30

Badel, L., 'Littéraires, libéraux et Européens: l'autre versant de la construction européenne', *Journal of European Integration History*, 3/2 (1997), 23–33

Badel, L., 'Trêve douanière, libéralisme et conjoncture (septembre 1929–mars 1930)', *Relations Internationales*, 82 (1995), 141–61

Badel, L., *Un milieu libéral et européen: le grand commerce français, 1925–1948* (Comité pour l'histoire économique et financière de la France, 1999)

Bairoch, P., 'European Trade Policy, 1815–1914', in P. Mathias and S. Pollard (eds.), *The Cambridge Economic History of Europe from the Decline of the Roman Empire* (Cambridge University Press, 1989), pp. 1–160

Bajor, F., 'Beneficiaries of Aryanization: Hamburg As a Case Study', *Yad Vashem Studies*, XXVI (1998), 173–201

Barclay, T., *Bearing and Importance of Commercial Treaties in the Twentieth Century* (Manchester University Press, 1906)

Barclay, T., *Problems of International Practice and Diplomacy* (Sweet and Maxwell, 1907)

Barclay, T., *La Seconde Conférence de la Haye: modèles des clauses et des conventions* (Pédone, 1907)

Barclay, T., *Thirty Years: Anglo-French Reminiscences (1876–1906)* (Houghton Mifflin, 1914)

Bariéty, J., *Les relations franco-allemandes après la Première-Guerre mondiale: 10 novembre 1918–10 janvier 1925, de l'exécution à la négociation* (Pédone, 1977)

Bashford, A., *Global Population: History, Geopolitics, and Life on Earth* (Columbia University Press, 2016)

Bátonyi, G., *Britain and Central Europe, 1918–1933* (Clarendon Press, 1999)

Baumgart, W., *Deutsche Ostpolitik, 1918: Von Brest-Litowsk bis zum Ende des Ersten Weltkrieges* (Oldenbourg, 1966)

Beck, K., *Wiener akademische Burschenschaft Albia, 1870–1930* (Selbstverlag der Wiener akademische Burschenschaft 'Albia', 1930)

Becker, P., 'Remaking Mobility: International Conferences and the Emergence of the Modern Passport System', in P. Becker and N. Wheatley (eds.), *Remaking Central Europe: The League of Nations and the Former Habsburg Lands* (Oxford University Press, 2020), pp. 193–211

Beckert, S., 'American Danger: United States Empire, Eurafrica, and the Territorialization of Industrial Capitalism, 1870–1950', *The American Historical Review*, 122/4 (2017), 1137–70

Beckmann, U., *Von Löwe bis Leontief: Pioniere der Konjunkturforschung am Kieler Institut für Weltwirtschaft* (Metropolis, 2000)

Bell, A. C., *A History of the Blockade of Germany and of the Countries Associated with Her in the Great War, Austria-Hungary, Bulgaria, and Turkey, 1914–1918* (H. M. G. Stationery Office, 1937)

Beller, S., 'Germans and Jews as Central European and "Mitteleuropäisch" Elites', in P. M. R. Stirk (ed.), *Mitteleuropa: History and Prospects* (Edinburgh University Press, 1994), pp. 61–85

Bemmann, M., 'Comparing Economic Activities on a Global Level in the 1920s and 1930s: Motives and Consequences', in W. Steinmetz (ed.), *The Force of Comparison: A New Perspective on Modern European History and the Contemporary World* (Berghahn Books, 2019), pp. 242–65 .

Berg, M., *Gustav Stresemann: Eine politische Karriere zwischen Reich und Republik* (Muster-Schmidt Verlag, 1992)

Berg, M., *Gustav Stresemann und die Vereinigten Staaten von Amerika: Weltwirtschaftliche Verflechtung und Revisionspolitik 1907–1929* (Nomos, 1990)

Bertilorenzi, M., 'Legitimising Cartels: The Joint Roles of the League of Nations and of the International Chamber of Commerce', in S. Fellmann and M. Shanahan (eds.), *Regulating Competition: Cartel Registers in the Twentieth-Century World* (Routledge, 2019), pp. 30–47

Beveridge, W., 'Sir Hubert Llewellyn Smith', *The Economic Journal*, 56/221 (1946), 143–50

Bhagwati, J. N., *Termites in the Trading System: How Preferential Agreements Undermine Free Trade* (Oxford University Press, 2008)

Biggeleben, C., *Das 'Bollwerk des Bürgertums': Die Berliner Kaufmannschaft 1870–1920* (C. H. Beck, 2006)

Biltoft, C., 'The League of Nations and Alternative Economic Perspective', in J. Ghosh, R. Kattel, and E. Reinert (eds.), *New Perspectives on the History of Political Economy* (Edgar Elgar, 2016), pp. 270–80

Biltoft, C., 'The Meek Shall Not Inherit the Earth: Nationalist Economies, Ethnic Minorities, and the League of Nations', in C. Kreutzmüller, M. Wildt, and M. Zimmerman (eds.), *National Economies: Volks-Wirtschaft, Racism and Economy in Europe Between the Wars* (Cambridge Scholars Publishing, 2015), pp. 138–54

Blackbourn, D., 'Das Kaiserreich transnational. Eine Skizze', in S. Conrad and J. Osterhammel (eds.), *Das Kaiserreich transnational: Deutschland in der Welt 1871–1914* (Vandenhoeck & Ruprecht, 2004), pp. 302–24

Bohling, J., 'Colonial or Continental Power? The Debate over Economic Expansion in Interwar France, 1925–1932', *Contemporary European History*, 26/2 (2017), 217–41

Bonn, M., 'The Austro-German Customs Union', *International Affairs*, 10/4 (1931), 460–76

Bonn, M. and A. Siegfried, 'Economic Tendencies Affecting the Peace of the World', *The Annals of the American Academy of Political and Social Science*, 50 (1930), 192–219

Booth, C. (ed.), *Life and Labour of the People in London* (Macmillan and Co., 1892), vol. I.

Borchard, E. M., 'The Customs Union Advisory Opinion', *American Journal of International Law*, 25/4 (1931), 711–16

Borgius, W. and J. P. Sevening, 'Die Gründung des internationalen Handelskammer- und Vereinskongresses', *Weltwirtschaftliches Archiv*, 4 (1914), 149–51

Collier, P., *The Bottom Billion: Why the Poorest Countries Are Failing and What Can Be Done about It* (Oxford University Press, 2007)

Boyce, R., *British Capitalism at the Crossroads, 1919–1932: A Study in Politics, Economics, and International Relations* (Cambridge University Press, 1987)

Boyce, R., *The Great Interwar Crisis and the Collapse of Globalization* (Palgrave Macmillan, 2009)

Boyer, G. R. and T. J. Hatton, 'New Estimates of British Unemployment, 1870–1913', *The Journal of Economic History*, 62/3 (2002), 643–75

Brettner-Messler, G. H., 'Richard Riedl – ein liberaler Imperialist: Biographische Studie zu Handelspolitik und "Mitteleuropa"-Gedanken in Monarchie und Erster Republik', PhD thesis, University of Vienna (1998)

Broadberry, S. and P. Howlett, 'The United Kingdom during World War I: Business As Usual?', in S. Broadberry and M. Harrison (eds.), *The Economics of World War I* (Cambridge University Press, 2009), pp. 206–34

Bruneteau, B., *'L'Europe nouvelle' de Hitler: Une illusion des intellectuels de la France de Vichy* (Rocher, 2003)

Burkman, T. W., *Japan and the League of Nations: Empire and World Order, 1914–1938* (University of Hawaii Press, 2007)

Bussière, E., 'Les aspects économiques du projet Briand: essai de mise en perspective de l'Europe des producteurs aux tentatives régionales', in A. Fleury and L. Jílek (eds.), *The Briand Plan of European Federal Union: National and Transnational Perspectives, with Documents* (Peter Lang, 1998), pp. 75–92

Bussière, É., *La France, la Belgique et l'organisation économique de l'Europe, 1918–1935* (Comité pour l'histoire économique et financière de la France, 1992)

Cabanes, B., *The Great War and the Origins of Humanitarianism: 1918–1924* (Cambridge University Press, 2014)

Capozzola, C., 'The United States Empire', in R. Gerwarth and E. Manela (eds.), *Empires at War, 1911–1923* (Oxford University Press, 2014), pp. 235–53

Carabelli, A. M. and M. A. Cedrini, 'Keynes and the Complexity of International Economic Relations in the Aftermath of World War I', *Journal of Economic Issues*, 44/4 (2010), 1009–28

Carson, R. L., *Comparative Economic Systems* (Macmillan, 1973)

Cassis, Y., *Capitals of Capital: The Rise and Fall of International Financial Centres, 1780–2009* (Cambridge University Press, 2006)

Chabot, J.-L., *Aux origines intellectuelles de l'Union européenne: l'idée d'Europe unie de 1919 à 1939* (Presses Universitaires de Grenoble, 2005)

Chase, K., 'Multilateralism Compromised: The Mysterious Origins of GATT Article XXIV', *World Trade Review*, 5/1 (2006), 1–30

Chatterji, B., *Trade, Tariffs, and Empire: Lancashire and British Policy in India, 1919–1939* (Oxford University Press, 1992)

Clark, C., *The Sleepwalkers: How Europe Went to War in 1914* (Allen Lane, 2012)

Clarke, P., *Liberals and Social Democrats* (Cambridge University Press, 1978)

Clavin, P., 'The Austrian Hunger Crisis and the Genesis of International Organization after the First World War', *International Affairs*, 90/2 (2014), 265–78

Clavin, P., 'Defining Human Security: Roads to War and Peace, 1918–45', in C.-C. W. Szejnmann (ed.), *Rethinking History, Dictatorship, and War: New Approaches and Interpretations* (Continuum, 2009), pp. 69–83

Clavin, P., *The Failure of Economic Diplomacy: Britain, Germany, France and the United States, 1931–36* (Macmillan Press, 1996)

Clavin, P., *The Great Depression in Europe, 1929–1939* (St. Martin's Press, 2000)

Clavin, P., *Securing the World Economy: The Reinvention of the League of Nations, 1920–1946* (Oxford University Press, 2013)

Clavin, P. and M. Dungy, 'Trade, Law, and the Global Order of 1919', *Diplomatic History*, 44/4 (2020), 554–79.

Clavin, P. and K. K. Patel, 'The Role of International Organizations in Europeanization: The Case of the League of Nations and the European Economic Community', in M. Conway and K. K. Patel (eds.), *Europeanization in the Twentieth Century: Historical Approaches* (Palgrave Macmillan, 2010)

Clavin, P. and J.-W. Wessels, 'Another Golden Idol? The League of Nations' Gold Delegation and the Great Depression, 1929–1932', *The International History Review*, 26/4 (2004), 765–95

Clavin, P. and J.-W. Wessels, 'Transnationalism and the League of Nations: Understanding the Work of Its Economic and Financial Organisation', *Contemporary European History*, 14/4 (2005), 465–92

Cohrs, P. O., *The Unfinished Peace after World War I: America, Britain and the Stabilisation of Europe, 1919–1932* (Cambridge University Press, 2008)

Collini, S., *Liberalism and Sociology: L. T. Hobhouse and Political Argument in England, 1880–1914* (Cambridge University Press, 1979)

Conze, E., *Die große Illusion: Versailles 1919 und die Neuordnung der Welt* (Siedler Verlag, 2018)

Conze, E., '"Titane der modernen Wirtschaft" Otto Wolff (1881–1940)', in P. Danylow and U. S. Soénius (eds.), *Otto Wolff: Ein Unternehmen zwischen Wirtschaft und Politik* (Siedler, 2005)

Coquet, L., 'L'Avenir économique de l'Alsace-Lorraine', *Revue Politique et Parlementaire*, 93/276 (1917), 209–23

Coquet, L. (ed.), *La France régionale: Annuaire régionaliste, touristique, économique et réertoire illustré des grandes marques françaises* (Dubois et Bauer, 1924)

Coquet, L., 'Les États-Unis d'Europe et l'Union douanière franco-allemande', *La Revue d'Alsace et de Lorraine* 9/91 (1926), 127–9

Coquet, L., *La paix monétaire et le problème européen-rhénan* (J. Vrin, 1947)

Coquet, L., 'La Percée des Vosges', *La Revue d'Alsace et de Lorraine*, 1/1 (1918), 3

Coquet, L., *La Percée des Vosges: Rapport général présenté aux Ministres, aux Membres des Parlements, des Chambres Consultatives, et des Conseils Généraux et Municipaux de France et d'Allemagne* (Comité commercial franco-allemand, 1909)

Coquet, L., 'Si nous parlions un peu d'économie . . . politique', *La Revue d'Alsace et de Lorraine*, 7/63 (1924)

Coudenhove-Kalergi, R., *Pan-Europa* (Pan-Europa Verlag, 1923)

Coyajee, J. C., *India and the League of Nations* (Thompson and Co., 1932)

Cristu, J., *L'Union douanière européenne: ses conditions et ses difficultés* (L. Chauny & L. Quinsac, 1928)

Cussó, R., 'Building a Global Representation of Trade through International Quantification: The League of Nations' *Unification of Methods in Economic Statistics*', *The International History Review*, 42/4 (2020), 714–36

d'Alessandro, M., 'Global Economic Governance and the Private Sector: The League of Nations' Experiment in the 1920s', in C. Dejung and N. P. Petersson (eds.), *The Foundations of Worldwide Economic Integration: Power, Institutions, and Global Markets, 1850–1930* (Cambridge University Press, 2013), pp. 249–70

Dahlmann, D., 'Das Unternehmen Otto Wolff: vom Alteisenhandel zum Weltkonzern (1904–1929)', in P. Danylow and U. S. Soénius (eds.), *Otto Wolff: Ein Unternehmen zwischen Wirtschaft und Politik* (Siedler, 2005)

Darwin, J., *After Tamerlane: The Rise and Fall of Global Empires, 1400–2000* (Allen Lane, 2008)

Darwin, J., *The Empire Project: The Rise and Fall of the British World-System, 1830–1970* (Cambridge University Press, 2009)

Das Handelsmuseum in Wien. Darstellung seiner Gründung und Entwicklung, 1874–1919 (Handelsmuseum in Wien, 1920)

David, T. and P. Eichenberger, '"A World Parliament of Business"? The International Chamber of Commerce and Its Presidents in the Twentieth Century', *Business History* (2022), 1–24

David, T. and P. Eichenberger, 'Business and Diplomacy in the Twentieth Century: a Corporatist View', *Diplomatica*, 2/1 (2020), 48–56

Davidson, R., 'Sir Hubert Llewellyn Smith and Labour Policy, 1886–1916', DPhil thesis, University of Cambridge (1971)

de Leener, G., 'L'organisation du commerce d'exportation et la concurrence internationale', *Ce qui manque au commerce belge d'exportation* (Misch & Thron, 1906), pp. 225–84

Decorzant, Y., 'La Société des Nations et l'apparition d'un nouveau réseau d'expertise économique et financière (1914–1923)', *Critique internationale*, 52/3 (2011), 35–50

Decorzant, Y., *La Société des Nations et la naissance d'une conception de la régulation économique internationale* (Peter Lang, 2011)

Dedinger, B., 'The Franco-German Trade Puzzle: An Analysis of the Economic Consequences of the Franco-Prussian War', *The Economic History Review*, 65/3 (2012), 1029–54

Degoutte, J., *L'Occupation de la Ruhr, Rapport d'ensemble* (Imprimerie de l'Armée du Rhin, 1924)

Degoutte, J., *L'Occupation de la Ruhr, Texte* (Imprimerie de l'Armée du Rhin, 1924)

Dehne, P. A., *After the Great War: Economic Warfare and the Promise of Peace in Paris 1919* (Bloomsbury Academic, 2019)

Dehne, P. A., *On the Far Western Front: Britain's First World War in South America* (Manchester University Press, 2009)

Delaisi, F., *Les deux Europes: Europe industrielle et Europe agricole* (Payot, 1929)

Delaisi, F., *L'Union économique européenne est-elle possible? Rapport présenté au 1er Congrès Paneuropéen, Vienne* (Le Monde Nouveau, 1926)

Denfeld, C., *Hans Wehberg (1885–1962): Die Organisation der Staatengemeinschaft* (Nomos, 2008)

Drossinis, C.-G., *Les chambres de commerce à l'étranger* (Payot, 1921)

Druelle, C., 'Un laboratoire réformateur, le département du commerce en France et aux États-Unis de la Grande Guerre aux Années Vingt', PhD thesis, Institut d'Études Politiques (2004)

Druelle-Korn, C., 'Étienne Clémentel président-fondateur de la Chambre de commerce internationale', in M. C. Kessler and G. Rousseau (eds.), *Étienne Clémentel (1864–1936) Politique et action publique sous la Troisième République* (Peter Lang, 2018), pp. 419–34

Drummond, I. M., *British Economic Policy and the Empire, 1919–1939* (Allen and Unwin, 1972)

Duchenne, G., *Esquisses d'une Europe nouvelle: L'européisme dans la Belgique de l'entre-deux-guerres (1919–1939)* (Peter Lang, 2008)

Dungy, M. L., 'The Global Agricultural Crisis and British Diplomacy in the League of Nations in 1931', *Agricultural History Review*, 65/2 (2017), 297–319

Dungy, M. L., 'International Commerce in the Wake of Empire: Central European Economic Integration between National and Imperial Sovereignty', in P. Becker and N. Wheatley (eds.), *Remaking Central Europe: The League of Nations and the Former Habsburg Lands* (Oxford University Press, 2021), pp. 213–40

Dungy, M. L., 'Writing Multilateral Trade Rules in the League of Nations', *Contemporary European History*, 30/1 (2021), 60–75

Ebeling, R. M., *Political Economy, Public Policy and Monetary Economics: Ludwig von Mises and the Austrian Tradition* (Routledge, 2010)

Eckes, A. E. and T. W. Zeiler, *Globalization and the American Century* (Cambridge University Press, 2003)

Eichengreen, B., *Golden Fetters: The Gold Standard and the Great Depression, 1919–1939* (Oxford University Press, 1992)

Ekbladh, D., 'American Asylum: The United States and the Campaign to Transplant the Technical League, 1939–1940', *Diplomatic History*, 39/4 (2015), 629–60

Ekbladh, D., *Plowshares into Swords: Weaponized Knowledge, Liberal Order, and the League of Nations* (University of Chicago Press, 2022), 166–172

Endres, A. M. and G. A. Fleming, *International Organizations and the Analysis of Economic Policy, 1919–1950* (Cambridge University Press, 2002)

Erker, L., A. Huber, and K. Taschwer, *Deutscher Klub: Austro-Nazis in der Hofburg* (Czernin, 2018)

Estevadeordal, A., B. Frantz, and A. M. Taylor, 'The Rise and Fall of World Trade, 1870–1939', *The Quarterly Journal of Economics*, 118/2 (2003), 359–407

Fairlie, J. A., *British War Administration* (Oxford University Press, 1919)

Fakhri, M., 'The 1937 International Sugar Agreement: Neo-Colonial Cuba and Economic Aspects of the League of Nations', *Leiden Journal of International Law*, 24/4 (2011), 899–922

Feinstein, C. H., P. Temin, and G. Toniolo, *The European Economy between the Wars* (Oxford University Press, 1997)

Fink, C., *Defending the Rights of Others: The Great Powers, the Jews, and International Minority Protection, 1878–1938* (Cambridge University Press, 2004)

Fink, C., *The Genoa Conference: European Diplomacy, 1921–1922* (University of North Carolina Press, 1984)

Fischer, C., *The Ruhr Crisis, 1923–1924* (Oxford University Press, 2003)

Fischer, C., 'Scoundrels without a Fatherland? Heavy Industry and Transnationalism in Post-First World War Germany', *Contemporary European History*, 14/4 (2005), 441–64

Fischer, P., 'Die österreichischen Handelskammern und der Anschluß an Deutschland. Zur Strategie der "Politik der kleinen Mittel" 1925 bis 1934', in Wissenschaftliche Kommission des Theodor-Körner-Stiftungsfonds und des Leopold-Kunschak-Preises (ed.), *Das Juliabkommen von 1936: Vorgeschichte, Hintergründe und Folgen* (Oldenbourg, 1977), pp. 299–314

Fleury, A., 'Paneurope et l'Afrique', in M.-T. Bitsch and G. Bossuat (eds.), *L' Europe unie et l'Afrique: de l'idée d'Eurafrique à la convention de Lomé I; actes du colloque international de Paris, 1er et 2 avril 2004* (Bruylant, 2005), pp. 35–58

Fleury, A. and J. Bariéty, 'Le plan Briand d'Union fédérale européenne: les dimensions diplomatiques, 1929–1932', *La Société des Nations et l'Europe, 1929–1932* (Presses universitaires de Strasbourg, 2007)

Frank, A., 'The Children of the Desert and the Laws of the Sea: Austria, Great Britain, the Ottoman Empire, and the Mediterranean Slave Trade in the Nineteenth Century', *The American Historical Review*, 117/2 (2012), 410–44

Frei, G. A., *Great Britain, International Law, and the Evolution of Maritime Strategic Thought* (Oxford University Press, 2020)

French, D., 'The Military Background to the "Shell Crisis" of May 1915', *Journal of Strategic Studies*, 2/2 (1979), 192–205

Frieden, J. A., *Global Capitalism: Its Fall and Rise in the Twentieth Century* (W.W. Norton, 2006)

Friedjung, H., *Das Zeitalter des Imperialismus, 1884–1914*, vol. 3 (Neufeld und Henius, 1919)

Friedlander, S., *Nazi Germany and the Jews: The Years of Persecution, 1933–1939* (Harper Collins, 1997)

Friedman, W. A., *Fortune Tellers: the Story of America's First Economic Forecasters* (Princeton University Press, 2014)

Garavini, G., *After Empires: European Integration, Decolonization, and the Challenge from the Global South 1957–1986* (Oxford University Press, 2012)

Geißler, F., *Österreichs Handelskammer-Organisation in der Zwischenkriegszeit: Eine Idee auf dem Prüfstand* (Österreichischer Wirtschaftsverlag, 1977)

Gerwarth, R., *The Vanquished: Why the First World War Failed to End, 1917–1923* (Allen Lane, 2016)

Gerwarth, R. and J. Horne (eds.), *War in Peace: Paramilitary Violence in Europe after the Great War* (Oxford University Press, 2012)

Gerwarth, R. and E. Manela (eds.), *Empires at War, 1911–1923* (Oxford University Press, 2014)

Gorman, D., *The Emergence of International Society in the 1920s* (Cambridge University Press, 2011)

Gram-Skjoldager, K. and H. A. Ikonomou, 'Making Sense of the League of Nations Secretariat: Historiographical and Conceptual Reflections on Early International Public Administration', *European History Quarterly*, 49/3 (2019), 420–44

Grimmer-Solem, E., *Learning Empire: Globalization and the German Quest for World Status, 1875–1919* (Cambridge University Press, 2019)

Gründer, H., *Walter Simons als Staatsmann, Jurist und Kirchenpolitiker* (Schmidt, 1975)

Grupp, P., 'Eugène Etienne et la tentative de rapprochement franco-allemand en 1907', *Cahiers d'études africaines*, 15/58 (1975), 303–11

Guieu, J.-M., 'The Debate about a European Institutional Order among International Legal Scholars in the 1920s and Its Legacy', *Contemporary European History*, 21/3 (2012), 319–37

Guieu, J.-M., *Le rameau et le glaive: les militants français pour la Société des Nations* (Presses de la fondation nationale des sciences politiques, 2008)

Guillen, P., 'La politique douanière de la France dans les années vingt', *Relations Internationales*, 16 (1978), 315–31

Hannigan, R. E., 'Reciprocity 1911: Continentalism and American Weltpolitik', *Diplomatic History*, 4/1 (1980), 1–18

Hansen, P. and S. Jonsson, *Eurafrica: The Untold History of European Integration and Colonialism* (Bloomsbury, 2014)

Harms, B., 'Der Außenhandel der Vereinigten Staaten von Amerika', *Weltwirtschaftliches Archiv*, 6 (1915), 341–48

Harms, B., 'Bestrebungen der Amerikaner, ihr Wirtschaftsleben durch den Krieg zu befruchten', *Weltwirtschaftliches Archiv*, 5 (1915), 385–8

Harms, B., 'England und Deutschland', *Deutsche Revue*, 35 (1910)

Harms, B., *Entstehung und Bedeutung der Weltwirtschaftlichen Aufgaben Deutschlands: Vortrag gehalten auf der Generalversammlung des Bundes der Industriellen* (Hauptverband Deutscher Flotten-Vereine im Auslande, 1911)

Harms, B., *Ferdinand Lassalle und seine Bedeutung für die deutsche Sozialdemokratie* (G. Fischer, 1909)

Harms, B., 'Strukturwandlungen der Weltwirtschaft', *Weltwirtschaftliches Archiv*, 25 (1927), 1–58

Harms, B., *Volkswirtschaft und Weltwirtschaft: Versuch der Begründung einer Weltwirtschaftslehre* (Gustav Fischer, 1912)

Harms, B., 'Die Weltwirtschaftskonferenz', *Weltwirtschaftliches Archiv*, 25 (1927), 211–44

Harms, B., 'Weltwirtschaftsrecht. Ein Beitrag zur sozialökonomisch-völkerrechtlichen Begriffsbildung', *Weltwirtschaftliches Archiv*, 20 (1924), 573–88

Harms, B., *Vom Wirtschaftskrieg zur Weltwirtschaftskonferenz: Weltwirtschaftliche Gestaltungstendenzen im Spiegel gesammelter Vorträge* (Gustav Fischer, 1927)

Hart, M., *A Trading Nation: Canadian Trade Policy from Colonialism to Globalization* (University of British Columbia Press, 2002)

Hauser, H., *Les Régions économiques* (Librarie Bernard Grasset, 1918)

Hautcoeur, P.-C., 'The Economics of World War I in France', in S. Broadberry and M. Harrison (eds.), *The Economics of World War I* (Cambridge University Press, 2009), pp. 169–205

Hellauer, J., *Die Organisation des Exporthandels: Eine allgemeine Darstellung und Untersuchung* (Handels-Museum, 1903)

Herren, M., 'Fascist Internationalism', in G. Sluga and P. Clavin (eds.), *Internationalisms: A Twentieth-Century History* (2016), pp. 191–212

Herren, M., *Hintertüren zur Macht: Internationalismus und modernisierungsorientierte Außenpolitik in Belgien, der Schweiz und den USA 1865–1914* (Oldenbourg, 2000)

Herren, M., '"They Already Exist": Don't They? Conjuring Global Networks Along the Flow of Money', in I. Löhr, and R. Wenzlhuemer (eds.), *The Nation State and Beyond* (Springer Berlin Heidelberg, 2013), pp. 43–62

Herren, M. and I. Löhr, 'Being International in Times of War: Arthur Sweetser and the Shifting of the League of Nations to the United Nations', *European Review of History: Revue européenne d'histoire*, 25/3–4 (2018), 535–52

Hirschman, A., *National Power and the Structure of Foreign Trade* (University of California Press, 1945)

Hirst, F. W., *Safeguarding and Protection in Great Britain and the United States* (Macmillan, 1927)

History of the Ministry of Munitions, 12 vols (H. M. G. Stationery Office, 1922), vols. I, II, IV.

Hochman, E. R., *Imagining a Greater Germany: Republican Nationalism and the Idea of Anschluss* (Cornell University Press, 2016)

Hoffer, R., 'Is the Business of Business Business Alone? The International Chamber of Commerce and the Origins of Global Business Diplomacy, 1920–1931', *LSE Economic History Student Working Papers*, 004 (2021)

Högselius, P., A. Kaijser, and E. van der Vleuten, *Europe's Infrastructure Transition: Economy, War, Nature* (Palgrave Macmillan, 2015)

Horn, M., *Britain, France, and the Financing of the First World War* (McGill-Queen's University Press, 2002)

Hörtlehner, A., 'Ludwig von Mises und die österreichische Handelskammer organisation', *Wirtschaftspolitische Blätter*, 28/4 (1981)

Howe, A., *Free Trade and Liberal England, 1846–1946* (Oxford University Press, 1997)

Hull, I. V., *Absolute Destruction: Military Culture and the Practices of War in Imperial Germany* (Cornell University Press, 2013)

Hull, I. V., *A Scrap of Paper: Breaking and Making International Law during the Great War* (Cornell University Press, 2014)

Hurrell, A., *On Global Order: Power, Values, and the Constitution of International Society* (Oxford University Press, 2007)

Ibs, H., *Hermann J. Held (1890–1963): Ein Kieler Gelehrtenleben in den Fängen der Zeitläufe* (Peter Lang, 2000)

Ikonomou, H. A., 'The Biography As Institutional Can-Opener: An Investigation of Core Bureaucratic Practices in the Early Years of the League of Nations Secretariat', in K. Gram-Skjoldager, H. A. Ikonomou, and T. Kahlert (eds.), *Organizing the 20th-Century World: International Organizations and the Emergence of International Public Administration, 1920–1960s* (Bloomsbury Academic, 2020), pp. 33–48

Ingulstad, M., 'Regulating the Regulators: The League of Nations and the Problem of Raw Materials', in A. R. D. Sanders, P. T. Sandvik, and E. Storli (eds.), *The Political Economy of Resource Regulation: An International and Comparative History, 1850–2015* (UBC Press, 2019), pp. 229–57

Ingulstad, M. and Lixinski, Lucas, 'Pan-American Exceptionalism: Regional International Law as a Challenge to International Institutions', in S. Jackson and A. O'Malley (eds.), *The Institution of International Order: From the League of Nations to the United Nations* (Routledge, 2018), pp. 65–89

Institut für Weltwirtschaft und Seeverkehr, *Der deutsche Außenhandel unter der Einwirkung der weltwirtschaftlicher Strukturwandlungen*, 2 (Mittler, 1932)

Irwin, D. A., *Clashing over Commerce: A History of US Trade Policy* (The University of Chicago Press, 2017)

Irwin, D. A., P. C. Mavroidis, and A. O. Sykes, *The Genesis of the GATT* (Cambridge University Press, 2009)

Jackson, J. H., *The World Trading System: Law and Policy of International Economic Relations*, 2nd ed. (MIT Press, 1997)

Jackson, P., *Beyond the Balance of Power: France and the Politics of National Security in the Era of the First World War* (Cambridge University Press, 2013)

Jackson, P. and A. O'Malley, 'Rocking on Its Hinges? The League of Nations, the United Nations and the New History of Internationalism in the Twentieth Century', in S. Jacksona and A. O'Malley (eds.), *The Institution of International Order: From the League of Nations to the United Nations* (Routledge, 2018), pp. 1–21

Jackson, S., 'Diaspora Politics and Developmental Empire: The Syro-Lebanese at the League of Nations', *Arab Studies Journal*, 21/1 (2013), 166–90

James, H., *The End of Globalization: Lessons from the Great Depression* (Harvard University Press, 2001)

James, H., *The German Slump: Politics and Economics, 1924–1936* (Clarendon Press of Oxford University Press, 1986)

Jančík, D. and H. Matis, '"Eine neue Wirtschaftsordnung für Mitteleuropa ..." Mitteleuropäische Wirtschaftskonzeption in der Zwischenkriegszeit', in A. Teichova and H. Matis (eds.), *Österreich und die Tschechoslowakei 1919–1938: die wirtschaftliche Neuordnung in Zentraleuropa in der Zwischenkriegszeit* (Böhlau, 1996), pp. 329–87

Jeannesson, S., *Poincaré, la France et la Ruhr, 1922–1924: histoire d'une occupation* (Presses universitaires de Strasbourg, 1998)

Jogarajan, S., *Double Taxation and the League of Nations* (Cambridge University Press, 2018)

Jones, G., *Multinationals and Global Capitalism: From the Nineteenth to the Twenty-First Century* (Oxford University Press, 2005)

Jones, H., 'The Great War: How 1914–18 Changed the Relationship between War and Civilians', *The RUSI Journal*, 159/4 (2014), 84–91

Kaiser, D. E., *Economic Diplomacy and the Origins of the Second World War: Germany, Britain, France, and Eastern Europe, 1930–1939* (Princeton University Press, 1981).

Kaiser, W. and J. W. Schot, *Writing the Rules for Europe: Experts, Cartels, and International Organizations* (Palgrave Macmillan, 2014)

Kant, I., *Perpetual Peace: A Philosophical Essay* (George Allen and Unwin, 1917)

Kapp, R., 'The Failure of the Diplomatic Negotiations between Germany and Austria-Hungary for a Customs Union, 1915–1916', PhD thesis, University of Toronto (1977)

Kauth, J. T., 'Fremdenrecht und Völkerbund: Das Scheitern der International Conference on the Treatment of Foreigners 1929', *Archiv des Völkerrechts*, 56/2 (2018), 202–28

Keene, E., 'The Treaty-Making Revolution of the Nineteenth Century', *The International History Review*, 34/3 (2012), 475–500

Kennedy, D. M., *Over Here: The First World War and American Society* (Oxford University Press, 2004)

Kenwood, A. G. and A. L. Lougheed, *Growth of the International Economy, 1820–2015*, 4th ed. (Routledge, 1999)

Keynes, J. M., *The Economic Consequences of the Peace* (Macmillan and Co., 1919)

Kill, T., 'Don't Cross the Streams: Past and Present Overstatement of Customary International Law in Connection with Conventional Fair and Equitable Treatment Obligations', *Michigan Law Review*, 106/5 (2008), 853–80

Kindleberger, C., 'Commercial Policy between the Wars', in S. Pollard and P. Mathias (eds.), *The Industrial Economies: The Development of Economic and Social Policies* (Cambridge, 1989)

Kissling, C., *Die Interparlamentarische Union im Wandel: Rechtspolitische Ansätze einer repräsentativ-parlamentarischen Gestaltung der Weltpolitik* (Peter Lang, 2006)

Klecker de Balazuc, M., *La République Rhénane* (La Revue d'Alsace et de Lorraine, 1924)

Kornberg, J., *Theodor Herzl: From Assimilation to Zionism* (Indiana University Press, 1993)

Koskenniemi, M., *The Gentle Civilizer of Nations: The Rise and Fall of International Law, 1870–1960* (Cambridge University Press, 2002)

Kott, S., 'Constructing a European Social Model: The Fight for Social Insurance in the Interwar Period', in J. Van Daele, M. Rodriguez Garcia, and G. van Goethem (eds.), *ILO Histories* (Peter Lang, 2011), pp. 173–96

Kott, S., 'Dynamiques de l'internationalisation: l'Allemagne et l'Organisation internationale du travail (1919–1940)', *Critique internationale*, 52/3 (2011), 69

Kott, S., 'From Transnational Reformist Network to International Organization: The International Association of Labour Legislation and the International Labour Organization, 1900–1930', in D. Rodogno, B. Struck, and J. Vogel (eds.), *Shaping the Transnational Sphere: Experts, Networks, and Issues from the 1840s to the 1930s* (Berghahn Books, 2015), pp. 239–78

Kott, S. and K. K. Patel (eds.), *Nazism across Borders: The Social Policies of the Third Reich and Their Global Appeal* (Oxford University Press, 2018)

Krobb, F. (ed.), 'Colonial Austria: Austria and the Overseas' special issue of *Austrian Studies* (2012)

Kuehl, W. F. and L. Dunn, *Keeping the Covenant: American Internationalists and the League of Nations, 1920–1939* (Kent State University Press, 1997)

Kuhn, A. K., 'The International Conference on the Treatment of Foreigners', *American Journal of International Law*, 24/3 (1930), 570–73

Kuisel, R. F., *Capitalism and the State in Modern France: Renovation and Economic Management in the Twentieth Century* (Cambridge University Press, 1981)

Lacour-Gayet, J., *La réforme douanière* (Comité d'action économique et douanière, 1926)

Lambert, N. A., *Planning Armageddon: British Economic Warfare and the First World War* (Harvard University Press, 2012)

Laqua, D., *The Age of Internationalism and Belgium, 1880–1930: Peace, Progress and Prestige* (Manchester University Press, 2013)

Laqua, D., 'Internationalisme ou affirmation de la nation? La coopération intellectuelle transnationale dans l'entre-deux-guerres', *Critique internationale*, 52/3 (2011), 51–67

Laqua, D., 'Transnational Intellectual Cooperation, the League of Nations, and the Problem of Order', *Journal of Global History*, 6/2 (2011), 223–47

Lavenex, S. and F. Jurje, 'The Migration-Trade Nexus: Migration Provisions in Trade Agreements', in L. S. Talani and S. McMahon (eds.), *Handbook of the International Political Economy of Migration* (Edward Elgar, 2015), pp. 259–81

Lawrence, G., *The Inquiry; American Preparations for Peace, 1917–1919* (Yale University Press, 1963)

Leal-Arcas, R., 'Proliferation of Regional Trade Agreements: Complementing or Supplanting Multilateralism?' *Chicago Journal of International Law*, 11/2, 597–629

Leffler, M. P., *The Elusive Quest: America's Pursuit of European Stability and French Security, 1919–1933* (University of North Carolina Press, 1979)

Lemercier, C. and J. Sgard, *Arbitrage privé international et globalisation(s). Rapport de recherche* (Archive ouverte en Sciences de l'Homme et de la Société, 2015)

Leonhard, J., *Der überforderte Frieden: Versailles und die Welt 1918–1923* (C. H. Beck, 2018)

Levy, H., 'Weltwirtschaft und territoriale Machtpolitik. Einige Bemerkungen kritischer Art über Norman Angell's Friedensargument', *Weltwirtschaftliches Archiv*, 1 (1913), 349–60

Lewis, A., *Economic Survey, 1919–1939* (Blakiston Co., 1950)

Lewis, A., 'The Rate of Growth of World Trade, 1830–1973', in S. Grassman and E. Lundberg (eds.), *The World Economic Order: Past and Prospects* (Macmillan, 1981), pp. 11–74

Lieven, D., *Towards the Flame: Empire, War and the End of Tsarist Russia* (Allen Lane, 2015)

Lisio, D. J., *British Naval Supremacy and Anglo-American Antagonisms, 1914–1930* (Cambridge University Press, 2014)

Llewellyn Smith, H., *The Board of Trade* (G. P. Putnam's Sons, 1928)

Llewellyn Smith, H., 'Economic Security and Unemployment Insurance', *The Economic Journal*, 20/80 (1910), 513–29

Llewellyn Smith, H., 'Introduction', *The New Survey of London Life and Labour*, 9 vols (P.S. King, 1930), vol. I, pp. 1–57

Llewellyn Smith, H., 'Introduction', *The New Survey of London Life and Labour*, 9 vols (P.S. King, 1932), vol. III, pp. 1–28

Llewellyn Smith, H., 'The New Survey of London Life and Labour', *Journal of the Royal Statistical Society*, 92/4 (1929), 530

Llewellyn Smith, H., 'Unemployment and Poverty', *The New Survey of London Life and Labour*, 9 vols (P. S. King, 1932), vol. III, pp. 153–87

Llewellyn Smith, H., 'Wages, Hours of Labour and Earnings', *The New Survey of London Life and Labour*, 9 vols (P. S. King, 1930), vol. I, pp. 111–42.

Lloyd, L. 'Loosening the Apron Strings', *The Round Table*, 92/369 (2003), 279–303

Löding, D., 'Deutschlands und Österreich-Ungarns Balkanpolitik von 1912–1914 unter besonderer Berücksichtigung ihrer Wirtschaftsinteressen', PhD thesis, University of Hamburg (1969)

Löhr, I., 'Lives beyond Borders, or: How to Trace Global Biographies, 1880–1950', *Comparativ: Lives beyond Borders: A Social History 1880–1950*, 23/6 (2013), 7–21

Loveday, A., 'The Economic and Financial Activities of the League', *International Affairs*, 17/6 (1938), 788–808

Loveday, A., 'The Measurement of Tariff Levels', *Journal of the Royal Statistical Society*, 92/4, 487–529

MacMillan, M., *Paris 1919: Six Months That Changed the World* (Random House, 2002)

Maier, C. S., 'Consigning the Twentieth Century to History: Alternative Narratives for the Modern Era', *The American Historical Review*, 105/3 (2000), 807

Maier, C. S., *Once within Borders: Territories of Power, Wealth, and Belonging since 1500* (The Belknap Press of Harvard University Press, 2016)

Maier, C. S., *Recasting Bourgeois Europe: Stabilization in France, Germany, and Italy in the Decade after World War I*, revised ed. (Princeton University Press, 2016)

Maiolo, J., 'Naval Armaments Competition between the Two World Wars', in T. Mahnken, J. Maiolo, and D. Stevenson (eds.), *Arms Races in International Politics: From the Nineteenth to the Twenty-First Century* (Oxford University Press, 2016), pp. 93–114

Manela, E., *The Wilsonian Moment: Self-Determination and the International Origins of Anticolonial Nationalism* (Oxford University Press, 2009)

Marcus, N., *Austrian Reconstruction and the Collapse of Global Finance, 1921–1931* (Harvard University Press, 2018)

Marin, S. A., 'Introducing Small Firms to International Markets: The Debates over the Commercial Museums in France and Germany 1880–1910', in H. Berghoff, P. Scranton, and U. Spiekermann (eds.), *The Rise of Marketing and Market Research* (Palgrave Macmillan, 2012), pp. 127–52

Marseille, J., *Empire colonial et capitalisme français: histoire d'un divorce* (Seuil, 1984)

Martin, J., *The Meddlers: Sovereignty, Empire, and the Birth of Global Economic Governance* (Harvard University Press, 2022)

Mavroidis, P. C., *The Regulation of International Trade, GATT, 2* (MIT Press, 2016), vol. I

Mazower, M., *Governing the World: The History of an Idea, 1815 to the Present* (Penguin Press, 2012)

Mazower, M., 'Minorities and the League of Nations in Interwar Europe', *Daedalus*, 126/2 (1997), 47–63

McDougall, W. A., *France's Rhineland Diplomacy, 1914–1924: The Last Bid for a Balance of Power in Europe* (Princeton University Press, 1978)

McKenzie, F., *GATT and Global Order in the Postwar Era* (Cambridge University Press, 2020)

McKenzie, F., *Redefining the Bonds of Commonwealth, 1939–1948: The Politics of Preference* (Palgrave Macmillan, 2002)

McKeown, A., *Melancholy Order: Asian Migration and the Globalization of Borders* (Columbia University Press, 2008)

Meade, J. E., *The Collected Papers of James Meade* (Unwin Hyman, 1988), vol. III: International Economics

Meade, J., 'International Economic Cooperation', in S. Howson (ed.), *The Collected Papers of James Meade* (Unwin Hyman, 1988), pp. 1–10

Mearns, A., *The Bitter Cry of Outcast London: An Inquiry into the Condition of the Abject Poor* (James Clarke, 1883)

Meunier, S. 'Managing Globalization? The EU in International Trade Negotiations', *JCMS: Journal of Common Market Studies*, 45/4 (2007), 905–26

Meyer, C., *Exportförderungspolitik in Österreich: Von der Privilegienwirtschaft zum objektiven Förderungssystem* (Böhlau, 1991)

Miller, D. H., *The Drafting of the Covenant*, 2 vols (G.P. Putnam's Sons, 1928), vol. II

Miller, M. B., *Europe and the Maritime World: A Twentieth-Century History* (Cambridge University Press, 2012)

Mises, L., 'Antimarxismus', *Weltwirtschaftliches Archiv*, 21 (1925), 266–93

Moeyes, P., 'Neutral Tones: The Netherlands and Switzerland and Their Interpretations of Neutrality 1914–1918', in H. Amersfoort and W. Klinkert (eds.), *Small Powers in the Age of Total War, 1900–1940* (Brill, 2011), pp. 57–84

Montarsolo, Y., 'Albert Sarraut et l'idée d'Eurafrique', in M.-T. Bitsch and G. Bossuat (eds.), *L'Europe unie et l'Afrique: de l'idée d'Eurafrique à la convention de Lomé I; actes du colloque international de Paris, 1er et 2 avril 2004* (Bruylant, 2005), pp. 77–96

Morrison-Bell, C., *Tariff Walls: A European Crusade* (J. Murray, 1930)

Muddiman, D., 'A Brain Centre of Empire: Commercial and Industrial Intelligence at the Imperial Institute, 1886–1903', in T. Weller (ed.), *Information History in the Modern World: Histories of the Information Age* (Palgrave Macmillan, 2011), pp. 108–29

Muddiman, D., 'From Display to Data: The Commercial Museum and the Beginnings of Business Information, 1870–1914', in W. B. Rayward (ed.), *Information Beyond Borders: International Cultural and Intellectual Exchange in the Belle Époque* (Ashgate, 2014), pp. 263–82

Mukherjee, A., 'British Industrial Policy and the Question of Fiscal Autonomy, 1916–1930', *Proceedings of the Indian History Congress*, 62 (2001), 726–55

Mulder, N., *The Economic Weapon: The Rise of Sanctions As a Tool of Modern War* (Yale University Press, 2022)

Müller, A., *Zwischen Annäherung und Abgrenzung: Österreich-Ungarn und die Diskussion um Mitteleuropa im Ersten Weltkrieg* (Tectum, 2001)

Müller, P., 'Coordonner le capitalisme européen. Les délégués français et allemands de la Chambre de commerce internationale des années 1930', in P. Müller and H. Joly (eds.),*Les espaces d'interaction des élites françaises et allemandes: 1920–1950* (Presses universitaires de Rennes, 2021), pp. 111–26

Nakhimovsky, I., *The Closed Commercial State: Perpetual Peace and Commercial Society from Rousseau to Fichte* (Princeton University Press, 2011)

Nautz, J., 'Historische Einführung', in R. Schüller, *Unterhändler des Vertrauens: Aus den nachgelassenen Schriften von Sektionschef Dr. Richard Schüller*, J. Nautz (ed.), (R. Oldenbourg Verlag, 1990), pp. 9–70

Nautz, J., *Die österreichische Handelspolitik der Nachkriegszeit 1918 bis 1923: Die Handelsvertragsbeziehungen zu den Nachfolgestaaten* (Böhlau, 1994)

Nautz, J., 'Tarifvertragsrecht und "Anschluss". Das Projekt einer gemeinsamen Tarifrechtsreform in Deutschland und Österreich 1919–1931', *Archiv für Sozialgeschichte*, 31 (1991), 123–35

Navari, C., 'Origins of the Briand plan', *Diplomacy & Statecraft*, 3/1 (1992), 74–104

Niemeyer, T. (ed.), *Der Völkerbundsentwurf der Deutschen Gesellschaft für Völkerrecht. Vorschläge für die Organisation der Welt* (Verlag Hans Robert Engelmann, 1920)

Offer, A., *The First World War: An Agrarian Interpretation* (Clarendon Press of Oxford University Press, 1989)

Orde, A., *British Policy and European Reconstruction after the First World War* (Cambridge University Press, 1990)

Orde, A., *The Eclipse of Great Britain: The United States and British Imperial Decline, 1895–1956* (St. Martin's Press, 1996)

Orde, A., 'The Origins of the German-Austrian Customs Union Affair of 1931', *Central European History*, 13/1 (1980), 34–59

O'Rourke, K. H., 'The European Grain Invasion, 1870–1913', *The Journal of Economic History*, 57/4 (1997), 775–801

O'Rourke, K. H., 'Tariffs and Growth in the Late 19th Century', *The Economic Journal*, 110/463 (2000), 456–83

O'Rourke, K. H. and J. G. Williamson, *Globalization and History: The Evolution of a Nineteenth-Century Atlantic Economy* (MIT Press, 1999)

Orzoff, A., *Battle for the Castle: The Myth of Czechoslovakia in Europe, 1914–1948* (Oxford University Press, 2009)

Oske, E., *Die Informationsstelle der Deutschen Liga für Völkerbund* (Verlag Hans Robert Engelmann, 1921)

Oske, E., 'Neuerrichtung von Auslandshandelskammern', *Weltwirtschaftliches Archiv*, 9 (1917), 104–6

Oske, E., 'Neuerrichtung von Auslandshandelskammern', *Weltwirtschaftliches Archiv*, 12 (1918), 414–24

Oske, E., 'Neugründungen von internationalen Vereinen und Gesellschaften', *Weltwirtschaftliches Archiv*, 8 (1916), 447–50

Oske, E., 'Neugründungen von internationalen Vereinen und Gesellschaften', *Weltwirtschaftliches Archiv*, 10 (1917), 439–41

Pahre, R., *Politics and Trade Cooperation in the Nineteenth Century: The 'Agreeable Customs' of 1815–1914* (Cambridge University Press, 2008)

Paparinskis, M., *The International Minimum Standard and Fair and Equitable Treatment* (Oxford University Press, 2014)

Patel, K. K., *The New Deal: A Global History* (Princeton University Press, 2016)

Patel, K. K., *Project Europe: Myths and Realities of European Integration* (Cambridge University Press, 2020)

Payk, M. M., *Frieden durch Recht? der Aufstieg des modernen Völkerrechts und der Friedensschluss nach dem ersten Weltkrieg* (De Gruyter, 2018)

Pedersen, S., 'Back to the League of Nations', *The American Historical Review*, 112/4 (2007), 1091–117

Pedersen, S., *The Guardians: The League of Nations and the Crisis of Empire* (Oxford University Press, 2015)

Pegg, C. H., *Evolution of the European Idea, 1914–1932* (University of North Carolina Press, 1983)

Pejovic, C., 'Civil Law and Common Law: Two Different Paths Leading to the Same Goal', *Victoria University of Wellington Law Review*, 32/3 (2001), 817–42

Petersson, N. P., *Anarchie und Weltrecht: Das Deutsche Reich und die Institutionen der Weltwirtschaft 1890–1930* (Vandenhoeck & Ruprecht, 2009)

Petersson, N. P., 'Legal Institutions and the World Economy', in C. Dejung and N. P. Petersson (eds.), *The Foundations of Worldwide Economic Integration: Power, Institutions, and Global Markets, 1850–1930* (Cambridge University Press, 2013), pp. 21–39

Picker, C. B., 'Regional Trade Agreements v. The WTO: A Proposal for Reform of Article XXIV to Counter This Institutional Threat', *University of Pennsylvania Journal of International Law*, 26/2 (2005), 267–319

Piétri, N., *La société des nations et la reconstruction financière de l'Autriche, 1921–1926* (Centre européen de la Dotation Carnegie pour la paix internationale, 1970)

Pinchis, M., 'The Ancestry of "Equitable Treatment" in Trade', *The Journal of World Investment & Trade* (2014), 13–72

Plehwe D. and Q. Slobodian, 'Landscapes of Unrest: Herbert Giersch and the Origins of Neoliberal Economic Geography', *Modern Intellectual History*, 16/1 (2019), 185–215.

Pohlmann, A., *Außenwirtschaftlicher Nachrichten-und Auskunftsdienst: Ein etwas verzwickte Geschichte* (Koehler & Hennemann, 1982)

Poidevin, R., *Les relations économiques et financières entre la France et l'Allemagne de 1898 à 1914* (Armand Colin, 1969)

Přibram, K., 'Die weltwirtschaftliche Lage im Spiegel des Schrifttums der Weltwirtschaftskonferenz', *Weltwirtschaftliches Archiv*, 26 (1927), 305–438

Prott, V., *The Politics of Self-Determination: Remaking Territories and National Identities in Europe, 1917–1923* (Oxford University Press, 2016)

Pulzer, P., 'Rechtliche Gleichstellung und öffentliches Leben', in S. M. Lowenstein, P. Mendes-Flohr, P. Pulzer, and M. Richarz (eds.), *Deutsch-jüdische Geschichte in der Neuzeit: Umstrittene Integration 1871–1918* (C. H. Beck, 1997), pp. 151–92

Reinalda, B., 'Biographical Analysis: Insights and Perspectives from the IO BIO Dictionary Project', in K. Gram-Skjoldager, H. A. Ikonomou, and T. Kahlert (eds.), *Organizing the 20th-Century World: International Organizations and the Emergence of International Public Administration, 1920–1960s* (Bloomsbury Academic, 2020), pp. 14–32

Richard, A.-I., 'Colonialism and the European Movement in France and the Netherlands, 1925–1936', PhD thesis, University of Cambridge (2011)

Richard, A.-I., 'Competition and Complementarity: Civil Society Networks and the Question of Decentralizing the League of Nations', *Journal of Global History*, 7/2 (2012), 233–56

Richard, A.-I., 'Les Pays-Bas entre l'Europe et le monde. L'européisme hésitant aux Pays-Bas durant l'entre-deux-guerres', *siècles*, 41 (2015)

Richarz, M., 'Berufliche und soziale Struktur', in S. M. Lowenstein, P. Mendes-Flohr, P. G. J. Pulzer, and M. Richarz (eds.), *Deutsch-jüdische Geschichte in der Neuzeit: Umstrittene Integration 1871–1918* (C. H. Beck, 1997), pp. 39–62

Ridgeway, G., *Merchants of Peace: Twenty Years of Business Diplomacy through the International Chamber of Commerce, 1919– 1938*, 2nd ed. (Columbia University Press, 1959)

Riedl, R., 'Äußere Handelspolitik', in V. Mataja (ed.), *Lehrbuch der Volkswirtschaftspolitik* (Österreichische Staatsdruckerei, 1931), pp. 441–521

Riedl, R., *Bemerkungen zu den deutschösterreichischen Friedensbedingungen. Handelspolitischer Teil* (Deutschösterreichische Staatsdruckerei, 1919)

Riedl, R., *Collective Treaties Facilitating International Commerce in Europe: Report of the Austrian National Committee to the Committee on Trade Barriers* (Vernay, 1926)

Riedl, R. *A Collective Treaty Relating to a Common Upper Limit of Customs Charges and to Reciprocal Most-Favoured Nation Treatment* (Vernay, 1927).

Riedl, R., *Exceptions to the Most-Favoured Nation Treatment: Report Presented to the International Chamber of Commerce* (P. S. King, 1931)

Riedl, R., *Die Industrie Österreichs während des Krieges* (Carnegie Endowment for International Peace, 1932)

Riedl, R., 'Innereuropäische Handelspolitik', *Weltwirtschaftliches Archiv*, 39 (1934), 13–66

Riedl, R., *La Réorganisation économique de l'Europe* (Le Foyer de la nouvelle Europe, 1930),

Riedl, R., 'Die Wirtschaftspolitik der Entente und Wilsons vor dem Frieden', *Deutsche Review*, 45/1 (1920), 97–117

Rietzler, K., 'From Peace Advocacy to International Relations Research: The Transformation of Transatlantic Philanthropic Networks, 1900–1930', in D. Rodogno, B. Struck, and J. Vogel (eds.), *Shaping the Transnational Sphere: Experts, Networks, and Issues from the 1840s to the 1930s* (Berghahn Books, 2015), pp. 173–96

Ritschl, A., 'The Pity of Peace: Germany's Economy at War, 1914–1918 and Beyond', in S. Broadberry and M. Harrison (eds.), *The Economics of World War I* (Cambridge University Press, 2009), pp. 41–76

Rodgers, D. T., *Atlantic Crossings: Social Politics in a Progressive Age* (Belknap Press, 1998)

Rodrik, D., *The Globalization Paradox: Democracy and the Future of the World Economy* (Oxford University Press, 2011)

Román, J. A. S., 'From the Tigris to the Amazon: Peripheral Expertise, Impossible Cooperation and Economic Multilateralism at the League of Nations, 1920–1946', in S. Jackson, A. O'Malley (eds.), *The Institution of International Order: From the League of Nations to the United Nations* (Routledge, 2018), pp. 59–64

Rosenberg, E. S., *Spreading the American Dream: American Economic and Cultural Expansion, 1890–1945* (Hill and Wang, 1982)

Rosenboim, O., *The Emergence of Globalism: Visions of World Order in Britain and the United States, 1939–1950* (Princeton University Press, 2017)

Rosengarten, M., *Die Internationale Handelskammer: wirtschaftspolitische Empfehlungen in der Zeit der Weltwirtschaftskrise 1929–1939* (Duncker & Humblot, 2001)

Rosental, P.-A. 'Géopolitique et État-providence. Le BIT et la politique mondiale des migrations dans l'entre-deux-guerres', *Annales. Histoire, Sciences Sociales*, 61/1 (2006), 99–134

Salmon, P., *Scandinavia and the Great Powers, 1890–1940* (Cambridge University Press, 1997)

Salter, A., 'The Contribution of the League of Nations to the Economic Recovery of Europe', *The Annals of the American Academy of Political and Social Science*, 134/1 (1927), 132–9

Salter, A., 'The Economic Conference: Prospects of Practical Results', *Journal of the Royal Institute of International Affairs*, 6/6 (1927), 350–67

Salter, A., *Recovery: The Second Effort* (G. Bell and Sons, 1933)

Salter, J. A., *Allied Shipping Control: An Experiment in International Administration* (The Clarendon Press, 1921)

Sauer, W. (ed.), *K.u.k. kolonial – Habsburgermonarchie und europäische Herrschaft in Afrika* (Böhlau, 2002)

Schirmann, S., *Crise, coopération économique et financière entre États européens, 1929–1933* (Comité pour l'histoire économique et financière de la France, 2000)

Schirmann, S., *Les relations économiques et financières franco-allemandes, 1932–1939* (Institut de gestion publique et du développement économique, 1995)

Schücking, W. and H. Wehberg, *Die Satzung des Völkerbundes*, 3 vols (Franz Vahlen, 1921)

Schüller, R., *Unterhändler des Vertrauens: aus den nachgelassenen Schriften von Sektionschef Dr. Richard Schüller*, J. Nautz (ed.), (R. Oldenbourg Verlag, 1990)

Schulz, M., *Deutschland, der Völkerbund und die Frage der europäischen Wirtschaftsordnung, 1925–1933* (Krämer, 1997)

Schwarte, C., *Le Plan Briand d'Union Européenne: De sa genèse au Quai d'Orsay à son échec dans la diplomatie des Grandes Puissances Européennes (1929–1931)* (Presses Académiques Francophone, 2014)

Serruys, D. 'L'Oeuvre économique de la S.D.N.', *La Revue des Vivants*, 3 (1929)

Sharp, A., *The Versailles Settlement: Peacemaking in Paris, 1919* (Palgrave Macmillan, 1991)

Shenoy, A. V., 'The Centenary of the League of Nations: Colonial India and the Making of International Law', *Asian Yearbook of International Law, Volume 24 (2018)*, 24 (2020), 3–23

Sinclair, G. F., 'A Bridge and a Pivot: The ILO and International Organizations Law in Times of Crisis', in G. Politakis (ed.), *ILO 100: Law for Social Justice* (International Labour Organization, 2019), pp. 123–34

Sinclair, G. F., *To Reform the World: International Organizations and the Making of Modern States* (Oxford University Press, 2017)

Skidelsky, R., *John Maynard Keynes: Hopes Betrayed, 1883–1920* (Macmillan, 1983)

Slobodian, Q., *Globalists: The End of Empire and the Birth of Neoliberalism* (Harvard University Press, 2018)

Slobodian, Q., 'How to See the World Economy: Statistics, Maps, and Schumpeter's Camera in the First Age of Globalization', *Journal of Global History*, 10/2 (2015), 307–32

Sluga, G., *Internationalism in the Age of Nationalism* (University of Pennsylvania Press, 2013)

Sommer, L., 'Der VII. Kongreß der Internationalen Handelskammer (Wien 1933)', *Weltwirtschaftliches Archiv*, 38 (1933), 284–90

Sommer, L., 'Freihandel und Schutzzoll in ihrem Zusammenhang mit Geldtheorie und Währungspolitik', *Weltwirtschaftliches Archiv*, 24 (1926), 33–72

Sommer, L., 'Die Mitteleuropäische Wasserstraßen-Konferenz (Budapest 1929)', *Weltwirtschaftliches Archiv*, 30 (1929), 447–57

Sommer, L., 'Sechste Mitteleuropäische Wirtschaftstagung am 18. und 19. März 1931', *Weltwirtschaftliches Archiv*, 35 (1932), 612–16

Sommer, L., 'Die Vorgeschichte der Weltwirtschaftskonferenz (Genf 1927)', *Weltwirtschaftliches Archiv*, 28 (1928), 340–418

Sommer, L., 'Die Vorgeschichte der Weltwirtschaftskonferenz (Genf 1927): Chronik und Archivalien', *Weltwirtschaftliches Archiv*, 28 (1928), 180–92

Sommer, L., 'Vom Zollwaffenstillstand zur Handelskonvention. Bericht über die Genfer Zollkonferenz vom 17. Februar bis 24. März 1930', *Weltwirtschaftliches Archiv*, 32 (1930), 274–82

Sommer, L., 'Zweite Konferenz für ein vereintes wirtschaftliches Vorgehen vom 17. bis zum 28. November 1930', *Weltwirtschaftliches Archiv*, 34 (1931), 284–96

Soutou, G.-H., *L'or et le sang: Les buts de guerre économiques de la Première Guerre mondiale* (Fayard, 1989)

Steen, K., *The American Synthetic Organic Chemicals Industry: War and Politics, 1910–1930* (The University of North Carolina Press, 2014)

Steiner, Z., *The Lights That Failed: European International History 1919–1933* (Oxford University Press, 2005)

Stern-Rubarth, E., *Aus zuverlässiger Quelle verlautet . . .* (W. Kohlhammer Verlag, 1964)

Stirk, P. M. R., 'Ideas of Economic Integration in Interwar Mitteleuropa', in P. M. R. Stirk (ed.), *Mitteleuropa: History and Prospects* (Edinburgh University Press, 1994), pp. 86–112

Stirk, P. M. R., 'Introduction: Crisis and Continuity in Interwar Europe', in P. M. R. Stirk (ed.), *European Unity in Context: The Interwar Period* (Bloomsbury, 2016), pp. 1–22

Stolleis, M., *A History of Public Law in Germany, 1914–1945* (Oxford University Press, 2004)

Stone Sweet, A. and F. Grisel, *The Evolution of International Arbitration: Judicialization, Governance, Legitimacy* (Oxford University Press, 2017)

Storli, E., 'The Global Race for Bauxite, 1900–1940', in R. S. Gendron, M. Ingulstad, and E. Storli (eds.), *Aluminium Ore: The Political Economy of the Global Bauxite Industry* (UBC, 2013), pp. 24–52

Strachan, H., *Financing the First World War* (Oxford University Press, 2004)

Strachan, H., *The First World War: To Arms* (Oxford University Press, 2001)

Sundhaussen, H. 'Die Weltwirtschaftskrise im Donau-Balkan-Raum und ihre Bedeutung für den Wandel der deutschen Außenpolitik unter Brüning', in W. Benz and H. Graml (eds), 'Aspekte deutscher Aussenpolitik im 20. Jahrhundert', special issue, *Schriftenreihe der Vierteljahrsheft für Zeitgeschichte* (1976), pp. 121–64.

Suppan, A., '"Germans" in the Habsburg Empire: Language, Imperial Ideology, National Identity, and Assimilation', in C. W. Ingrao and F. A. J. Szabo (eds.), *The Germans and the East* (Purdue University Press, 2008), pp. 147–269

Suppan, A., 'Mitteleuropa Konzeptionen zwischen Restauration und Anschluss', in R. G. Plaschka, H. Haselsteiner, A. Suppan, A. M. Drabek, and B. Zaar (eds.), *Mitteleuropa-Konzeptionen in der ersten Hälfte des 20. Jahrhunderts* (Verlag der Österreichischen Akademie der Wissenschaften, 1994), pp. 171–97

Sykes, A. O., 'Protectionism As a "Safeguard": A Positive Analysis of the GATT "Escape Clause" with Normative Speculations', *The University of Chicago Law Review*, 58/1 (1991), 255

Taft, W. H., 'Reciprocity with Canada', *Journal of Political Economy*, 19/7 (1911), 513–26

Take, G., '"Die Objektivität ist durch sein Wesen verbürgt": Bernhard Harms' Gründung des Kieler Instituts für Weltwirtschaft und sein Aufstieg im Ersten Weltkrieg', *Demokratische Geschichte*, 26 (2015), 13–74

Take, G., '"One of the Bright Spots in German Economics": Die Förderung des Kieler Instituts für Weltwirtschaft durch die Rockefeller Foundation, 1925–1950', *Jahrbuch für Wirtschaftsgeschichte/Economic History Yearbook*, 59/1 (2018), 251–328

Take, G., *Forschen für den Wirtschaftskrieg: Das Kieler Institut für Weltwirtschaft im Nationalsozialismus* (De Gruyter, 2019)

Taylor, A. J. P., *The Origins of the Second World War* (Fawcett, 1961)

Teichova, A., *An Economic Background to Munich: International Business and Czechoslovakia, 1918–1938* (Cambridge University Press, 1974)

Thompson, H., 'The Habsburg Myth and the European Union', in F. Duina and F. Merand (eds.), *Europe's Malaise: The Long View* (Emerald Publishing Limited, 2020), pp. 45–66

Thorpe, J., *Pan-Germanism and the Austrofascist State, 1933–38* (Manchester University Press, 2011)

Thorpe, J., 'Pan-Germanism after Empire: Austrian "Germandom" at Home and Abroad', in G. Bischof, F. Plasser, and P. Berger (eds), *From Empire to Republic: Post-World War I Austria* (UNO Press, 2010) 257–62

Tollardo, E., *Fascist Italy and the League of Nations, 1922–1935* (Palgrave Macmillan, 2016)

Tooze, A., *The Deluge: The Great War and the Remaking of Global Order, 1916–1931* (Allen Lane, 2014)

Tooze, J. A., *Statistics and the German State, 1900–1945: The Making of Modern Economic Knowledge* (Cambridge University Press, 2001)

Tooze, A., *The Wages of Destruction: The Making and Breaking of the Nazi Economy* (Allen Lane, 2006)

Tooze, A. and T. Fertik, 'The World Economy and the Great War', *Geschichte und Gesellschaft*, 40/2 (2014), 214–38

Torp, C., *The Challenges of Globalization: Economy and Politics in Germany, 1860–1914* (Berghahn Books, 2014)

Trachtenberg, M., '"A New Economic Order": Étienne Clémentel and French Economic Diplomacy during the First World War', *French Historical Studies*, 10/2 (1977), 315–41

Trachtenberg, M., 'Poincaré's Deaf Ear: The Otto Wolff Affair and French Ruhr Policy, August–September 1923', *The Historical Journal*, 24/3 (1981), 699–707

Trachtenberg, M., *Reparation in World Politics: France and European Economic Diplomacy, 1916–1923* (Columbia University Press, 1980)

'Trade Organization', *The Encyclopædia Britannica: A Dictionary of Arts, Sciences, Literature, and General Information*, Eleventh ed. (Cambridge University Press, 1910), pp. 135–9

Trentmann, F., *Free Trade Nation: Commerce, Consumption, and Civil Society in Modern Britain* (Oxford University Press, 2008)

Tucker, R. W., *Woodrow Wilson and the Great War: Reconsidering America's Neutrality, 1914–1917* (University of Virginia Press, 2007)

Tworek, H., 'Magic Connections: German News Agencies and Global News Networks, 1905–1945', *Enterprise and Society*, 15/4 (2014), 672–86

Tworek, H., *News from Germany: The Competition to Control World Communications, 1900–1945* (Harvard University Press, 2019)

Ullmann, H.-P., 'Staatliche Exportförderung und private Exportinitiative. Probleme des Staatsinterventionismus im Deutschen Kaiserreich am Beispiel der staatlichen Außenhandelsförderung (1880–1919)', *Vierteljahrschrift für Sozial- und Wirtschaftsgeschichte*, 65/2 (1978), 157–216

Unger, C. R., *International Development: A Postwar History* (Bloomsbury Academic, 2018)

Varian, B. D., 'The Growth of Manufacturing Protection in 1920s Britain', *Scottish Journal of Political Economy*, 66/5 (2019), 703–11

Vermeiren, J., *The First World War and German National Identity: The Dual Alliance at War* (Cambridge University Press, 2016)

Watson, A., *Ring of Steel: Germany and Austria-Hungary at War, 1914–1918* (Allen Lane, 2014)

Wehberg, H., 'Aus der Zeit, Bernhard Harms', *Friedens-Warte*, 33/10 (1933), 279–80

Wehberg, H., 'Verkehrsfreiheit und Völkerbund', *Weltwirtschaftliches Archiv*, 15 (1919), 468–80

Wehberg, H. (ed.), *Der Völkerbundvorschlag der Deutschen Regierung: Flugschrift der Deutschen Liga für Völkerbund* (Verlag Hans Robert Engelmann, 1920)

Wertheim, S., *Tomorrow, the World: The Birth of U.S. Global Supremacy* (The Belknap Press of Harvard University Press, 2020)

Wessels, J.-W., *Economic Policy and Microeconomic Performance in Inter-war Europe: The Case of Austria, 1918–1938* (Steiner, 2007)

Wildner, H. and Agstner, R. (ed.), *1915/1916. Das etwas andere Lesebuch zum 1. Weltkrieg. Heinrich Wildner: Tagebuch* (Lit Verlag, 2014)

Willson, F. M. G. and D. N. Chester, *The Organization of British Central Government, 1914–1956* (Allen and Unwin, 1957)

Wintzer, J., *Deutschland und der Völkerbund, 1918–1926* (Schöningh, 2006)

Wolf, N., M.-S. Schulze, and H.-C. Heinemeyer, 'On the Economic Consequences of the Peace: Trade and Borders After Versailles', *The Journal of Economic History*, 71/4 (2011), 915–49

Wolff, L., *Woodrow Wilson and the Reimagining of Eastern Europe* (Stanford University Press, 2020)

Wrigley, C., 'The Ministry of Munitions: An Innovatory Department', in K. Burk (ed.), *War and the State: The Transformation of the British Government, 1914–1919* (Routledge, 1982), pp. 32–56

Zahra, T., *The Great Departure: Mass Migration from Eastern Europe and the Making of the Free World* (W.W. Norton & Company, 2016)

Ziegerhofer-Prettenthaler, A., *Botschafter Europas: Richard Nikolaus Coudenhove-Kalergi und die Paneuropa-Bewegung in den zwanziger und dreißiger Jahren* (Böhlau, 2004)

Index

Printed in the United States
by Baker & Taylor Publisher Services